# ETHICS IN THE HISTORY
# OF WESTERN PHILOSOPHY

*Also by Robert J. Cavalier*

LUDWIG WITTGENSTEIN'S TRACTATUS
LOGICO-PHILOSOPHICUS:
A Transcendental Critique of Ethics

*Also by James Gouinlock*

JOHN DEWEY'S PHILOSOPHY OF VALUE
THE MORAL WRITINGS OF JOHN DEWEY

*Also by James P. Sterba*

JUSTICE: ALTERNATIVE POLITICAL PERSPECTIVES
THE DEMANDS OF JUSTICE
JUSTICE IN THEORY AND PRACTICE

# ETHICS IN THE HISTORY OF WESTERN PHILOSOPHY

Edited by
Robert J. Cavalier
*Coordinator*
*'Project Theoria: Interactive Video Media for Moral Reasoning'*
*Carnegie Mellon University*

James Gouinlock
*Associate Professor of Philosophy*
*Emory University*
*Atlanta*

and

James P. Sterba
*Professor of Philosophy*
*University of Notre Dame*
*Notre Dame, Indiana*

St. Martin's Press     New York

First published in the United States of America in 1989

Printed in the People's Republic of China

ISBN 0-312-02145-3 (cloth)
ISBN 0-312-03211-0 (pbk)


Library of Congress Cataloging-in-Publication Data
Ethics in the history of western philosophy.
Includes index.
1. Ethics—History.    I. Cavalier, Robert J.
II. Gouinlock, James.    III. Sterba, James, P. .
BJ71.E84  1989      170'.9      88–18182
ISBN 0-312-02145-3 (cloth)
ISBN 0-312-03211-0 (pbk)

# Contents

# List of Figures

# Preface

Comprehensive and sustained work in the history of ethics has been suprisingly meagre, especially in light of the dictum that 'an understanding of philosophy often entails an understanding of the history of philosophy'. Henry Sidgwick's *Outlines of the History of Ethics for English Readers* (1886) is the one durable work of the past while Vernon J. Bourke's *History of Ethics* (1968) and Alasdair MacIntyre's *A Short History of Ethics* (1967) are the only works of the present that can be genuinely recommended. And each of the above contain differences in method and points of emphasis, making them far from the final word on the subject.

The weakness of scholarly work in this area can be explained in two ways. The first has to do with the extreme difficulty that a single person would have in trying to think through the entire history of moral philosophy. The difficulty arises from the fact that a true history of ethics is deeper and far more complex than a mere 'summary of positions'. To understand a philosopher's ethical theory, that philosopher must be placed within the immediacy of the specific philosophical issues and the general cultural problems that confronted the writer at the time of his work and that formed the frame of reference for the meaning of his position. A true history of ethics takes the form of a historical narrative which contextualises a moral theory in order to achieve a correct understanding of that moral theory. Research into this kind of approach to the history of ethics is critically lacking.

The lack of work in this area comes not only out of the difficulty of the task, but also out of a certain attitude taken by 20th-century Anglo-American philosophers with regard to the very idea of moral philosophy itself. MacIntyre, in *After Virtue* (Indiana: University of Notre Dame Press, 1981), sees this attitude in 'the persistently unhistorical treatment of moral philosophy by contemporary philosophers in both the writing about and the teaching of the subject' (p. 11). He amplifies this by noting that 'we all too often still treat the moral philosophers of the past as contributors to a single debate with a relatively unvarying subject-matter, treating Plato and Hume and Mill as contemporaries both of ourselves and of each other'. With this attitude, history has become irrelevant to the subject-matter of ethics.

This book hopes to overcome both the difficulty of and the attitude towards doing a history of ethics. It seeks to provide a prolegomenon to the writing of a historical narrative through a series of single-author chapters which discuss the context of selected ethical theories as those theories are found in key figures of western philosophy. The emphasis in each case will be on the development of the theory within the specific historical context that formed its immediate frame of reference. The criterion used for choosing the philosophers to be discussed is that the philosopher chosen should be a major systematic writer in the history of western philosophy. The only exception to this rule is in 20th-century Anglo-American ethical theory, where the analytic method tended to produce a series of specialised works and articles that are best represented by a collection of writers rather than a single figure.

This is a 'history of ethics' that is valuable for the student wishing to know a certain theory, a scholar wishing to criticise a certain theory, and a person wishing to study the history of ethics in the sense of seeking themes, divergences and convergences. No attempt is made here to draw sweeping conclusions or to make comparative judgements regarding the whole of the history of ethics.

Furthermore, our task is not to produce an encyclopaedic view of the entire history of ethics nor to pronounce the final word on any particular philosopher within that history. Rather, we seek to join the recent move in philosophy that recognises the importance of history and context in the ongoing activity of philosophy. We hope that by taking this route we have provided access to these ethical theories, and in such a way that they will become understandable to a broad range of readers.

Robert J. Cavalier
Carnegie Mellon University

# Acknowledgements

A collaborative effort involving years of preparation naturally owes a great many debts to a number of individuals and institutions. We would like first of all to express our gratitude to the Matchette Foundation for supporting a conference on this topic that was held at the University of Notre Dame in the Spring of 1985. Our appreciation also extends to the Philosophy Departments of Emory, Notre Dame and Towson State universities.

Individuals who have offered helpful comments, encouragements, suggestions and criticisms or who have otherwise enabled the book to reach its finished state include: Tom Beauchamp, Jude Dougherty, Wolfgang Fuchs, Jerald Kreyche, James Rachels, J. B. Scheewind and Calvin O. Schrag. There have been many others besides, and we appreciate all who have helped.

# Notes on the Contributors

**Arthur Adkins** was educated at Merton College, Oxford and is currently Edward Olsen Professor of Greek and Professor of Philosophy and Early Christian Literature at the University of Chicago. His books include *Merit and Responsibility: A Study in Greek Values* and *Moral Values and Political Behavior in Ancient Greece*.

**Hazel E. Barnes**, recently retired from the University of Colorado at Boulder, has been a long-standing interpreter of Sartre's work. She translated *Being and Nothingness* and is author of *An Existentialist Ethics*.

**Vernon J. Bourke**, Professor Emeritus at St Louis University, is one of the world's foremost authorities on Thomas Aquinas. His works include *History of Ethics*, the *Thomistic Bibliography*, *St. Thomas and the Greek Moralists*, *The Pocket Aquinas* and *Aquinas' Search for Wisdom*.

**Robert J. Cavalier** received his degrees from New York University and Duquesne University and taught philosophy at Towson State University from 1981 to 1986. He is currently at Carnegie Mellon University, where he is working on 'Project Theoria: Interactive Video Media for Moral Reasoning'.

**Stephen Darwall**, Professor of Philosophy at the University of Michigan, is the author of *Impartial Reason* and numerous articles on contemporary ethics.

**Alfonso Gomez-Lobo** has attended the University of Athens and has degrees from the universities of Tübingen and Munich, Germany. He is Professor of Philosophy and Director of the Greece Program at Georgetown University. His many articles include studies of Aristotle that have appeared in Spanish as well as English philosophical journals.

**James Gouinlock** received his Ph.D. in Philosophy from Columbia University in 1969. He has been teaching in the Department of Philosophy at Emory University since 1971. Before that he taught at the State University of New York at Buffalo and at DePauw University.

He has served as both Director of Graduate Studies in Philosophy and as Chairman of the Department at Emory.

Dr Gouinlock's scholarly publications have been principally in the field of American philosophy, especially the philosophy of John Dewey. He is the author of *John Dewey's Philosophy of Value* and *Excellence in Public Discourse: John Stuart Mill, John Dewey, and Social Intelligence*. He is also the editor of *The Moral Writings of John Dewey*. He was on the Executive Committee of the Society for the Advancement of American Philosophy from 1978 to 1981 and was President of the Society from 1983 to 1986.

**Christine Korsgaard** received her degree from Harvard and currently teaches at the University of Chicago. Her articles on Kant include 'Kant's Formula of Humanity' in *Kant-Studien*, 'Aristotle and Kant on the Source of Value' in *Ethics* and 'The Right to Lie: Kant on Dealing with Evil' in *Philosophy and Public Affairs*.

**John Lachs** received his degree from Yale and is currently Professor of Philosophy at Vanderbilt University. His writings on Mill include 'Mill on the Happy Man' in *Journal of Philosophy* and 'Two Views of Happiness in Mill' in *The Mill News Letter*.

**Thomas Losoncy**, Associate Professor of Philosophy at Villanova University, is founder of the *International Patristic, Mediaeval, and Renaissance Conference* and author of many articles and papers on medieval philosophy.

**Larry May** is Associate Professor of Philosophy at Purdue University, and received his degree from the New School of Social Research. His publications on Hobbes include 'Hobbes's Contract Theory' in the *Journal of the History of Philosophy* and 'Hobbes on Equity and Justice' in *Hobbes's Science of Natural Justice*.

**David Fate Norton** is one of the foremost authorities on Hume's thought. He is Professor of Philosophy at McGill University and from 1986 to 1987 was a Fellow of the Institute for Advanced Studies in the Humanities, University of Edinburgh. Former editor of the *Journal of the History of Philosophy*, his works on Hume include *David Hume: Common Sense Moralist, Sceptical Metaphysician* and *David Hume: Philosophical Historian*, edited with R. H. Popkin.

**Richard Schacht** currently holds the Chair of the Philosophy Department at the University of Illinois at Urbana. His is the author of *Nietzsche* and of many articles on Nietzsche.

**James P. Sterba** is Professor of Philosophy at the University of Notre Dame. He specialises in political philosophy and practical ethics. The books he has written or edited include *Justice: Alternative Political Perspectives*, *The Demands of Justice*, *Morality in Practice*, *The Ethics of War and Nuclear Deterrence*, *Contemporary Ethics* and *How To Make People Just*. He is also general editor for Wadsworth's *Basic Issues in Philosophy Series*.

# 1

# Plato
## *Arthur Adkins*

My task is to relate Plato's ethical thought to its historical context. For the authors of later chapters in this book, 'historical' will include both the history of philosophy and other aspects or fields of history; but since, in the words of Cicero, Socrates 'was the first [to bring philosophy away from the study of nature] and to lead it to the study of ordinary life, in order to investigate the virtues and vices and good and evil', and I do not here propose to distinguish between Socratic and Platonic ethics, there is no history of philosophical ethics prior to Socrates and Plato to discuss.[1] In consequence, I shall begin with a sketch of the salient points of the 70 years of Greek military and political history immediately prior to Plato's birth. These events, occurring in a context of traditional Greek values, posed some of the problems in ethics and politics which Plato addresses in his moral and political thought. Next, I shall briefly describe some important events in Athenian military and political history which occurred during Plato's formative years, ending with the death of Socrates, the Athenian who more than any other influenced Plato's thought. It will become apparent that Plato came to the conclusion that a change in Greek values was urgently necessary. I shall discuss the identity and nature of those who were responsible for the propagation of existing Greek values, and the character and history of those values. Having thus established the nature of the problem with which Plato was faced, I shall discuss the methods which he employed to solve it.

## MILITARY AND POLITICAL HISTORY

Plato was born in Athens in 428 BC, in the fourth year of the Peloponnesian War. The condition of Athens at the beginning of that war, the condition that Plato was subsequently to criticise, was the result of a series of events and decisions which began certainly

1

no later than the Persian Wars. For the Athenians the significant events of those wars were three battles: Marathon (490 BC), Salamis (480 BC), and Plataea (479 BC). At Marathon the Athenian army almost single-handed defeated what the Athenians chose to regard as the full might of the Persian army; at Salamis they furnished the largest contingent of warships in the battle which virtually eliminated the Persian fleet from a war in which Persian strategy required the close cooperation of navy and army; and at Plataea they played a significant part in the allied defeat of the Persian expeditionary force. (The skeletal details of this account can be fleshed out with the aid of any outline history of Greece, for example [10] or [14]. All figures in square brackets refer to the bibliography.)

At the beginning of the Peloponnesian War Athens had a standing fleet with highly trained crews, defensive walls and dockyards, and a considerable amount of money (Thucydides, 2.13), all derived from the tribute of the poleis of the empire that the Athenians had developed from the league of free poleis formed for mutual protection against the common Persian foe. Athens had always been a large polis; to many, both in Athens and elsewhere, she must have appeared virtually invincible against Sparta and the other poleis of the Peloponnesian League.

Pericles, who had for many years been the most influential leader of the Athenian democracy (Thucydides, 2.64), established Athens' strategy in the war: the Athenians should all withdraw behind the Great Walls, make no attempt to defend Attica, and rely on the command of the sea for all necessary supplies. An unforeseen consequence was the Great Plague, whose ravages were intensified among the Athenians in their overcrowded city (Thucydides, 2.47–53). But Pericles' general evaluation of the situation was correct: despite many setbacks and disasters, Athens was not defeated until—in an episode of folly which it would be difficult to match—she lost command of the sea and was starved into surrender (Xenophon, *Hellenika*, 2.1.22–2.2.23).

Into this beleaguered Athens, ravaged by disease but still materially strong and in no danger of defeat, Plato was born.[2] As he grew up, Athens experienced the vicissitudes characteristic of wars. I select a few of the most significant. In 415 BC, when Plato was 13 years old, the Athenians, while technically at peace with their original enemies, sent out a large expedition to Sicily which, together with copious reinforcements, came to complete disaster in 413 BC (Thucydides, 6 and 7). In 404 BC Athens was finally starved into surrender, and 30 prominent citizens were put into power and given the task of drafting a constitution with a severely limited franchise. In fact, the Thirty, now usually referred to as 'The Thirty Tyrants', retained all power for themselves and instituted a lawless Reign of Terror, seizing and murdering wealthy citizens and resident aliens out of greed for their money (Plato, *Apology*, 32c–d, Lysias 12, Xenophon, *Hellenika*, 2.3.1–2.4.4). In 403 the Thirty were defeated in battle by the democrats who had left the city, and fell from power (Xenophon, *Hellenika*, 2.4.2–2.4.23). Democratic government was restored. In 399 BC three Athenian democrats—Anytus, Meletus and Lycon— brought against Socrates a rather vague charge of believing in gods other than those the city worshipped, and corrupting the young. Socrates was found guilty and condemned.

Now any thinking Athenian who had lived through the Pelopon- nesian War is likely to have thought long and hard in an effort to determine what had gone wrong. The Athenians had not expected to lose. How could a city of outstandingly intelligent, courageous and energetic citizens, a city richly endowed with material resources, have passed from prosperity and glory to defeat and shame? Indeed, anyone whose early years, like Thucydides', had been passed in the golden light of Periclean Athens might perhaps have been even more puzzled than those who, like Plato, knew those glories only by report. (Thucydides gives his answer, 2.65 and elsewhere; and in their own way Anytus, Meletus and Lycon were giving theirs.) But Plato had particular reasons for hard thought. On both his paternal and maternal side he was descended from the old nobility of Athens. This fact does not in itself demonstrate that he grew up in a household hostile to the democracy. Pericles' family tree was similar, and even if they took no active part in politics Plato's family need not have been hostile to the policies of the democracy while they prospered. However, after the disasters of 413 and 404 BC, families like Plato's, members of the class which traditionally governed and formed policy in Greek poleis, must have resolved that it was time for the 'better' (more *agathoi*, a word I shall discuss below), more prudent and substantial citizens, people like themselves, to take over. The Thirty included several of Plato's close relatives; and he was unfeignedly appalled by their behaviour.[3] The prosecution of Socrates, whom Plato regarded as the finest man he had known (*Phaedo*, 118),[4] provided further stimulus to thought about values, for Plato's evaluation was shared by few. Traditional values, as we shall see, would lead the Athenians to admire Plato's bloodthirsty, greedy and lawless relatives—before they showed their true colours[5]—much more than they had admired Socrates. (Socrates had to be rehabilitated on two counts: he had not succeeded in the ways desiderated by traditional values, and several of his associates—not only some members of the Thirty, but also Alcibiades[6]—had proved to be enemies of the democracy. Socrates was suspected of having taught them their evil ways, of having 'corrupted' them, in the terms of the indictment.)[7] A thinker of Plato's social background might well have preferred a more traditional type of polis, in which the landowner and the land army played a more prominent role, to imperial Athens, materially prosperous to an extent unparalleled elsewhere in the Greek world, and resting her power on the poorer citizens and the navy. When such an Athens proved to be not merely distasteful but unsuccessful, Plato was stimulated to search for the reasons and prescribe for a better kind of polis.

## THE TEACHERS OF VALUES

If Plato wished to change Greek values, or rather the interpretation of Greek values, he had to displace all rival teachers of values, both traditional and more recent. The earliest teachers were the poets, among whom Homer and Hesiod held pride of place. (They were believed to teach not merely values, but the skills of politics and war. See Plato, *Ion, passim.*) The influence of Homer and Hesiod continued to be powerful in Plato's day: the Homeric poems constituted a large part of the Athenian schoolboy's literary education. The tragedians were important too: any Athenian citizen might attend tragic performances several times each year and absorb any values that the playwright favoured. Less renowned teachers, but ever present, were the prominent citizens of each polis, who possessed such rule-of-thumb political wisdom as was available. In earlier periods in Greece the younger members of each generation, or those of its members who had the status and leisure to aspire to an active political role, must have learned their practical politics from this source (Plato, *Meno*, 92e, [*Theages*] 126d). But in the later decades of the 5th century a new phenomenon appeared in Greece. Teachers made their way from polis to polis, giving instruction to those who could afford to pay (Plato, *Apology*, 19d–20c, *Protagoras*, 316c). Their views and values were far from uniform [18], and they professed a variety of skills and areas of knowledge; but the skills needed for success in politics were, as we shall see, most in demand.[8] Her empire rendered Athens more prosperous. A significant number of the wealthier citizens must have been able to pay the high prices that the sophists charged for their tuition, if they wished. Athens' position must also have engendered administrative, legal and political problems of a complexity greater than those which can have faced the majority of Greek poleis at any period. Anyone who, with however little justification, claimed to be able to solve the problems and to enable the aspiring young to succeed in politics was assured of a ready hearing. For some purposes it is useful to divide these itinerant teachers into sophists and rhetoricians, but for the present purpose it is unnecessary. From Plato's point of view both, like the poets and the prominent politicians, imparted values which he regarded as unsatisfactory and dangerous. In time, Plato came to realise that everyone took part in the socialisation of the young, and labelled the general public as the greatest sophists (*Republic*, 492a8–b1; compare the attitude of the sophist Protagoras as portrayed by Plato in *Protagoras*, 327e–28b).

## THE VALUES OF THE HOMERIC POEMS

Most of the important value-terms found in the Homeric poems remained important in Plato's own day. This fact might have little significance; a word might continue to be the most important word to commend a man while the qualities which it was used to commend changed radically. After all, Athens in the 5th and 4th centuries, a democracy under the rule of law, surely cannot value most highly in its citizens the qualities valued most highly in Homeric Ithaca or in the Greek army before Troy. But in fact the resemblances are remarkably close; and therein lies Plato's problem.

In the Homeric poems, the adjective *agathos* is used to commend the most admired type of man, and the noun *arete* to commend his most admired qualities.[9] I take these, and many other important terms of value, to be untranslatable, and have in most of my other publications on Greek values simply transliterated the key terms. In accordance with the desire of the editors of this volume, however, I have usually furnished translations, with 'scare quotes' to remind the reader that the word does not have its characteristic English use. Only the most admired qualities are commended by *arete* (which I shall in future render by 'virtue'), and the *agathos* (hereafter 'good', or, when a noun is needed, 'goodman'),[10] remains 'good' insofar as he manifests those qualities. Those qualities which are admired to a lesser degree are not 'virtues'. (At this period there is no Greek word which denotes and commends all the qualities, and only the qualities, which are generally termed 'virtues' by users of modern English.) The Homeric poems portray a world of small groups whose existence, like that of most small groups, is precarious. Their members naturally value most highly those of their number who seem most able to ensure their continued existence, and in those persons the characteristics which seem most relevant to the performance of that most important function. The first need is evidently defence againt other similar virtually autonomous small groups. Homer's Ithaca gives us an example of these 'virtues' in action, and indicates the vital importance of the Homeric oikos, or noble household, and the relative unimportance of the polis.[11]

In such a situation, those persons who can most effectively defend their own will be most valued, and valued for those characteristics which seem most relevant to their primary task: courage, a strong right arm, and effective weapons, so wielded as to bring about a successful conclusion.

The most effective weapons in Homeric society are very elaborate: body-armour, a helmet, large shield, two throwing-spears, a sword and a two-horse chariot. Such armour is expensive. Few are well-armed. The individual purchases his own weapons. In the money-less society of the Homeric poems, wealth consists of land and the movable and immovable goods thereon. This wealth is controlled by the head of the noble oikos, who obtained it by inheritance. Only the heads of noble oikoi (plural of 'oikos') and any adult male members of the immediate family can hope to possess the essential weapons, and so manifest their 'virtue'. Other members of society cannot be 'good', and the other qualities of the 'goodman' will be regarded as less important.

In such a society, an agglomeration of virtually autonomous oikoi, to settle disputes between 'goodmen' peacefully is likely to be difficult, if not impossible. Odysseus could not have returned openly to Ithaca and taken up the reins of government. The reins are very tenuous; and the suitors make it clear that he would have been killed had he tried to do so (*Odyssey*, 2.242–56). He had to do what he did: overcome and kill the suitors by a mixture of force and fraud. This behaviour is not regarded, either by Odysseus or by the relatives of the suitors as an imposition of judicial punishment, but rather as multiple homicide (*Odyssey*, 23.118–22), or as the beginning of a war. As the language of *Odyssey*, 2.237 and 3.24 shows, the suitors had engaged in the equivalent of a war or piratical expedition against the oikos of Odysseus, and in the absence of Odysseus had done so scot free: an *aischron* (hereafter 'shameful') situation, or *lobe*, a shameful hurt, for the oikos (*Odyssey*, 18.225). On discovering the death of their relatives the surviving members of the families propose to continue the war, for the situation is now a *lobe* for them, and they will appear to be *kakoi* (hereafter 'bad' or 'badmen') if they are unable to take vengeance.[12]

In the larger-scale war against Troy, it is equally difficult to settle disputes between 'goodmen', or the most prominent 'goodmen', the leaders of contingents; for though Agamemnon is in some sense Commander-in-Chief, as Odysseus is in some sense the Paramount Chief of Ithaca, the contingent leaders are virtually autonomous. Achilles cannot be accused of desertion in the face of the enemy when, after his quarrel with Agamemnon, he withdraws his contingent and sulks in his tent. The quarrel is a consequence of 'virtue'-values. Agamemnon and Achilles each claim to be the most 'good' of the Greeks, Agamemnon on the basis of his greater political power, Achilles as the greatest warrior.[13]

In the earliest extant documents, then, to be 'good' and possess 'virtue' is desirable. It is true that the exercise of one's 'virtue' may at times be dangerous or even fatal; but the lot of the live 'goodman', successful, prosperous, admired, in a position of political power, credited with political acumen, listened to respectfully in assembly, is evidently preferable to that of the 'bad'. Any move down the scale, however small, in the direction of *kakotes* (hereafter 'badness') will be bitterly resented. The position of Achilles and Agamemnon, vying for the evaluation *'aristos* (most "good") of the Greeks', occasions even greater tensions. The self image of each as supremely 'good', as possessed of preeminent 'virtue', is of such importance to him that he is willing to prejudice the attainment of goals which, once achieved, would have greatly increased his reputation for 'virtue' [1], [4], [6].

The conflicts which constitute the main plots of the *Iliad* and *Odyssey* arise directly out of the institutions and most powerful values of the society of the poems. Since no society could exist in which the state of war was constant, in general values which did not produce conflict must have guided action for much of the time. Provided that no one disparages the 'virtue' or threatens the *time* (hereafter 'honour') of a 'goodman', crises may be averted; and it is only in a crisis, where the 'goodman' is faced with two courses of action, one involving cooperation (with the possibility of appearing unable to manifest his 'virtue'), the other competition, that the competitive value take precedence and conflict occurs, regardless of the consequences.

Accordingly, something must be said of less important value-terms found in the Homeric poems and in other early Greek works, for though they do not prevail in crises, they will be employed where appropriate in other situations. For example, *moira* lessens the likelihood of conflict by keeping the potential combatants apart as much as by inducing them to cooperate. In Homer and in early Greek generally, society is thought of as consisting of persons with *moirai*, 'shares', of *time*. *Time* denotes this world's goods, and also endows these goods with a high emotive charge. 'Honour', though I shall use the word here, is not a satisfactory translation, for the early Greek concept of punishment is entwined with the meaning of *time* and related words [2]. A very striking use of the term is made by the god Poseidon in *Iliad*, 15, 185–95, when the goddess Iris brings him Zeus' instructions to leave the battlefield.

> 'Good' though he is, he has spoken excessively if he means to restrain me who am equal in 'honour' with him, by force and against my will. We are three sons whom Rhea bore to Kronos, Zeus and I, and thirdly Hades who rules among the dead. All things are divided into three, and each has a 'due share' of 'honour'. When the lots were cast, I received the grey sea to dwell in for ever, Hades received the dank darkness, and Zeus drew the broad heavens among the clear sky and the clouds. The earth and mighty Olympus were left common for all. So I will not live at Zeus's behest [and leave the battlefield, which is on earth]. Strong though he is, let him remain in his own third 'due share'.

This speech evidently reflects human practice. Just so might three human brothers have divided up the family estate, each having the unchallenged use of his share. Just so might the 'goodman' have viewed his own oikos, in which he had virtual autonomy, so that he need rarely come to the place of common assembly to discuss matters which concerned more than one oikos. Divisions of family property may well be equal, but not all 'due shares' in a community will be equal. The 'due share' of a king will not be equal with that of a bard, nor that of a bard with that of a beggar. In a society both stratified and static, the existing distribution of 'shares' is likely to be treated as the correct one. It is for this reason that 'shares' are 'due shares' and to speak or act 'in accordance with one's due share' is to speak or act in the approved manner—a manner different for a king and a beggar, or for a 'goodman' and a common soldier [1], [4], [5]. In different mouths the same speech may be differently evaluated: it has often been observed that Achilles' criticism of Agamemnon (*Iliad*, 1. 225–44) closely resembles Thersites' criticism of him (*Iliad*, 2. 225–42). The 'goodman' Achilles cannot even be effectively censured; the 'badman' Thersites has his ears boxed by Odysseus for his pains. One ought to act in accordance with one's 'due share', and the social inferior, the 'badman' who has no 'virtue', will usually do so, since his superiors will ensure that any other behaviour does not pay by taking 'honour' for themselves from him.[14] But the 'ought' of 'virtue'—or rather the desire to be 'good' and possess 'virtue', since the possession of 'virtue' is a desirable condition—is stronger than the 'ought' associated with one's 'due share'. It is more important to show oneself to be 'good' than to behave in accordance with one's 'due share', particularly if one has placed oneself in a position hazardous to life, well-being or reputation. The suitors of Penelope are not acting in accordance with their 'due shares', for Odysseus' oikos is Odysseus' 'due share', not theirs; but so long as they can succeed in their enterprise, they remain 'good-men' nonetheless. It is only when they fail to string Odysseus' bow that they become alarmed, for the failure reflects upon their 'virtue' (*Odyssey*, 21, 320ff.), and it would be intolerable if the 'beggar' (the disguised Odysseus), necessarily 'bad' qua beggar, who has asked to try, should succeed where they have failed. They are not afraid that Penelope will marry the beggar if he is successful: Ithaca is not the land of fairy-tale, but (323–29)

> We *aischunesthai*, feel shame, at the talk of men and women, lest at some time some 'more bad' person from among the Greeks may say 'Men much "more bad" are wooing the wife of an excellent man. They cannot draw the polished bow. But another man, a wandering beggar, came and easily strung the bow and shot through the iron'. So they will say, and these things will become a reproach to us.[15]

In fact, once a Homeric hero regards an action as demanded by his

*Plato*

'virtue', he will attempt to perform it. Achilles and Agamemnon had evidently long resented each other, and Achilles had regarded his 'due share' of *time* (status-producing material goods, here his share of the booty) [2], as inadequate; but only when the quarrel had broken out, and each regarded compromise as a slur on his 'virtue', did cooperation between them become impossible, even though, as Nestor pointed out, cooperation and compromise would have been in the interests of both, since both would have benefited from the defeat of the Trojans and the sack of Troy (*Iliad*, 1.254–84).[16]

Consequently, breaches of the cooperative excellences must be shown not to pay; and if the 'goodman's' human peers cannot achieve this, the gods must do so. As Hesiod said (*Works and Days*, 271–73), 'Now may neither I nor my son be just among men, if the unjust is to fare better'. Justice must pay if justice is to be pursued. There were many problems facing any Greek of this period who wished to believe in the unfailing profitability of justice. Some of the problems were related to the character and behaviour of the gods in some myths, some to the necessity of the gods' rewarding and punishing in this life, since the predominant belief in our texts portrays a Hades dank and unpleasant for all, just and unjust alike, with neither rewards nor punishments. The gods were believed to reward and punish in this life by sending good or ill fortune. It must be believed to be impossible, or at all events unusual, to be unjust and prosper.[17] Despite its difficulties, the belief—or hope—that the gods would punish injustice or *hubris* persisted until about the middle of the 5th century in Athens, when it began to fade, at least in the circles of society with which Plato was primarily concerned when philosophising. We have his testimony, and the testimony of other documents, that the belief was still prevalent elsewhere.[18]

To sum up the values of earlier Greece. The 'goodman', who is so termed because he possesses both certain excellences and a certain social and economic position, employs his 'virtues' to defend his own well-being, and that of his *philoi*, 'friends',[19] and if possible increase it. That well-being is usually interpreted in material terms, and the excellences are the competitive ones. The cooperative excellences are rendered choiceworthy for those who are too powerful to be constrained by their fellow-men, by the belief that the gods will punish the unjust or the over-successful, by reducing their material well-being.[20]

Now if the competitive 'virtues' are valued for the direct contribution that they make to the well-being of the group—oikos or polis—and the gods are firmly believed to ensure the desirability of the cooperative excellences by inflicting damage on those who do not behave in accordance with them, a stable situation may result. But for anyone who holds these values and ceases to believe either that the gods exist or that, if they exist, they interest themselves in human behaviour,[21] the cooperative excellences will cease to be attractive unless some other reason for their attractiveness can be discovered. Several methods of increasing their attractiveness suggest themselves: (a) the less powerful members of society may believe that if they commit injustice they will be haled before the courts by those whom they have wronged, and punished. But detection and punishment must be quite likely if even these members of society are to be convinced; and in ancient Athens the absence of an investigative police force rendered a high level of detection and punishment unlikely. The more powerful members of society will be less restrained; and their crimes may be on a larger scale; (b) in addition, one might attempt to give the cooperative excellences the status of 'virtues' by demonstrating that their instrumental relationship with the desired goal of prosperity and stability for the individual and the polis was so important that they merited inclusion among the 'virtues'; (c) one might attempt to reach the goal of (b) by simple suasion. Since the 'goodman' was a member of an admired social class, a 'gentleman', the moralist might attempt to include the practice of the cooperative excellences under the rubric of 'gentlemanly behaviour'.[22] All these methods were attempted, as can readily be demonstrated from the literature of the later 5th century, and from Plato's own works.

A fourth possibility, that of demonstrating the intrinsic benefits of justice and other cooperative excellences, will be discussed below.

## PLATONIC SOLUTIONS OF PROBLEMS IN GREEK ETHICS

The list of the 'virtues' in later 5th century Greece contained a number of recent recruits, whose requirements in a given situation might conflict with the requirements of the traditional 'virtues'. Much hard thought, of a kind not yet to be found in Greece, was needed before such conflicts could be resolved. The competitive excellences had deeper historical roots, and their contribution to the well-being of the 'goodman' and his 'friends' was more readily apparent. They were likely to be given precedence in a crisis. Since the result might be the disruption of civic order and harmony, one of Plato's goals when portraying Socrates in conversation with the well-meaning who accepted—at least in some circumstances—the addition of cooperative excellences to the 'virtues' was to ensure that they were not discarded in a crisis.

In the *Crito* Plato portrays Crito in just such a crisis. Crito is Socrates' oldest friend, and, though evidently in no sense a philosopher, he has previously agreed with Socrates in regarding the cooperative excellences as 'virtues', and therefore desirable. In this crisis he reverts to traditional values: any 'goodman' should help his friends when their well-being is threatened, and be ready to spend money and hazard his life if need be. Socrates himself is betraying himself and his family by his refusal to escape from prison. The situation is not merely *kakon* (hereafter 'harmful') for Socrates but also *aischron* (hereafter 'shameful/ugly') for him.[23] Socrates is showing himself deficient in 'virtue' and his refusal to let his friends help him causes them to seem deficient in 'virtue' too.

In reply, Socrates asks Crito whether he has abandoned his former agreement that living *dikaiôs* ('justly') is to be equated with living *kalôs* ('honourably/beautifully'), and living *eu*, ('well', in the sense of 'efficiently' or 'in a flourishing manner', not in the sense of 'justly'). Crito replies that he has not. The reply commits him to the pursuit of any course of action of whose justice he is convinced, or can be convinced by Socrates, for *eu zen* (hereafter 'living well' in the sense explained above) is synonymous with *eudaimonia* (hereafter 'human flourishing') which all pursue as their goal.[24] Socrates accordingly devotes the rest of the dialogue to demonstrating that it is just for him to remain in prison.

But if the cooperative excellences merit being enrolled as 'virtues', they must be beneficial in the same sense as the traditional 'virtues', that is, to the 'goodman' himself. No one can maintain that justice is (a) a 'virtue' and (b) other-regarding to the detriment of the 'goodman'; for what is other-regarding is an *allotrion agathon*, someone else's 'good', and therefore, as we shall see, not a 'virtue'. (Thrasymachus in *Republic* 1 makes the point most strongly.) Accordingly, to be consistent, one must either grant justice the status of a 'virtue' and accept the consequences or deny that justice is a 'virtue'.[25]

The *Crito* shows how readily the inclusion of the cooperative excellences as 'virtues' may be abandoned in a crisis. Other Greeks, of whom Polus in Plato's *Gorgias* is an example, adopt an incoherent position. If anyone agrees that the cooperative excellences are 'virtues', he should have a reason for so doing; and the only sound reason for so doing, in a Greek context, is that they make the same contribution to the life of their possessor (and to the polis) as do the traditional 'virtues'. If they do so, then they are *agatha* (hereafter 'beneficial') for their possessor, and actions that express them should be termed *kala* (hereafter 'honourable/beautiful') as are, and traditionally have been, actions which are expressions of courage and successful competition. Polus, however, maintains that committing injustice is more 'shameful/ugly' than suffering it, but more beneficial for the unjust agent, while suffering injustice is less 'shameful/ugly' but more harmful for the person who suffers it. A clearer-headed person than Polus, as portrayed by Plato, could have successfully sustained his position in argument. A clear head is needed, since Polus is abandoning the customary alignments of traditional Greek values, in terms of which the behaviour of the 'goodman' is both 'honourable/beautiful' and beneficial for the 'goodman' himself (as well as for the members of his group). As soon as Socrates begins to question him, Polus grants that the more 'honourable/beautiful' exceeds the more 'shameful/ugly' in respect of either pleasantness or benefit or both. Since committing injustice, agreed by Polus to be more 'shameful/ugly', is evidently not more painful than suffering it, it must be more harmful to the person who commits it, and so is not only more 'shameful/ugly' but also more harmful for the unjust agent.

(If Polus were alert, and more conscious of the history of Greek values, he would reply that what Socrates says is true of traditional usages of 'honourable/beautiful' and 'shameful/ugly', but that the usage has recently been extended, and it rests with Socrates to prove that the same is true of the new usages. If Polus were really committed to the new usages himself, Socrates could reasonably ask Polus to accept the consequences: either the 'logic' of the new 'shameful/ugly' and 'honourable/beautiful' is the same as that of the old, or Polus has no justification for accepting the usage.)

Callicles and Thrasymachus are more worthy and more formidable opponents. Like Socrates and Greeks in general, they are agreed that what is 'honourable/beautiful' is also beneficial for its possessor and that the 'goodman', the finest specimen of human being, uses his 'virtue' or 'virtues' to secure 'flourishing' (for himself and his group). If we render the Greek in this manner, it becomes apparent that nothing very determinate is being expressed. Two or more persons—for example, Socrates and Thrasymachus—could agree

on the form of words without agreeing in any way on their interpretation of the goal or the human qualities needed to achieve it.
This fact indicates that it is misleading to term Thrasymachus and
Callicles immoralists. They are not immoralists in Greek terms,
since they subscribe to the most powerful values of the Greeks, and
interpret them in a manner far more familiar in ancient Greece than
does Socrates. They are not nihilists [17]; they have standards, even
if not what the modern reader would term ethical standards. They
are not hedonists, if hedonists always seek to maximise their
pleasure, irrespective of other criteria: when Socrates 'proves' fallaciously to Callicles that cowards and fools sometimes enjoy more
pleasure than the wise and brave, Callicles responds by drawing a
distinction between classes of pleasures (Plato, *Gorgias*).[26] They are
not concerned with their own well-being alone; they have friends as
well as enemies. In fact, they exemplify 'goodmen' who regard
themselves as qualified to rule by the qualities they possess, including
their intelligence, and who in ruling will exploit the citizens who are
outside their own group.

Such men as these are fearless, intelligent and skilful. They are
also ruthless, bloodthirsty and unjust. The Thirty Tyrants, and
members of factions in poleis all over the Greek world, were very
similar. Plato must try to convince them that his favoured set of
human excellences, his account of intelligent behaviour, his account
of 'human flourishing', more successfully satisfy criteria on which
he and they will agree than do their versions of human excellences,
intelligent behaviour and 'human flourishing'.

If Thrasymachus' and Callicles' positions are coherent, and Plato
does his best for them in argument, Socrates' logic cannot refute
them. He certainly cannot thus refute the best case that can be made
for their position. What he does is to maintain that the very idea of
leading one's life in an intelligent manner must resemble a life justly
lived rather than one unjustly lived.

In the second book of Plato's *Republic*, Plato's brothers, Glaucon
and Adimantus, utter a complicated challenge to Socrates. Glaucon
asks Socrates whether he wants merely to seem to have convinced
them, or really to convince them that 'in every way it is more
beneficial (for the agent) to be just than unjust' (357a–b). He distinguishes three classes of 'beneficial things', those which are chosen
for their own sake, those chosen both for themselves and for their
results, and those chosen not for themselves but only for their
results. The first class is exemplified by harmless pleasures, the

second by thought, sight and health, the third by gymnastic training and being treated when ill. Most people, according to Glaucon, place being just in the third category, as did Thrasymachus in Book 1. Socrates would place it in the second category. Glaucon now challenges Socrates to put it into the first, and discuss the effect which justice has in itself when present in the *psuche* (hereafter 'soul'), setting all extrinsic goods on one side.[27] Socrates must show that justice is an intrinsic good so valuable that it outweighs all the ills and woes that may come on the just man because of his justice and all the extrinsic benefits that he might have gained by being unjust. Socrates must demonstrate the falseness of the common view that, for anyone, committing injustice is beneficial to himself, but suffering it harmful. Yet the harm of suffering injustice out-weighs the benefit of committing it, with the consequence that those who cannot avoid the harm and secure the benefit think it profitable to make an agreement with one another neither to commit nor suffer injustice. This agreement is the source of laws and contracts. Justice, accordingly, is the mean between the best state of affairs, commit-ting injustice and not being punished for it, and the worst, suffering injustice and being unable to obtain any requital. It is not welcomed as a good, but is esteemed because one has not the strength to commit injustice and get away with it. Anyone who could get away with committing injustice and was a real Man would never make an agreement with anyone neither to suffer nor commit injustice: he would be insane to do so. If we gave the just and the unjust man the ability to do whatever they wanted, we should find them following the same course, motivated by *pleonexia*, a desire for more, which all (every?) *phusis* (hereafter 'nature') pursues as a good, though it is constrained by *nomos* (hereafter 'law') to value equality.[28] At this point Glaucon tells the story of Gyges' ring. He concludes that if Gyges did not use his opportunities to commit injustice, to those who knew the situation he would appear most *athlios* (the contrary of *eudaimon*, and hence 'wretched, miserable') though they would praise him in each other's sight, and deceive each other out of fear of suffering injustice at his hands.

Glaucon insists that Socrates discuss with them a perfectly just man and a perfectly unjust man. The unjust is to have the ability to commit the greatest injustices while maintaining a reputation for justice. Should any unjust act come to light, he is to be able to restore his position by persuasion (having presumably taken the courses of the rhetoricians) or, if need be, by force, using his courage, his strength, his wealth and his 'friends'. The corresponding just man, on the other hand, is to possess his justice but none of its good (extrinsic) consequences. He must be really just, but have a reputation for injustice, and suffer the utmost rigours of the law. The unjust man, with his reputation for justice, rises to high office in his polis, marries a wife from any family he chooses, betrothes his daughter to anyone he chooses, and engages in cooperative transactions with anyone he chooses. Since he is not squeamish about committing injustice, in any transaction he *pleonektein* over (gets the better of) his 'enemies within the polis' and in so doing becomes rich and helps his 'friends' and harms his 'enemies within the polis'. Being rich, he can make much more sumptuous sacrifices and offerings to the gods than the just man has the resources to do, and so will presumably be more favoured by them. (Note that Glaucon is speaking not only of tyrants, but also of 'respect-able' citizens in a democracy.)

Adimantus now joins the fray. Glaucon challenged Socrates to refute the views of those who hold that injustice is preferable to justice for a real Man. His brother finds fault with the manner in which justice is praised by its advocates. It is not justice itself that they praise, but its (extrinsic) rewards. They allocate to the just man the glittering and successful career that Glaucon allocated to the unjust. The just man is favoured by men and by gods, who furnish him with material rewards. Adimantus quotes texts from Hesiod and Homer to prove his point. The rewards that they offer are confined to this life; but Musaeus and Orpheus offer an eternal drinking-party in the next, as if this were the finest reward for 'virtue'. Others promise that the family of the pious man who keeps his oaths will continue from generation to generation. The advocates of justice threaten the impious and unjust with terrors in Hades, and with the ill-repute and punishments in this life which Glaucon enumerated as the lot of the just man who is believed to be unjust. Adimantus now approaches Glaucon's position more closely. He maintains that 'everyone with one voice'—an evident exaggeration, even if we cite only Callicles and Thrasymachus as exceptions[29]— 'proclaims that *sophrosune*, "self-control", and *dikaiosune*, "justice", are "honourable/beautiful" but difficult and toilsome, whereas license and injustice are pleasant and easy to attain, and "shameful/ ugly" only by common report and by "law/custom/convention"'. They say that unjust acts are for the most part more profitable than just ones, and they are willing to account as 'flourishing' and to honour 'bad' men who are rich and powerful, and to dishonour the weak and poor, though they admit that the latter are more 'good' than the former. (Once again, there are evident exceptions to what 'they' say.)[30] Adimantus then expresses amazement at those who say that the gods allot a 'bad' life to many 'goodmen', and vice versa, and at the claims of those who profess to be able to free wrongdoers from divine punishment by ritual means.

Glaucon argued that the social contract benefits only the inferior; real Men abide by it only because they are deceived by the weak. The unjust man, furthermore, is able to serve the Greek gods as they are often portrayed in belief and cult much better than can the just. To this Adimantus adds that the rewards offered by the partisans of justice are often vulgar, and that other beliefs render it possible for the unjust to obtain them as well as the just. Adimantus concludes that no reason is given by current values and beliefs for preferring justice to the greatest injustice, if one has any power based on one's 'soul', one's body, one's material resources or one's family. (Note the range of different types of people who, it is implied, have no sound reason for preferring justice to injustice.) Combine injustice with a specious façade of justice and one will fare as one would wish in this world and the next. 'Since if anyone can declare that these beliefs are false, and is sufficiently aware that justice is most beneficial (for its possessor), he feels great compassion and is not angry with the unjust. He knows that except for any man there may be who feels distaste for injustice in consequence of his *theia phusis* ("divine nature"; the phrase is related to Plato's view of the divine, *Republic* 379a–83c, not to the myths about the gods reprehended above), or gains knowledge (of the effects of injustice) and abstains from it, no one is voluntarily just. If he finds fault with injustice, the reason is inability to commit injustice and get away with it.'[31]

It seems evident that this indictment of Greek values and beliefs is intended to be comprehensive. It includes touches which are little attested in our literary sources (for example, the graphic pictures of the priests going from door to door promising to obtain forgiveness from the gods through pleasures and feasting, or to harm any enemy, just or unjust, for a small fee). But everything fits into the framework which is found in other documents. Justice will be valued precisely as far as it is conducive to the good of the just agent, injustice disvalued precisely as far as it leads to disaster. Since, as is plain from other documents and as Plato tells us here, the gods are not reliably just and are widely believed to be moved by ritual, sacrifice or mere caprice, Greek religion as Plato, Glaucon and Adimantus know it is of little use in rendering justice attractive even to those who believe that the gods exist and take an interest in human affairs. The picture is unrelievedly bleak.

All of the beliefs reprehended here cohere with beliefs that are otherwise attested. They are all teleological, and the goal is interpreted as 'human flourishing', 'living well' and *'eu prattein'* in the sense of 'faring well'.[32] The debate concerns the most effective route to the goal, the nature of the goal to a much lesser extent. The phrase 'human flourishing' [11] and the others which appear above evidently leave some room for debate about the criteria for the condition; but in fact there is more agreement than is prima facie likely.

For most Greeks of Plato's day of whom we know anything, the 'goodman' is envisioned as seeking his 'human flourishing', his fully satisfactory life with no regrets,[33] in a public, political context; or at all events as holding that 'goodmen' should discharge such a role, and have a claim to do so *qua* 'goodmen'. The expectation, as we have seen, goes back to Homer, and continues through Plato's contemporaries. Isocrates (*to Nicocles*, 14) thinks it monstrous that the more 'bad' should rule the more 'good' and that the more foolish should give orders to those who are wiser, more *phronimoi*, 'practically wise'. In Aristotle's 'best polis' of the *Politics*, we find (1329a17–24):

Besides, the ruling class should be the owners of property, for they are citizens, and the rulers of a polis should be in good circumstances; whereas mechanics, and any other class which is not a producer of 'virtue', have no share in the polis. This follows from our first principle, for 'human flourishing' cannot exist without 'virtue' and a polis is not to be termed 'flourishing' in regard to a proportion of its citizens, but in regard to them all.

Compare what Callicles says in Plato's *Gorgias* (491a7–b4):

By 'stronger'[34] I do not mean shoemakers or cooks, but those who are *phronimoi* (hereafter 'practically wise') in that they know how to *eu oikein* (hereafter 'manage well') the affairs of the polis, and not only 'practically wise' but *andreioi* (hereafter 'manly'),[35] being (thereby) capable of carrying out in action the plans which they form; men who will not grow weary from softness of 'soul'.

Again, in the *Protagoras*, Protagoras in discussion with Socrates defines his teaching in this way (318e–319a):

> What they learn is sound judgement about their own affairs—how best they may manage their own households and about the affairs of the polis—how they may be most competent to handle its business both in speech and in action.

In reply, Socrates asks:

> Do I understand you correctly? You seem to mean the political art, and to be promising to make men into *agathoi politai*, 'good citizens'.[36]

Protagoras agrees.

Consider also some of Meno's attempted definitions in the *Meno*. The first occurs at 71e2:

> If you want a definition of the 'virtue' of a man, that is easy enough: the 'virtue' of a man is to be capable of taking part in politics—the same Greek phrase as Protagoras used above—and while doing so, to be capable of helping one's friends and harming one's enemies, while taking care to suffer no harm oneself at their hands.

Other definitions given by Meno are: 'the capacity for ruling men' (73c9), 'to desire what is "honourable/beautiful" and to be able to obtain it' (77b4), and 'the power to obtain "good things"' (78c1).

These definitions and uses of 'virtue', 'human flourishing', and other important Greek terms would be interpreted very differently by those who put them forward, particularly so far as concerns the cooperative excellences. Plato's Protagoras seems to be a law-abiding citizen, and does not challenge the claims of the cooperative excellences to be 'virtues'; Isocrates is similar; Meno adds justice and 'self-control' to his definitions when pressed to do so by Socrates, but it should be noted that the cooperative 'virtues' are not the first to come to his mind; Aristotle's account of 'virtue' in the passage quoted depends on the *Ethics* and *Politics* as a whole. Callicles on the other hand, holds that ordinary men

> 'Praise "self-control" and "justice" through their own *anandria*, "lack of manliness".' For if a man were born a king's son, or if he

were himself a man capable of providing himself with a tyranny or
some other position of power,

'What in truth could be more "shameful/ugly" and more harmful for such a man than "self-control" and justice? . . . Luxury,
intemperance and license, provided that they have the means to
gain their ends—these are "virtue" and "human flourishing".'

The modern reader leaps to label this position 'immoralist'. But it
should be noted that, if we think not of what we term ethical/moral
values but the most important values of the Greeks, not merely is
there agreement on the terms 'virtue' and 'human flourishing',
there is a broad agreement linking the attainment of 'human flourishing' with the intelligent use of one's 'virtue' in the public life of one's
polis. (For different reasons, the lives of Socrates, Plato and Aristotle
run counter to this.) 'In the public life of one's polis' need not mean
'with an eye to the good of one's polis'. Not only Callicles and
Thrasymachus, but Meno, Crito and Polemarchus believe that it is a
mark of 'virtue'—and indeed of justice—to help one's friends and
harm one's enemies within the polis; and we have seen that this
evaluation posed urgent practical problems in Greek civic life.

The beginning of *Republic* 2 marks a dissatisfaction with the results
that can be obtained by logic and elenchus. The challenge expressed
by Glaucon and Adimantus is the challenge of traditional Greek
values to the contemporary moral and political philosopher, whose
task it must be to solve the problems posed by the values ascribed to
their gods by the Greeks and by the secularised values of some late
5th-century and 4th-century Greeks. The range of solutions is
limited by the values already present in the culture. The goal of all is
'human flourishing', or the possession of such goods as are deemed
to be necessary to produce or constitute 'human flourishing'. There
is no material from which a more powerful deontic 'ought' might be
generated.[37] How one ought to live is equated with the way of life
that will render one most 'flourishing' (for example, *Republic* 352d2,
Aristotle, *Nicomachean Ethics* 1095a 17–30). Social contract theory is
evidently known, but is of little use to Plato. Where some modern
social contract theorists, doubtless under the influence of Hobbes'
grim account of the *bellum omnium contra omnes*, would accept
virtually without question that it is more advantageous for all to
keep to the terms of the contract, in Plato's day it seemed evident to
all that a man sufficiently 'good' in the competitive sense would lose
by so doing, and would therefore be mad to enter into the contract[38];

and it is precisely that kind of 'goodman' who poses Plato's problem in its most acute form.[39]

In the circumstances, it was imperative to affix justice and 'self-control' so firmly to 'human flourishing', the 'good life', 'living well' and 'faring well', all of which express the goal of life, as to make separation impossible. Justice and 'self-control', accordingly, must be intrinsic goods, benefits, so important that no aggregate of extrinsic harms could outweigh them, and their contraries must be harms so important that no aggregate of extrinsic goods, benefits, could outweigh them.

The challenge addressed to Socrates derives from Greek values. His attempt to meet it naturally does so too. He can hope to convince only if he provides an account of the cooperative excellences, and justice and 'self-control' in particular, which all will accept as producing a condition which satisfies the criteria of 'human flourishing' more successfully than any competitor. In those circumstances, justice and 'self-control' will be accepted as 'virtues'. Socrates must now try to attain his goal by some means other than logic or elenchus.

It is now apparent that Socrates is not entirely without resources. Since there is general agreement that 'virtue' and 'human flourishing' are linked with an active life in politics lived as intelligently as possible, though the 'human flourishing' with which one is concerned may well be one's own and one's friends'—sometimes a political faction—rather than that of the polis as a whole, Socrates has a point from which to begin. If he can delineate for his challengers a way of life in the polis which they will admit satisfies the criteria for a 'flourishing' life better than any competing view, a way of life in which justice and 'self-control' are undeniably choiceworthy *per se*, he has satisfied their demands.

Socrates begins by looking for justice in the polis. His alleged reason for so doing is that it will be easier to see there than in the individual. The relationship of 'virtue' and 'human flourishing' to public life may have had an important part to play in his—or rather Plato's—decision. He sketches in a polis *ab initio*, beginning from a handful of craftsmen. A weaver, a shoemaker, a farmer and a builder come together. It is evidently more efficient if each does the work for which he is best fitted by *phusis* ('nature') than if each does everything for himself. The principle of 'one man, one job' having been invoked at this uncontroversial level, Socrates employs it to argue that the soldiers of their polis should engage in no other activity. In their case it is more important, since the *ergon* ('task') is greater. From the soldiers are to be drawn such older men as prove suitable, to govern the polis; but no one is to be a soldier and a governor at the same time. The result is a polis in which each person has one and only one *ergon* ('task/function'),[40] that for which he is fitted by his *phusis* ('nature'). In reading the *Republic* it is useful to remember that Plato has other problems to solve in addition to replying to the challenge that he put into the mouth of Glaucon and Adimantus. The urgent problem of civic strife, the development of values that will rather produce civic harmony, must have been always in his mind. It is for this reason that he forbids the guardians and auxiliaries to own property, or even handle money (417a–b).

Plato is concerned with preventing conflict between rulers and ruled, and between factions of the rulers, such as occur in other poleis. The polis of the *Republic* will be one polis; all others are at least two, and sometimes many more, in number (422e). The community of women and children among the guardians and auxiliaries has the same goal of preventing civic strife. Socrates points out that in other poleis there exist bonds of association between some of the rulers and not others (463e10–c2); whereas in their polis every member of the guardians and auxiliaries will regard every other member as a relative.

The proposal is bizarre, and Aristotle makes appropriate criticisms (*Politics*, 1261a2–22); but Plato does not put it forward dispassionately. If Thucydides is to be believed (3.83), civic strife was endemic in Greece during the Peloponnesian War. His account of the strife at Corcyra shows the extremes to which the opposing factions could go. Plato was aware of recent Greek history. The behaviour of the Thirty occasioned less bloodshed than did the civic strife at Corcyra; but in every sense it came closer to home for Plato. To view the polis of the *Republic* as a desperate remedy for a desperate situation does not make the proposals any more practical, but it perhaps helps to explain why Plato put them forward.

To return to the challenge of Glaucon and Adimantus. Having divided his polis into three groups—the guardians, who are to govern it, the auxiliaries, who are to defend it, and the rest—Socrates returns to the quest for justice. He says (427d): 'I expect that we shall find that if the polis has been correctly founded it is perfectly "good". And if so, it is clear that it is *sophos* ("wise") and "manly" and "self-controlled" and just.'

Since no one objects,[41] Socrates goes on to claim that the wisdom of their polis resides with the guardians (428b–29a), and the 'manliness' with the auxiliaries (429a–30c).[42] 'Self-control' is present (431b) because the more 'good' part of it rules the more 'bad' part. He adds (432a7–10) that the agreement of the more 'bad' part and the one more 'good' by 'nature' as to which should rule, whether in a polis or in each individual, is 'self-control'. Justice is present when each of the three elements in the polis discharges its proper task (433a–434a).

Socrates then turns to the 'soul' of the individual (435c–444a). He distinguishes three 'parts' of the 'soul', the 'rational', the 'spirited', and the part which is 'concerned with the desires and affections'.[43] Wisdom is evidently the 'virtue' of the 'rational', 'manliness' that of the 'spirited' part. 'Self-control' is present when the ruling part of the 'soul' and the two ruled parts ('spirited' and 'desirous') agree that the 'rational' should rule and do not engage in civic strife against it. (Plato uses *stasiazein*, the technical term for civic strife, metaphorically here. The metaphor helps to bind more closely together the analogy of the polis and the 'soul'.)

Evidently one may debate whether what Socrates has identified as justice in the polis and the 'soul' is the justice whose intrinsic choiceworthiness as a 'good' for its possessor Adimantus and Glaucon challenged him at the beginning of *Republic* 2 to demonstrate. But the concern here is rather to demonstrate the link between Socrates' answer and the values and attitudes already present in Greece. I have already argued that anything that is to be choiceworthy must be something 'good' for the chooser; and we have seen that the traditional competitive 'virtue' of the traditional 'goodman' was choiceworthy in this manner. Traditional 'virtue' might demand the running of risks, or even death; but the 'goodman' perceived himself and was perceived by others as a good, effective and flourishing specimen of human being; and such a condition was evidently preferable to being an inferior and ineffective specimen of human being.

Socrates has invoked the idea of successful flourishing in his account of the best 'soul' and the best polis. He is concerned to demonstrate that the excellence(s) of each will make each flourish: a very different matter from arguing that the virtues of each will make each happy. From the beginning of his account of the genesis of the polis he has emphasised that each citizen should perform only one task, and that task the one for which he is best fitted by 'nature'; and he insists that the polis he has described is a polis established in accordance with 'nature'; (428e). If one cannot find any fault with the argument—and the participants in the dialogue are not given the opportunity to do so by Plato—it would be difficult to claim that a polis whose every inhabitant was thus employed was not a 'good' and 'flourishing' polis, or that its possession of the excellences with which it was thus endowed was not an intrinsic 'good' or 'benefit' for it. The argument that a 'soul' similarly organised and endowed is 'good' and 'flourishing' is essentially similar. If the arguments are accepted, Socrates has met the challenge of Glaucon and Adimantus. The manner in which their challenge was put explicitly depended on the non-philosophical values of Greece from Homer onwards; and Socrates' answer is achieved by drawing out other implications of those self-same values.

Plato's solution in the *Republic* requires a type of polis whose occurrence is very unlikely, and even more unlikely when the philosopher-rulers are introduced (473c). Since every citizen must possess all the necessary 'virtues', whose appropriate interpretation in each case depends on his position in the hierarchy, which in turn depends on the type of metal in his 'soul' (415a–d), it is perhaps impossible to claim that any 'virtue' is more important than any other, though the wisdom of the rulers and the courage of the auxiliaries might well appear to have a stronger claim: the city's need to defend itself successfully is as urgent as that of any other Greek polis, even though Plato argues that his polis will have certain advantages peculiar to itself, and the wisdom of the philosopher-rulers is essential if any polis is ever to be 'flourishing' (473c–d). The 'package' must be accepted as a whole; one cannot take over any insights it may contain piecemeal.

It was not until the appearance of the *Laws*, written at the end of his life, that Plato attempts to give rank-order to the 'virtues'. In the guise of lawgiver for a polis which is to have no philosopher rulers,[44] he is in a position to utter fiats; he need not prove his case. The child in the *Laws*-polis will be taught from earliest years that the truly pleasant, the truly 'honourable/beautiful' and the truly beneficial for himself coincide. He will consequently pursue the truly 'honourable/beautiful', so defined that civic harmony is assured (654a). Much admiration was felt by some very prominent Athenian 'good-men' for Crete and Sparta, in which martial courage was the most highly esteemed of the 'virtues'. Plato offers a critique of Crete and Sparta.[45] In the *Laws*-polis there will be a type of education as a result of which a man would be not only 'good' in war, but also capable of administering his polis; the type of man who . . . is really more skilled in war than the warriors of Tyrtaeus; the man who honours courage as the fourth grade of 'virtue', not the first, whether it is manifested in individuals or in the polis as a whole.

Elsewhere the brave deeds of the soldier are ranked second (922a):

So let this law mingled with praise be laid down for the mass of the citizens—a law which counsels but does not compel: that they should give the second grade of honour to the 'good' men who preserve the polis whether by acts of courage or by stratagems of war; for the greatest honour is to be given to those who are able to observe to an outstanding degree the written pronouncements of their good legislators.

Plato justifies his reranking of justice in the following manner (*Laws* 688c):

For I certainly expect that if you follow the reasoning that I put forward just now, you will discover that what caused the downfall of these kingdoms . . . was not cowardice or ignorance of warfare on the part of the rulers or of those who should have been their subjects, but that what ruined them was 'badness' of all other kinds, and especially about the greatest of all human interests.

Plato here writes 'kingdoms', since he has been discussing Troy and other early cities that were governed by kings; but there can be little doubt that he has in mind not merely the legendary past but also the Athens in which he grew up, the Athens which against all expectations had lost the Peloponnesian War. There is, after all, no great interest in trying to improve poleis which no longer exist. To the end, then, Plato's ethics is designed to offer solutions to the urgent practical problems posed by the values of the Greek polis.

# Notes

1. So far as concerns the theory of Forms, Plato's metaphysics and epistemology are a response to the philosophies of Parmenides and Heraclitus [9], [13], [14], and the theory of Forms with the accompanying doctrine of *anamnesis* (recollection), affects the ethics of Plato's maturity, but this lies beyond the scope of the present essay. For a recent discussion of the question see [17].

2. If Plato's *Seventh Letter* is genuine—and most Plato scholars now seem to agree that it is at least a 4th-century composition produced by someone well acquainted with Plato's life—we have the evidence of Plato himself for many of the statements of the next few pages.

3. Even if the evidence of the *Seventh Letter* is rejected, the whole of Plato's moral and political philosophy makes it impossible to doubt this claim.

4. This judgement, like every other in Plato's dialogues, is passed by a character in the dialogue, not by Plato himself, but I cannot believe that the evaluation is not also Plato's own.

5. Indeed, even after the fall of the Thirty, Lysias, prosecuting one of them, Eratosthenes, for the murder of Lysias' brother Polemarchus, is afraid that Eratosthenes will be successful in pleading that his 'virtue', manifested in the expensive services he has performed for the polis, should outweigh the injustice of the crime with which he is charged (Lysias, 12.38, discussed in [1], p. 201).

6. Alcibiades' advice to the Spartans, given after his flight to Sparta when summoned home from the Sicilian Expedition to stand trial on charges of sacrilege, to fortify a permanent strongpoint in Attica and deny the Athenians access to their farms throughout the year, caused great deliberate harm to the Athenians. His justification for his behaviour (Thucydides, 6.92) draws on the values discussed in this chapter.

7. The charges against Socrates were vague, and necessarily so. The restored democracy had proclaimed an amnesty for crimes committed during the period in which the Thirty were in power. Socrates—at great risk to himself—had declined to be implicated in one of their crimes (Plato, *Apology*, 32c–d). It would have been difficult as well as illegal to charge him with some *explicit* responsibility for having taught the Thirty to behave in a manner which he so patently abhorred. 'Corrupting the young' allowed the jury to think of Critias, Charmides and the rest without either contravening the provisions of the amnesty or becoming too aware of the illogicality of the charge.

8. See [1], chapters 10–13.

9. For evidence and arguments for the account of Homeric values given here, see [1], [2], [3], [4], [5], [6], [7], [8].

10. The translation 'goodman', which is my own, should both remind the Greekless reader that the Greek is a nominalised adjective, and that the adjective is customarily rendered by 'good', but not in a sense familiar to us. (Reference to the *OED*, s.v. will demonstrate that when the term was in use, its connotations were not altogether different from those of

26

*agathos* [*aner*].) 'Goodity', a word attested in *OED* as having been used once in the 17th century, might be proposed as an equivalent for *arete* with practically no connotations in 20th-century English, if it did not sound rather frivolous as an equivalent for such an important term.

11. Telemachus is regularly termed *pepnumenos* (for instance, *Odyssey*, 1. 213, 230, 306), a word which praises his behaviour as prudent and 'co-operative'; but he is unable to defend Odysseus' oikos—now his own, if Odysseus is really dead, as the suitors believe—against the suitors of Penelope. It is not surprising that the competitive, combative excellences are more highly regarded or that, though the other members of the oikos naturally prefer their head, their 'goodman', to be *pepnumenos* too, they perceive a stronger need for his martial qualities than for his cooperative behaviour towards them.

12. Had not the goddess Athena herself come from Olympus—as a partisan of Odysseus rather than as an impartial dispenser of justice—to administer oaths to the combatants, the war would have continued. (Note the 'virtue'-language of *Odyssey*, 24.504–15.)

13. See, for example, [1], [4], [6]. I use 'most "good" rather than "best", and similarly most "bad" rather than "worst",' as an additional reminder that 'good' is not used in a familiar sense here.

14. This rendering of *'timesthai'* must appear implausible to readers unacquainted with Homeric values. See [2] for the pattern of values into which it fits.

15. See also [1], p. 39.

16. When, as a result of Achilles' mother Thetis obliging him, and Zeus obliging Thetis, it became apparent to Agamemnon that he could not both keep Briseis and defeat the Trojans without Achilles, he tried to placate Achilles. Since the fear of seeming to be deficient in 'virtue' is so powerful a motive, Agamemnon might not have been deterred had failure been guaranteed at the time of the quarrel: but certainly nothing less could serve as a deterrent.

17. There can be few societies in which the belief is not empirically falsified with some regularity. Some scholars dislike this account of early Greek belief; but as we shall see, Plato confirms it. Plato of course was not infallible; but it would perhaps be rash to claim that he was mistaken about the beliefs of the society in which he was living, particularly when the other documents of the society uniformly support him. In any case, the question is irrelevant to the present chapter: Plato's philosophy is naturally based on Plato's own view of the values and beliefs of the society.

18. Injustice and *hubris* are not necessarily the same thing. Petty larceny is unjust, but unlikely to be considered to be *hubris*. Claiming that one can play the lyre better than Apollo is *hubris*, but hardly unjust.

19. The word *philos* serves to demarcate those persons, and indeed things, on which the 'goodman' should be able to rely—a small number, particularly in Homer—from persons in general, from whom hostility or indifference is to be expected. See [3], [5].

20. However, the words used—*olbos, eudaimonia, eu zen, eu prattein*, and so forth—do not simply denote material well-being. There is room to

debate what constitues *olbos* or *eudaimonia*, at least as early as Herodotus' fictitious acount of the meeting of Solon and Croesus (1.30–3, discussed in [4]).

21. The earlier Presocratic philosophers eliminated anthropomorphic deities, not deities as such, from their accounts of the cosmos. However, such deities played the role of efficient causes, to account for movement in the cosmos, and took no interest in the doings of mankind.

22. Since the heavy infantry and the cavalry at Athens still purchased their own weapons, those who could afford to do so constituted a socio-economic class, as did the Homeric warriors. They continued to be termed 'goodmen' even when, as in later 5th-century Athens, the contribution of the poorer citizens who rowed the triremes was more significant. See [Xenophon], *Constitution of the Athenians, passim*, for a splenetic but shrewd account of the situation.

23. In general, I have not placed 'harmful', 'beneficial', 'just' or 'unjust' or the nominal or adjectival forms of these words within 'scare quotes', since I have discussed no Platonic arguments in which their absence seems likely to mislead the Greekless reader.

24. See [1], chapter 13, 281–86. The question sounds trivial in an English translation but, as I there argue, it, and Crito's answer, are the foundation for the arguments of the rest of the dialogue. For the phrase 'human flourishing', see [11].

25. For the consequences, see, for example, the arguments against Callicles and Thrasymachus put forward by Socrates (discussed in [1], chapter 13). The extension of 'good' and 'bad' to the cooperative excellences produces the 'Socratic paradox'. 'No one is voluntarily "bad"' is a truism so far as concerns competitive 'virtue', for then 'bad' decries poverty and failure. The phrase is confusing so far as concerns cooperative 'virtue', for then 'bad' decries injustice. That agents are always involuntarily unjust reads very strangely, partly because it seems likely to conflict with the idea of being an agent. But for any 5th- or 4th-century Greek who accepted justice as a 'virtue', a human excellence, and therefore beneficial to its possessor, while regarding injustice as a human 'badness', a mark of an inferior human being, and hence harmful to its possessor, the Socratic paradox must have been difficult to clarify or disprove.

26. He could have replied by arguing that the fool and the coward may in a particular case enjoy more pleasure than the brave and intelligent 'goodman', but that the latter by employing his 'manliness' and intelligence will be able to get more pleasure over even a comparatively short period, and much more over a complete lifetime.

27. 'Soul' is misleading. No Greek, whether atomist, Platonist, Peripatetic, Stoic or 'ordinary Greek', ever discusses the dominant question concerning the 'soul' in more recent times, whether the *psuche* exists. The Greek discussion concerns the nature of *psuche*, which denotes that which constitutes the difference between a live rabbit and a dead one. One may dispute whether the difference consists in the presence or absence of light round atoms, dispersed at death, or in the presence or absence of a non-material immortal substance which passes through a variety of

incarnations, or any of a number of other possibilities, but that there is a difference between a live rabbit [lettuce, human being] and a dead one is hardly likely to be disputed.

28. *Nomos* and *phusis* are concepts of great importance in the later 5th and earlier 4th centuries. For a discussion, see [15]. (*Phusis* spans 'birth'—in a sense which includes not merely the event of being born but whatever results from being born at a particular place and time into a particular social or economic group—and 'nature'. *Nomos* spans 'law', 'custom' and 'convention'.)

29. Callicles and Thrasymachus evidently represent a type of person, not merely themselves.

30. Examples abound of men who are 'bad' in a cooperative sense being regarded as 'flourishing'. It is more difficult to discover anyone treating the weak and poor just person as 'good'. But see [1], chapter 9.

31. Only a person who regarded justice as a 'virtue' would be voluntarily 'just'.

32. *Eu prattein* is used in the sense both of 'doing good' and of 'doing/faring well', and thus lends itself to a variety of equivocations. See Plato, *Gorgias*, 507c, *Charmides* 172a1, *Euthydemus* 281c1, and so on.

33. *Eudaimonia* is objective as 'happiness' is not. However, for the most part Plato and Aristotle, unlike the Stoics later, do not suppose that 'human flourishing' is compatible with suffering violent and unpleasant physical sensations, that the 'goodman' can be 'flourishing' even on the rack. (Note Aristotle's comments, *EN* 1096a1–2, 1100a8–9. Plato's Socrates sometimes takes a more extreme view, for instance, *Crito* 44c–d.)

34. *Kreittous*, often used as the comparative of *agathos*. From Homer onwards, strength is an essential criterion for being a 'goodman'.

35. *Andreios*, the usual Greek word for 'brave', is sexist in its implications, being formed from *aner*, 'man, warrior'. ('Human being' is 'anthropos'.)

36. Note the difference between the sense of *agathos polites* and 'good citizen'. The English phrase has connotations of obeying the laws and cooperating with one's fellow-citizens, whereas the Greek at this period has connotations of skill and daring. See [1], chapters 10–16. Plato and Aristotle try in different ways at least to give different emphases to the words.

37. Such an 'ought' may perhaps require the earlier presence of a deity or deities believed to be more just, or just in a higher sense, than mere mortals can aspire to. No such deities are available in early Greece. (Alasdair MacIntyre has some interesting speculations on this theme in [19].)

38. This seems different from the problem of the 'free-rider', who on particular occasions finds it profitable to behave in contravention of the contract into which he has entered.

39. In ancient Greece only the atomists are staunch adherents of social contract theory; and the atomists tend towards quietism, and set little value on competitive 'virtue'.

40. For a discussion of the problems involved in translating *ergon*, see [8].

41. As Thrasymachus should have been permitted by Plato to point out, Socrates is begging the question here. Since Thrasymachus does not

accept that 'justice' and 'self-control' are 'virtues', he has no reason to grant that a 'good', 'flourishing' specimen of a polis should be 'self-controlled' or 'just'. Socrates should have said 'if it is "good", our polis must have all the *aretai*, "virtues/excellences", that a polis should have. Let us now consider what these "virtues/excellences" are'.

42. Some of the auxiliaries were to be women, however. Plato knew that the proposal would not be popular, *Republic*, 502d ff.

43. So LSJ, *A Greek/English Lexicon* compiled by Henry George Liddell and Robert Scott, revised by Sir Henry S. Jones (Oxford University Press, 1968), sub v. There seems to be no neat rendering.

44. Plato no longer believed that any human being could possess either so much wisdom or so much 'self-control' as a philosopher-ruler would need, *Laws* 874e ff. However, even as late as the *Politicus* (293a–b, 297d, 301c), the Stranger—and so presumably Plato—still maintains that *if* a person with real knowledge should appear, he should be given a free hand in governing the polis. The same point is made in the *Laws*, 875c.

45. Plato's choice of a Cretan and a Spartan to converse with the Athenian in the *Laws*, and his initial praise of the Cretan and Spartan constitutions, would be likely to attract Laconophile readers in Athens. Once attracted, they would find Plato critical of important features of their favourite poleis. Plato presumably hoped that his readers would agree that his proposed changes were indeed improvements.

# Bibliography

1. Adkins, A. W. H. (1960) *Merit and Responsibility: a Study in Greek Values* (Oxford: Clarendon Press).
2. Adkins, A. W. H. (1960) ' "Honour" and "Punishment" in the Homeric Poems', *Bulletin of the Institute of Classical Studies*, 7: 23–32.
3. Adkins, A. W. H. (1963) ' "Friendship" and "Self-sufficiency" in Homer and Aristotle', *Classical Quarterly*, 13: 29–45.
4. Adkins, A. W. H. (1972) *Moral Values and Political Behaviour in Ancient Greece* (London: Chatto & Windus; Toronto: Clarke, Irwin).
5. Adkins, A. W. H. (1972) 'Homeric Gods and the Values of Greek Society', *Journal of Hellenic Studies*, 92: 1–19.
6. Adkins, A. W. H. (1982) 'Values, Goals, and Emotions in the Iliad', *Classical Philology*, 77: 292–326.
7. Adkins, A. W. H. (1985) 'Cosmogony and Order in Ancient Greece', in Robin W. Lovin and Frank E. Reynolds (eds), *Cosmogony and Ethical Order* (Chicago and London: University of Chicago Press) pp. 39–66.
8. Adkins, A. W. H. (1984) 'The Connection between Aristotle's *Ethics* and *Politics*', *Political Theory*, 12: 29–49.
9. Barnes, J. (1979) *The Presocratic Philosophers*, vol. 1 (London, Henley and Boston: Routledge & Kegan Paul).
10. Bury, J. B. (1951) *A History of Greece to the Death of Alexander the Great*, revised by R. Meiggs (London: Macmillan).
11. Cooper, J. M. (1985) *Reason and Human Good in Aristotle* (Cambridge, Mass.: Harvard University Press).
12. Guthrie, W. K. C. (1962) *A History of Greek Philosophy*, vol. 1 (Cambridge: Cambridge University Press).
13. Guthrie, W. K. C. (1965) *A History of Greek Philosophy*, vol. 2 (Cambridge: Cambridge University Press).
14. Hammond, N. G. L. (1959) *A History of Greece to 322 B.C.* (Oxford: Clarendon Press).
15. Heinimann, F. (1945) *Nomos und Physis* (Basel: Reinhardt).
16. Irwin, T. (1977) *Plato's Moral Theory* (Oxford: Clarendon Press).
17. Kerferd, G. B. (1947) 'The Doctrine of Thrasymachus in Plato's *Republic*', *Durham University Journal*, December.
18. Kerferd, G. B. (1981) *The Sophistic Movement* (Cambridge: Cambridge University Press).
19. MacIntyre, A. (1984) *After Virtue*, 2nd ed. (Notre Dame: University of Notre Dame Press).

# 2

# Aristotle
## *Alfonso Gomez-Lobo*

### THE MAN AND HIS TIMES

Aristotle, son of Nicomachus, was born in the small city of Stageira in northern Greece in 384 BC (in what follows all dates are BC). It still happens today in Greek villages that when family and friends perceive exceptional talent in a young member of the community considerable effort is invested in providing him with the best education available. In Aristotle's case, his guardian, a certain Proxenos, made provisions to send him to Athens where he joined Plato's Academy at the age of 17.

Aristotle remained in the Academy approximately 20 years, a lengthy period of apprenticeship corresponding to Plato's remarkable last phase of philosophical production. During these years, which range from his 60th birthday to his death at 81, Plato had doubtless been composing, among other writings, the *Theatetus* and the *Sophist*, two dialogues in which his analytical powers are applied to the difficult domains of logic, epistemology and metaphysics. The *Gorgias* and *The Republic*, with their impassioned moral claims, lay in the past. But Plato's interest in ethical matters had not waned in the least, as attested by the *Philebus* and the *Laws*.

At Plato's death in 347 his nephew Speusippos (who was already over 60 years old at the time) succeeded him as head of the Academy. Due to reasons which are not totally clear (but which probably have more to do with the political, anti-Macedonian climate than with intellectual or personal quarrels among the Academics), Aristotle left Athens and embarked on a lengthy period of wanderings and instability.

After three years in Assos, on the coast of Asia Minor, where he married Pythias, the sister (or niece and adopted daughter) of Hermias, the local ruler, Aristotle moved to Mytilene on the island of Lesbos. Here he started his lifelong collaboration in the study of zoology and botany with Theophrastus, a native of the island.

In 343 Aristotle received one of the highest honours that could be granted to someone of his intellectual stature: he was invited by Philip II to the court of Macedonia to become the tutor of the crown prince. About the relationship between the philosopher and Alexander the Great—who was then 13 years old—we know next to nothing. Apparently, in keeping with standard Greek custom, the *Iliad* was used as the main source of moral education for the young man. Alexander's romantic decision to place a garland on the tomb of Achilles after crossing over to Asia many years later attests to this. But as time went by and Alexander had to organise the territories he had conquered, it became more and more evident that he had radically rejected Aristotle's political ideas whose cornerstone was the small, self-governing and self-centred polis with its emphasis on the radical difference between Greeks and Barbarians.

Alexander's education was cut short in 340 when the 16-year-old prince had to serve as regent of the Macedonian kingdom during his father's absence. Aristotle, it seems, remained in Macedonia, perhaps in Stageira, or moved for some time to Delphi to compile on behalf of the Amphictyonic Council a list of the victors in the Pythian games.

We may conjecture that in 335 Aristotle saw and grasped the opportunity he had been expecting for a long time: due to Alexander's accession to the throne, he was now in a position to return to Athens under Macedonian protection.

The next 12 years represent the culmination of Aristotle's life. He founded his own school, the Lyceum (later also known as the Peripatos). At this time he must have been quite an attraction in Athens for those sensitive to his achievements. He often gave public lectures, he reworked earlier material and gave more or less final form to works on a wide variety of topics including logic, physics, metaphysics, theology, ethics, politics, aesthetics and literary criticism, general biology, zoology and meteorology. He also organised collective research projects such as the study of Greek political institutions based on a vast compilation of constitutions from different Greek states, and gave support to research done by his students in such areas as botany, descriptions of moral characters, the history of geometry, arithmetic and astronomy, and the history of medicine, to mention just a few of the domains that attracted the interest of the early Peripatetics.

In 323, in the midst of the aforementioned encyclopaedic activities, Aristotle received the news of Alexander's death. 'Lest the Athenians commit a second crime against philosophy' (the first one being, of course, the execution of Socrates) Aristotle withdrew to his mother's house in Chalkis on the island of Euboea where he died a natural death a few months later at the age of 62.[1]

Aristotle's will gives us an insight into the affectionate nature of one of the most powerful intellects in western history. After making provisions for the marriage of his daughter, for the well-being of his son Nicomachus, and for the manumission of some of his slaves, he adds in general:

> Do not sell any of the slaves who served me, but employ them; and when they come of age, send them away free men as they deserve.

Later on he continues:

> They [the executors of will] are to dedicate the statue of my mother to Demeter in Nemea or wherever seems best. Wherever they make my grave they are to take and deposit there Pythia's [his wife's] bones too, just as she instructed. And Nicanor [his future son-law], if he is preserved (which is a prayer I have offered on his behalf) is to set up statues in stone four cubits in height to Zeus Saviour and Athena Saviouress at Stageira.[2]

During Aristotle's lifetime the political scene in Greece went through two different stages. The first was a brief period of Theban hegemony (371–362) and the second was the dramatic rise of Macedonian power in the north which finally engulfed the whole of Hellas.

The Peloponnesian War (431–404) had put an end to Athenian domination of the Aegean sea and to a period of astonishing intellectual and artistic creativity. After Athens' unconditional surrender to the Spartans a dictatorship (the Thirty) was set up under their protection, but when the new rulers were defeated by a democratic uprising, Sparta was generous (or weak) enough to allow the restoration of the old democratic institutions. Under this regime Athens did not recover her lost pre-eminence, but she certainly remained a city full of vitality and dynamism. The extreme humiliation came when finally a Macedonian governor, Aristotle's friend Antipater, was imposed on her.

Aristotle's relationship to Athens was very different from that of his teacher. Plato was an Athenian citizen. His own life and thought were indissolubly linked to the fortunes of his city. He had seen his friend Socrates tried and condemned to death by the same groups which had been chiefly responsible for the insolence and blindness of Athenian imperialism which had inevitably led to the catastrophe of 404. Remotely to blame were the 5th century sophists for their moral relativism and agnosticism, directly guilty were in his opinion those Athenians who, like Callicles in the *Gorgias*, had endorsed a might-makes-right theory of international and civic relations. It is against these forces that Plato reacts; it is to these ideas that Plato's moral philosophy is to supply a radical and sound alternative.

Nowhere in Aristotle's writings do we find the intensity and the passion which strike the reader of some of the Platonic dialogues. Aristotle faces Athens not as an active participant in the life of the city, but rather as a detached though sympathetic observer. The causes of the fall of the empire are no longer a living issue for him. What attracts his eye and awakens his admiration are the institutions which allow the Athenians more than anyone else in the Greek world to lead a kind of life essentially worth living. It is not un-reasonable to conjecture that during his early stay in Athens as a student, Aristotle learnt about most of the basic values (or *aretai*, 'virtues') which he later included in his conception of the good life. There is indeed a sense in which Aristotle's ethics is basically Athenian ethics, that is, not a revisionist system of morality (as was perhaps that of Socrates and Plato), but a refined version of the best ideals that the educated Athenian of his day would in principle accept. Thus, magnanimity, for example, though not practicable by all, was doubtless held in high esteem, and even detached intel-lectual pursuits (or *theoria*), we may conjecture, would have been admired even by those who could not engage in them, something that still happens today in Greece.

Although Aristotle's ethics reflects many of the Greek values current then in everyday life, it should not be forgotten that the very core and structure of the system owes much to specialised philo-sophical reflection, that is, to the sustained inquiries of Socrates and Plato. Most of the basic Aristotelian concepts were developed either in direct acceptance of Platonic material or in its explicit rejection.

Keeping all of the foregoing in mind we may now turn to Aristotle's moral philosophy.

## PRACTICAL KNOWLEDGE

In its present form the *Corpus Aristotelicum* (or collection of Aristotle's writings) contains three works that have the Greek word ethika in their title. They are the *Eudemian Ethics* (*EE*, a treatise in a poor state of textual preservation which is generally believed to be the earliest of the three), the *Nicomachean Ethics* (*NE*, reasonably well preserved, it has three of its 'books' in common with the *EE*) and the *Magna Moralia* (*MM*, which many scholars believe to be by a student of Aristotle).[3]

Aristotle occasionally refers to the aforementioned works by means of the expression *en tois ethikois*, 'in the ethical [books]',[4] but he seems to reserve for their content a rather suggestive title: *he peri ta anthropeia philosophia*, 'the philosophy of human affairs'.[5] In the context in which he uses this expression he makes it clear that the philosophical territory he is referring to includes the subject-matter of what is called today his *Politics*. Indeed, since the ultimate goal of politics embraces every other human goal[6] and since the life of man as a member of the *polis* determines his very nature,[7] it is not surprising to see that the philosophy of human affairs is for the most part called simply *politike*, 'politics'. This is in fact the standard way of referring to the discipline itself in the *NE*.[8]

If we now look for the most general way of characterising 'politics', we shall discover the label 'practical knowledge'. This is particularly interesting because it gives some indication about the place that Aristotle assigns to ethics within his philosophical system.

According to Aristotle's most general classification there are three basic forms of knowledge: practical, productive and theoretical.[9] Taking this enumeration in the reverse order, we can say that these labels serve to convey the idea that, first, the human mind can apply itself to the contemplation (*theoria*) of things without any possibility or intention of changing or affecting them. Among such objects of contemplation are the natural bodies, namely, those things that move or develop according to immanent principles, viz. according to what Aristotle calls their *physis*, 'nature', in the strict sense. Physics, the study of things endowed with such a *physis*, is therefore one of the theoretical sciences.[10] But, second, the human mind can also originate motion or change.[11] If its aim is to create a tangible object, for example, a pair of sandals or a piece of furniture, then reason proceeds productively, usually by means of the rationally motivated moves prescribed by some *techne* or craft. This accomplish-

ment is called *poiesis*, 'production'. It is not, however, the only kind
of motion or change we originate. Our productions are only a subset
of our actions, that is, they are subordinate to what we intend to do
with the products we have created. We need clothes and furniture in
order to pursue further goals. There is, then, a third use of reason,
the use that is at work when one tries to attain certain ultimate ends
which cannot be 'produced' but which affect one's life as a whole.[12]
In Aristotle's terminology this use of reason is called 'practical
science' or knowledge pertinent to action. Ethics falls within its
province.[13]

Contrary to his Plato, Aristotle sharply distinguishes between
theoretical and practical knowledge. Theoretical science is the result
of the operation of a human faculty or power which he calls *to
epistemonikon*, 'the scientific [part of the rational soul]'. Likewise,
practical science corresponds to the operation of *to logistikon*, 'the
calculative [part of the rational soul]'.[14] The names given to these
faculties or powers by later philosophical tradition are 'theoretical
reason' and 'practical reason', respectively.

When Aristotle discusses theoretical and practical reason he holds
explicitly that 'truth is the work [*ergon*] of both rational parts'.[15]
These 'parts' are indeed nothing but two different modes of operation
of the chief cognitive faculty in the human soul.

But how are we to distinguish truth of the theoretical part from
truth attained by the practical part of reason? What is the distinguishing mark of practical truth as opposed to theoretical truth? The
classification of Aristotelian disciplines introduced earlier is useful
at this point because it is the aim of human reason in the pursuit of
truth that determines whether a given kind of truth is to be understood to fall within one domain or the other. Truth, of course, is
primarily sought as a property of a declarative sentence or proposition
(*apophantikos logos*).[16] Hence, it seems more appropriate to phrase
the question as a question about such propositions or *logoi*. With
these considerations in mind the difference may be set out as follows:

(1) a declarative proposition is theoretical if and only if its truth is
sought for its own sake;
(2) a declarative proposition is practical if and only if its truth is
sought for the sake of something else, viz. action.[17]

How exactly can the truth of a practical proposition affect action?
How does this congnitive element enter into the motivation for action?

For Aristotle, practical thought grasps a *possible* object of desire (namely, something worth desiring) which the faculty of desire then turns into an actual object of desire (namely, something actively pursued). Thus a practical proposition affects action by stating that something is desirable or good.

But since there are things that really are good and things that only appear to be good,[18] then if the practical proposition is *true*, we are moved to action by the real good; if it is *false*, the motivation for action is the apparent good.[19]

Thus, Aristotle's characterisation of ethics as a practical science should lead us to expect that it will consist basically in the presentation and dialectical defence of something like a catalogue of real goods, namely, a set of true propositions about the goals for human action. With this in mind we now turn to the *Nicomachean Ethics*.

## ARISTOTLE'S CONCEPTION OF THE GOOD

In the opening chapters of Book I of the *NE* the central question of Aristotelian ethics is raised and in chapter 7 an outline of an answer is given. Since that answer involves the notion of excellence or virtue (*arete*), two kinds of virtue are distinguished in chapter 13, thus providing an organisational principle for the rest of the work. Books II to V discuss moral virtue while Books VI–VII deal with intellectual virtues and some related problems. Books VIII and IX are devoted to an excellence which in a sense represents both kinds of virtue, viz. friendship, and finally in Book X an ultimate effort is made to provide a definitive reply to the original question and to initiate the transition to the *Politics*.

The road towards the formulation of the central question takes the following turns: we are first invited to consider the fact that there is a multiplicity of goods or ends (indeed every human activity has its own end)[20] and that there is a subordination of such ends, that is, there are ends that we pursue for the sake of other ends.[21] This latter point holds not only for production where the end is an artifact (for example, a vase) which in turn is used for some further end (offering wine to friends), but also for the case in which the ends of action are the actions themselves.[22] This last idea is difficult to understand because it would seem that there is an inconsistency in saying that something was done for its own sake and at the same time for the sake of something else. The difficulty vanishes if we assume that the former is one of the things that count as doing the latter. Thus, to contemplate the East pediment of the temple of Apollo may be an end in itself, but it also counts as part of what admiring the whole sanctuary of Delphi consists in. This point will later be seen to be of considerable importance.

From the idea that in action there is subordination of ends, Aristotle moves to a somewhat stronger claim:

> If, then, there is some end of the things we do, which we desire for its own sake (everything else being desired for the sake of this), and if we do not choose everything for the sake of something else (for at any rate the process would go on to infinity, so that our desire would be empty and vain), clearly this must be the good and the chief good.[23]

Here Aristotle seems first to posit hypothetically the existence of an ultimate end and then confirm it by means of the consideration that otherwise our desire would be empty and vain.[24] Such an end would be *the* good, namely, the best thing there is for human beings to pursue.[25]

But what is the best thing? What is the chief good at which we ultimately aim for its own sake? In Book I of the *NE* Aristotle takes two steps leading to an answer: (1) he advances a conceptual clarification of the question itself; and (2) he gives an initial sketch of his own reply.

In dealing with (1) Aristotle starts by saying that there is general agreement on calling the chief good *eudaimonia*[26] and by specifying two marks that are tied to this concept: *eudaimonia* is something complete (or final) and self-sufficient.[27] The standard translation of *eudaimonia* into English is 'happiness' but it has often been observed that this is misleading and definitely wrong in some contexts. 'Happiness' points primarily to a state of feeling. One does or does not *feel* happy, whereas in Greek one *is* or *is not eudaimon*, one possesses or does not possess a property which usually lasts through time and which is characteristically predicated of cities. To be *eudaimon* is to be prosperous, to be well-off, to flourish. It is to attain the best possible condition for a human being.

I take it that by saying that the human good is called '*eudaimonia*' Aristotle is uttering what we would call a logical truth.[28] He makes a further analytic move when he specifies that it must be complete and self-sufficient. The test for completeness is whether something is said to be chosen for its own sake only or for its own sake *and also* for the sake of something else. In the former case we have complete-ness, in the latter we do not.[29]

In turning now to the self-sufficiency property of happiness we find Aristotle writing:

> . . . the self-sufficient we now define as that which when isolated makes life desirable and lacking in nothing; and such we think happiness to be; and further we think it most desirable of all things, without being counted as one good thing among others— if it were so counted it would clearly be made more desirable by the addition of even the least of goods; for that which it added becomes an excess of goods, and of goods the greater is always more desirable.[30]

The idea that Aristotle tries to convey in this passage is that happiness must be thought of as analogous to a self-sufficient individual. An individual (or a city) is self-sufficient if he can pro-duce everything he requires to satisfy his needs. He does not depend on barter, just as a self-sufficient city does not depend on foreign trade: nothing needs to be brought in for it from the outside. Self-sufficiency, however, may be achieved by two different ways: either by lowering one's needs or by producing more without diminishing one's needs. It seems clear that Aristotle wants to stress that the concept of happiness should be understood according to the second model, that is, according to the model in which nothing needs to be added to it from the outside not because of low internal demand but because of ample internal supply.

This logical feature of the concept of happiness is further stressed by noting that if happiness is by definition the most desirable of all things it logically cannot have any goods added to it from the outside. *All* goods lie *within* its borders.

The logical point made in the passage is therefore that a correct answer to the question 'What is happiness?' must be an inclusive one. It must specify a *collection of goods* and not just a single one.[31]

In the course of clarifying the kind of self-sufficiency he has in mind, Aristotle also gave an important hint in the direction of his final reply. For in a passage preceding the former quote, he wrote:

> Now by self-sufficient we do not mean that which is sufficient for man by himself, for one who lives a solitary life, but also for

parents, children, wife, and in general for his friends and fellow citizens, since man is sociable [= political] by nature.[32]

That is, a human being does not flourish in isolation but only in the context of a family and of a wider community, the city-state.

The two formal characteristics of flourishing, viz. completeness and self-sufficiency have thus led to the same conclusion. The human good does not consist in a single thing but rather in a collection of goods. But how can these goods come to be specified? In order to do this Aristotle proposes what has come to be known as the *ergon* argument, an argument based on the consideration of the function or characteristic activity of man.[34]

For the historian of ethics this is a step of considerable importance because it is here that Aristotle seems to be laying the ultimate foundations of his ethical system.

The general form of the argument seems to be as follows:

(1) for any $x$ there is a characteristic activity $y$ such that if $x$ exercises $y$ well, then $x$ is a good $x$
(2) man has a characteristic activity $C$. Therefore
(3) if a man exercises $C$ well, then he will be a good man.

Conclusion (3) is equivalent to a definition stating that the human good consists in exercising well the characteristic activity or 'work' of man. And this, Aristotle adds independently of the argument, 'in a complete lifetime', that is, in a lifetime in which there are no periods in which the work of man is not well exercised. If such periods do exist, then that would be an incomplete token of the good.[35]

In analysing the argument leading to the definition we must first observe that Aristotle assumes without question that it is good for man to be a good man. Flourishing is accordingly the state which is best for me and in which I am at my best.

It must be further taken into account that 'to do something well' and 'to do it according to virtue (or excellence, *kat'areten*)' are synonymous expressions. Moreover, they are both primarily expressions used to evaluate and commend actions. If we take this into account plus the occurrence of the predicate 'good' in premise (1), we see that Aristotle's starting point is a general principle of evaluation and commendation which could be plausibly accepted by Aristotle's fellow Greeks as true. It is indeed in premise (2) where most of the difficulties seem to arise.

Initially Aristotle argues for (2) by invoking psychological doctrines from the *De Anima*. The life of nutrition and growth and the life of perception are ruled out. They are not peculiar to man. But the introduction of reason seems to anticipate a way of viewing this faculty which corresponds to what we read later on in the *NE*:

> There remains, then, an active life of the element that has a rational principle (*tou logon echontos*] (of this, one part has such a principle in the sense of being obedient to one, the other in the sense of possessing one and exercising thought).[36]

The mention of what is 'obedient to *logos*' is an early reference to the part of the soul which may or may not conform to reason[37] and in consonance with this the work of man is presented in a value neutral way with regard to action.[38]

What Aristotle is saying, then, is that it is peculiar to man to act either rationally or irrationally, neither of which possibilities is open to brutes. Premise (2), then, makes a value neutral statement about human nature, but no evaluation is directly inferred from it. The value judgement which the antecedent of conclusion (3) requires so that its consequent can be affirmed should be made on other grounds, namely, on the basis of the logically independent standards for what is to count as doing the work of man well. Such standards are the virtues and to their definition and analysis Aristotle devotes the rest of the *NE*. In other words, human beings should be evaluated by focusing on what is most characteristic of their nature, namely, their (good or bad) use of reason. But the judgement that some uses of reason are good (for example, the use involved in guiding temperate or just actions) is not grounded on theoretical considerations about human nature but on evaluative, that is, independent practical principles.

If the foregoing interpretation of Aristotle's argumentation is correct, then he may be cleared of the charge of inferring evaluative conclusions from descriptive premises in the derivation of his initial definition of human flourishing. The exact wording of the definition itself, however, deserves further commentary.

> [The] human good turns out to be activity of soul in conformity with excellence [*arete*, virtue], and if there are more than one excellence, in conformity with the best and most complete.[39]

What is in our best interests, that is, what makes us be good human beings, is, according to this definition, action in accordance with the standards for good use of reason. If there is more than one such standard, then 'in conformity with the best and most complete (*teleiotaten*)'. For a long time scholars have been misled into thinking that this phrase denotes a single virtue among a plurality of virtues. In retrospect this is rather surprising given the fact that Aristotle had previously defined 'complete' in a way that indicates rather clearly that this predicate applies only to an inclusive end, that is, an end that includes many ends aimed at for their own sake and for the sake of the collective one as well. The best and most complete excellence is then the one that includes all the other ones and is, in this sense, self-sufficient.[40]

But the interpretation I am presenting is controversial. The claim that according to Aristotle flourishing consists in enjoying a collection of goods seems at first sight to be contradicted by passages that apparently commit him to the view that happiness is reached in the exercise of a single virtue.

The purported contradiction seems to come most conspicuously to the fore in the opening section of chapter 7 of Book X where the initial definition of human flourishing in I.7 is explicitly recalled:

> If happiness is activity in accordance with excellence, it is reasonable that it should be in accordance with the highest excellence; and this will be that of the best thing in us. Whether it be intellect [*nous*] or something else that is this element which is thought to be our natural ruler and guide and to take thought of things noble and divine . . . the activity of this in accordance with its proper excellence will be complete happiness [*he teleia eudaimonia*]. That this activity is contemplative we have already said.[41]

The text is unambiguous in calling 'complete happiness' the activity of a single human capacity, namely, the human intellect, which in I.7 had been included in the list of items which *did not* count as complete ends.[42]

Is there a serious incoherence at the very heart of Aristotle's ethical system? Are we facing a contradiction which forces us to conceive in two radically different ways Aristotle's conception of the relation of the right and the good? If perfect happiness includes the exercise of the moral virtues then the right would be part of the good, but if the good is exclusively identified with contemplative activity, then the right would be excluded from the good and would presumably have to be interpreted as conducive to the good.

This latter alternative has the unpalatable consequence that sometimes doing the morally wrong thing might be the most efficient way of producing conditions for theorising. Thus, the system would justify morally wrong actions on the basis of the paramount pursuit of the highest good.[43]

Is it fair to attribute this kind of immoralism to Aristotle's *NE*? I think not. In the first place Aristotle is quite firm in his conviction that certain actions are wrong regardless of consequences: 'It is not possible, then, ever to be right [*katorthoun*, to do the right thing] with regard to them [sc. adultery, theft, murder]; one must always be wrong [*amartanein*, do the wrong thing].'[44]

Second, the view that Aristotle could be advocating contemplation as happiness to the exclusion or postponement of every other kind of action fails to take into account a pervading feature of his thought, namely the idea that there is a natural hierarchy of layers of life such that the activation of the higher ones rests on the activation of the lower ones. Just as the life of the senses continually presupposes the life of nutrition and growth, and the life of reason that of the senses, similarly the full exercise of contemplation presupposes that the requirements of the moral life have been satisfied and continue to be satisfied. On this view, to say that contemplation is complete happiness is to say that it is the coping stone of an edifice which without it would be incomplete.

The evidence for the suggested solution seems to be scant, but this is due, I think, to the fact that it was obvious to Aristotle that 'no one would call happy [flourishing] someone who does not have a portion of courage or temperance or justice'[45] and that moreover the definition of happiness as contemplation without morality is an easy prey to his own self-sufficiency argument. Contemplation *with* the exercise of moral virtue would be more desirable than contemplation alone and hence would be more likely to constitute that which by definition is the most desirable of all things.

In Book X we read that

> such a life [sc. the life of contemplation] would be too high for man; for it is not in so far as he is man that he will live so, but in so far as something divine is present in him; and by so much as this is superior to our composite nature is its activity superior to that which is the exercise of the other kind of excellence. If intellect is

divine, then, in comparison with man, the life according to it is divine in comparison with human life.

And further down Aristotle adds

> For deeds many things are needed, and more, the greater and nobler the deeds are. But the man who is contemplating the truth needs no such thing, at least with a view to the exercise of his activity; indeed they are, one may say, even hindrances, at all events to his contemplation; but in so far as he is a man and lives with a number of people, he chooses to do excellent acts.[46]

These passages draw a contrast between what man does in so far as there is something divine in him and what he does in so far as he is a man. To the former corresponds contemplation, to the latter the moral life.

Man can be considered in so far as there is something divine in him but this does not mean that he can lead the life of the gods and cut himself off from the human community. Indeed, there seems to be deep Aristotelian wisdom in the well-known dictum: *primum vivere, deinde philosophari*. One should strive for philosophy but first more elementary requirements of life have to be satisfied.

These prior requirements are perhaps less valuable than the ultimate ones, but they are the more stringent ones. In fact, as I have been trying to argue, Aristotle does not seem to entertain the idea that human goodness can be obtained through purely intellectual pursuits, but he does countenance the notion of a second best life, of life 'in accordance with the other kind of excellence', that is, in accordance with moral virtue and, by implication, with prudence (*phronesis*, practical reasonableness).[47] This would be a life without the coping stone of philosophical contemplation but it would be a good life none the less because it implies the ability to secure external goods and the enjoyment of a set of basic goods, viz., the moral goods.[48]

I think that misunderstandings have arisen in this area of thought because there is a tendency to suppose that Aristotle favours some sort of maximisation doctrine to the effect that if contemplation is the greatest good, then it would have to be secured *at any price*. Aristotle does indeed exhort us to 'make ourselves immortal' [*athanatizein*, 'act as immortals'] by engaging in contemplation, but he adds a restriction: 'so far as it is possible'.[49] The possibility of engaging in contemplation is in fact limited by a number of factors, among them by life in the community. Sometimes the choice between contemplating or doing something else will be neutral and in those cases we ought (that is, it would be in our best interests) to choose contemplation. But in other circumstances the choice will not be neutral. The more basic requirements of morality will indicate that contemplation has to be given up because we would otherwise be giving up the more basic goods that make us *agathoi*, 'good men'.

Aristotle's ethics is not an ethics of maximisation of some commodity either for the individual or for the greatest number. It is first and foremost a prudential ethics, a guide to action such that what ought to be done is determined by what in the given circumstances appears as the appropriate good to be pursued.

In retrospect we can now say that for Aristotle there are two possible degrees of human flourishing. The gods (or the god) flourish by engaging in *their* characteristic activity, viz. contemplation. If a man crowns a life of excellent performance towards himself, his family, his friends and his city by the practice of contemplation, then he will have attained the highest degree of human flourishing. The characteristic work of man, namely, the use of reason, will have been fulfilled. But if political life proves to be too absorbing or if he simply does not have the necessary taste and talent for abstract studies, or if external circumstances prevent him from engaging in them, he can still be a good man and hence flourish at a second level. He can certainly perform the work of man well although one of his capacities will not have been activated.[50]

Both forms of genuine happiness, then, consist in engaging in action in a broad sense (one does not flourish just by being fortunate enough to possess wealth, good health or good looks) and moreover engaging in action according to reason. Action in accordance with reason is equivalent to action according to certain standards that the community agrees on and that philosophers help clarify. There are two sets of such standards: the moral virtues and the intellectual virtues. The intellectual virtues in turn display two major divisions: the ones that pertain to the use of reason in attaining truth for the sake of action in a narrower sense (of which the chief one is prudence) and those that pertain to the use of reason in attaining truth for its own sake (of which *sophia* or theoretical wisdom is the most important one).[51] Actions according to these standards then are the basic human goods. One should strive to attain them all but there are circumstances in which the moral goods should take precedence over the theoretical ones. It befalls prudence to decide this not by giving orders to theoretical wisdom[52] but by pointing to the fact that the overall good of the agent is in jeopardy.

This last remark takes us to the third part of this exposition, viz. Aristotle's doctrine of the right and the role of prudence in action.

## ARISTOTLE'S CONCEPTION OF THE RIGHT

When are actions right according to Aristotle?[53] They are right if they are performed in accordance with the corresponding moral virtue. Not only must a certain standard be followed but the agent has to be in a certain state of mind when he acts:

> Again, the case of the arts and that of the excellences [*aretai*] are not similar; for the products of the arts have their goodness in themselves, so that it is enough that they should have a certain character, but if the acts that are in accordance with the excellences have themselves a certain character it does not follow that they are done justly or temperately. The agent also must be in a certain condition when he does them; in the first place he must have knowledge; secondly he must choose the acts, and choose them for their own sakes; and thirdly his action must proceed from a firm and unchangeable character.[54]

Virtuous action then requires knowledge, choice and a steadfast way of reacting to similar passions or affections. This last feature of virtue is further emphasised when Aristotle argues that its proximate *genus* is habit or dispositional state, that is, an habitual manner of responding to episodes of such 'undergoings' as 'appetite, anger, fear, confidence, envy, joy, love, hatred, longing, emulation, pity, and in general the feelings that are accompanied by pleasure or pain'.[55]

The central element of virtuous action, however, is choice and choice of something for its own sake. This latter requirement reinforces the view that the right is conceived as a good in itself and not as conducive to some further first order good.[56]

Distinctly Aristotelian is the doctrine concerning the object of virtuous choice: we act virtuously when we choose a mean (*meson*) between two extremes which constitute the corresponding vices. The notion of a mean is doubtless quantitative. Its application is warranted by the common sense view that both in passions and actions we can distinguish between excess and deficiency. We know what it means to be excessively afraid or to be overconfident. Someone charging the enemy in front of the line of hoplites can be said to be foolhardy or rash and thus to display 'too much' courage while the coward who deliberately stays behind when the phalanx advances may be accused of having too little of it. But these quantitative judgements are not conceived by Aristotle as reducible to strict arithmetical calculations. There is in the first place the problem of changing circumstances. No mathematical calculation of the right times, the right objects, the right people, the right aim, the right way, and so on, is possible.[57] Similarly, subjective conditions vary widely so that the mean has to be determined by reference to one's own constitution. Too little food for Milo, the famous wrestler, may be too much for the beginner in athletic exercises.[58] The trainer in their cases will have to find a different mean for each one of them.

Aristotle wants us to think of the moral agent as the gymnast and the trainer blended into one individual. Temperance (*sophrosyne*) requires that I consider my constitution in deliberating whether to have another cup of strong Parian wine (if I am thin and small I may become drunk with a very small amount) and it also requires that I determine the mean without leaving this task to someone else. But the determination will be prudential, not arithmetical. Indeed, this feature of virtuous action is built into the official definition of moral virtue in Book II:

> Excellence [*arete*, moral virtue], then, is a state [*hexis*, habit] concerned with choice, lying in a mean relative to us, this being determined by reason [*logos*] and in the way in which the man of practical wisdom [*phronimos*, the prudent man] would determine it.[59]

Virtuous action demands that I regularly and habitually prefer the mean as determined by *logos*, that is, I should proceed in the same way a prudent man would if he were in my case. In a later reference back to this definition Aristotle adds the precision that the *logos* involved should be 'the right *logos*'[60] or, as he says elsewhere, 'the true *logos*'.[61] The qualification is understandable since a wrong *logos* corresponds to a mistaken identification of the mean in a given set of circumstances and thus would lead to action which could not count as performed in accordance with virtue.

The true or right *logos* involved in right moral choice is probably equivalent to a singular sentence identifying some determinable amount of emotion or some particular action as the goal or good which the agent should try to attain, for instance, in these circumstances and given my physical constitution 'drinking two cups of wine is the mean'. Deliberation follows as a reasoning about the way to achieve such a goal, for example, avoiding spicy food which might lead me to drink more than my due.

A right *logos* of the kind just described is objective in the sense that although it is relative to the circumstances and the conditions of the agent, it is nevertheless true or false; that is, it is true (or false) that for agent *a* in the set of circumstances *c* action *m* is the mean, that is, the thing to choose. Such an action is good for this agent at this time. Thus the *logos* functions as the *arche* or principle for a particular action.

The right reason, however, is neither an empirical nor a mathematical proposition and Aristotle is probably correct in warning us that its grasp is subjectively conditioned by the moral character of the agent. Someone accustomed to choosing primarily according to the dictates of pleasure will be liable to make certain intellectual mistakes, but, Aristotle explains,

> it is not any and every belief that pleasant and painful objects destroy and pervert, for instance, the belief that the triangle has or has not its angles equal to two right angles, but only beliefs about what is to be done. For the principles of the things that are done consist in that for the sake of which they are to be done, but the man who has been ruined by pleasure or pain forthwith fails to see any such principle—to see that for the sake of this or because of this he ought to choose and do whatever he chooses and does; for vice is destructive of the principle.[62]

The central doctrine of the quotation is that one's intellectual grasp of moral goods can be seriously impaired by morally wrong habits. To the intemperate the mean does not 'appear';[63] he does not see what would be the right amount, say, of Parian wine for him in the present circumstances. Aristotle also expresses this idea in a picturesque way which has caused unnecessary confusion:

> excellence makes the aim right, and practical wisdom [*phronesis*, prudence] the things leading to it.[64]

Virtue 'makes the aim right' in that it allows the agent not to be misguided in the apprehension of the end of a particular action. But the apprehension itself should not be attributed to any of the moral virtues for they are not excellences of any cognitive faculty. The apprehension of the end is a function of practical reason.[65]

From these considerations Aristotle draws the generalising conclusion that 'it is impossible to be practically wise [*phronimos*, prudent] without being good'.[66] This is indeed a generalisation because prudence is not limited to the grasp and evaluation of the moral goods. It extends to all human goods.[67] Moral uprightness, then, is not only good in itself, it is also a necessary condition for the adequate pursuit of other goods, such as the external or the intellectual goods.

## SUMMARY AND CONCLUDING REMARKS

If we now turn back in order to give a sketch of Aristotle's conception of the process of moral choice, we shall have a better view of the role of prudence in morally right action. First (in the logical sense of first) an agent has a prudential conception of the human good. He knows that it is composed of many goods, the chief among which are the actualisations of his moral and intellectual capacities. Since he knows that virtuous activity is a basic good for him, that is, a good which contributes to his ultimate goal, he chooses to pursue such a good. The agent has a general notion of each of the moral virtues. Prudentially he can determine which circumstances provide him with an opportunity to exercise a particular one. He knows that in general virtue requires him to choose a mean and hence make a judgement as to what, in these particular circumstances, constitutes the mean. This he now lays down as the end for a particular action. Deliberation ensues as to how the end is to be attained. The deliberation in many cases will be quite brief. The means will be obvious and choice will follow without further ado.

The actual choice with which the action (as opposed to the thinking process) begins will be a good one if two conditions are met: (1) The practical proposition must be true. If it is false the choice will be vicious. For example, an intemperate person will typically think that having two or three extra drinks is fine and an unjust agent that paying a labourer less than agreed is all right.

But correct intellectual grasp is not enough. Thought by itself does not generate any motion unless desire comes to play. If I know something to be good but do not desire it, I will take no steps to secure it for myself. Hence a second condition, one applying to the impulsive ingredient of action, must be satisfied: (2) The desire must be right, namely, directed towards that which the practical proposition presents as good. If the desire is not right, if it is moved primarily by pleasure and pain in spite of awareness of the true practical proposition, the choice will be an instance of incontinence (*akrasia*)—for example, an Athenian at a drinking party who is aware of the fact that two extra drinks will give him a severe headache and yet goes on drinking, or a Corinthian merchant who knows that it is unfair not to return certain wares received as a deposit and yet fails to return them because he wants to keep them for himself.[68]

We now have before us the essentials of what I take to be Aristotle's doctrine of morally right choice.

In retrospect we may now see in a better light what he meant by classifying his philosophy of human affairs as a practical science. His works on ethics discharge the function of presenting to the student or reader the contents of the first and most basic elements in any process of practical decision making, namely, the general description of the human good and the specific configuration of the virtues both moral and intellectual. He painstakingly analyses such shared values as courage, temperance, liberality, magnificence, magnanimity, proper ambition, patience, truthfulness, wittiness, friendliness, modesty and righteous indignation. The proper attainment of these ethical excellences requires the guidance of prudence or practical wisdom in both private and public affairs. If someone manages to habitually act in conformity with these standards of excellence, then he will be a good man but not the best possible human being. This last label Aristotle reserves for the man who over and above the display of moral virtue illuminated by prudence also finds time and leisure to engage in contemplation and to do it in excellent fashion, that is, in accordance with its specific excellence: theoretical wisdom. It is this kind of integrated life, the most divine for a mortal being, that we should constantly keep before our eyes.

Aristotle seems to have kept his word of providing his readers with a target so that we may have, like archers, a mark to aim at.[69]

# Notes

1. For a critical summary of the biographical information cf. Flashar [4] 230–34. The most important source-book for such information is I. Duering, *Aristotle in the Ancient Biographical Tradition* (Goeteborg: Studia Graeca et Latina Gothoburgensia, 1957).
2. Barnes [1] 2464–2465. Unless otherwise noted, translations from the works of Aristotle are taken from this edition, generally referred to as The Revised Oxford Translation.
3. Apart from the *Politics* the *corpus* also includes a small treatise called *De Virtutibus et de Vitiis* which is probably spurious (cf. Aristoteles, *Ueber die Tugend*, uebers. von E. A. Schmidt, Berlin: Akademie Verlag, 1980).
4. Cf., for instance, *Politics* VII.13.1332 a 8.
5. *NE* X.9.1181 b 15. Cf. *Met.* I.1.981 b 25.
6. *NE* I.2.1094 a 27 – b 7.
7. *NE* I.7.1097 b 11; IX.9.1169 b 18–19.
8. Cf. *NE* 1094 a 27, b 11, 15; 1095 a 2, 16; 1099 b 29; 1102 a 12, 21; 1105 a 12; 1130 b 28; 1141 a 20, 29, b 23 sqq.; 1145 a 10; 1152 b 1; 1177 b 15; 1180 b 31; 1181 a 11.
9. Cf. *Met.* VI.1.1025 b 25.
10. *Met.* VI.1. 1025 b 18–21 and *Phys.* II.1 *passim*.
11. *Met.* VI.1.1025 b 22–24.
12. *NE* VI.2.1139 b 1–4.
13. To say that ethics is a practical discipline may give rise to an important misunderstanding which is prompted, moreover, by Aristotle's own words. He says literally that 'the end aimed at [in politics, that is, ethics] is not knowledge [*gnosis*] but action [*praxis*]' (*NE* I.3.1095 a 5–6). Such a statement can be easily misconstrued as implying that the aim of theoretical disciplines is truth, whereas the aim of practical science would not be truth but action. This kind of misunderstanding is usually linked to the conviction that there is only one mode of truth and that if truth is put to the service of action it inevitably suffers significant distortions and abridgements. An example of this misunderstanding is found in the otherwise interesting commentary by H. H. Joachim. He writes ([8] 15–16):

> The reasoning about human conduct and character, he [sc. Aristotle] insists, is only with a view to influencing action. His object is not to understand . . . but to guide and improve life. And being thus subordinate to practice (so he seems to argue), the thinking is here necessarily curtailed and perverted: thought is here pressed into the service of an end other than its own, i.e. not exercised with a view solely to the attainment of truth. It aims not at the whole truth and nothing but the truth, but only at so much of the truth, or at such a rough and distorted version of the truth, as is required for action.

Clearly, Joachim assumes that there is one and only one mode of truth.

14. *NE* VI.1.1139 a 5–17. There are difficulties involved in the criterion used to make the distinction, viz. the nature of the objects of each of the two *dynameis* or faculties, but this is not the adequate place to discuss them.
15. *NE* VI.2.1139 b 12. Cf. 1139 a 29.
16. Cf. *De Interpretatione* 4.17 a 2–4.
17. The textual evidence for drawing the distinction in these terms is not uncontroversial. At *De An.* III.10.433 a 14 Aristotle mentions a *nous* or intellect which is *ho heneka tou logizomenos kai ho praktikos* and which differs from theoretical *nous* because of its *telos* or end. I follow Loening ([7] 28–31) in taking here *logizomenos* as a general term for 'thinking' which is not limited to 'calculating' (Loening quotes *Met.* VIII.4.1047 b 7 for the use of *logizomenos* with reference to a geometrical problem, and in our context, namely, at 432 b 26, the cognate term *to logistikon* is used to cover both theoretical and practical reason). If this is right, then *ho heneka tou logizomenos* does not mean 'the (intellect) which calculates (means) for the sake of something (that is, a particular goal)' but rather 'the intellect which thinks for the sake of something', that is, for the sake of something external to the thinking itself, viz. action (*praxis*). The conjunction linking *ho heneka tou logizomenos* and *ho praktikos* is therefore an explicative *kai*. Theoretical *nous*, by contrast, does not have such a goal. Cf. further *NE* VI.2.1139 a 32–3, 36. In these and related topics I am heavily indebted to Loening's book.
18. *De An.* III.10.433 a 28–9.
19. Some of the features of Aristotle's ethics which follow from its being conceived as a branch of practical knowledge are of interest for present-day discussions about the nature of moral thought. I list four of those features. (1) The fact that Aristotle is committed to the notion of true and false practical propositions implies that he would reject what is generically called today the non-congnitivist thesis. The assertion that something is good (or right) is not just the evincing of the agent's attitude or an expression of his subjective preferences. According to Aristotle there is knowledge, that is, objective truth, involved, and this can (and should) be critically ascertained. (2) The idea that ethics involves objective truth does not make it a theoretical discipline. For Aristotle our current label 'ethical theory' would be a misnomer because a theoretical approach to ethics (in his sense of 'theoretical') would yield either descriptive propositions about human action or exclusively intensional evaluative propositions. We would learn what people do or what they think or esteem to be good or worth doing. But this is insufficient to guide action. The role of guiding and justifying action which is essential to the idea of practical knowledge can only be played by extensional evaluative propositions, that is, by propositions stating that something is good. (3) The introduction of a distinction between the good and the apparent good, that is, admitting that extensional evaluative propositions can be true or false, implies furthermore that there can be right and wrong desires (*De An.* III.10.433 a 26–7 and *NE* VI.2.1139 a 24). A desire is right if the practical proposition that presents something as good is true, and a desire is wrong if the corresponding proposition is false. This implies that there is a strong anti-naturalistic strain in

Aristotle's ethics: not everything that is desired is good. The good is not equivalent to what is desired. It may be objected that this interpretation is directly contradicted by the well-known opening sentence of the *NE* ('the good has rightly been declared to be that at which all things aim' I.1.1094 a 2–3). I cannot here discuss this passage in full. Suffice it to say that it should probably be understood as a forefather of the axiom *nihil appetimus nisi sub ratione boni*, that is, that the notion of good is what gives direction to our desires in that we desire what we conceive as good, but this does not exclude the possibility of our conception being wrong. Compare the more careful wording at *Politics* I.1.1252 a 2–3 'for everyone always acts in order to obtain that which they *think* good'. (4) From this it follows that the method of Aristotelian ethics cannot be empirical observation of what people in fact desire or think good. It is rather some form of dialectic by means of which Aristotle can expect to persuade in principle reasonable members of the community by leading them to reflect in certain ways on their experience of human affairs.

20. Cf. *NE* I.1.1094 a 1–9.
21. Cf. *NE* I.1.1094 a 9–16.
22. Praxis is here used in the more or less technical sense in which it stands in opposition to *poiesis*, 'production'. Cf. *NE* I.1.1094 a 16–18. Cf. J. L. Ackrill, 'Aristotle on Eudaimonia', in Rorty [12], 15–33.
23. *NE* I.1.1094 a 18–22.
24. Commentators sensitive to logical nuance have intimated that there is a fallacy implicit in the argument, the fallacy namely of going from 'all human activities tend to some end', which was argued for in the preceding chapter, to 'there is one end to which all activities tend'. (Cf. A. Kenny, 'Happiness' in J. Feinberg (ed.), *Moral Concepts* (Oxford University Press, 1975) pp. 43–5 where earlier discussions by G. H. Von Wright, B. A. O. Williams and W. F. R. Hardie are mentioned.) It is of course true that if an agent aims at ends A, B and C, we are not necessarily justified in positing a further end D and saying that the agent ultimately aims at this beyond A, B and C. But if we assert that for such an agent there is an ultimate end, namely the set [A, B, C], then of course the logical move would not be invalid. The challenge for the interpreter is to show from the text that Aristotle has this latter schema in mind.
25. When Aristotle (and his translators) uses singular expressions for his key concepts ('the good', 'the human good', 'the best', 'the highest of all goods achievable by action' or, at least in some passages '(the) virtue') it is a mistake to assume without argument that he intends to denote one singular thing. In all these cases he might aim at a collective notion.
26. *NE* I.1.1095 a 17–20; I.7.1097 b 22–4.
27. *NE* I.7.1097 a 25 – b 21.
28. At I.5.1095 b 14–15 the two terms are used virtually as synonyms.
29. In the terms of the example given in footnote 24 this means that the collective or inclusive end [A, B, C] is more complete, in the sense just defined, than the end A because we may choose A for its own sake *and* for the sake of [A, B, C], whereas we do not choose the latter for the sake of anything else. We examine the temple of Apollo for its own sake and

for the sake of contemplating the whole sanctuary at Delphi, but we do not admire the whole sanctuary for the sake of admiring one of its parts.

30. *NE* I.7.1097 b 6–20.
31. Self-sufficiency provides the evidence for the view that Aristotle is anticipating a chief good which has the nature of a set. The set would have to be such that there is no basic good which is not encompassed by it.
32. *NE* I.7.1097 b 8–11.
33. *NE* I.7.1097 b 24 – 1098 a 20.
34. The argument has been traditionally read as inferring a definition of happiness from considerations about the nature of man and has accordingly led to the belief that Aristotle commits some form of the naturalistic fallacy, that is, the fallacy of deriving evaluative conclusions from descriptive premises. My interpretation tries to argue that this is not the case.
35. This remark is intended to show that the adjective equivalent to 'complete' is predicated of a lifespan in a sense not dissimilar to the one defined as a formal requirement of the concept of happiness.
36. *NE* I.7.1098 a 3–5.
37. *NE* I.13.1102 b 13 – 1103 a 3.
38. *NE* I.7.1098 a 7–8 and 13–14. I think that 1111 b 1 ('the irrational passions are thought not less human than reason is') tends to confirm this view in spite of the superficial harshness of having to equate things which are *me aneu logou*, 'not without reason' with *aloga pathe*, 'irrational passions'. At VI.13.1144b 26–7 *meta logou*, 'with *logos*' is opposed to *kata logon*', 'according to *logos*' and used to convey the notion of internalising the standard in accordance with which action proceeds.
39. *NE* I.7.1098 a 16–18.
40. If we turn to the Eudemian Ethics we cannot fail to admit that the wording of the definition of happiness in that work is very similar to that of the *NE* and differs from it only in the way the inclusiveness factor is formulated. Let me quote it in full:

> But happiness, we saw, was the best of things; therefore happiness is the activity of a good soul. But since happiness was something complete, and living is either complete or incomplete and so also excellence—one excellence being a whole, the other a part—and the activity of what is incomplete is itself incomplete, therefore happiness would be the activity of a complete life in accordance with complete excellence. (*EE* II.1.1219 a 35–8. Cf. 1219 b 22–3)

This last expression clearly denotes the totality of the virtues.
41. *NE* X.7.1177 a 12–18.
42. *NE* I.7.1097 b 2.
43. A. Kenny, *The Aristotelian Ethics* (Oxford University Press, 1978) p.214 n.1 using an example by D. Devereux poses the problem as follows: 'he [sc. the Aristotelian contemplative man] may by betraying a friend gain a large sum of money and thereby assure himself years of leisure for philosophizing. What would hold him back?' A. W. H. Adkins has also often raised this objection to what he takes to be the Aristotelian position.

Cf. his *Merit and Responsibility* (Oxford University Press, 1970) pp. 345–46: 'On Aristotle's principles, it seems impossible to persuade anyone who could now be solving a particular geometrical problem, thereby securing the highest kind of *eudaimonia*, that he should instead perform some moral act, since this would secure him only an inferior kind of *eudaimonia*, and *eudaimonia* is universally admitted to be the end of life. A man must put his emotional and impulsive life in order, so that in the ensuing calm he may pursue his theorizing more readily; but once this is accomplished there seems to be no reason why he should prefer any given moral claim—say that of defending his friend's interests, expected even by traditional standards of *arete*—to his desire to philosophize.' Cf. also his *From the Many to the One* (London: Constable, 1970) p. 204: 'As it is, since *eudaimonia* is the end and *theoria* furnishes the highest type of *eudaimonia*, then, even though one cannot, being human, engage in *theoria* continually, *theoria* is always to be preferred to any other kind of activity whatsoever: if one at any moment has the choice between a good practical moral action, one should always choose *theoria*.' Prof. Adkins' position is further defended in '*Theoria* versus *praxis* in the *Nicomachean Ethics* and the *Republic*', *Classical Philology* 73 (1978) 297–313.

44. *NE* II.6.1107 a 14–15. See also the stern denunciation of someone 'who will sacrifice his dearest friend for the sake of half a farthing' at *Politics* VII.1.1323 a 31–2.

45. *Politics* VII.1.1323 a 27–8.

46. *NE* X.8.1178 b 1–6.

47. *NE* X.8.1178 a 9 and 16–22. On the related question of the use of *bios*, 'life', in this context, cf. the lucid article by D. Keyt, 'Intellectualism in Aristotle', *PAIDEIA*, Special Aristotle Issue, 1978, pp. 138–57. My views here owe much to Keyt's paper.

48. In reply to Kenny (cf. above note 43). we may now say that the man who betrays a friend to assure himself a large sum of money and thus years of leisure for philosophising would be defective in at least two virtues which receive extensive treatment in the *NE*, viz. the fundamental virtues of justice and of friendship. And who would say that such a man is a good man? I think the prospect of being, and being considered to be, *kakos* (bad), *phaulos* (bad, worthless), *adikos* (unjust), *aphilos* (a man without friends), which he would be according to the *NE*, should be sufficient to hold him back. A similar reply would have to be given to Adkins by calling attention to Aristotle's dictum that 'in so far as he [= the contemplative man] lives with a number of people, he chooses to do excellent acts [*ta kata ten areten prattein*, to engage in action according to the moral virtues]'. (X.8.1178 b 5–6). I take these lines to imply roughly the following consequences. Life in a community sometimes requires the defence of that community against external aggression. In so far as a philosopher is a member of a city under such threat, he will *choose*, that is, he will find sufficient reason to prefer, to abandon *in those circumstances* his theoretical contemplation and join the ranks of his fellow citizens and thus perform acts in accordance with the virtue of courage. Indeed, it would be *aischron* (base) for him not to do so. His fellow citizens would certainly react with anger and contempt were he

to argue that his *eudaimonia* requires him to choose instead the excellence of the best part in him, viz. of his theoretical reason. Any *phronimos* (prudent, reasonable man) would see that this is an appropriate time for moral action rather than for contemplation. And who would wish to deny that Aristotle's happy man is prudent as well? Indeed, to attribute to Aristotle a view so drastically opposed to Greek popular morality as to favour idleness in the presence of unjust aggression seems to me so absurd that I am inclined to count this consideration as a major argument against such an attribution.

49. *EN* X.7.1177 b 33.
50. In contrast with him a man who betrays family, friends and city for the sake of contemplation cannot be said to perform *well* the characteristic activity of man. From the initial definition of flourishing (to which Aristotle refers at the opening of his treatment of contemplation in *NE* X.7) it follows that he is not a flourishing human being.
51. *EN* VI.11.1143 b 14–17.
52. Cf. Adkins, '*Theoria* versus *Praxis*', p. 304.
53. There is a reply that has to be rejected at the outset if the foregoing exposition of Aristotle's notion of the good is correct. Actions cannot be said to be right because they are conducive to a single highest good called 'contemplation'. Actions according to Aristotle are right or wrong regardless of whether they produce, or are conducive to, contemplation. Because of this Aristotle's ethics cannot be said to be teleological, that is, to take the good as primitive and to define the right as that which is conducive to the good. Nor is it deontological either in defining the right independently of the good (cf. Cooper [10], 87–8). The rejection of the deontological interpretation of the structure of Aristotelian ethics follows from the fact that morally right actions are included both in the perfect and in the imperfect form of flourishing, that is, in the one that includes and the one that does not include contemplation. Thus the right is either the whole or an important part of the good and therefore not logically independent of it.
54. *NE* II.4.1105 a 27–33.
55. *NE* II.5.1105 b 21–3.
56. The reference to a *first order* good is added to indicate that flourishing, of course, is not excluded as an ultimate object of pursuit. On the contrary, we may want to remind ourselves that in the passage defining the term 'complete', moral virtue appeared explicitly as one of the things 'we choose indeed for themselves (for if nothing resulted from them we should still choose each of them), but we choose them also for the sake of happiness' (*NE* I.7.1097 b 2–4).
57. Cf. *EN* II.6.1106 b 21–2.
58. Cf. *NE* II.6.1106 b 3–4.
59. *NE* II.6.1106 b 36 – 1107 a 2.
60. *NE* VI.1.1138 b 20, 25 and 29. In this passage the ROT [1] surprisingly enough fails to translate *orthos*. Cf. II.5.1114 b 29 ('right reason' ROT).
61. *NE* VI.2.1139 a 24.
62. *NE* VI.5.1140 b 13–20.
63. *NE* VI.12.1144 a 34–1144 b 1.

64. *NE* VI.12.1144 a 7–9.
65. Cf. *NE* VI.9.1142 b 32–3. For the correct interpretation of this passage see Cooper [10], 64 n.84. The allusions to the eye in Aristotle's analysis of prudence and virtue, viz. VI.11.1143 b 13–14 and VI.12.1144 a 29–31, should probably be understood as metaphors for the prudential grasp of ends.
66. *NE* VI.12.1144 a 36 – b 1. Cf. III.4.1113 a 29 – b 2.
67. *NE* VI.5.1140 a 25–8.
68. I have here made use of the difficult passage on good choice at *NE* VI.2.1139 a 24–5. For an alternative analysis cf. Adkins, *From the Many to the One*, p. 189. On the topic of incontinence, cf. *NE* VII, *passim*.
69. I would like to express my thanks to Robert Cavalier for his patient review of my original draft.

# Bibliography

1. Barnes, J. (ed.), *The Complete Works of Aristotle* (The Revised Oxford Translation), 2 vols. (Princeton University Press, 1984). The best complete trans. includes a revised version of W. D. Ross' translation of the *NE*.
2. Bywater, I., *Aristotelis Ethica Nicomachea* (Oxford University Press, 1894; (reprint 1970). Standard edition of the Greek text of the *NE*.
3. *The Ethics of Aristotle* trans. by J. A. K. Thompson (Harmondsworth: Penguin, 1978). Includes a useful bibliography by J. Barnes.
4. Flashar, H. (ed.), *Aeltere Akademie-Aristoteles-Peripatos*, vol. 3 of Part One of Ueberweg, *Grundriss der Geschichte der Philosophie* (Basel/Stuttgart: Schwabe Verlag, 1983). Very valuable, for specialists.
5. Ross, D. *Aristotle* (London: Methuen, 1923; 5th ed. 1971). A conservative overall exposition which follows closely the Aristotelian texts.
6. Ackrill, J. L. *Aristotle the Philosopher* (Oxford University Press, 1981). An exposition of Aristotle's thought aimed at the contemporary reader.
7. Loening, R., *Die Zurechnungslehre des Aristoteles* (Jena: G. Fischer and Olms Verlag, 1903; reprint Hildesheim, 1967). Particularly good on the foundations of Aristotle's ethics.
8. Aristotle, *The Nicomachean Ethics*, a commentary by the late H. H. Joachim (Oxford University Press, 1951; 1970).
9. Hardie, W. F. R., *Aristotle's Ethical Theory* (Oxford University Press, 1980; 2nd ed.). Useful as a commentary on the *NE*.
10. Cooper, J., *Reason and Human Good in Aristotle* (Cambridge, Mass.: Harvard University Press, 1975).
11. Barnes, J., Schofield, M., Sorabji, R. (eds), *Articles on Aristotle*, vol. 2: Ethics and Politics (London: Duckworth, 1977).
12. Rorty, A. O. (ed.), *Essays on Aristotle's Ethics* (Berkeley: University of California Press, 1980).

# 3

# St Augustine
## *Thomas Losoncy*

'Faith, Hope, and Charity, and the Greatest of These is Charity'
(1 Cor 13, 13)

The quote is not the typical beginning to a study of someone's ethics; yet, if at all, it is fitting in St Augustine's case. This middle-class Roman citizen was born in Tagaste, Africa, today's Souk Ahras in Algeria near the Tunisian border, in 354 AD.[1] His was to be a life enmeshed in love, unconscious—in one sense at least and by his own admission[2]—and conscious, illicit and licit, and ultimately all-consuming. In stages he went from grammar school student to playboy-student, to a career-seeker using grammar and rhetoric as a means to a bureaucratic position in the Roman government. In his early 30s he experienced a career jolt as a result of reading St Paul that is reminiscent of Paul's own sudden reversal in mid-life and at the outset of that famous person's own career.

Subsequently, Augustine would seriously entertain taking up a monastic life, become ordained a priest, consecrated bishop, and live out the remainder of his life working as one of the most remarkable bishops and prolific writers the Christian Church has known. All this would transpire while he vigorously pursued responsibilities to his diocese of Hippo, engaged in vast correspondence, attended councils and meetings, and combatted such major heresies as those of the Donatists, Manicheans and Pelagians until his death on 28 August 430 AD.

At the time of Augustine's death the Vandals were laying siege to his familiar and beloved Hippo. Within a few years all was laid waste. Within 60 years sand covered much of its remains and Hippo vanished until excavations in the early 20th century recovered some of the original glory beneath nearly 20 feet of sand. Had one suggested such a prospect for Hippo's future to the average citizen of Augustine's day, the likely reaction would have been disbelief; yet one wonders what a frontier soldier might have said about the same outcome. Such a soldier would be well-acquainted with the 'uncivilised' reaches existing in Africa beyond the Empire's official control and removed from the daily experience of Hippo's inhabitants.

This energetic figure of the latter 4th and early 5th centuries after Christ never wrote a work on ethics. He did, however, write numerous pieces on clearly ethical issues and many of these have endured as some of the most profound and provocative insights on ethics ever developed. For this reason one cannot legitimately present a system of ethics in Augustine's name but neither can one ignore his ethical impact on future centuries. In the face of these two inseparable facts, the path taken here is a presentation of his ethical thinking which follows the course of his own life, thus trying to capture Augustine's ethical views in their historical development.

## QUASI-SYSTEMATIC TREATMENT

Taking a cue from the previous remark about Augustine's own life as a way to present his ethics, a two-dimensional and quasi-systematic treatment of his ethics will be undertaken. First, a number of ethical issues and problems, pertaining to the moral individual, will be examined. These, in a sense, parallel the historical sequence of Augustine's own life. Topics such as: the goal of the good life, human free will, divine foreknowledge and issues of determinism, moral evil, certain and ethical normative judgements, temporal and eternal law in ethics, the virtues and the vices, the roles of reason and desire in moral action, and joy as the outcome of the morally good life all belong to this consideration of the moral individual in relation to others. They include such matters as: friendship, lying, human and divine society, and predestination.

The topical order listed above involves a contextual and a historical schema that intertwines with these issues and often serves as the catalyst for Augustine's treatment of a given problem. In this respect one could say that the period of Augustine's early works (386–397) until the *Confessions* shows that his ethical concerns are prompted and handled in respect to his earlier life experience. Thus the Manicheans, the Academics, Neoplatonists and Stoics provide a diverse backdrop for his many discussions in ethics.[3] This is obvious in the early works.

From about 397–410 the ethical issues are influenced by, as well as arise from, his deeper understanding of Christian writings and issues related to these concerns. His treatment of the virtues and vices and the leading of a virtuous life for a Christian are pronounced indications of this change.[4] A third period of development (410–430) shows an increasing interest in the society of man and in issues relating to a Christian community or society.[5] In this period there is added emphasis on Christianity's extension, grace and forgiveness for the human being, and an awesome sense of *mankind* as being engaged in a historical destiny and, at the same time, a lesser emphasis on isolated moral individual matters. It is here that Augustine's working out of the two themes of a City of Man and a City of God takes place and lays to rest any concern with the City of Rome as a historical entity. This seems to be linked directly with the view of the impending historical demise of Rome, an earthly endeavour that is necessarily a passing affair.

The series of ethical problems cited and the historical features of Augustine's own life experiences require some additional ingredients for the understanding of his ethical thought. There is a schema of reality in which the moral enterprise is set and in relation to which moral actions gain their value. Also love is presented as the catalyst and moving force of the beings and actions in this universe.

Augustine's schema of reality possesses three levels of being. At the summit of reality he maintains the existence of the Christian God as an immutable being and the possessor of divine ideas, the immutable measure of all beings and the source of all created species and their individual members. These created or caused beings are further divided into two distinct categories. One category consists of beings, which, once they begin to exist, will continue to exist forever. These are angelic beings and human souls both of which are everlasting but not eternal, since they come into existence as creatures. Human beings, consisting of souls and bodies, are also mutable as subject to material change and corruption.

In yet another division of created beings there exist all wholly material beings or bodies which are subject to continual change, temporal and material, in the same fashion as Plato depicted corporeal beings. Still Augustine separates himself from the Platonic tendency to view the material world negatively. In the former outlook every being, including the being of bodies, is good insofar as it is a creation of God.

Actually there exist sizable differences between the Augustinian view of reality and the Platonic and/or Neoplatonic versions which sharply affect his moral thought and separate it from that of Plato and Plotinus. Whereas for Plato several beings are immutable and for Plotinus the One is immutable and above being, Augustine maintains that God is the *one immutable being* which stands as creator of all others.[6] Intellectual and volitional beings such as angels and men are assigned a moral mutability. This means that they may turn to and seek their happiness with the source of their being that is superior to them or instead they may prefer themselves and/or beings below them in place of their creator.

Admittedly the upward motif and seeking of wisdom and the good, which Augustine maintains is open to human and angelic beings, locates human destiny in an immaterial realm suggestive of Plato's and Plotinus' respective immaterialisms. Augustine, however, posits a kind of moral freedom here, as well as an ontological freedom on God's part in creating such beings, which is foreign to these Greek philosophers. A more pronounced change of perspective is to be found in his explanation of the force that moves this universe of beings, namely, the impact of love on the totality.

In Augustine's view, creation is the *freely given result* of God's love. It does not benefit the Creator, but is for the well-being of the created. In this scenario the freely willed decision to return to its creator by human and angelic beings imitates, in a lesser way, the creative act itself and the yet greater paradigm of this love, the Trinity.

What Augustine discovers in his ethical analysis of human action is that the created will, man's in this case, can freely decide to direct its many loves to other goods besides God. Thus in his early works one finds Augustine singling out the tendency of man to love things beneath him or even himself in preference to God. This is a case of loving what is both good and deserving of love but in a disordered fashion. While the emphasis in the early works is on this disorder as a wrongful desire of things mutable and beneath man, Augustine's later writings concentrate more on the love man bears towards God and his fellow man. Here the disorder of the will's love is described as a wrong desire seen primarily as 'pride'.

The two great Scriptural commands to love God and to love one's neighbour occupy most of Augustine's later writings about love. In the first instance Augustine thinks this commandment means to love God as the true good or fulfilment of human existence, not in some selfish sense of using God[7] but in the sense of the refined notion of friendship found in Aristotle and Cicero—loving God for God's own goodness and love. Such a love is also seen as the key to love of one's neighbour since love of one's fellow man should mean willing the same fulfilment and good love to exist in him. Such loves are selfless, the opposite of pride. Pride, as self-love, strikes at the very heart of these relationships with God and neighbour.

Psychologically, Augustine's positioning of pride as the opposite of love, in this context of personal relationships, appears to follow from taking pride as rooted in a person's fear that to be obligated in love to another somehow threatens or detracts from one's independence and freedom by making demands which are demeaning rather than enhancing.[8] It is this disorder in the appreciation of love, seeking one's own will or pride, that Augustine clearly fastens on as the source of moral evil. Wrongly assessing love's place in the universe brings calamitous moral consequences. The host of moral issues this position of Augustine raises *vis-à-vis* the universe of being he accepts will be better recognised by turning directly to these specific moral issues.

## THE GOOD LIFE AND THE DESTINY OF MAN

Augustine's early writings speak of the 'good life' as the moral agent's primary concern. His endeavours are directed towards making the good life intelligible in terms of the philosophies or wisdoms already familiar to him, namely, Neoplatonism, Manicheism and Stoicism. On the other hand, as he studies Scripture more extensively his account becomes decidedly more Christian.

In *The Happy Life* (*De beata vita*), for instance, he speaks of this goal of man as truth and the good, both of which are located in one being, God, the highest truth and the highest good.[9] His interest here seems clearly to be one of depicting the good life in philosophical terms. Man seeks the truth as his greatest good, but the supremely true is also what is supremely good for man. One detects here strong overtones of Plato's view that knowledge is virtue. But Augustine proceeds to identify and place the epitome and source of all truth and goodness in God.[10]

Augustine is here invoking some rather common classical philosophical notions. First, he sees philosophy as a way of life or, in today's terms, a lifestyle, something that one loves as an active pursuit and not just as a subject to study. To the Platonists and Neoplatonists this meant the pursuit of truth, an unchanging wisdom, as opposed to preoccupation with the changing sense input of the material world. Nor is this to be taken as simply a case of man trying to attain a certain object or goal that will be *used* as his truth and good. Rather Augustine's description of this good as man's 'plenitude' carries with it the added implication of something fulfilling, a satisfying of a need in man's very being.[11]

Augustine's remarks in the *Confessions*, acknowledging that he could not decipher God's ways or intent in his younger years, are instructive here.[12] What was mysterious to him is that rooted in one's very being is a hunger for the truth and the good that is God, a truth and good which he had been unable to recognise. Augustine's heart was, accepting the witness of the *Confessions*, indeed restless. Among various misdirected loves, he had deluded himself into thinking that a Roman governorship and the misplaced love he had bestowed on his concubine of some nine years could somehow satisfy his longing and thereby bring the plenitude and fulfilment that his very being so desperately sought.[13] This further explains Augustine's repeated declamations against placing one's love in such mutable things as corporeal beings and pleasures inferior to man or even in man himself.

Augustine brings these notions together in striking fashion in chapter 3 of the *Moral Behaviour of the Catholic Church (De moribus ecclesiae)*:

> For what do we call enjoyment but having at hand the objects of love?
> And no one can be happy who does not enjoy what is man's chief good, nor is there any one who enjoys this who is not happy. We must then have at hand our chief good, if we think of living happily . . . For if happiness consists in the enjoyment of a good than which there is nothing better, which we call the chief good, how can a man be properly called happy who has not yet attained to his chief good? or how can that be the chief good beyond which something better remains for us to arrive at? Such, then, being the chief good, it must be something which cannot be lost against the will.[14]

And in chapter 8 he invokes St Paul to specify further what this chief good is:

> What does Paul say on this? 'We know,' he says, 'that all things issue in good to them that love God.' . . . We have heard, then, what and how much we must love; this we must strive after, and

to this we must refer all our plans. The perfection of all our good things and our perfect good is God. We must neither come short of this nor go beyond it; the one is dangerous, the other impossible.[15]

In short, it is somehow not sufficient for man merely to exist. Over and above existing man needs to exist or live 'well' as befits a human being. Augustine sees this completion as residing in man's enjoyment of his highest good—a union and/or friendship with God and the society of morally good beings who comprise the City of God. In this respect Augustine's Ethics is eudaimonistic and his stand that man's fulfilment lies in this higher goal beyond him is a position he never abandons.[16]

The mysterious yet positive orientation in man's being towards happiness and self-fulfilment in communion with God and other good beings as well makes moral evil an even more perplexing occurrence in the world. Augustine finds it necessary to search for the reason why there is moral evil in human experience both to better understand man and also the will's functioning in the moral journey that constitutes human destiny. This whole investigation, on his part, will lead to an account of the will itself.

## FREEDOM IN THE HUMAN WILL

No single aspect of St Augustine's moral thought is so central, complex and even controversial as his account of the human will. It is of prime concern in his ethical writings from his earliest to his very latest works.

In the early writings Augustine's previous philosophical background and experience are ready grist for his inquiries and thoughts on the subject. In the *Confessions* he admits how the Manichean doctrine to which he turned seemed a welcome relief for his own misgivings about his early irresponsible lifestyle. With their belief that there exist two wills in man, one good and one evil, and the further claim that one could do nothing about either, Augustine discovered what appeared to be an escape from all responsibility for the evil in his life.[17]

He also was well aware of the Roman pagan acceptance of fate and the use of auguries. Such pagan practices are amply described in *The City of God (De civitate dei)*[18] and there is indication of paganism's revival in the later years of Augustine's life. In the light of his own experiences he turns first to the question of the will's freedom. He then continues to treat this problem in a closely related area, that of the will's capacity to seek evil when it was created to seek good.

In the work *On Free Decision of the Will (De libero arbitrio)*,[19] Augustine observes in Book I, that 'nothing lies more in the power of the will than the will itself'.[20] Later he reminds one that while a person grows old against his will and dies of necessity against his will, the will cannot be changed against one's will and the will lies ready at hand to act (will) as one wants.[21] The importance of the insight is that no one can prevail on or change another's will about something, for example, bringing one to enjoy paying taxes, without that individual's willing assent. Thus one may find taxation inescapable but it does not follow that one has to submit willingly.

This assertion that one has dominion over the will initiates Augustine's effort to free man from the attractions of Manicheism and Fate. He then proceeds to locate this limited freedom of the human will in the hierarchical world of beings more precisely. And so from another angle he introduces the kinds of causes which one might discover at work in the universe. These are given as: necessary or natural causes, violent or unnatural causes, chance causes, and voluntary causes. The list is partially found in *On Free Decision of the Will*,[22] and expanded in *The City of God*.[23]

In Book II, chapter 1, of *On Free Decision of the Will*, Augustine refers to a stone thrown into the air as a way of illustrating how free will should be understood. The stone, if unimpeded, will of necessity fall back to the earth. Its movement upwards was a violent motion proceeding contrary to its natural tendency to rest on the earth's surface. He then claims that the will's decision to turn to good or evil is neither violent nor necessitated as an action. It is the agent's decision that directs the will's movement.

The will is, in a sense, poised between good and evil so that it can arrest any downward tendency towards evil and also direct itself upwards to its true immutable and immaterial good. It can also, of course, freely abandon that good and descend to evil which is not its good. But this argument scarcely settles all of the difficulties Augustine finds connected with the issue of necessity regarding the will.

He raises one difficulty that hearkens back to a worry of Cicero. Cicero had feared that if the gods do indeed watch over and know everything that occurs in the universe then surely man cannot enjoy freedom in willing. Cicero's response to this difficulty was simply to deny any divine foreknowledge regarding man's actions. Augustine reacts to this position by labelling it a blasphemous thought to entertain about an immutable and all-knowing God. This is seen in Evodius' presentation of the issue of God's foreknowledge in Book III, chapter 3, of *On Free Decision of the Will*, and, by implication, chapter 2 as well.

Augustine furnishes two short and direct arguments in support of his view. First, he argues that if God is truly all-knowing then God must know all things as they, in truth, actually are. This, it turns out, means God must know a freely willed decision of the will as just such an action. As a consequence, rather than compromising the freedom of decision in any way divine foreknowledge proves to be the surest guarantee of its existence.[24]

In a second argument Augustine rhetorically queries whether or not one's knowledge of the past affects, in any way, the peformance of that past action. Obviously such knowledge cannot alter the past as past. He then observes, 'As you remember certain things that you have done and yet have not done all the things that you remember, so God foreknows all the things of which He Himself is the Cause, and yet He is not the Cause of all that He foreknows'.[25] What the passage quoted and Augustine's immediately preceding remarks are attempting to show Evodius is that knowledge pertains to the knower and not the thing known as regards the action involved. Knowledge is not transitive in its effect. For Augustine divine foreknowledge encompasses all of time in its eternity. God knows all that will come to pass in time, as it comes to pass, either necessarily or voluntarily. All such causes of these future occurrences are *bona fide* causes *sui generis*.

In the defence of the will's free decision elaborated by Augustine one detects a serious and constant counterpoint to the ever progressing and complex difficulties he encounters and engages. This hint of another and related issue is to be found in his lengthy attempts to fathom how it is that the will, although free, could ever turn to evil. After all, in retrospect, his own life is a graphic instance of that very enigma. It is through Augustine's studied effort to explain moral evil that one attains a richer insight into the many workings of the will.

## MORAL EVIL

St Augustine develops his interpretation of moral evil in response to a plethora of contemporary opinions. He is familiar with the Platonic and Neoplatonic views that for man to run away from the true and the good and to succumb to the pleasures of the senses is to become ensnared by the world's attractiveness. The additional Neoplatonic position that matter was nearly nothing because not a definite being seems to have some influence on the notion of evil Augustine adopts. The Manicheans, for their part, had been so impressed with evil in the world that they maintained the existence of a supremely evil being along with a supremely good being.[26] Man, according to their teaching, possessed a mixture of evil and good and, as a result, two wills, a good and an evil one. Finally, Scripture, both Old and New Testaments, repeatedly presented evil as a turning away from God and/or rejection of God's will.

In an early observation about moral evil, Augustine leads Evodius[27] to the conclusion that moral evil stems from or lies in the will's wrong desire or lust (a general term for wrongful desire [*cupiditas*] pertaining to the senses). When he returns to the topic again in Books II and III of *Free Decision of the Will* he tries to identify just what accounts for the existence of evil in the will and what the nature of evil is.

He has by now formulated his basic notion, metaphysically grounded, of evil as 'the absence of good in a being'.[28] This notion needs to be understood with precision. Here Augustine rejects the Manichean notion of evil by maintaining that evil can *only* exist *in* a being or in that which is good. He has also identified the highest reality in the universe, God, as being *and as good*. Evil cannot be a supreme being because of good's metaphysical precedence. There also cannot be two supremely good beings. But then how is it that evil actually does affect being?

Augustine goes on to describe this lack in the being of things as the lack of what *normally speaking ought to be in a thing by nature*.[29] For example, a person born blind would display this sort of lack. However, this lack or absence of being does not always and necessarily mean something subtracted or omitted from a being. A thing may be deprived of what, normally speaking, its being or nature requires by way of excess. An overweight person would be a case in point.

This two-dimensional sense of absence (or lack in a being of what is normally good for it) suggests to Augustine that basically one is dealing with a disorder in the thing. Employing this refined sense of 'disorder' to explain a thing's lack of being places Augustine in a better position to treat of moral evil. Moral evil, in the human will, is a disorder, as wrong desire which inclines one to desire either something that one should not, an apparent good, or to desire ineffectively the means towards one's goal or a real good. He illustrates the first kind of disorder in an analysis of what occurs mentally in the case of a suicidal person.

The suicide seeks peace from what troubles him but mistakes death, as an imagined final state of non-being that will convey peace, for a genuine state of peace. Genuine peace, he notes, can only be realised by one who exists to enjoy it.[30]

However, when it comes to the case of those who take an ineffective means to an end, he resorts to an evaluation of a perplexing phenomenon in life. Apparently all humans seek and will happiness, yet many fail to achieve this goal. If one's will is truly in one's power then this does pose a puzzling situation.

Augustine's procedure, in this instance, is to focus on the importance of the means to an end. Anyone may will a given end but a failure to will the appropriate means to reach that end prevents one from ever fulfilling one's aim. Again, the will discloses a disorder, but this time in regards to the full capacity of its willing power. These frailties and failures, which can beset the human will, reveal what transpires within the individual psychologically. Their presence is seen to produce an impact on the human being that will amount to a failure in the being, a kind of paralysis when it comes to willing what, normally speaking, one ought to will.[31]

In yet another analysis of the evil in wrongful desire or of the disordered will, Augustine thinks of the problem in terms of being and God. Here the Scriptural sense of evil is seen to mesh with his philosophical analysis. He now recalls, first, the previous notion of plenitude as man's goal in existing and, second, that man is constituted to seek being and permanence with a capacity of will that allows him to act accordingly.

Now the apex of being and the good in the universe is God Himself. Thus, the more man approaches this end and becomes godlike, the more he achieves being and approaches the good, the good that is immutable, eternal and unable to be taken from man against his will. The more man, on the other hand, turns inward on himself or becomes attracted to beings beneath him the more he veers towards that which is mutable and able to be taken from him against his will.[32]

This dual-directional motif deftly portrays the Scriptural notion that moral evil is a turning away from God, an aversion or defection, and that moral good is a turning towards God, a conversion that results in the good will or benevolent moral action.[33] It is this broader Scriptural sense that comes to preoccupy Augustine later in life when he again reflects on the will, but then in regard to the issue of predestination and God's will.

What Augustine does think, however, at this point in his examination of human failure, is significant both for his basic position and subsequent exploration of the problem. *Evil* is the result of *disorder in a being* and, in the case of a rational and/or created intellectual being, a further *disorder of its love*. This disorder in love affects the will in such manner as to frustrate the tendency towards fulfilment in the being as such and to render the moral actions issuing from such a being deficient. Thus the will is not free by nature, that is, in its orientation towards good (God) for its completion in existence nor is it wholly free subsequently when affected by its failings, sin and evil. In the first case man's very satisfaction and fulfilment of being by communion with God means a built-in orientation for human nature's perfection, its *plenitudo*. In the latter condition the same nature is crippled and disoriented in making its decisions. Yet there always remains a freedom of decision in the directing of one's love.[34] The same will, whether in a state of original nature or as fallen, always needs assistance from God to become a *benevolent will* but such assistance was and is always available to the will that decides to will, in accordance with its constituted nature.[35]

## CERTAINTY AND ETHICAL NORMATIVE JUDGEMENTS

From his earliest works, *On Free Decision of the Will*, *On Order (De ordine)*, and *On the Teacher (De magistro)*, Augustine was proposing and claiming a normative guide and source for the certainty of one's moral judgements. In these early works different influences operate as he discusses with his small circle of friends at Cassiciacum the kind of lifestyle one should pursue as a Christian. An immediate concern is to reject the sceptic's positions. The Sceptics had taken the Academy in a direction quite contrary to Plato's intent. Thus in the work, *On Free Decision of the Will*, one finds Augustine citing his famous claim of certainty regarding his own existence, '*si fallor, sum*' (If I doubt, then I am). But there is also present a direct appeal to the Platonic-Neoplatonic tradition for a certainty rooted in the unchanging realm of the immaterial.

Augustine does not invoke the world of Platonic Ideas here since he has taken the stand that the exemplars of all things and the norms of all mathematical, moral judgements, and so forth, are rooted in God's immutable being and truth. How then is the human being to gain access to these unchanging normative truths? It is Augustine's view that, under the influence of Scripture, man enjoys a kind of divine illumination and assistance in seeing these truths rightly. There are many interpretations and controversies about what Augustine means by this.[36]

It is generally conceded he does not hold for a kind of vision of God, nor of these normative truths themselves as they are in God. He is, however, backed into a position that sounds Platonic inasmuch as he does not think one has access to such truths in the sensory world of experience nor does he allow for the abstraction of universals from the sensory world.

The theory of divine illumination, as developed, reveals a three-fold aspect to the illumination: metaphysical, epistemological and moral. In the treatise, *Against Faustus the Manichee (Contra Faustum Manichaeum)* he writes:

> Far different from the cognition whereby I think about limited and familiar bodies is that incomparably distinct cogitation in which I understand justice, chastity, faith, truth, charity, goodness, and whatever else is like these. Now tell me, if you can, in regard to this cogitation known by trustworthy evidence, what kind of illumination is identified with this cogitation, whereby all those things that are not this light are both distinguished among themselves and shown to be different from the light. Yet even this light is not the Light that is God: the former is created, the latter is the Creator. . . . From it come the beginning of our act of being (*initium existendi*), the principle of our act of knowing (*ratio cognoscendi*), and the law of our act of loving (*lex amandi*).[37]

Now the above passage is but a fuller statement and development of what Augustine was already saying in the dialogue, *On Order*, when he wrote:

> By degrees the soul leads itself toward good habits and the best life (*ad mores vitamque optimam . . . perducit*), not only through faith but by sure reasoning (*certa ratione*).[38]

Again, in *On Free Decision of the Will*, Augustine speaks of man's access to the divine guidance of illumination and further asserts that it is open to all men:

> You will not deny, therefore, that immutable truth, comprising everything that is immutably true, exists; and you cannot say that immutable truth is yours, or mine, or anyone else's. It is present and shows itself as a kind of miraculously secret, yet public, light for all who see what is immutably true.[39]

Finally, Augustine articulates the full range, moral, mathematical, and so on, of this illumination in the *Literal Commentary on Genesis* *(De Genesi ad litteram)* when he writes:

> So also among the objects of the intellect there are some that are seen in the soul itself: for example the virtues (to which the vices are opposed), either the virtues which will endure, such as piety, or virtues that are useful for this life and not destined to remain in the next, as faith, by which we believe what we do not see, and hope, by which we await with patience the life that shall be, and patience itself, by which we bear every adversity until we arrive at the goal of our desires. These virtues, of course, and other similar ones, which are quite necessary for us now in living out our exile, will have no place in the blessed life, for the attainment of which they are necessary. And yet even they are seen with the intellect; for they are not bodies, nor have they forms similar to bodies. But distinct from these objects is the light by which the soul is illumined, in order that it may see and truly understand everything, either in itself or in the light.[40]

Evidently, then, Augustine supports the position that man can achieve sound moral judgements. To assure the certainty of these value judgements there exists a kind of illumination which enables one to see the truth in an immaterial and unchanging realm when the intellect is turned towards the divine reasons themselves. In support of this position he cites a whole list of judgements such as 7 plus 3 always equals 10, justice is to be rewarded and injustice punished, the eternal is better than the temporal, and the incorruptible is preferable to the corruptible.[41] All have a kind of immaterial permanence and are truths against which the intellect's judgements are measured.

## LAW: TEMPORAL AND ETERNAL

The theme of an immutable norm for moral action is also evident in Augustine's treatment of temporal and eternal law. It is first presented in the work, *On Free Decision of the Will*. Here Augustine observes that temporal law is that law which changes with time and the vicissitudes of human temporal existence. Yet the rightness of such laws and their need for change is recognised through man's awareness of justice, goodness, and so forth, as rooted in the unchanging domain of eternal law. The temporal law is evaluated in the light of its appproximation to the eternal law. And, again, he thinks the ability to realise when temporal law is closer to or more remote from the justice demanded by the eternal law discloses a relationship on the part of the intellect to these immutable truths. In fact, he thinks this ability of mankind is enjoyed generally. Thus he writes:

Augus. What of the law called the highest reason (*summa ratio*), which ought always to be obeyed, the law through which evil men deserve a wretched life and good men a happy one, and through which, finally, the law that we have just called temporal is rightly passed and rightly changed? Can anyone who understands it think it is not immutable and eternal? Can it ever be unjust that the evil are wretched and the good happy, or that the well-ordered and serious nation should elect its own officials while the wicked nation should be deprived of this power?
Evodius. I see that this law is eternal and immutable.
Augus. I think too that you understand that in temporal law there is nothing just and lawful which men have not derived from eternal law. . . .
Evodius. I agree.
Augus. To put in a few words, as best I can, the notion of eternal law that has been impressed upon our minds: it is that law by which it is just that everything be ordered in the highest degree (*ordinatissima*).[42]

It is with this assurance about a normative guide for moral behaviour that Augustine can proceed to present a doctrine of the virtues and vices.

## VIRTUES AND VICES: THE ROLES OF DESIRE AND REASON

Augustine's treatment of the virtues and vices in his ethical view is remarkably similar to Stoic and classical Greek presentations, at least in his early writings. Thus, in *On Free Decision of the Will* one finds a straightforward presentation of the moral virtues of prudence, fortitude, temperance and justice in Book I, chapter 13. Moreover, it is *reason* that is assigned the role of guiding desire in moral action. When this relationship is rightly ordered man has a kind of 'dominion' over his emotions and can act in a morally upright fashion. Consequently Augustine writes:

> When reason is master of these emotions (*motus animae*), a man may be said to be well ordered (*ordinatus*). No order in which the better are subject to the worse can be called right, or can even be called order at all . . . Therefore, when reason, whether mind or spirit, rules the irrational emotions, then there exists in man the very mastery which the law that we know to be eternal prescribes.[43]

Book I of *On Free Decision of the Will* seems to be a natural law theory of ethics. However, in Book II, Augustine's approach changes. Now it appears that man definitely needs some assistance from God in order to learn to exercise these same virtues:

> No one becomes prudent through another's prudence, or brave through another's courage, or temperate through another's temperance. So too, no one becomes just through the justice of another. Instead, man obtains virtues by adapting his spirit to the immutable rules and lights of those virtues which dwell incorruptible in truth itself and in common wisdom, to which the virtuous man has adapted himself and fitted his spirit.[44]

In a letter (*Epistola* 155, 4, 13) Augustine plainly connects one's ability to exercise these moral virtues with the love of God. It is only when the love of God motivates a person, as the highest object of love, that one can pursue other loves prudently, temperately and as the moral virtues demand:

> In this life, although there is no virtue save that of loving what ought to be loved, prudence lies in choosing it; fortitude in not being turned from it by any troubles; to be allured from it by no

seductions is temperance, and by no pride is justice. But what
ought we to choose as the object of our principal love but that
which we find to be better than anything else? This object is God;
and to set anything above or even equal to Him is to show that we
do not know how to love ourselves. For our good becomes the
greater the more we approach Him . . .[45]

Augustine's emphasis on divine assistance has changed in the
above, but only in terms of order and ordering. Whereas he has
regularly been speaking of a need for God's assistance in order for
one to see aright in practising the moral virtues, the above letter
points out that God's assistance in knowing is tied to a love of God
that alone will clear the way for one to see and know how to act
correctly. Previously it was noted that Augustine views the universe
as resulting from a freely willed act of creative love. As a result of this
creative act the beings themselves are held to be impressed with a
kind of love as well. In these beings love is a motive force that drives
such beings to strive to exist in imitation of the source of their being.
Their very existence, therefore, both makes an addition (contribution) to the universe of beings and involves them in a dynamic
movement of love.

When speaking of how this love affects man Augustine refers to it
as a kind of inner inclination and tendency which is depicted in
images of weight much like the pull of gravity. Impelled from within
man seeks his highest good in God. However, this will to good and
joy is implanted in a being (man) that possesses heterogeneous outlets for this desire. As a result, the direction of man's love towards
God as its plenitude may be obscured in many ways. One recalls
here Augustine's own early years.

In Augustine's writings the complex relations and movements of
love are nuanced by a careful and selective terminology which might
best be grasped by means of the following diagram[46] of how love
(*amor*), which, in a broad sense, signifies almost psychic or physical
attraction, affects the universe he describes. The diagram should be
read from left to right. The first three categories are overviews of
how love might be taken in a broad sense as encompassing man in
the universe. The four levels on the right represent the major
channels for man's love.

As Augustine gradually establishes the characteristics of these
different outlets which the human will seeks and experiences in its
love, he comes to realise how certain events had transpired in his own

*Love* in the *universe*:
1. as 'cosmic love'—encompasses the universe and sees man at the mid-point between the Fall and the Redemption.

2. as 'positive love'—(*delectatio*) stands for man's response to this universe in terms of use and enjoyment.

3. as '*caritas*'—stands for the highest kind of spiritual love that man can practise. It is the love of God and of other beings as God's creatures. Consequently each creature is to be loved in terms of its special relation to its creator.

1. has a metaphysical character.
2. suggests man's natural love at work in this universe.
3. represents the natural love of man in the universe placed in full attunement with that universe through *caritas*.

1) *Love of God* (and other spiritual beings): when properly directed is *caritas*.

2) *Love of self*:
(a) favourable—(*dilectio*). This is benevolent love when man discovers and promotes his true welfare in God;
(b) neutral—the natural condition either of man's animal or rational nature;
(c) wrongful—when man's love represents the root of all sin and rebellion against love— pride. Or this may also mean the disordered love of the body and material things and pleasures—lust or wrong desire.

3) *Love of neighbour*:
May be a love that amounts to use. When it is the proper love of *caritas* then one loves his neighbour as a creature of God made to be in communion with God and other morally good beings.

4) Love of the body and things beneath man:
*Voluptas*—stands for any sort of pleasure but frequently means lower sensual satisfaction.
*Libido* and *cupiditas*—usually indicates the lustful and perverse craving of sexual and other attractions of bodies.

FIGURE 1 *AMOR*

earlier years when the pure love for God had been so blindly and mistakenly directed towards other goals and objectives. It was not the Manichean explanation that would resolve these problems of man's wayward tendencies. For all things of this universe, and even the objects of man's diverse loves, are good. Still man's love towards them had become disordered and not subject to reason's dominion as Book I of *On Free Decision of the Will* had indicated they should be.

Augustine comes thus to a realisation of the implications of the Scriptural accounts of man's original fault or sin. It brought disorder into man's pursuit of his diverse loves. Thus he begins, under the influence of Paul, to insist more and more on the moral virtues being rooted in *caritas* if they are to issue in good works and be efficacious. Only a generous assistance from God can enable man to see aright once more the ultimate goal and highest end of the weight of his love:

> These fruits of the spirit reign in the man in whom sins do not reign. These goods reign in him because they delight (*delectant*) him so much that they restrain his mind from consenting to temptations. For we must perform our actions in accord with that which brings us most delight (*quod amplius nos delectat*). Thus, the appearance of a beautiful woman may come to mind and stimulate the delight (*delectatio*) associated with fornication. But if the inner beauty and pure appearance of chastity gives more delight (*plus delectat*), through the grace that is found in the faith of Christ, then we live and act in accord with it. Thus when sin does not reign in us, so as to promote obedience to its desires, but rather when righteousness (*justitia*) reigns in us through charity, then with great delight (*cum magna dilectatio*) we do whatever we know as pleasing to God. Now what I have said of chastity and fornication I wish to be understood of other objects.[47]

In addition to its display of the considerable range of Augustine's references to love the text shows how he brings *caritas*, as charity, to apply to man's right love and willing of everything in the universe. In this sense it can truly be said that charity is the greatest of all virtues for Augustine.

## JOY AS THE OUTCOME OF THE MORALLY GOOD LIFE

In many of his writings Augustine treats of the themes of 'using' (*uti*) and 'enjoying' (*frui*). These notions pertain particularly to what might be called positive love according to the diagram given above. Generally Augustine will allow that man may 'use' things beneath him but will claim one should never use God or his fellow man.

The joy man will reach and experience as the outcome of the moral life is described in Pauline terms, 'How great will that happiness (*felicitas*) be, where there will be no evil and no lack of good!'[48] This emphasis on God as the joy that awaits man as the fulfilment of the morally good life commences with his growing interest in St Paul, usually thought to originate about the time of the *Confessions* (397–401), and, as has been indicated elsewhere above, stresses the importance of the benevolent will for man to see aright and to act aright. Further reflection on the dynamics of Trinitarian love and on the great brotherhood of mankind in the historical drama of its pilgrimage towards God as it final goal and place of peace open yet another dimension in Augustine's moral thinking. He will explore the social implications of *caritas* in one's moral living.

## FRIENDSHIP: LOVE OF GOD, NEIGHBOUR AND ONE'S ENEMIES

That 'nothing is closer to man than man' is a theme which, for Augustine, reflects mankind's direction towards God as the goal of human existence. As Professor Vernon Bourke has put it:

> Human nature is essentially sociable and men are united by bonds of kinship. In all ordinary circumstances a man should live with his fellow man. The life of the wise man both on earth and in heaven is social.[49]

This is not to deny that for man the model of all friendships is the love of God; but rather to acknowledge that all men share in the invitation to this loving friendship. It is, after all, that great and mysterious circle of love in the Trinity that Augustine holds to be the paradigm of all love. For just as the love of the Trinity freely flows into the progression of persons constituting the Trinity, and is found in the third person to be mutually returned to Father and Son, Augustine thinks creation's return of love to the Creator of its goodness constitutes its well-being. On this earth, Augustine sees the human being as possessing an image of this Trinitarian dynamism in one's psychological makeup of intellect, will and memory.

Augustine's notion of friendship has many sources and is ultimately marked by his insights into the Christian teaching about love as related to the two great commandments of Scripture: 'Love God with your whole heart and soul', and 'Love your neighbour as yourself'.[50] He was aware of the Platonic notion of friendship and the later Greek views of Aristotle which differentiated among the friendships of pleasure, use and the true friendship between virtuous parties loving the other for the virtue they possessed. Cicero also contributed to this classical discussion of friendship. From this background Augustine could accept the high-minded ideal of friendship as a kind of altruistic notion that respected the other person as another self. Still another dimension to the notions of love and friendship was that found in the tradition of Neoplatonism. From the Neoplatonists Augustine would learn of mystical unions born out of love in which the self was lost in flight to the One, a union that seemed to overwhelm any further sense of self. However, through the insights of Christianity Augustine would invoke the love found in the Trinity and the love of God for man as the major inspirations of his own views.

Trinitarian love, as it involved the respective persons, was not as something possessive, but rather a beneficent and delightful experience. One person does not desire the prerogatives of the other but rejoices in them and finds the presence of the other delightful, not from a sense of use but of appreciation. Such love is unifying without effacing a real distinction among persons and without detracting from the inherent goodness and worth of each person of the Trinity. In a lesser degree God's love of creation was in the same image. This was not a jealous God who creates for personal use, but rather for the good and well-being of the created itself. Creation was good and all together very good; hence to be loved and praised by God and man alike. It was this sense of love as *caritas* that would permeate Augustine's thinking about the second great commandment and even extend to that ironic Christian obligation to 'love one's enemies'.

One could always love one's neighbour as a result of the motivation of a kind of 'positive love', namely, that somewhat neutral love whereby one feels a certain kinship of nature towards one's fellow man. In its most sublime aspect this neutral love could even lead to the philosophical notion of 'true friendship'. But Augustine finds in Scripture a need of assistance from God in order for man to see his destiny clearly and to be able to act effectively towards that end.

Once granted, this assistance marks the love of the recipient with a benevolent will, the ability to will rightly. With such benevolent will one loves his neighbour both as a nature that is good by its very existence and also for the perfection of that nature in God. To love another properly, with *caritas*, one must comprehend that nature as it was ultimately intended to be perfected in the company of God and other good beings. In this fashion Augustine recasts old philosophical notions of friendship to fit within the universe of order and love which he accepts.

Augustine proceeds further to explain how the benevolent love effected by *caritas* even extends to one's enemies. In loving the fruition and completion of an enemy's nature, as intended from the very beginning of its existence, one is not loving the wounding of that nature by the individual who fails to live properly. In fact, it is from a true love of nature, a human being with all its implications, that one tries to lead another away from immorality.[51]

Augustine's growing sense of humanity as a society in relation to God is evident in *The City of God*. This work about the course and history of mankind presents a much more encompassing use of 'society' than the previous membership in the Roman Empire or the Stoic 'universe of mankind' could express.[52] In a sense, Augustine replaces these worldwide and horizontal unions of mankind, with an enduring and hierarchical society, the society of the elect—a union that will comprise God, angelic beings and the just—in a friendship of *caritas*. Charity, in this context, effects a union of mutual respect and appreciation that shows it to be a virtue of humility in contrast to the vice of pride that leads to self-centred individualism.

But how does this new social outlook fit within Augustine's ethical views? One can note first the Platonic precedents of two patterns as a possible source for his two cities theme. For Plato had written in the *Theaetetus* (176E–177A) that there are two patterns laid up for man in the world of ideas. In the *Republic* (IX, 592B) he added that the philosopher always lives for the better city even if he never sees it copied here. He will live in this world as if a citizen of that other-worldly City.

As one studies the 'two-city' confrontation one begins to realise that Augustine is undertaking a historical depiction of the basic human moral struggle. Man is engaged in a working out of citizenship in one of these two cities via his love(s). But establishing one's citizenship amounts to a moral struggle internal to the individual as

such. Thus Augustine captures the titanic proportions of this struggle
in the following words:

> There are two wills, struggling between themselves within man:
> one old, the other new; one carnal, the other spiritual, and they
> are dissipating my soul in their discord.[53]

Man, then, has a two-directional ability of will which spills over
into the two cities to two loves which both afflict and benefit human
progress in the course of human history. One is dealing here with
the Pilgrim City on earth, not all that clear to men now, but a City
formed under the rubric, 'by their loves you shall know them'.
Whether one fails to discern the true object of one's love and how
that love should be practised because of ignorance or troublesome
inclinations and desires or not, the commandment of charity is
immutable. One is simply obliged to love one's fellow man aright,
whether neighbour, friend or foe, by that benevolent will that is
concerned for their ultimate union with God and other men. It is
under this principle that Augustine finds it acceptable for the civic
powers to restrain evil doers in society as best an *imperfect* human
society in this world can manage.[54]


## LYING

Because of man's historical moral struggle in the two cities of this
world Augustine places stress on lying as an anti-social fault of the
severest sort. Since the highest good for man also coincides with the
highest truth about his being and destiny man needs the truth about
himself in order to acquire that benevolent will whereby he can live
rightly. Lying threatens to keep one in ignorance about their being
and destiny and hence strikes at the very roots of the human being's
psychological and metaphysical constitution. When one realises the
influence of Plato's connection of knowledge and the good in his
doctrine of virtue on Augustine along with the Christian view of
God as the highest truth and good, it is easy to appreciate his harsh
words about lying:

> To speak of what is, is to speak the truth; to speak of what is not, is
> to tell a lie. Therefore, says that Psalmist, *Thou wilt destroy all* that
> speak a lie, since in turning their backs upon that which has
> existence, they turn aside to that which has none.[55]

## PREDESTINATION AND WILL ONCE MORE

A final issue in Augustine's view of human free will is his thinking about predestination. To begin with, there exists a somewhat complex and varied background to his thinking about this issue. Up to the time of the *Confessions* and while under the influence of Neoplatonism Augustine apparently thought one could, by human efforts, achieve some sort of mystical experience and union with God in this life.[56] Increasing familiarity with the writings of St Paul led him to abandon this belief.

Later in his life and during his episcopacy he encountered Pelagianism and its teaching that man could merit salvation by his good works alone. These various experiences all appear to turn Augustine to the stand that man is dependent on God's grace to gain the benevolent will necessary for performing morally good works. The position is explicit in the *De Spiritu et Littera*:

> If therefore the Apostle, when he mentioned that the Gentiles do by nature the things contained in the Law, and have the work of the law written in their hearts, he intended those to be understood who believed in Christ (*illos intelligi voluit qui credunt in Christum*) . . . so that belonging to the new testament means having the law of God not written on tables but on the heart—that is, embracing the righteousness of the law with innermost affection, where faith works by love. 'Because it is by faith that God justifies the Gentiles' (*Quia ex fide justificat gentes Deus*).[57]

Although Augustine might sound harsh in affirming a doctrine of predestination where only those whom God elects will reach their final good two features of Augustine's thinking and the times in which he lived ought to be kept in mind. First, his growing sensitivity to mankind, as being destined to enjoy God as its supreme good, was being sorely tried by the divisive impact of Pelagianism on the Christian Church. Second, Augustine's abandonment of the belief that man could raise himself to the experience of a mystical encounter with God such as Plotinus' encounter of the One was a lesson in personal humility. If this was not enough, Augustine's charitable effort to dissuade the Pelagians from their cherished ideas was often met by an incorrigible refusal. Finally, there was a certain mystery about God's bestowal of grace that probably reminded Augustine of the mystery of his own striking conversion. At any rate, his thoughts in the *De gratia et libero arbitrio*, 15, 31, some four years prior to his death, are neither harsh nor pessimistic about man's reaching his ultimate goal:

> Free will (*voluntas libera*) *is always present in us*, but it is not always good. It is either free from righteousness, when it is in the service of sin, and then it is evil: or it is free from sin, when it is in the service of righteousness, and then it is good. But the grace of God is always good and brings about a good will in man who before that was possessed of an evil will. It is by this grace, too, that this same good will, once it begins to exist, is expanded and made so strong that it is able to fulfill whatever of God's commandments it wishes, whenever it does so with a strong and perfect will.[58]

## CONCLUDING REMARKS

The Christian universe to which Augustine subscribed and in which he explores a host of moral topics resulted in the original moral vision he bequeathed to the history of ethics. His prolonged efforts to set the human will free from fate, from determinism, from the attractiveness of the mutable things of this world, not to mention the impact of sin, all mark the disappearance of an era. Although deeply concerned with evil and its reality in human experience he was most effective in combatting the idea that a *supremely* evil being existed in the universe. In fact, his emphasis is on the force of love in the world, on the joy of existence, on history as a positive experience for man as he progresses towards a goal of permanent happiness and personal as well as social fulfilment in an eternal communion of true friends. These inspirations and insights have all acted on the western world to give it a hope such as the classical era, and especially the stagnant times of the Roman Empire, never produced.

# Notes

1. The biographical work on Augustine still continues and poses many challenging questions and issues for his investigators. Following are some of the studies which indicate the vastness of this field: Bonner, Gerald, *St. Augustine: Life and Controversies* (Philadelphia, Pennsylvania: Westminster Press, 1963); Bourke, Vernon J., *Augustine's Quest of Wisdom* (Milwaukee, Wisconsin: Bruce, 1945) and *Wisdom from St. Augustine* (Houston, Texas: The Center for Thomistic Studies, 1984); Brown, Peter, *Augustine of Hippo* (Berkeley and Los Angeles: University of California Press, 1967); Marec, E., *Hippone-la-royale: antique Hippo Regius* (2me ed.: Alger: Imprimerie Officielle, 1954) and *Monuments chrétiens d'Hippone, ville épiscopale de saint Augustine* (Ministère de l'Algérie. Sous-direction des Beaux-Arts. Paris: Arts et Métiers graphiques, 1958); Perler, Othmar, *Les Voyages de saint Augustin* (Paris: Études Augustiniennes, 1969); Pope, Hugh, OP, *St. Augustine of Hippo* (Westminster, Maryland: Newman Press, 1949), Pottier, René, *Saint Augustin le Berbère* (Paris: 1945); Van der Meer, F., *Augustinus de zielzorger* (Utrecht: 1947; trans. Brian Battershaw and G. R. Lamb as *Augustine the Bishop*, London and New York: Sheed Ward, 1961).
2. 'Late have I loved Thee, O Beauty so ancient and so new, late have I loved Thee! And behold, Thou wert within and I was without. I was looking for Thee out there, and I threw myself, deformed as I was, upon those well-formed things which Thou has made. Thou wert with me, yet I was not with Thee.' A21, X, 27, 297. Cf. ibid., 'I invoke Thee, O my God, my Mercy, who hast made me—Thou didst not forget even when Thou wert forgotten. I invoke Thee into my soul, which Thou dost prepare to receive Thee through the desire that Thou inspirest into it. Do not abandon me as I invoke Thee now, Thou who didst come to my aid before I uttered any invocation, and who didst repeatedly instruct me by many sorts of calls, so that I might listen from afar off and be turned back, and call upon Thee as Thou wert calling me.' XIII, 1, 407. The translation is that of Vernon J. Bourke as found in *The Fathers of the Church Series* vol. 21 (Washington, D.C.: Catholic University of America Press, 1953). Notes will refer in the following fashion to the Works and Studies of Augustine's Ethics as listed in the Bibliography: For Works, A3, A4, and so on will mean a work followed by book and chapter and section if appropriate. More available works from English series or volumes translating a large number of Augustine's writings are generally employed. In these instances, the page number of the translation is the last number given. Studies will be cited according to list number and then page number. For example, 2, 20 will mean the second work in the list of studies, page 20.
3. See the discussions in the following: (6, 82–4; 109; 112; 138–9), (8, 46–60; 93–100; 245–46; 302–12; 317–24), (15, 47–8; 56–7, 71–5; 77–8; 105–111; 134–36), (16, entirety), (25, 56; 68–74; 88–92; 94; 135–36; 139–42). Other

notable studies are: the chapters on Augustine by R. A. Markus in *The Cambridge History of Later Greek and Early Medieval Philosophy*, ed. A. H. Armstrong (Cambridge University Press, 1967); A. C. Pegis 'The Mind of St. Augustine', *Mediaeval Studies*, VI (1944), 1–61; and Raymond D. DiLorenzo's 'Ciceronianism and Augustine's Conception of Philosophy', *Augustinian Studies*, XIII (1982), 171–76.

4.  See Bourke (6, 67–71; 140–42) and O'Donovan (25, 48–59; 75–92; 93–8).
5.  See Bourke (6, 71–4; 143–51) and O'Donovan (25, 112–36).
6.  'Indeed, just as Thou dost exist absolutely, Thou alone dost really know—Thou who existest immutably and knowest immutably and willest immutably, as Thy essence knows and wills immutably, Thy knowledge exists and wills immutably, and Thy will exists and knows immutably.' A21, XIII, 16, 424. Cf. ibid. XI, 30, 364–65: and 'There is a nature which is susceptible of change with respect to both place and time, namely, the corporeal. There is another nature which is in no way susceptible of change with respect to place, but only with respect to time, namely, the spiritual. And there is a third Nature which can be changed neither in respect to place nor in respect to time: that is, God. Those natures of which I have said that they are mutable in some respect are called creatures; the Nature which is immutable is called Creator. A1, 18, translation from *The Works of Aurelius Augustinus*, vol. VI (ed. Marcus Dods), 15 vols (Edinburgh: T. and T. Clark Co., 1871–76).
7.  Consult O'Donovan (25, 124–36). See especially *De catechizandis rudibus* 4, 7 and *De trinitate* VI, 5, 7 as quoted on pages 124 and 128 respectively.
8.  In this connection see the contemporary reflections of Karl Stern in *The Flight from Woman*, 'A Note on Dependence' (New York: The Noonday Press, 1965) pp. 296–305.
9.  ' "Therefore, we do not have the slightest doubt that anyone out to be happy must obtain for himself that which always endures and cannot be snatched away through any severe misfortune."
    Trygentius said: 'We have already agreed to this."
    "Is God, in your opinion, eternal and ever remaining?" I asked.
    "This, of course, is so certain," replied Licentius, "that that question is unnecessary." All the others agreed with pious devotion.
    "Therefore," I concluded, "whoever possesses God is happy." ' A2, II, 11, 58–9. Cf. ibid., 'This, then, is the full satisfaction of souls, this the happy life: to recognize piously and completely the One through whom you are led into the truth, the nature of the truth you enjoy, and the bond that connects you with the supreme measure.' IV, 35, 83. The translation is that of Ludwig Schopp as found in *The Fathers of the Church Series*, vol. 5, 1948.
10. 'If, then, it be asked what the City of God has to say upon these points, and, in the first place, what its opinion regarding the supreme good and evil is, it will reply that life eternal is the supreme good, death eternal the supreme evil, and that to obtain the one and escape the other we must live rightly. . . . As for those who have supposed that the sovereign good and evil are to be found in this life, and have placed it either in the soul or the body, or in both, or, to speak more explicitly, either in pleasure, or in virtue, or in both; in repose, or in virtue, or in both; in

pleasure and repose, or in virtue, or in all combined; in the primary
objects of nature, or in virtue, or in both—all these have, with a
marvellous shallowness, sought to find their blessedness in this life and
in themselves.' A27, XIX, 4, 1. The translation is that of Dods as found in
Bourke (3, 88–9). Cf. nn. 14 and 15.

11. The following text illustrates how Augustine connects the recom-
mendations for Christian living with 'a way of life', 'a lifestyle' (in the
sense of a philosophy of life in his day) and how he maintains that such
a practice brings man to his ultimate perfection and fulfilment:

> Our righteousness in this pilgrimage is this that we press forward to
> that perfection and fullness of righteousness where there shall be
> perfect and full love in the sight of his glory; and that we now hold to
> the rectitude and perfection of that course, by chastising our body
> and bringing it into subjection, by doing our almsgiving cheerfully
> and from the heart, while bestowing kindness and forgiving the
> trespasses which have been committed against us, and by continuing
> steadfast in prayer . . . and doing all these things with sound
> doctrine, upon which are built a right faith, a firm hope, and a pure
> charity. This is now our righteousness, in which we run our course
> hungering and thirsting after the perfection and fullness of righteous-
> ness, in order that we may hereafter be satisfied therewith. Therefore
> that Lord in the Gospel (after saying, 'Take heed that you do not your
> righteousness before men, so that you may be seen by them') in order
> that we should not measure our life by the goal of human glory,
> declared in his exposition of righteousness itself that there be none
> except these three—fasting, almsgiving, and prayer. Now by *fasting*
> He means the entire subjugation of the body; by *almsgiving*, all kinds
> of will and deed, either by giving or forgiving; and by *prayer* He
> implies all the rules of holy desire . . . Let us run, believing, hoping,
> longing; let us run, chastising the body, cheerfully and from the heart
> giving alms—in giving kindnesses and forgiving injuries, praying
> that our strength may be helped as we run; and thus let us so listen to
> the commandments which urge us to perfection, that we do not fail to
> run towards the fullness of love.

(A28, VIII. Translation and emphasis mine.) See also the discussions in
O'Donovan (25, 56–9; 156–58) and O'Connor (24, entirety).

12. See n. 2.
13. These various loves which had attracted Augustine's heart at various
periods in his earlier years are indicative of how one's heart could be
restless until it achieved union with its true good and thus would come
to rest.
14. A5, 3, trans. Dods as reprinted in *Basic Writings of Saint Augustine*, ed.
Whitney J. Oates, vol. 1 (New York: Random House, 1948) p. 321.
15. A5, 8, ibid., p. 325.
16. This is emphatically claimed by 'O'Donovan (25, 168–69, n. 20) and the
span of texts he cites in this note amply support the position.
17. Considering Augustine's opportune encounter with and fascination

with Manicheism as well as its stress on two wills, good and evil, the following texts suggest that the result was a salving of conscience for current immoralities. See A21, IV, 1, 73–4 and ibid., VIII, 10, 218:

> During this same period of nine years, from my nineteenth to my twenty-eighth year, we were led astray and we led others astray, deceived and deceiving, through a variety of passions; openly, through teachings which they call liberal; secretly, through the false name of religion. In the former, we were proud; in the latter, superstitious; in all, vain. . . . On the other, desirous of cleansing ourselves from these sordid things, we brought food for those who were called the 'elect' and the 'saints,' so that they might fashion from it, in the workshop of their paunches, angels and gods for us, through whom we might be made free. I was one of these pursuers and I did these things along with my friends, who were deceived by me and along with me.

> Just as vain talkers and those who seduce the mind perish from before Thy presence, O God, so let those perish who, noticing the two voluntary tendencies in the process of deliberation, maintain that there are two natures belonging to two minds: the one a good nature; the other, bad. Truly, they themselves are evil when they entertain these bad opinions.

Cf. ibid., VIII, 10, 219:

> Indeed, if there are as many opposed natures as there are voluntary inclinations which offer mutual resistance, then there will be not two wills, but many. If a person deliberates whether he will go to one of their meetings, or to the theatre, they cry out: 'See, two natures; the good one draws in this direction, the bad one draws away in that. Otherwise, whence comes this hesitation of opposed wills within him?'

18. In the following passage of his *Letter to Firmius*, Augustine states his purpose to be that of refuting the teaching of the pagans in the first ten books:

> If you wish that two volumes be made of them, they should be so apportioned that one volume contain ten books, the other twelve. For in those ten the empty teachings of the pagans have been refuted . . . If, however, you should prefer that there be more than two volumes, you should make as many as five. The first of these would contain the first five books, where argument has been advanced against those who contend that the worship, not indeed of gods, but of demons, is of profit for happiness in this present life. The second volume would contain the next five books, where a stand has been taken against those who think that, for the sake of the life which is to come after death, worship should be paid, through rites and sacrifices, whether to these divinities or to any plurality of gods whatever.

The parts of the passage are quoted from Vernon J. Bourke, *The Essential Augustine* (Indianapolis, Ind.: Hackett Publishing Company, 1964) p. 199, as taken from the *Fathers of the Church*, ed. R. Deferrari *et al.*, vol. VI (New York: Fathers of the Church, Inc., 1950) pp. 399–401. Moreover, both Bourke, *op. cit.*, p. 197 and R. A. Markus, *Saeculum: History and Society in the Theology of St. Augustine* (Cambridge University Press, 1970) pp. 56–7, take this as evidence of a late revival of paganism and/or a sign of moral decline.

19. This signifies a change of title translation from more traditional translations like 'On the Free Will' or 'On the Freedom of the Will'. The purpose here is to avoid any suggestion that Augustine means something like Aristotle's notion of choice.

20. 'Quid enim tam in voluntate quam ipsa voluntas sita est?' A7, I, 12, 86, 228.

21. A7, III, 3, 92:

> For you could not maintain that anything is in our power except actions that are subject to our own will. Therefore, nothing is so completely in our power as the will itself, for it is ready at hand to act immediately, as soon as we will. Thus we are right in saying that we grow old by necessity, not by will; or that we die by necessity, not by will, and so on. Who but a madman would say that we do not will with the will?
>
> Therefore, though God foreknows what we shall will in the future, this does not prove that we do not will anything voluntarily. In regard to happiness, you said (as if I would deny it) that you do not make yourself happy. I say, however, that when you are to be happy, you shall not be happy against your will, but because you will to be happy. When, therefore, God foreknows that you will be happy, it cannot be otherwise, or else there would be no such thing as foreknowledge. Nevertheless, we are not forced to believe, as a consequence of this, that you are going to be happy when you do not want to be. This is absurd and far from the truth.

The translation is that of Anna S. Benjamin and L. H. Hackstaff in The Library of Liberal Arts paperback edition (Indianapolis, Ind.: Bobbs-Merrill, 1964).

22. A7, III, 1, 7–12, 175–276. Besides enumerating these different causes this extensive passage contains Augustine's detailed argument as discussed in the text.

23. A27, V, 9.

24. A7, III, 3, 93:

> So it follows that we do not deny that God has foreknowledge of all things to be, and yet that we will what we will. For when He has foreknowledge of our will, it is going to be the will that He has foreknown. Therefore, the will is going to be a will because God has foreknowledge of it. Nor can it be a will if it is not in our power. Therefore, God also has knowledge of our power over it. So the power is not taken from me by His foreknowledge; but because of His foreknowledge, the power to will will more certainly be present in me, since God whose

foreknowledge does not err, has foreknown that I shall have the power.

25. A7, III, 4, 95:

> Your recollection of events in the past does not compel them to occur. In the same way God's foreknowledge of future events does not compel them to take place.

The treatment of this issue is focused improperly in Rowe (30, 209–17) where he confuses the inevitability of aging, which is outside one's power, with one's will about the fact, a matter that is quite within the power of one's will. If such were not the case then the cosmetic and plastic surgery practices of today would hardly be explainable. (One simply is not willing to go along with the inevitability of aging.) It is one's will towards the matter that is Augustine's concern. Furthermore, Rowe quite neglects Augustine's principal arguments against claiming that God's foreknowledge constrains the human will as discussed in the text, pages 67–8.

26. This is, at least, the Manichean position as understood in Augustine's time. See, for example, the passages in n. 17 and elsewhere in Augustine's writings.

27. A7, I, 4, 10: 'E. I have come to my senses. Now I am glad that I clearly know the nature of that blameworthy desire called lust (*libido*). It now appears to be the love of those things which a man can lose against his will.'

28. A7, III, 14, 120: 'Since an imperfection is opposed to the nature, the degree to which the imperfection is evil is equal to the amount by which the completeness of the nature is decreased. Therefore, when you blame an imperfection, are you not really praising that in which you desire completeness?' And see the earlier chapter 7 of Book III for its discussion of existence as background for Augustine's statement about evil as the absence of good. Cf. *The Nature of the Good* (*De natura boni*) 4: 'When accordingly it is inquired whence is evil, it must first be inquired, what is evil, which is nothing else than corruption, either of the measure, or the form, or the order, that belong to nature.' Trans. Dods as found in Oates, vol. I, p. 432; and ibid., 6; vol. I, p. 433.

29. See A7, II, 18, 183–85, 269–70 for a full account of Augustine's thought on this point.

30. This is a summary of Augustine's argument as presented in A7, III, 8, 76–84, 288–89.

31. See Augustine's treatment of this theme in A7, I, 14, 99–102, 231–32.

32. See A7, III, 7, 69–75, 287. Cf. *The Nature of the Good*, 1–3, and A5, II, 6, 8.

33. See A7, III, 7, 71–3, 287. Cf. ibid., II, 19, 196–200, 272; II, 20, 201–02; 204–05, 272–73, and A21, X, 8–26, 12–37, 161–75.

34. A33, 15. The English translation of this passage is taken from Bourke (3, 54). Cf. Augustine, *Enchiridion* IX:

> 'Man misusing his free will destroys both himself and it. A man who kills himself does so, indeed, while he is living; but, in killing himself,

no longer lives and cannot restore himself to life. So also, when he has sinned through free will, sin is victorious and his free will is lost, "for by whatever a man is overcome, of this also he is the slave." The sentence quoted is from the Apostle Peter. Since it is surely true, what liberty, I ask, can a slave have except when it pleases him to sin. For that service is liberty which freely does the will of the master. Accordingly, he is free to sin who has not been freed from sin and begins to be the servant of justice. And such is true liberty because he has the job of right-doing, and at the same time dutiful servitude because he obeys the precept. But, for the man sold into the bondage of sin, where will that freedom of right-doing come from unless he be redeemed by Him who said: "If the Son makes you free, you will be free indeed"? If this operation has not begun in a man and he is not yet free to do right, how can he glory in free will and in good works, unless he puffs himself up with foolish pride? And this it was that the Apostle spoke against when he said: "By grace you have been saved through faith." '

This translation is that of Bernard M. Peebles in *The Fathers of the Church Series*, 1947; vol. 2, p. 395; A35, I, 9, 4; A27, XXI, 15.
35. A14, 93, 18 as translated by Bourke (6, 150–51):

> Don't try to twist the will of God to your will; rather, correct your own in terms of God's will. For the will of God is certainly a rule (*regula*): now think, do you twist the rule that serves as a standard for your own correction? Indeed, this rule endures without corruption: it is an immutable rule. As long as this rule is unbroken, you have something to which you may turn and correct your iniquity, you have a means of correcting what is twisted in you. What is it that men will? It's of little importance, because they have each his own twisted will: in their hearts they wish to make God's will twisted, so that God may do what they will, when they themselves ought to be doing what God wills.

Similarly, O'Donovan writes, 'In saying that self-love finds its only true expression in love of God Augustine is formulating in one of many possible ways a principle fundamental to his metaphysical and ethical outlook, namely that all moral obligation derives from an obligation to God which is at the same time a call to self-fulfillment.' 25, 138 and ibid., 157–58.
36. See, especially, Bourke (6, 96–100) for the scriptural impact. In addition, extensive discussions of the various approaches to the 'Divine Illumination Doctrine' can be found in Gilson (15, 77–96), Ronald H. Nash, *The Light of the Mind: St. Augustine's Theory of Knowledge* (Lexington, Kentucky: University of Kentucky Press, 1969) chapter 7, and Bourke (6, 108–10).
37. *Contra Faustum Manichaeum* XX, 7, as translated in Bourke (6, 110–11).
38. A3 II, 19, 50, 134, as translated by Bourke (6, 110).
39. A7, II, 12, 33, 130–31, as translated by Anna S. Benjamin and L. H. Hackstaff in *On Free Choice of the Will* (New York: Bobbs-Merrill, 1964) pp. 65–6.

40. Augustine continues: 'For the light is God Himself, whereas the soul is a creature; yet since it is rational and intellectual, it is made in His image'. XII, 31, 59, as translated in Bourke (6, 112–13).

41. A7, II, 12, 34, 133–34, 260.

42. A7, I, 6, 15, 48–51, 220, as translated by Benjamin and Hackstaff, pp. 14–15.

43. A7, I, 8, 18, 64–5, 223), as translated by Benjamin and Hackstaff, p. 82.

44. A7, II, 19, 52, 198, 272, as translated by Benjamin and Hackstaff, p. 82.

45. A1, CLV, 4, 13, as found in Bourke (6, 98). See also O'Donovan's observations (25, 157–59).

46. This diagram represents a condensation of the complexities of Augustine's terminology and his distinctive themes of how man and God's love function and are directed. For excellent background material see O'Donovan (25, 10–36), Bourke (6, 116–20) and especially for its extensive and helpful analyses (3, 30–49).

47. *Expositio Epistolae and Galatas*, 5, 49. The translation is taken from Bourke (3, 36–7).

48. A27, XXII, 30.

49. Bourke, 6, 164.

50. Mark 12, 30–1; Matt. 19, 19 and 22, 37–8; Luke 10, 27; Romans 13: 9; Gal. 5:14; James 2: 8. See O'Donovan (25, chapter 2, 37–59 and chapter 5, 112–35), for his discussion of these two commandments and Augustine's treatment of each respectively.

51. See O'Donovan (25, 23) for further discussion of this point and page 193, ns. 27 and 28 for the pertinent texts from Augustine.

52. See the penetrating anlaysis of this change in Markus, *Saeculum*, pp. 76–104, where he traces Augustine's development of a distinction between the classical conception of the *polis* and a *civitas*, as arranging for human fulfilment in the *polis* and that of a Christian Society of men and angels whose fulfilment lies in communion with God. Realisation of this latter *plenitudo* in communion requires divine providence or the assistance of God to bring about the right ordering of wills to such a society. Consult also Gilson's analysis (15, 168–84) and the parallel views of those issues, as maintained by Markus, in Cranz (11, entirety) and Bourke (6, 159–68).

53. A21, VIII, 5. Translation mine.

54. See O'Donovan (25, 120–27) and the extended discussion (127–36). There are many issues which branch out from Augustine's central thesis of the love of God as the paradigm for love of one's fellow man. However, the extensions of these themes must recognise and incorporate certain key elements in Augustine's thought to remain authentic reflections of his views. In this case, Augustine's view of man's nature as prevented from normal direction of its loves by sin along with the corresponding result that all human efforts at society in this world are 'imperfect' are essential to any assessment or presentation of his position(s). Brown (8, 311–35) provides a rather harsh assessment of Augustine's political views. See Bourke (6, 169–87) for a detailed commentary on Brown's account of Augustine's political thought in various publications. Studies such as those of Markus, *Saeculum*, O'Connor (23, entirety and 24, entirety) as well as George J. Lavere's, 'The Problem of the Common

Good in Saint Augustine's *Civitas Terrena'*, *Augustinian Studies* 14 (1983), 1–10, and the annual 'patristic, Mediaeval, and Renaissance Conference' at Villanova University regularly present a number of articles and papers respectively on these issues. Finally, regarding Augustine's views on war, especially a just war, two comments seem in order: first, his concern in the case of the political realm is always a moral one extending beyond any particular political system or nation (see *Epistola 138* and recall his position that man's political efforts at society in this life are laden with imperfection stemming from human weakness and sin); second, Augustine himself is primarily and principally a man of peace. He searches for it to the extent possible in this life (remembering here that his efforts in various controversies and heresies of his own day were to try to bring about reconciliation and peace) and further that he longed as much as or more than most men for true peace, the peace of that heavenly society such as has not 'entered the heart of man' in this world. See Bourke (6, 166) and the accompanying notes. The following words of George J. Lavere ('The Problem . . .', p. 7) sum up the position and reflect Augustine's enduring eudaimonism:

Augustine's political philosophy—his political realism—is based upon his realization of the inability of the earthly city to accomplish its task of mediation. The two cities cannot agree on single purpose, a comprehensive common good which would sustain a unified community. The operative values of those who love God inevitably conflict with the values of those who love themselves and the things of this world. Logically, the outcome would be constant struggle, even warfare, between the conflicting parties; but the Christian wayfarer in the earthly city is a social being by doctrinal commitment and bound to love his fellowman for the sake of God.

This is the stand that Augustine could take, the position of one who could see the demise of a world superpower and realise that man's true peace was not of this world.

55. A14, 5, 7. The translation is taken from Vernon J. Bourke, *The Essential Augustine*, 2nd ed. (Indianapolis, Ind.: The Hackett Publishing Company, 1974), p. 170. See also Sissela Bok, *Lying: Moral Choice in Public and Private Life* (New York: Random House, 1979) pp. 34–6.
56. On this specific issue consult F. E. Van Fleteren, OSA, 'Augustine's Ascent of the Soul in Book VII of the *Confessions*: A Reconstruction', *Augustinian Studies*, V (1974), 29–72. Also see n. 4.
57. *De spiritu et littera*, 46. Translation that of P. Holmes, Oates, *Basic Writings*, I, p. 497.
58. A33, 15, 31.

# Bibliography

The standard complete edition of St Augustine's works has been that of the Benedictines of St Maur (1679–1700) reprinted in J. P. Migne, *Patrologia Latina*. Paris: 1844–49; vols. XXXII–XLV. (Current: Turnhout: Brepols; Brill, 1971). The critical editing of Augustine's writings was begun in the series *Corpus Scriptorum Ecclesiae Latinorum*, Vienna: Tempsky, 1864– ; and continued in the *Corpus Christianorum, Series Latina*, Turnhout: Brepols; The Hague: Nijhoff, 1953– . English translations of most of his writings are available in *Ancient Christian Writers*, eds J. Quasten and J. C. Plumbe (Westminster, Maryland: Newman Press, 1964– ); and *The Fathers of the Church Series* (New York: Fathers of the Church, 1947–60); and numerous translations by individuals of various major works outside these series. Besides these editions and various translations a concordance to the writings of St Augustine by the German Augustinian Province is nearly complete and should be available in a few years. Bibliographical information and chronological details about his works are available in the following: C. Andresen, *Bibliographia Augustiniana* (Darmstadt: Wissenschaftliche Buchesewellschaft, 1973) and *Zum Augustinespräch der Gegenwart*, Wege der Forschung, 5 (Darmstadt: Wissenschaftliche Bucheswellschaft, 1962); *Augustine Bibliography*, riprod. dei *Fichiers bibliographiques* della *Études Augustiniennes*, Paris-Boston, 1972; G. Bardy, *Les révisions in Oeuvres de s. Augustin* vol. XII (Paris: Desclée, 1950); T. v. Bavel, *Répertoire bibliographique de Saint Augustin 1950–1960* (The Hague; Nijhoff, 1963); E. S. Lodovici, *Agostino* in *Questioni di Storiografia Filosofica*, I (Brescia: 1975) pp. 445–501; Terry L. Miethe, *Augustinian Bibliography, 1970–1980* (Westport, CT: Greenwood, 1982); and S. M. Zarb, *Chronologium Operum S. Augustini* (Roma: Angelicum, X 1933, 359–96, 478–512; XI 1934, 78–91). The following list of Augustine's works with ethical content is in the chronological order found in Vernon J. Bourke's *Wisdom from St. Augustine*, chapter 1 (Houston, Texas: Center for Thomistic Studies, 1984), pp. 8–13. The chronological order is practically a necessity to follow Augustine's shifting interests and focus. Only works of major importance for the themes treated in the text are listed.

## WORKS

| | |
|---|---|
| 1.386/430 | Letters (*Epistulae*) |
| 2.386 | The Happy Life (*De beata vita*) |
| 3.386 | On Order (*De ordine*) |
| 4.387/390 | On Prosody (*De musica*) |
| 5.387/389 | The Customs of Catholics and Manichees (*De moribus ecclesiae catholicae et manichaeorum*) |
| 6.388/389 | On Genesis against the Manichees (*De Genesi contra manichaeos*) |

7.388/395    On Free Decision of the Will* (*De libero arbitrio*)
8.389        The Teacher (*De magistro*)
9.391/430    Sermons (*Sermones*)
10.391       On True Religion (*De vera religione*)
11.388/395   Eighty-three Different Questions (*De diversis quaestionibus 83*)
12.392       The Advantage of Believing (*De utilitate credendi*)
13.392/393   On Dual Souls against the Manichees (*De duabus animabus contra manichaeos*)
14.392/426   Enarrations on the Psalms (*Enarrationes in Psalmos*)
15.394       The Sermon of Our Lord on the Mount (*De sermone Domini in monte*)
16.395       On Lying (*De menadacio*)
17.395       On Continence (*De continentia*)
18.395       Answers to Simplicianus' Various Questions (*De diversis questionibus ad Simplicianum*)
19.396/426   Christian Doctrine (*De doctrina Christiana*)
20.397/401   Questions on the Gospels (*Quaestiones Evangeliorum*)
21.397/401   The Confessions (*Confessiones*)
22.399/419   The Trinity (*De Trinitate*)
23.401       On Baptism against the Donatists (*De baptismo contra Donatistas*)
24.411       The Deserts and Forgiveness of Sins (*De peccatorum-meritis et remissione*)
25.413/415   On Nature and Grace (*De natura et gratia*)
26.413/418   Treatise on John's Gospel (*Iohannis Evangelium, Tractatus 124*)
27.413/426   The City of God (*De civitate Dei*)
28.415/416   Man's Perfection under Justice (*De perfectione iustitiae hominis*)
29.417       The Correction of the Donatists (*De correptione Donatistarum*)
30.418       The Grace of Christ and Original Sin (*De gratia Christi et de peccato originali*)
31.419/421   Marriage and Concupiscence (*De nuptiis et concupiscentia*)
32.422       Against Lying (*Contra mendacium*)
33.426       Grace and Free Decision of the Will* (*De gratia et libero arbitrio*)
34.426       Correction and Grace (*De correptione et gratia*)
35.426/427   Retractations (*Retractationes*)
36.429       The Predestination of the Saints (*De praedestinatione Sanctorum*)
37.429       The Gift of Perseverance (*De dono perseverantiae*)

## STUDIES OF AUGUSTINE'S ETHICS

This listing is neither comprehensive nor weighted towards any one analysis of interpretation of Augustine's ethical thought. It is selected with the intention of giving the initiate to Augustine's thought, or at least the beginner in studying his ethics, a broad sampling of the international effort to make his thought in this area more accessible and better understood. One

*This signifies a change of title translation from that found in Vernon Bourke's list for purposes of avoiding any suggestion that Augustine means something like Aristotle's notion of choice.

feature of this listing that should be noted is the growing tendency, in more recent years and works, to take account of developments in Augustine's lifetime and the considerable impact these changes had on his ethics.

1. Armas, P. Gregorio, *La moral de San Agustin* (Madrid: Difuso del Leiro, 1954).
2. Bourke, Vernon J., *History of Ethics* vol. I (Garden City, New York: Image Books, 1970) pp. 80–4.
3. ——, *Joy in Augustine's Ethics* (Villanova, Pennsylvania: Villanova University Press, 1979).
4. ——, 'Voluntarism in Augustine's Ethico-Legal Thought', *Augustinian Studies*, I (1970), 3–17.
5. ——, *Will in Western Thought* (New York: Sheed & Ward, 1964).
6. ——, *Wisdom from St. Augustine* (Houston, Texas: Center for Thomistic Studies, 1984).
7. Boyer, C., *San Agustin. Sus normas de Moral* (Buenos Aires: 1945).
8. Brown, P. R. L., 'Political Society', *Augustine*, ed. R. A. Markus (Garden City, New York: Doubleday Anchor Books, 1972) pp. 38–58.
9. Combes, G., *La charité d'après S. Augustin* (Paris: Desclée de Brouwer, 1934).
10. Cranz, F. Edward, 'The Development of Augustine's Ideas on Society before the Donatist Controversy', *Augustine . . .* ; pp. 336–403.
11. ——, '*De Civitate Dei*, XV, 2, and Augustine's Ideas of the Christian Society', *Augustine . . .* ; 404–21.
12. de Lubac, Henri, SJ, *Augustinianism and Modern Theology* (trans. Lancelot Sheppard) (New York: Herder & Herder, 1968); originally published under the title *Augustinisme et théologie moderne* (Paris: F. Aubier, Editions Montaigne, 1965).
13. Di Giovanni, A., *La dialettica dell'amore 'Uti-frui' nelle preconfessioni di S. Agostino* (Roma: 1965).
14. Fortin, Ernest L., 'The Political Implications of St. Augustine's Theory of Conscience', *Augustinian Studies*, I (1970), 133–52.
15. Gilson, Etienne, *The Christian Philosophy of Saint Augustine* (trans. L. E. M. Lynch) (New York: Random House, 1960).
16. Holloway, Alvin J., SJ, *The Transformation of Stoic Themes in St. Augustine* (unpublished PH.D. Thesis) (New York: Fordham University, 1966).
17. Holte, R., *Béatitude et Sagesse. Saint Augustin et le problème de la fin de l'homme dans la philosophie ancienne* (Paris: Etudes Augustiniennes, 1962).
18. Jolivet, R., *Le problème du mal chez S. Augustin* (Paris: Archives de Philosophie, vol. VII, 2 (1930), 1–104).
19. Madec, G., 'Verus philosophus est amator Dei', *Revue Sc. Phil. Théol*, 61 (1977), pp. 549–66.
20. Mausbach, J., *Die Ethik des Hl. Augustimus* 2 vols. (Freiburg: Herder, 1909).
21. O'Connell, Robert J., SJ, 'Action and Contemplation', *Augustine . . .* ; 38–58.
22. ——, *De Libero Arbitrio I*; 'Stoicism Revisited', *Augustinian Studies*, I (1970), 49–68.

23. O'Connor, William Riordan, 'The Concept of Person in St. Augustine's *De Trinitate*', *Augustinian Studies*, XIII (1982), 133–43.

24. ——, 'The *Uti/Frui* Distinction in Augustine's Ethics', *Augustinian Studies*, XIV (1983), 45–62.

25. O'Donovan, Oliver, *The Problem of Self-Love in St. Augustine* (New Haven and London: Yale University Press, 1980).

26. Pedone, *Il problema della voluntá in S. Agostino* (Lanciano: 1940).

27. Ramirez, J. Roland E., 'Demythologizing Augustine as Great Sinner', *Augustinian Studies*, XII (1981), 61–88.

28. Rist, John M., 'Augustine on Free Will and Predestination', *Augustine* . . . ; 218–52.

29. Roland-Gosselin, R., *La morale de S. Augustin* (Paris: Rivière, 1925).

30. Rowe, William L., 'Augustine on Foreknowledge and Free Will', *Augustine* . . . ; 336–403.

31. Stark, Judith Chelius, 'The Problem of Evil: Augustine and Ricoeur', *Augustinian Studies*, XIII (1982), 111–22.

# 4

# Aquinas
## *Vernon J. Bourke*

As professor of theology at the University of Paris in the mid-13th century, Thomas Aquinas (1224–74) made the study of morality a major part of his course.[1] He had taken a degree in liberal arts, with philosophy as core subject, at the state university in Naples and then studied theology at Paris and Cologne under Albert the Great as key teacher. In Cologne Albert's lectures on the *Nicomachean Ethics* of Aristotle (as transcribed by Aquinas) opened the door to the ethical thinking of the ancient Greek and Latin philosophers, as well as to the Fathers of the early Christian Church (such as Augustine, Ambrose, Gregory the Great, John Chrysostom and John Damascene), to the Greek and Latin commentators on Aristotle, to Boethius and Dionysius the Pseudo-Areopagite, to the classics of Roman and ecclesiastical law, and to the ethical writings of Moses Maimonides and of Avicenna and Averroes.[2]

The Bible (both Old and New Testaments) was also a most important influence on Thomas' practical philosophy. The ten commandments from the Book of Exodus, for instance, had a strong impact on his approach to many problems in applied ethics. And the New Testament injunctions, to love God above all and one's neighbour as one's self, introduced an emphasis on charity, mercy and a future life that was absent from ancient philosophical ethics.[3] Yet Thomistic ethics is much more than a simple distillation of biblical morality. Indeed some writers on Christian ethics regard Aquinas as more an Aristotelian philosopher than a Christian theologian. Closer to the historical truth, however, is the view that Thomas Aquinas came at a time when Graeco-Roman ethics was rediscovered by teachers in the first Christian universities of Europe. St Thomas rethought this complexus of philosophical ethics in the light of his Christian beliefs. The result was a combination of secular moral science with a theistic and other-worldly outlook.

Aquinas' ethics emerged in a multi-faceted contemporary setting.[4] From the early decades of the 13th century came the establishment of the first European universities. These institutions, like cathedrals, burst on Europe as a result of immense energy, local pride and even competition. As cathedrals captured enormous space in a vertical fashion, the universities sprawled out in urban centres and adjacent to towns. But the energies loosed in them and by them were not simply architectural and urban in scope. They lived with new ideas and endured large mixtures of students.

The University of Naples was founded by Frederick Barbarossa to rival the papal-chartered University of Paris. The University of Cambridge was to result from disagreements between the students and faculty of Oxford University and the town's citizenry. And the University of Bologna was initially run and controlled by its students.

At first professors posted notices of courses to be offered and waited, perhaps anxiously, for students to enroll. The students themselves would either occupy rows of hard benches or sit on straw strewn about the floor, raising their knees to serve as desks. The teacher would enter and start a series of lectures which, with brief interruptions, went on for hours. The students would take notes on wax tablets which would eventually be rewritten on parchment sheets. Evenings were spent either in study or in the taverns with which the university towns abounded. Except for a few late night revellers, a town curfew sent students and citizens to bed at nine o'clock.

Thomas' career at Naples, Paris and Cologne made him a cosmopolitan academic. Although he taught at Paris in the faculty of theology his relations with the liberal arts teachers there were friendly and close. It was a time in which many of the classics of Greek, Hebrew and Arabic philosophy were being translated into Latin. A little before mid-century the *Nicomachean Ethics* of Aristotle became available in a complete Latin version with notes by Robert Grosseteste. Fragments of this first great work of academic ethics had been extant in Latin even in the 12th century but its full impact was not felt in the western schools before the 1240s.[5] Scholars in Spain and southern Italy provided Latin translations of Jewish and Moslem commentaries on Greek ethics, as well as original moral writings.

These new works circulating in the Arts and Theology Faculties appeared to pit Aristotle and Greek pagan thought against Christianity and a Platonism approved by St Augustine. Yet what was authenti-

*Aquinas*

cally Aristotelian versus Arabic innovation and accretions required great scrutiny. And even authentic Augustinianism had become entwined with Arabic and Neoplatonic teachings. Confronted with these entanglements of doctrine and ideas, professors attempted to sort things out and engaged in vigorous debate.

Up to the 13th century the dominant philosophy in Europe had been a Christianised Platonism. With the making of Latin versions of Aristotle and his early commentators, something like a medieval Renaissance occurred. Differences of opinion appeared with this new appreciation of the classics. Some Christian thinkers favoured continued adherence to the traditional view of St Augustine and other religious writers, while other philosophers and theologians advocated the adoption of the more naturalistic and empirical features of Aristotelianism. Evidence of this tension is found in the condemnation by Bishop Tempier of Paris of many propositions in philosophy and theology which he considered anti-Christian. Concern focused on questions such as the immortality of the human soul, the natural end of man, the possibility of happiness in an earthly life, and even on the necessity of philosophy to the living of a good life.[6] Thomas Aquinas taught, wrote and developed his ethical theories in the midst of all this intellectual turmoil.

In the 13th century the three dominant religious cultures, Judaic, Moslem and Christian, were all strongly theistic. Particularly at the University of Naples Thomas encountered representatives of all three religions. Christianity was developing several institutions of ethico-religious significance. Religious Orders (Benedictines, Augustinians, Dominicans, Franciscans and Carmelites) provided a context in which scholarly monks had the means to pursue philosophical and theological studies and to teach in key centres of learning. As a Dominican friar, Thomas Aquinas was given a personal assistant and, at times, several secretarial scribes to copy his many writings from dictation and from his own almost illegible handwriting. By no means a religious recluse, Thomas travelled to many parts of Europe, attended meetings in various places and visited relatives and friends.

While he taught twice at the University of Paris (1256–59 and 1269–72) and later at the University of Naples (1272–73), Thomas also served for many years as Lector in various Dominican monasteries in Italy. His religious congregation had been founded in 1217 by Dominic Guzman (hence the name 'Dominicans') with the primary purpose of preaching (hence the more formal name 'Order of

Preachers') but within a few years the hearing of confessions was also stressed.[7] A Dominican Lector was required to give regular lectures with special emphasis on the pastoral and moral training of all the priests in his monastery. The hearing of confessions brought the Dominicans into contact with a wide variety of possibly sinful acts. For their guidance these confessors had to study (in addition to the Bible and other doctrinal works) collections of typical moral 'cases' (such as Raymond of Pennafort's *Summa de casibus*). So Thomas was expected to make his instructions as practical and detailed as possible. There was a consequent emphasis in his ethics on how to distinguish good from bad acts. This influenced his thinking in the direction of what today would be called an act ethics.

But Thomas Aquinas was not satisfied with a casuistry[8] that had little grounding in doctrinal theology and theoretical philosophy. He determined to give equal stress to practical judgement and the more universal consideration of divinity, creation, and especially of the nature of man and his typical activities. This is evident in the structure of his *Summa of Theology*, in which the first part deals with God as Creator, the products of creation, and the place of man in the created universe. The second part (with two sections, I–II and II–II) continues the treatment of man as intelligent and free to make his own decisions, who is able to develop good or bad moral habits (virtues and vices) and thus to grow as a moral and spiritual character. Also included is a discussion of moral laws as expressions of rules governing the development of the moral person. The focus in this second part is on the human person, rather than his particular acts. The result is what would be called today a rule ethics. The second section of Part II contains detailed studies of hundreds of virtues and vices, probably owing much to a *Summa de vitiis et virtutibus* by an older Dominican, Guillelmus Peraldus; it still maintains Aquinas' emphasis on personal character formation. So one finds in this ethics a delicate balance between universal and particular judgements. It also means that Thomas used both utilitarian and deontological approaches in his ethics.

Politically still feudal, the society of 13th-century Europe was undergoing many changes.[9] Thomas' father was a justiciar in the Norman kingdom of Sicily. It was the period of Magna Carta, of the Crusades, of papal wars (in which Thomas' brothers fought on both sides), and of the introduction of somewhat democratic practices in the management of the Dominican Order. Canon (church) law courts treated many cases that would be settled in civil courts today.

Latin was the language of law, of scholarship and of university instruction. Thomas' students at Paris, Rome and Naples came from many different parts of Europe but they had the advantage of one language of learning. Public officials sought Aquinas' advice on various socio-political problems: the practice of lending money at high rates, the treatment of religious minorities, and the rules for the establishment of a viable city-state (*De Regno*, On Kingship).

## ETHICAL WRITINGS

In the 20 years of his teaching career Aquinas developed different facets of his ethics in nine major works, all in Latin.[10] (1) His early lectures at Paris on Peter Lombard's *Books of Sentences* (*Scriptum in IV Libros Sententiarum*) are a complete theology course: the second and third books are chiefly ethical. (2) From 1256 to 1259 he conducted academic disputations on truth and goodness (*Quaestiones Disputatae de Veritatae*). In them he outlined a moral psychology and theory of knowledge leading to a discussion (in qq. 21 to 29) of what it means to be good, ontologically and ethically. (3) Started in 1258 at Paris and finished in 1264 at Dominican monasteries in the vicinity of Rome is one of his most readable works, the *Summa contra Gentiles* which contrasts the teachings of Christianity with those of paganism and other religions. It was written in short chapters (most of his other major treatises are in question style). Its four books cover much the same material as the *Commentary on the Sentences* but more briefly. Book III treats ethical questions from the point of view of divine law. Yet the ethics of Aristotle and other philosophers plays a prominent part in this *Summa*. (4) In the early 1260s Thomas produced a biblical commentary *On the Book of Job* (*Expositio in Job*) which explores many of the moral problems in man's relations to God. This work, too, emphasises an ethics based on divine law. (5) A short treatise on *Kingship* (*De regno*), written for the King of Cyprus, throws some light on Thomas' socio-political views.

At some point in the last decade of his life Aquinas wrote a commentary entitled (6) *On the Nicomachean Ethics of Aristotle* (*Sententia in X Libros Ethicorum*). Thomas analyzes the text, section by section, and explains how he understands Aristotle's ethical theory. He rarely criticises Aristotle but in a few places indicates differences from Christian theology. Modern interpreters, such as A. E. Taylor and W. D. Ross, consider this a helpful commentary.

Most modern expositions of Aquinas' ethics are based almost exclusively on (7) the *Summa of Theology* (*Summa Theologiae*) composed from 1266 to 1273 and left incomplete. Its Part II is devoted to ethics. This *Summa* is lengthy but it actually condenses longer explanations of similar topics found in the *Disputed Questions* from the latter part of his life. One series (8) deals with the problem of evil and its many ramifications (*De Malo*). Another series on the virtues (9) (*De Virtutibus*) treats the problems of charity, the correction of others, the virtue of hope, and the four cardinal virtues.[11]

Several brief writings (some are letters) show Aquinas' views on special ethical problems. The morality of buying and selling on credit and the related question of usury are treated in *De emptione et venditione ad tempus* (1262–63). Thomas' own way of living as a monk is discussed in *De perfectione spiritualis vitae* (1269–70). The problem of just treatment of Jews in a Christian state is encountered in *De regimine Judaeorum ad Ducissam Brabantiae* (1270–71). At about the same time a layman named James consulted Thomas on the morality of gambling and the result was the letter *De sortibus ad Dominum Jacobum de Burgo* (1271). A similar inquiry about the use of astrology produced the *De judiciis astrorum* (1272). Similar problems in special ethics are faced in all the major works listed above.

## BASIC ETHICAL THEORY

Aquinas' ethics is constructed as a practical study (*scientia practica*): it is an organised type of knowledge leading to certain general judgements about what is right or wrong in human activity.[12] Its development starts with experience of the ordinary facts of human living, plus some insight into interpretive principles. As such, Thomistic ethics does not deal directly with individual particular actions (this is the sphere of personal prudential judgement and conscience). Rather, this ethics is concerned with general practices (such as giving to the needy, controlling one's excessive emotions, procreating offspring, stealing, homicide, and so on). Since it is *universal* in its conclusions (a requirement of Aristotelian 'science', *episteme*, *scientia*), Thomistic ethics is designed to be teachable. An ethics that attempts to judge individual deeds is not considered communicable because it is trying to judge private decisions.

One basic characteristic of this sort of ethics is its stress on ends or goals of human activity (ST I–II, q. 1, 1–8, InS II, d. 40, 1; Vir art. 2, ad

3m; CG III, 2; *EE* I, lect. 2). As a teleological study this ethics judges various types of action in terms of the end-directed character of human nature. For a person to be reasonable involves acting well for some intended purpose; conversely, unreasonable human action is either without conscious purpose, or it employs means not calculated to achieve a properly intended end. In a very broad sense a morally good action is one consciously chosen on the basis of honest thinking about its suitability to achieve an appropriate goal. This teleological orientation does not imply that a good end justifies the use of merely any means that will work (ST I–II, q. 18, 4–6). Aquinas recognised the importance of the moral agent's prior attitude (intelligent thinking, reasonable willing, controlled emotions) as well as attention to the consequences of one's moral actions to self and society.

Thomistic moral psychology focuses on three distinctively human functions (ST I, qq. 75–88). He accepted the ancient definition of man as a rational animal but reinterpreted it in terms of intelligence, volition and emotion (ST I–II, qq. 8–17). Most characteristic of man is his intellect: this includes the ability to understand the universal meanings (*rationes*, intelligibilities) of the facts of sense experience, and the further ability to reason to theoretical and practical conclusions entailed in the comprehension of such experience. In the second place, human understanding provides a stimulus for positive or negative will-acts in regard to what is understood. It is, for instance, one thing to understand the meaning of peace, and quite another thing to will to do something about it.

Apart from sensory appetition (emotional and affective responses to individual aspects of sense objects), there is a higher level of appetitive response (pro or con) to what is grasped intellectually as a *universal* good or evil. Thus one may desire to drink some orange juice, because it tastes good (sense appetite) and/or because it is understood to promote good health (intellectual appetite, will). Volition (from the Latin for will, *voluntas*) is quite different from passion, emotion, sensory affectivity. One wills for a universal reason but one feels affectively as a response to quite particular attractions or repulsions of sensed objects.

Intellectual and volitional functions play a key role in the exercise of personal freedom. Choice and the direction of one's moral actions depend on prior considerations that are both cognitive and volitive, as the following analytic figure suggests.[13]

In this series of rational steps man is envisioned as thinking and willing, first of all, about some sort of goal. One might consider, for

| | INTELLECT | WILL |
|---|---|---|
| In regard to end | I. Apprehension of end (*intelligere*) | II. Willing the end (*velle*) |
| | III. Judgement of attainability (*judicium de fine*) | IV. Intending the end (*intentio*) |
| In regard to means | V. Deliberation on means (*consilium, deliberatio*) | VI. Consenting to means (*consensus*) |
| | VII. Judgement of choice (*judicium electionis*) | VIII. Choosing (*electio*) |
| In regard to execution | IX. Commanding external act (*ordinare, imperium*) | X. Executing the act (*usus*) |
| | XI. Apprehending suitability (*perceptio convenientiae*) | XII. Fruition |

FIGURE 2  *Analysis of Choice*

example, how good it would be to live forever. But then one would usually realise that this is not possible. Cognitively these thoughts reduce to the apprehension of the meaning of this end and the judgement that it is not attainable. Volitionally one might briefly wish never to die then with the realisation that this objective is impossible one would will to reject it. Such rejection terminates the consideration in this case but an end judged to be possible may lead to positive adoption (intention). It is not that intellect and will are viewed as two separate agencies but rather that the whole person is the agent who must both judge various goals and adopt or reject them willingly.

If one decides that a certain end is attainable (say, for example, getting a better education), then practical consideration turns next to the things that may be done (the means) to attain this end which has been judged possible and which one intends to achieve. Think of a farm boy who would like to go to college. He may weigh (the literal meaning of deliberation) the various means that he might use: ask his skinflint father to pay his tuition, get his rich aunt to help him, or work for a while as a hired hand to raise the money. If he decides on the last means, he may then willingly adopt it (consent to the means) as the best available thing to do. However, this need not lead to immediate bodily action: the young man may judge that it would be better to wait a few years and help his father on the farm. But if he decides intellectually (the judgement of choice) that it is better to start to work right away on his paying job, then he may elect willingly to do this (the choice act). At this point personal freedom is most evident both in his understanding of the situation and in his willing commitment to the means. Such choices usually entail further implementation by carrying out either bodily or mental actions (commanded acts) under the guidance of such intellection and volition. Clearly, too, one's emotions are involved throughout such decisions but not, in a rational agent, to the extent of dominating the process. In this area of execution, the understanding of how the proposed external act must be ordered is called command but the actual translation of such thinking into deeds is named use. One must finally will to do it, or not. The physical and mental activity involved in working and saving the tuition money may be a lengthy commanded action, done as a result of prior understanding, judging and willing that it must be done. At any point in the implementing of one's choice, it is possible to decide for or against the appropriateness of the commanded act. If the young man realises eventually that his savings will never enable him to go to college, he may terminate his efforts. But if he decides that he is doing well and may have enough money to start college next year, then he approves his work, so far, and enjoys a certain satisfaction (fruition) in his accomplishment.

The foregoing 12 steps are parts of a schematic analysis: one does not usually go through such a process of moral consideration in such detailed fashion. The point of the analysis is not that one must think: now I am adopting my objective, now I am selecting appropriate means, and now I am ordering myself to use or enjoy a given deed. Rather, the intellective-volitive analysis can be valuable, if there is some failure to act reasonably. Just as the person who has lost the ability to walk or talk properly may have to consider the various steps involved in such apparently simple functions, so may the moral agent (or his adviser) need to break down his unsuccessful moral action into the various points at which his failure to think or will properly might be corrected.

Thomistic moral psychology also places much stress on habit formation.[14] Three kinds of conscious powers are regarded as capable of development by the acquisition of permanent dispositions or habits (*habitus*). These powers are capacities flexible enough and free enough to be improved by appropriate usage. Intellect, will and emotive capacity are of this type. Intellectual understanding may become more proficient with use: some trained people can solve difficult mathematical problems and untrained ones cannot. Aristotle taught that there are five distinctive intellectual habits (*hexeis*): the ability to grasp the starting-points (principles, definitions) of reasoning; the skill to reason step-by-step to well-established conclusions (*episteme, scientia,* scientific thinking); the ability to evaluate one's experience in terms of the highest standards (*sophia,* wisdom); the acquired ability to reason to good practical conclusions concerning one's free actions (*phronesis,* prudence, practical wisdom); and finally, the acquired ability to make things reasonably well (*poiesis,* art).[15] Thomas Aquinas adopted much of this Aristotelian teaching on intellectual habits and he particularly emphasised the ethical importance of the primary intuition of first practical principles by the intellectual habit of *synderesis.*[16]

As will be seen later (in connection with natural moral laws) the role of synderesis was not to provide man with an insight into detailed moral standards, or special rules of behaviour. What Aquinas thought was that, just as theoretical reasoning begins with certain initial axioms (such as the principles of non-contradiction or of identity) which are not demonstrable but are grasped by natural insight, so in practical reasoning there are primary indemonstrable principles (such as, good is to be done and evil avoided, or, no harm should be done to others). If their terms are understood, these are intellectually self-evident. More specific ethical judgements are made, Thomas thought, in the light of such guiding principles but with a content supplied by further experience of life (DV XVI, 1 and 2; ST I–II, 94, 1). For example, one might readily subscribe to the general principle that harm should not be done to others. On the other hand, it may not be obvious, usually and in the first instance, that cheating on one's just taxes would be a case of violating this principle.

The power of willing (intellectual appetite) was viewed by Aquinas as able to be actualised (perfected) by many habits. The repeated practice of diligent study, a regular tending of the sick or frequent efforts to assist the poor would all dispose one to perform such actions with increased ease and desire. Correspondingly, constant cheating, lying, excessive drinking or eating would readily dispose one to perform such actions with greater and greater ease and desire.

Such actions, reasoned as desirable for one, become crystallised as habits.

The chief naturally acquired habit of will he called justice: the virtue of willing and doing what is good for others, as for one's self. The reason why such altruism is rooted in willing lies in Aquinas' view that the good of other persons is always a somewhat abstract and universal object, as compared with one's own concrete advantage. He discussed many kinds of justice and lesser virtues associated with it (ST II–II, qq. 57–122). However, Thomas saw the great importance of another will-habit that was almost unknown to Aristotle. This is charity (*caritas*), the habit of loving other persons as special creatures that God has made. This sort of divinely-motivated love is called a theological virtue. As far as Thomistic ethics is concerned, it is much more important than justice. Of course, even Aristotle saw that the 'love of friendship' values the other person and his/her good for its own sake, and so for something more than one's own private advantage. This aspect of justice is an approach on the natural level to the level of supernatural charity.[17] In Aquinas' teaching charity is the 'form' of all moral virtues: it gives an essential and superior character of excellence to the well-developed moral person.[18]

In the sphere of emotional responses (sensory appetition) Thomas distinguished two different general types: the sort of feelings that culminate in sensory desires (concupiscible appetites) and the affective reactions to various difficulties and threats presented in sensory experience (irascible appetites).[19] Desires for food, intoxicants and sexual pleasure tend to become excessive (sometimes defective) and the habit of moderation in such matters is temperance. It is developed in the concupiscible appetite under the regulation of intellect and will. The notion of the golden mean between excess and defect of feeling is incorporated from ancient classical ethics into Aquinas' account of temperance. Besides the major species of habitual moderation in regard to food, intoxicants and sexual pleasure, many other forms of reasonable self-control are studied in his treatises on the virtues. The influence of Stoicism as well as Aristotelianism is evident in these discussions of moral moderation.

A quite different field of human emotions (*passiones animae*) is associated with movements of the irascible appetite (DV XXV, 2; DM VIII, 3; ST I, 81, 2 and 3). This power is the seat of feelings such as hope and despair, daring and fear and the complex emotion of anger. The chief problem that Thomas saw here was man's tendency to submit weakly to various attacks on his well-being. So fortitude (emotional strength) is the primary good habit in this area. It is a virtue which enables one to bear up courageously, when the tendency is to despair about some perceived evil, and to attack and overcome such threats, when they seem reasonably open to such positive action (InJ, *passim*). Here again Stoic ethics had an impact but Aquinas broadens his treatment of these emergency passions to include many habits of courage in regard to dangers both physical and spiritual.

From the foregoing it may become clear that this moral psychology is an essential basis for all other themes in Thomistic ethics. It has ramifications in Thomas' treatment of freedom and voluntarism, in the explanation of moral law in terms of inclinations, and indeed of almost every aspect of his moral philosophy. Since this psychology leads to a study of hundreds of moral virtues and vices, Thomism might well be named an *aretaic* ethics—for it is an ethics of self-perfection through the growth of many virtues.[20]

## DISTINGUISHING MORAL GOOD FROM EVIL

Some evils that beset mankind are physical: blindness, illness, pain, starvation are examples. These may occur quite apart from our ability to cause or control them. When they are thus involuntary, physical evils are not moral. On the other hand, when these and other evils are self-inflicted, voluntarily inflicted on others or subject to some degree of rational control, they do become part of our moral life. So there is an important difference between moral goods and evils and those that are physical. A key problem in Thomistic ethics has to do with establishing some norm or standard by which moral good may be distinguished from moral evil.[21] Of course, this is a major issue in any kind of ethics. However, we are not thinking here about how the individual agent makes his own moral decisions on what to do or avoid: that is a matter of conscience. What we need to consider in ethics is the question: what general types of voluntary activity are morally good and what kinds of actions (and omissions) are morally evil?[22] And we need some explanation of how these practices are ethically differentiated.

Ancient philosophy frequently suggested that good kinds of human acts are those which are in accord with human nature. Sometimes the 'nature' of man was viewed universally; in other cases it was interpreted in terms of individual differences. Thus Socrates' nature might not be the same as that of Protagoras. When Aquinas speaks of actions being in accord with man's nature, and so good, he is thinking universally. This norm of judgement is man-in-general, viewed as an animated body capable of distinctive functions, intellectual, volitional and emotional. Thus, speaking generally, Thomas says that the kinds of voluntary acts that are good are those which promote the proper use of understanding, will and the emotional powers.[23] Such use is proper when it leads to the well-being (*felicitas*, *beatitudo*) of the human person. So, if Thomistic ethics teaches that the young should respect their parents, or that theft is ethically wrong, these are general judgements of what is, or is not, in accord with the nature of the *species* man.

But Aquinas also writes, over and over again, that right reason (*recta ratio*) is the norm of moral judgement.[24] This is a complex notion, for reason (*ratio*, the Greek *logos*) has both a logical and an ontological signification. To use one's intelligence in a typically human way is to reason. Thomas believed that there are other intelligent creatures (angels) who intuit truths without having to go through any step-by-step process of ratiocination, but he strongly maintained that humans must work out most of their judgements about what is true or good by a laborious series of steps. Syllogistic reasoning is one kind of ratiocination but Thomas knew that there are other types of sequential thinking to conclusions. Obviously such ratiocination is one meaning of 'reason'. When it is done in accord with the laws of logic and the facts of experience, it is right.

Another meaning of *ratio* (reason) has to do with the relations between different kinds of existing beings.[25] We still speak of the relation of any two numbers as a 'ratio'; one is to five in a meaningful relationship. Similarly father is to son in an understandable general relationship. The artist is to his picture in another real ratio. Such metaphysical relations, as capable of being understood, are called 'reasons' (*rationes*) by Thomas Aquinas. They are of great importance in this ethics. It is quite a different thing for a man to kill his son and for him to kill a dog. This is because the ratio between father and son is really different from the relation between a man and a dog. Of course, these rational but real relations among beings are ethically significant to the extent that man's psychological reasoning can grasp them and form judgements according to them. So it is not merely human 'nature' expressed in some abstract definition that is the standard of ethical judgement for Aquinas. Man's reason is not only 'right' when used with logical correctness: it is right in a more realistic sense when it operates with an understanding of the intelligible relations that exist between man and all other 'natures' of things in the world in which humans live and act. (People who say that all life is sacred and that it is just as immoral to kill a flea as to kill a man ignore that metaphysical character of right reason. Similarly people who say that to act 'naturally' means to follow one's instincts or emotional tendencies overlook these other significant features of the total milieu of man as an ethical agent.) Right reason is a complex norm; to oversimplify it is to misunderstand it.

There is also the theme in Thomistic ethics which can be expressed as follows: every voluntary act is good which promotes the well-being of man and leads to the attainment of his ultimate end (ST I–II, qq. 18–21). Aquinas distinguishes proximate ends (which become means to the achievement of more distant goals) for one's ultimate end (which is the final reason or objective for a good human life). He thinks that all men, because they are of the same species, share in one and the same ultimate end. Viewed subjectively, from the side of what happens within the successful moral agent, this end is happiness (*felicitas, beatitudo*). But the objective reality that would provide for such felicity by being known and loved would have to be perfect and available to all humans. In a lengthy series of arguments by exclusion,[26] Thomas rejects a large number of important goods that have been proposed in earlier kinds of ethics (bodily goods such as health, strength, beauty; social goods such as political power, wide recognition; and mental goods such as great knowledge or virtue itself) and he concludes that a perfect being (God) is the only reality that could satisfy all man's aspirations.

It is here that we find the greatest difference between the ethics of Aquinas and that of Aristotle. St Thomas thought that God gives direction to ethical thinking, not simply by special inspiration of favoured individuals such as prophets, but more so by existing as the highest good (*summum bonum*) and thus providing a prototype for all lesser goods. In this, Thomas was nearer to Plato than to Aristotle but his position here owes most to Christian theism. The view that ultimately all human acts are good if they help man to arrive at the loving vision of God, in a future life, is an essential part of the theory of right reason. As Aquinas sees the situation, the moral agent is in constant relationship with large numbers of beings in his environment. Some of these beings are below man in the scale of reality, others are equal, and there is one highest being that is above man. Right reason consists in the intelligent acknowledgement of the differences in these various contextual relations (*rationes*) to material things, to other humans and to God. These relations require a readiness to respect the rights and duties that arise in human living. As a theist Aquinas looked to God as the highest justification for the performance of moral duties and for the exacting of natural rights.

Thus another dimension of Thomistic ethics extends to the field of natural law.[27] Sometimes Aquinas uses the term *jus naturale* which means natural right (*droit*, *Recht*) and at other times he speaks of *lex naturalis* which means natural law (*loi*, *Gesetz*). Most English versions use 'natural law' to translate both phrases but other modern languages have separate words for *jus* and *lex*. There is disagreement among interpreters of Thomas' works as to the precise meanings of these terms but it would appear that *jus* (from which our word justice is derived) is more fundamental, in the sense that it designates some essential rightness in man and his actions, while *lex* names some expression of what is right, rather than the rightness itself.

There are several simplistic ways of interpreting the teaching of natural moral law found in Aquinas' treatises. One such interpretation simply identifies natural law with the Decalogue and the New Testament injunctions to love God and one's neighbour. This reduction to simplified biblical morality is less than what Thomas intended. Another set of interpreters seem to think that any common-sense person can intuit all the basic goods of human life. From these one works out specific ethical regulations.[28] Thomas' teaching on synderesis may give some apparent credence to this interpretation but the main principle that Thomas cites as so known (ST I–II, 94, 2) is: 'Good is to be done and promoted and evil to be avoided' (*bonum est faciendum et prosequendum et malum vitandum*). Since this rule does not specify *what* is good, it cannot be further analyzed to find more specific moral rules. It is a principle formally governing practical reasoning and in this sense Thomas calls it the first precept of natural law. To determine what are the proximate natural goods for man, Aquinas suggests that reason naturally apprehends as goods those objects that satisfy man's basic inclinations. On the lowest level are those physical goods that all beings incline to, such as self-preservation. Second are biological goods that men tend towards, as do all living things: the procreation and care of offspring, for instance. In the third and highest place he puts those values that satisfy man as a rational being: the knowledge of truth about God and the advantage of living in the society of other humans. These natural inclinations suggest the sort of secondary natural goods that are to be sought in order eventually to attain to the ultimate good.

Thomas' famous treatment of the *lex naturalis* is more than an ethical intuitionism and more than a mere analysis of human instincts. His treatise on laws in the *Summa of Theology* follows and summarises a long discussion of the criteria of ethical judgement.[29] He presents natural law as a summary of much that we have seen above in regard to the meaning of right reason, for Thomas defined all law as a rational ordering (*ordinatio rationis*).[30]

A still different aspect of Aquinas' natural-law approach to ethics lies in the assertion that natural law is what man can learn from his ordinary experience about that part of God's eternal law which applies to human behaviour.[31] He never claimed that we can know the entirety of God's law. Some portion of divine justice may be known by reflection on man's life experiences. In this sense men 'naturally' participate in the law of God. Of course Thomas also taught that God reveals more of this supreme law through special communications to certain favoured people, prophets. Special revelations, however, cannot belong to philosophical ethics.

## PERSONAL MORAL REASONING

What each human person does in thinking through to a decision to do, or not to do, a given concrete action is not part of Thomas' ethics. He does offer a general description of how this process of private decision-making may be well conducted. This is another area for the application of right reason. Any person may develop a sort of practical skill in doing this thinking, a good habit which Aquinas called *prudentia* (from *pro-videntia*, foresight).[32] Five components of prudence are concerned with knowing the precise problem that is faced and three other factors deal with ordering one's self to act (or not) in regard to this particular problem.[33] In the phase of prudential thinking one should: (1) try to grasp the exact moral significance of the problem; (2) remember one's past experience with similar problems; (3) be ready to take useful advice from others; (4) use as much skill as possible in reasoning to a decisive judgement; and (5) promptly make one's best judgement on the matter, having regard to all pertinent circumstances that are known. The practical moral judgement that one should do, or omit, this concretely proposed action is what Thomas called moral conscience.[34]

Three more components of the habit of prudential reasoning are concerned with commanding one's self to action. A person needs a certain skill in looking ahead to appraise a contemplated act in relation to the end in view: this is foresight, the central feature of prudent behaviour. Again, one must develop some ability to appraise quickly the pertinent circumstances of a proposed action: this is circumspection.[35] Finally, the translation of this thinking into actual performance requires a certain carefulness in commanding the execution of one's decision. All eight of these prudential components indicate something of what it means to govern one's actions in a wise and practical manner. Some interpreters prefer terms such as practical wisdom or practical reasonableness to translate the latin *prudentia*.

Moral conscience plays a key role in this application of practical reasoning to one's actions. As a personal and private judgement, conscience is not something taught in an ethics course.[36] Nor should it be regarded as a source of general ethical rules, rights or duties. It is possible for one's moral conscience to be faulty (in the sense that a wiser person, or certainly God, might judge otherwise) but if it is a judgement carefully made, to the best of one's ability, then Aquinas thinks that one should act in accord with it. Moral conscience does not necessitate such accord: one may act against one's best judgement, or fail to act when one thinks that one should. This is simply to say that a person does not always do what he knows to be the right thing. Both intellect and will are involved in the process of self-guidance to action.

## SOME SPECIAL ETHICAL PROBLEMS

The way that Thomas Aquinas treated certain problems in what today is called 'applied ethics' throws some light on his general theory of ethics.[37] It has become customary in recent ethics to consider a given system of ethics as either deontological or teleological. The supposition is that the ethicist must either stress the prior moral attitude of the agent (respect for duty, habitual love of God, self-interest, and so on) or that one must rather look to the consequences of a proposed act in order to determine its ethical value. Some interpreters of Aquinas are much opposed to consequentialism.[38] They think that it is a non-Thomistic approach. Others limit consequentialism to the 'double-effect' principle and appear to extend this decision-making device into a general principle of Thomistic ethics.[39] In fact Aquinas rarely discussed this double-effect rule. Its main occurrence is in an answer to the problem of killing in self-defence (ST II–II, 64, 7), where he says:

> Nothing prohibits one act from having two effects, only one of which is intended, the other [being] not intended. Moral actions take their specific character from what is intended and not from what is unintended, since that is incidental. So a double effect (*duplex effectus*) can follow from the act of a person defending himself: one is the preservation of his own life, the other effect is the killing of the aggressor. An act of this kind, from the fact that the preservation of one's life is intended, is not essentially illicit, since it is natural for anyone to preserve himself in existence as far as is possible.

Such intending is right and good, Thomas thinks, if directed to the naturally appropriate purpose of saving one's life. He admits that there are two results to such commanded action and he judges that to intend the bad physical result (death of the aggressor) is immoral. Here Aquinas is obviously considering both the prior attitude of the moral agent and the value of the consequences of the whole action. His position is neither exclusively deontological nor completely consequential.[40]

Much the same conclusion can be drawn from Aquinas' discussion of the famous medieval problem of usury.[41] In the simple economics of the 13th century it was generally thought that to charge interest on a loan, as compensation for the time in which the lender had to wait for repayment, was immoral. The point was that, in an era in which investment was practically unknown, one lost nothing by lending money that was not in use. In a letter to a fellow Dominican priest (James of Viterbo) Thomas said the same thing about charging for deferred payments in a buying-selling contract. Both from the point of view of intention and of consequences such contracts were usurious, as Thomas saw it.

If we consult the corresponding treatment of buying and selling on credit, in the *Summa of Theology*, we can see some justification for this view of usury. Such contracts were introduced to facilitate exchanges between two parties, 'for the common advantage of both' (*pro communi utilitate utriusque*, ST II–II, 77, 1; cf. DM XIII, 4). From the point of view of the common good (or public welfare) there is no reason why one party should profit more than the other. The just ideal in such exchanges is equality; if the price exceeds the value of what is purchased, or if the converse is so, then the contract is contrary to justice. Here again the insistence on promotion of the common good is clearly consequential.

Nor is it essentially immoral to risk money on a matter of chance, as Thomas sees it.[42] This may be done for recreation, provided none of the circumstances associated with wagering is unreasonable. Because of unjust circumstances betting may become an offence against a number of virtues: temperance, justice and prudence. But in itself betting need not be contrary to either one's private good or that of the community.

Similarly it is not necessarily immoral to attempt to foretell future events by consulting the positions of heavenly bodies. In the ancient and medieval world astrology was not always clearly distinguished from the science of astronomy. Thomas explains that it is not wrong to foretell eclipses or forecast the weather and then use this knowledge to guide one's actions, for instance, in farming or taking a trip.[43] However, dependence on horoscopes and similar types of divination is condemned by Aquinas. Here the importance of using appropriate means is stressed.

Of more significance is the treatment of the problem of justifying going to war. Thomas was not unacquainted with military life. Many members of his family were soldiers.[44] His basic political philosophy is found in the short treatise *On Kingship*. In his view a sovereign state could justly fight a war for two reasons: self-defence against attack and in order to expand its territories. The conditions for engaging in war justly, according to Aquinas (ST II–II, 40, 1) were three: (1) it had to be waged under the authority of the chief of state (*auctoritas principis*); (2) there must be a just cause (*causa justa*), that is, the enemy must be guilty of serious wrongdoing; and (3) the state authority must wage the war with a right intention (*intentio bellantium recta*), to promote some good or to prevent some evil. Later, in the Renaissance, commentators on Aquinas, suh as Francis de Vitoria and Francis Suarez, developed this into a much more complicated just war theory. This continues to influence present-day writers on international relations.[45]

Indeed the ethics of Thomas Aquinas has continued to be influential in every century since the 13th. It had an impact on British ethicists from the 14th century onwards.[46] Some early English Catholic scholars (Robert Kilwardby and John Peckham) were very critical of Thomism. Later, Reginald Pecocke (15th century) and Richard Hooker (16th century expounded moral philosophies that retained the essential features of Aquinas' thought. Both the Cambridge Platonists and the Caroline Casuists made some use of Thomistic ethics, sometimes with approval and sometimes critically. Early British jurisprudence, running through John Fortescue (15th century), Christopher St Germain (16th century), Edward Coke (17th century) and William Blackstone (18th century), exhibits the continued influence of Aquinas' teachings of law and morality.[47]

Commentators in Spain and Italy during the later middle ages and the renaissance (Cajetan, Sylvester of Ferrara, Antonino of Florence, Francis Vitoria and Francis Suarez) expanded the moral view of Aquinas much beyond his original thought. The *Treatise on Laws* (*De legibus*) of Suarez had an impact on legal and ethical thinking in nearly all the universities of early modern Europe.[48] Immanuel Kant's first course of lectures in ethics used the textbooks written by Alexander Baumgarten which were condensations of Thomistic moral philosophy.[49]

Of course, the broadest continued influence of Thomistic ethics is to be found in Roman Catholic educational institutions but recent ethicists of other religious persuasions (such as E. L. Mascall, Jaroslav Pelikan, Mortimer Adler and Henry Veatch) make noteworthy use of this type of moral philosophy.[50]

# Notes

1. On the life and works of Thomas Aquinas see J. A. Weisheipl, *Friar Thomas d'Aquino* (Garden City, New York: Doubleday, 1974). For the extensive literature of Thomistic studies see P. Mandonnet et J. Destrez, *Bibliographie Thomiste* (Paris: J. Vrin, 1960); V. J. Bourke, *Thomistic Bibliography, 1920–1940* (St. Louis, Mo: University Press, 1945); T. Miethe and Bourke, *Thomistic Bibliography, 1940–1978* (Westport, CT: Greenwood, 1980). P. Wyser, *Thomas von Aquin* in Bibliographische Einführungen in das Studium der Philosophie 13–14 (Bern: A. Franke, A. G. Verlag, 1950).

2. See H. V. Jaffa, *Thomism and Aristotelianism* (Chicago: University of Chicago Press, 1952); J. Owens, 'Aquinas as Aristotelian Commentator', in *St. Thomas Aquinas, Commemorative Studies* vol. I (Toronto: PIMS, 1974) pp. 213–38; V. J. Bourke, 'The Nicomachean Ethics and Thomas Aquinas', ibid., pp. 239–60. For the background in patristic and medieval ethics see Bourke, *History of Ethics* Part II (Garden City, New York: Doubleday, 1968).

3. On the religious background see M. D. Chenu, *Toward Understanding St. Thomas* (Chicago: Regnery, 1964).

4. For the social context of Aquinas' thoughts see A. W. Levi, *Philosophy as Social Expression* (University of Chicago Press, 1974) chapter 3, 'Medieval Philosophy. The Age of the Saint. Aquinas,' pp. 101–62. For discussions of the medieval university see Frederick Artz, *The Mind of the Middle Ages* (University of Chicago Press, 1980), Charles Haskins, *The Rise of the Universities* (Ithaca, New York: Cornell University Press, 1957), Nathan Schnachner, *The Mediaeval Universities* (New York: A. S. Barnes & Company, 1962) and Paul Oskar Kristeller, 'The Curriculum of the Italian Universities from the Middle Ages to the Renaissance', *Proceedings of the Patristic, Mediaeval and Renaissance Conference*, IX (1984) pp. 1–16.

5. Much information on the 13th-century rediscovery of Aristotle's *Nicomachean Ethics* is found in R. A. Gauthier's *Praefatio* to the Leonine edition (vol. 47) of Thomas' *Commentary on the Nicomachean Ethics*.

6. The condemnation of 7 March 1277, by Stephen Tempier, Bishop of Paris, marks the culmination of some 60 years of trying to seek some accommodation between the newly introduced writings of Aristotle, other ancient Greek authors, Arab writers, and the Christian Universities of Europe, especially Paris. In 1210, 1215 and 1223 the teaching of Aristotle's works had been prohibited by bishop, cardinal and pope respectively. In 1267 St Bonaventure was voicing his upset at the boldness of certain philosophical teachings and investigations by the Arts Faculty at Paris. And on 10 December 1270 Stephen Tempier had condemned 13 propositions as not to be taught at the University. Some of the propositions in the 1277 Condemnation pertaining to matters ethical are the following: (1) that there is no more excellent state than to study philosophy; (2) that the only wise men in the world are the

philosophers; (53A) that an intelligence or an angel or a separated soul is nowhere; (133) that the soul is inseparable from the body, and that the soul is corrupted when the harmony of the body is corrupted; (172) that happiness is had in this life and not in another; (174) that after death man loses every good; and (216) that a philosopher must not concede the resurrection to come, because it cannot be investigated by reason (this is erroneous because even a philosopher must bring his mind into captivity to the obedience of Christ [II Cor. 10:5]. For an English translation of 216 condemned propositions see A. Hyman and J. J. Walsh, *Philosophy in the Middle Ages* (Indianapolis: Hackett, 1973) pp. 543–49.

7. On the influence of Thomas' work as a Dominican Lector see L. Boyle, *The Setting of the Summa Theologiae of Saint Thomas* (Toronto: PIMS, 1982) and his references to earlier sources in Dominican records.

8. 'Casuistry' originated in the 16th century and is usually associated with the Jesuit schools of that time and the following few centuries. It represented an attempt to determine choices of whether to act or not to act in terms of which means was more probably the best one among several to choose. The discussion could take one into a whole series of probable and/or equiprobable reasons for or against acting in a certain way. With its endless hairsplitting over which opinions were most weighty, it soon acquired a reputation as a less favourable approach to what ethics was about.

9. Still useful on the political and historical situation in the 13th century is C. J. H. Hayes and M. H. Baldwin, *History of Europe* (New York: Macmillan, 1949) pp. 223–339.

10. Details on Latin editions and English versions of Aquinas' writings are provided in Weisheipl, pp. 358–404; and more recently in Miethe-Bourke, pp. 20–57.

11. Except for the *Commentary on the Sentences* and the *Commentary on Job*, all these ethical works are available, at least in part, in English.

12. After saying that logic deals with the ordering of reason's own acts of understanding, Aquinas explains that 'the order of voluntary actions pertains to the consideration of moral philosophy', *EE* I, lectio 1; for the English: *Commentary on the Nicomachean Ethics*, trans. Litzinger, vol. I, p. 6.

13. ST I–II, qq. 11–16; and InS II, 38, art. 3; for a more complete analysis of these steps see Bourke, *Ethics* (1966) pp. 58–66.

14. Thomas' main treatise on *habitus* is ST I–II, qq. 49–55; see also InS III, 23, q. 1; *EE* VI, lect. 3 to 5. Cf. G. Klubertanz, *Habits and Virtues* (New York: Appleton-Century-Crofts, 1963).

15. Aristotle, *Nicomachean Ethics*, 1103a4 and 1139a17–1143b15. Cf. A. C. Pegis, 'St. Thomas and the Nicomachean Ethics: Some Reflections on SCG III, 44, 5', *Medieval Studies* (Toronto) 25 (1963) 1–25.

16. InS II, 24, q. 2, art. 3; DV XVI, art. 1 to 3. *Synderesis* meant an intellectual habit or ability, in the practical order, whereby the intellect immediately intuited the 'principle(s)' of the practical order (for example, 'Good is to be done and evil avoided'). Aquinas speaks of this principle as 'in some way innate' but he means that the principle(s) becomes immediately evident to the agent through sense experience and memory. See Michael

Crowe, 'Synderesis and the Notion of Law in Saint Thomas', *L'Homme et son Destin* (Actes du premier Congrès International de Philosophie Médiévale) (Louvain and Paris: Nauwelaerts, 1960) pp. 601–09; G. Grisez, 'The First Principle of Practical Reason', *Natural Law Forum* 10 (1965) pp. 168–201; Bourke, 'The Synderesis Rule and Right Reason', *The Monist* 66, 1 (1983) pp. 71–82; and 'El principio de la sinteresis: Fuentes y funcion en la etica de Thomas de Aquino', *Sapientia* (Buenos Aires) ns. 137–38 (1980) pp. 615–26.

17. For a development of this point see C. J. O'Neil, 'Is Prudence Love?' *The Monist* 58, 1 (1974) 119–39. Regarding the Theological Virtue of Charity Thomas' sources would have been threefold: The Gospel of St John, the Epistles of St Paul, and the writings of St Augustine (especially *The Trinity*, the *Treatise on the Gospel of St John*, the *Treatise on the First Epistle of John, Epistles*, and *Enarrations on the Psalms*).

18. InS III, qq. 26 and 27; DM VIII, art. 2; *De caritate* art. 1–5; DV XIV, art. 5; ST I–II, 65, 5 and II–II, qq. 23–7. Cf. G. Gilleman, *The Primacy of Charity in Moral Theology*, trans. W. F. Ryan and A. Vachon (Westminster, MD: Newman, 1959) for an extension of Aquinas' view.

19. InS III, d. 15, qq. 15 and 26; DV XXVI, art. 1 and 2; *EE* II, lect. 5; DM III, art. 11; ST I–II, qq. 22–48. Cf. M. D. Chenu, 'Les passions vertueuses. L'Anthropologie de saint Thomas', *Revue Philosophique de Louvain* 72 (1974) pp. 11–18.

20. General expositions of the moral virtues are in ST I–II, qq. 55–61 and of the theological virtues in I–II, qq. 62–7; detailed treatments in ST II–II, qq. 1–44 (on faith, hope and charity) and II–II, qq. 47–170 (on prudence, justice, fortitude and temperance, plus many associated virtues and vices); parallel treatises are indicated in the footnotes to the Ottawa edition of ST. Cf. J. Pieper, *The Four Cardinal Virtues* (Indiana: Notre Dame University Press, 1967).

21. The chief treatise on moral good and evil is ST I–II, qq. 18–21; see also InS II, d. 36, art. 5, and q. 40, art. 3; CG III, ch. 1–16; DM II, art. 4 and 7.

22. On the meaning of voluntary see InS II, d. 25, art. 1; DV XXIII, art. 1; *EE* III, lect. 4; ST I–II, q. 1, art. 1 and q. 6 in toto. Cf. Bourke, *Ethics* (1966) ch. 3.

23. Each cardinal virtue perfects a different human power: prudence for the intellect, justice for will, fortitude for irascible appetite, and temperance for concupiscible appetite; see ST I–II, 57, 4 and 61, 4.

24. CG III, ch. 9, 'moralium autem mensura est ratio'; cf. ST I–II, 19, 5. Several articles in *The Monist* 66, 1 (1983) examine the notion of right reason.

25. On the order of reason ('ordo rationis') in nature and in human action see the Prologue to Thomas' *Commentary on the Nicomachean Ethics*; also CG III, 10; ST II–II, 154, 12. Cf. Sister Theresa Clare Morkofsky, 'Morality and Real Relations', *The Thomist* 29 (1965) 396–419.

26. CG III, ch. 26–63; ST I–II, qq. 1–7. An argument by exclusion, as employed by Aquinas, consists of listing the various solutions proffered to solve a problem throughout the history of philosophy and then demonstrating how all fail to meet the required answer except one. A famous instance of this procedure occurs in the *Summa Contra Gentiles* (II, 56–68). In this particular case Aquinas reviews numerous philosophical

views of how man is constituted as a being and eliminates all the candidates except one.

27. In the whole treatise on law (ST I–II, qq. 90–108) natural law is treated in six articles of q. 94. Cf. P. A. Armstrong, *Primary and Secondary Precepts in Thomistic Natural Law Teaching* (The Hague: Nijhoff, 1966); M. B. Crowe, *The Changing Profile of Natural Law* (The Hague: Nijhoff, 1977); and for criticism, D. J. O'Connor, *Aquinas and Natural Law* (London: Macmillan, 1968).

28. See G. Grisez and R. Shaw, *Beyond the New Morality* (Indiana: University of Notre Dame Press, 1974) and J. Finnis, *Natural Law and Natural Rights* (Oxford: Clarendon Press, 1980).

29. This starts with the treatise on good and evil in human actions, ST I–II, qq. 18–21.

30. ST I–II, 90, 4 c: [*lex est*] *rationis ordinatio ad bonum commune, ab eo qui curam communitatis habet, promulgata.*

31. CG III, ch. 114 ff.; ST I–II, 90, 4 *ad primum: per naturalem legem participatur lex aeterna secundum proportionem capacitatis humanae naturae.*

32. On prudence as a virtue see InS III, d. 33, q. 3; *De virtutibus cardinalibus*, art. 1; *EE* VI, lect. 8 and 9; ST I–II, 57, art. 4 to 6; II–II, qq. 47 to 56.

33. For the 'integral parts' of prudence, ST II–II, q. 49, arts. 1 to 8.

34. One of the best explanations of conscience is, DV, XVII, arts. 1 to 3; see also ST I, q. 79, art. 13; I–II, q. 19, art. 5.

35. DM II, arts. 6 to 8; ST I–II, q. 72, art. 9.

36. Cf. Eric D'Arcy, *Conscience and Its Right to Freedom* (London and New York: Sheed & Ward, 1961).

37. M. V. Murray, *Problems in Ethics* (New York: Holt, Rinehart and Winston, 1960) is a typical modern Thomistic study of special problems.

38. See G. Grisez, 'Against Consequentialism', *American Journal of Jurisprudence* 23 (1978) pp. 21–72.

39. Peter Knauer, 'The Hermeneutic Function of the Principle of Double Effect', *Natural Law Forum* 12 (1967) pp. 132–62; R. A. McCormick, *Ambiguity in Moral Choice* (Milwaukee: Marquette University Press, 1973); and McCormick and Paul Ramsey (eds) *Doing Evil to Achieve Good* (Chicago: Loyola University Press, 1978).

40. On the deontology/teleology dichotomy see Henry Veatch, *Human Rights. Fact or Fancy?* (Baton Rouge and London: Louisiana State University Press, 1985) pp. 93–104.

41. *De emptione et venditione ad tempus (On Buying and Selling on Time)*, trans. A O'Rahilly in *Irish Ecclesiastical Record* 31 (1928) pp. 164–65; complete English text in Bourke, *Pocket Aquinas* (New York: Washington Square Press, 1976) pp. 223–25. For the medieval problem of usury see John Noonan, *The Scholastic Analysis of Usury* (Cambridge, Mass: Harvard University Press, 1957).

42. *De sortibus* ch. 5; ST II–II, q. 92, art. 8.

43. *De judiciis astrorum* (a brief answer to questions on the use of astrology) no English version, Latin in *Opera Omnia* (Parma, 1852–75) vol. xvi, p. 317; see also ST II–II, q. 95, arts. 1 and 2.

44. For military prudence see ST II–II, q. 50, art. 4; InS III, d. 33, q. 3, art. 1, 4.

45. See E. B. F. Midgley, *The Natural Law Tradition and the Theory of International Relations* (New York: Harper & Row, 1975) pp. 43–55 and 69–74.
46. See Bourke, 'Thomas Aquinas and Early British Ethics', *Rivista di Filosofia Neo-Scolastica* (Milan) 66, 2–4 (1974) pp. 818–40.
47. A. P. D'Entreves, *The Medieval Contribution to Political Thought* (Oxford: Clarendon Press, 1939).
48. On Suarez see F. C. Copleston, *A History of Philosophy: Late Medieval and Renaissance*, vol. 3, part II (New York: Doubleday, 1963).
49. See I. Kant, *Lectures on Ethics*, trans. L. Infield (New York: Harper & Row, 1963); the 'Introduction' by J. MacMurray (p. XVII) indicates Kant's debt to Baumgarten.
50. Cf. Jacques Leclercq, *La philosophie morale de s. Thomas d'Aquin devant la pensée contemporaine* (Paris: Spes, 1954); and several essays in *St. Thomas Aquinas, 1274–1974: Commemorative Studies*, 2 vols., ed. A. Maurer *et al.* (Toronto: Pontifical Institute of Mediaeval Studies, 1974).

# Bibliography

## WORKS OF THOMAS AQUINAS WITH ETHICAL CONTENT

1. *Scriptum in libros Sententiarum*, AD 1252–56, *Commentary on Peter Lombard's Sentences*, no English version (cited as InS).
2. *Quaestiones Disputatae de veritate*, 1256–59, *Disputed Questions on Truth*, trans. Mulligan, McGlynn and Schmidt, 3 vols. (Chicago, Regnery, (DV) 1952–54).
3. *Summa contra Gentiles*, 1259–64, *On the Truth of the Catholic Faith against the Gentiles*, trans. Pegis, Anderson, Bourke, O'Neil, 5 vols. (New York: Doubleday, 1955–57; reprinted Indiana: Notre Dame University Press (CG) 1975).
4. *Expositio in librum Job*, circa 1261–62, no English version (InJ).
5. *Quaestiones Disputatae de malo*, 1266–67, *Disputed Questions on Evil*, trans. John and Jean Oesterle (Indiana: Notre Dame University Press, (DM) 1986).
6. *De regno*, ante 1267, *On Kingship*, trans. Phelan and Eschmann (Toronto: Pontifical Institute of Mediaeval Studies (DR) 1949).
7. *Quaestiones Disputatae de virtutibus*, 1269–72, partial versions: *On the Virtues in General*, trans. J. P. Reid (Indiana: Providence College Press, 1951; *On Charity*, trans. L. H. Kendzierski (Milwaukee: Marquette University Press (Vir) 1960).
8. *Expositio in libros Ethicorum*, 1265–70, *Commentary on the Nicomachean Ethics*, trans. C. I. Litzinger, 2 vols. (Chicago: Regnery (EE) 1964).
9. *Summa Theologiae*, Part II, 1269–70, *Summa of Theology*, trans. English Dominicans, 22 vols. (London: Burns, Oates & Washbourne, 1912–36; reprint in 3 vols. New York: Benziger, 1947–48); Latin-English edition, by T. Gilby *et al.*, 60 vols. (New York: McGraw-Hill (ST) 1964–74).

Critical editions of most of the Latin works are to be found in: S. Thomae Aquinatis, *Opera Omnia*, jussu Leonis XIII (Romae: Editori di San Tommaso, 48 vols. 1882– ). This Leonine edition is still in course of publication. Excellently annotated is the Ottawa edition of *Summa Theologiae*, 5 vols. (Ottawa, Canada: Studium Generalis Ordinis Praedicatorum, 1941).

## SECONDARY WORKS

1. Armstrong, P. A., *Primary and Secondary Precepts in Thomistic Natural Law Teaching* (The Hague: Nijhoff, 1966).
2. Bourke, V. J., *St. Thomas and the Greek Moralists* (Milwaukee: Marquette University Press, 1948); *Ethics. A Textbook in Moral Philosophy* (New York: Macmillan, 1966).

3. Chenu, M. D., *Toward Understanding St. Thomas*, trans. A. M. Landry and D. Hughes (Chicago: Regnery, 1964).
4. D'Arcy, E., *Conscience and Its Right to Freedom* (London and New York: Sheed & Ward, 1961).
5. Finnis, J., *Natural Law and Natural Rights* (Oxford: Clarendon Press, 1980).
6. Grisez, G., *Christian Moral Principles* (Chicago: Franciscan Herald Press, 1983).
7. Grisez, G. and R. Shaw, *Beyond the New Morality* (Indiana: University of Notre Dame Press, 1974).
8. Jaffa, H. V., *Thomism and Aristotelianism. A Study of the Commentary by Thomas Aquinas on the Nicomachean Ethics* (University of Chicago Press, 1952).
9. Klubertanz, G., *Habits and Virtues* (New York: Appleton-Century-Crofts, 1965).
10. Kluxen, W., *Philosophische Ethik bein Thomas von Aquin* (Mainz: Gruenewald, 1964).
11. McInerny, R., *Ethica Thomistica. The Moral Philosophy of Thomas Aquinas* (Washington, D.C.: Catholic University of America Press, 1982).
12. Midgley, E. B. F., *The Natural Law Tradition and the Theory of International Relations* (New York: Harper & Row, 1975).
13. O'Connor, D. J., *Aquinas and Natural Law* (London: Macmillan, 1968).
14. Oesterle, J., *Ethics. Introduction to Moral Science* (Englewood Cliffs, N.J.: Prentice-Hall, 1957).
15. Pieper, J., *The Four Cardinal Virtues* (Indiana: Notre Dame University Press, 1967).
16. Tranoy, K. E., *Thomas av Aquino som Moral Filosof*. Prefaced by English summary (Oslo: Universitetsforiget, 1957).
17. Veatch, H., *Rational Man* (Bloomington: Indiana University Press, 1964).
18. Weisheipl, J. A., *Friar Thomas d'Aquino* (Garden City, New York: Doubleday, 1974).

# 5

# Hobbes
## *Larry May*

After Aquinas, the two most notable developments in ethical theory are to be found in the turn from Aristotelian realism to Ockhamist nominalism on the one hand, and the turn towards a prudence-based understanding of right and justice epitomised by Machiavelli on the other hand. In the 13th century, Ockham combined a theory of divine omnipotence with a nominalist metaphysics. The result was an ethical theory which was strongly voluntarist in the sense that 'goodness is dependent on obligation, obligation on volition, and volition unbound by reason or anything else'. (James Walsh, 'Nominalism and the Ethics', Journal of the History of Philosophy, January 1966, vol. IV, no. 1, p. 2.) Thomas Hobbes (1588–1679) made much of Ockhamist nominalism in his own ethical writings. And Hobbes was also influenced by the 14th century pragmatic political philosophy, in which Machiavelli, most importantly, had argued that rights and civic virtue were circumscribed by such practical considerations as the fact that a ruler must remain in power in order to accomplish anything at all. These pragmatic and nominalist departures from Aquinas reached their most forceful articulation in Hobbes' writings.

During the 17th century a moral philosophy arose which focused almost exclusively on the secular human person, rather than on community or church. Its proponent, Hobbes, became the symbol of all that is wrong, or right, with the turn away from a theological or communitarian approach to ethics. In the 17th century there was also a major break with the Aristotelian understanding of human nature, of science and of the proper methods of philosophical inquiry. Hobbes epitomised the turn among philosophers towards the new science of Coppernicus, Newton and Galileo which set out a mechanical model of understanding human beings. His natural philosophy infused his ethics with an egoistic psychology according to which people only did what they agreed to be best for themselves. Changes in legal theory in the late 16th and early 17th century, especially concerning contract and obligation, had a profound impact on Hobbes' moral philosophy as well. In general, the 17th century was a period of radical change and by its end Hobbes' espousal of a legally oriented, prudential contractarianism was recognised to be the most radical moral philosophy of the time. In this chapter I will attempt to assess the portrait of Hobbes sketched by his contemporaries, namely, as the chief exponent of an amoral philosophy which challenged all that was good in the classical natural law tradition, epitomised by Aquinas.

While Hobbes did break with classical traditions in ethics, his break was consistent with certain developments in political and legal theory at his time. Indeed it is my contention that, rather than rejecting the natural law tradition, Hobbes is best appreciated as having found a non-theological basis for the doctrine of moral obligation. In Hobbes' view, the dictates of conscience, encapsulating the voice of God, were not the sole or even the most important source of morality. Instead, prudentially based consent and conformity to the properly authorised dictates of the sovereign lawmaker were the chief ingredients in Hobbes' theory of obligation. Thus Hobbes' critics were not fully justified in regarding him as the chief enemy of the classical tradition. It is true that Hobbes came to moral and political disputes from a very different starting point from that of classical authors, but the conclusions that he reached were often not so greatly at odds with these authors as his contemporaries claimed. Finally, while putting Hobbes into historical context, I will also consider the extent to which Hobbes' views are unique and whether or not those views lead us to a plausible basis for ethics.

## SOVEREIGNTY AND ASSUMPSIT

In the late 16th and early 17th century two concepts, sovereignty and assumpsit, were developed which greatly affected Hobbes' understanding of the contractual obligation a citizen owed to a ruler. I will briefly survey the development of these two concepts. First, I will look at the writings of Jean Bodin and Richard Hooker on sovereignty, a concept which epitomised the modern turn in political and moral thought. From Bodin Hobbes borrowed the new concept of sovereignty; and from Hooker he borrowed the notion that the social contract was between individuals, not between a people and a ruler. I will then look at various legal writings on the emerging doctrine of assumpsit which significantly changed contract law in England at Hobbes' time, and may have been a model for Hobbes' own understanding of the social contract.

At the end of the 16th century the social contract was linked with a new notion of rulership, which the French theorist Jean Bodin called sovereignty. Bodin argued that a ruler derived unlimited power from a transfer of power from the people; that is, he argued that the people, by a contract, gave up any claim to retain rulership in their own hands by contracting with and subjecting themselves to a ruler. He defined sovereignty as 'the most high, absolute, and perpetuall power over the citisens and subjects in a commonwealle . . . that is to say, the greatest power to command'. (*The Six Bookes of a Common-wealle*, K. D. McRae, ed., Cambridge, Mass.: Harvard University Press, 1962, p. 84). There had been many theories of absolute ruler-ship before Bodin; and there had been many theories of obligation based on contract. But Bodin was one of the first to combine these two notions to form the modern notion of sovereignty.

The main feature of Bodin's contract-based sovereignty was that it was not limited by other persons or political bodies, although it remained limited by various natural law factors. Here is how Bodin put it: 'the chiefe power given unto a prince *with charge and condition* is not properly soveraigntie, nor power absolute.' (*The Six Bookes*, p. 89.) Power must be given absolutely, that is, given as unlimited, in order to be properly sovereign power. Hobbes' own notion of sovereignty drew heavily on that of Bodin. But Bodin and Hobbes were not in complete agreement. Bodin, like his predecessors, con-tinued to cling to the natural law foundation of rulership. He saw the relationship between sovereign monarch and subjects as an ex-tension of the relation between a father and his family. Bodin also retained the idea that the subjects, as a 'people', relinquished power to the sovereign, rather than relinquishing power as individual citizen-subjects. The people had a position analogous to the family, and as a result the individual members had no status apart from their group in respect to the grant of sovereignty. For Bodin, the people were a type of 'corporation'. But he gave little indication how this corporation, as a body, related to its individual members. This was typical of the writers prior to Hobbes: the people were not seen as a collection of individuals each giving assent to the ruler.

On the other side of the English Channel, Richard Hooker's notion of a covenant-based rulership varied from that of Bodin. Hooker introduced the idea that covenants, especially the covenant between God and man, needed to be conceived in individualistic terms. In both religious and political contexts there must be a compact between individual subject and sovereign ruler; and the terms of this compact must be well understood in order for the subject to be obligated to obey the dictates of the ruler. Here is the way he put it:

> the articles of compact between them must shew: not only the articles of the first beginning, which for the most part are clean worn out of knowledge, or else known unto very few, but whatsoever hath been after in free and voluntary manner condescended unto, whether by express consent, whereof positive laws are witnesses, or else by silent allowances famously notified through custom reaching beyond the memory of man.[1]

For Hooker, moral obligation is created by the explicit or implicit consent of individuals. Unless the individual person, not merely that person's group, consents to the law-maker, the individual is not properly obligated. On this point, Hobbes and Hooker were in complete agreement.

But Hooker also held that the 'best established dominion [is] where the law doth most rule the king'. Hooker wanted not only to establish the contractual basis of the obligations of citizens, but also the contractual limitations on the power of the ruler. Of all the advocates of religious toleration during this period, Hooker presented the most legally oriented attack on the absolute power of the king. His general maxim was that 'power may be limited ere it be granted'. Hobbes, to the contrary, followed Bodin in thinking that sovereignty was not properly so called when it was limited. To support his view Hobbes proposed a quite different maxim from Hooker's: power always seeks after more power until an absolute dominion is achieved. To place limits on one ruler's power is merely to open the door for another person to supplant this ruler.

One other historical development may have had an influence on Hobbes' attempt to ground ethics in a social contract. Contract law before Hobbes' time was seen mainly as a branch of property law. It was not sufficient to show that there had been an agreement between two parties and a violation of that agreement in order to establish that one of the parties had a basis of legal action. In addition there had to be some 'consideration' at stake. Only when there was something done to or given by one party to another, and one had thereby established the *quid* of the *quid pro quo*, could a claim be made for the *quo*. It was not the promise *per se* that created the obligation, but the debt.[2]

By the end of the 16th century contract law was changing. The doctrine of assumpsit arose which allowed one to sue merely for the violation of a promise, regardless of whether there had been a 'consideration' or not. It was thought to be sufficient that one person had raised the expectations of another through the spoken act of promise making, that is, through beginning an 'undertaking' which expressed the voluntary relinquishing of what one would otherwise have been free to do. Once the doctrine of assumpsit established a foundation for legal actions based on promises alone, the stage was set for the creation of obligations which could not be removed merely by withdrawing from the agreed-on undertaking. By the end of the 16th century assumpsit actions had established the theory that irreversible legal rights and duties resulted from agreements and contracts.[3]

Of equal importance, developments in the doctrine of assumpsit led to the establishment of the legitimacy of 'third-party beneficiary contracts'. By the middle of the 17th century it had become well accepted in English common law that the beneficiary of a promise, even when that person was not one of the contracting parties, had a legitimate right to the benefit. *Lever v. Heys* (1599), for instance, concerns a marriage agreement struck between two fathers. The one father promised to pay a certain sum of money as dowry to the second father's son if the second father agreed to give his consent to the marriage and assure that it would take place. Properly, then, the contract was made between the fathers, with the son being only a third party to the contract and incurring no obligations thereby himself. The legal question was this: once the marriage had taken place, did the son have a legal right to the dowry, and could he sue on his own behalf to secure it. The judges of the King's Bench ruled that the son did have standing to sue.[4]

As we shall see in a moment, Hobbes made his sovereign a third-party beneficiary to the contract which each person makes with each other person in the state of nature. This doctrine, although fraught with problems, constitutes one of the unique contributions Hobbes made to social contract theory. While it is not possible to prove that Hobbes was influenced by the legal developments in assumpsit at his time, his doctrine of contract is so similar to that of the common law defenders of assumpsit that the influence seems quite likely. In any event, Hobbes explicitly acknowledged his reliance on a large number of other common law doctrines. And as we shall see later, his moral concepts of right, justice and equity are all framed within a legalistic structure.

## SELF-INTEREST AND NATURAL RIGHT

Psychology is as important to Hobbes' ethics as is law and, interestingly, the two combine together in an important way. Surely the most famous passages from *Leviathan* deal with the highly imaginative thought experiment which Hobbes developed to test his views of human nature and the psychological motivation to obey the law, namely the state of nature. It is quite clear that Hobbes did not envision the state of nature as a historical condition. He said:

> It may peradventure be thought, there was never such a time, nor condition of war as this; and I believe it was never generally so, over all the world . . . yet in all times, kings, and persons of sovereign authority, because of their independency are in continual jealousies, and in the state and posture of gladiators . . .[5]

But it is equally clear that Hobbes used this thought experiment to set out his views on the relation between psychology and ethics, especially the centrality of self-interest to the concept of natural right.

Hobbes begins his discussion of the mythical state of nature by drawing our attention to three conditions of equality that exist in nature: equality of strength, equality of prudence or ability, and equality of hope. Equality of strength does not imply that each person possesses the same amount of physical strength as the next person, but only that 'the weakest has strength enough to kill the strongest'. (*Leviathan*, EW III 110.) People are of equal strength in the sense that each is endowed with enough physical strength to put the other in fear. Even the strongest must sleep, and then even the weakest can sneak up and put a dagger to such a person's heart. Hobbes regards this vulnerability as a basis for the motivation of fear in human psychology.

The second equality, of prudence or the ability to pursue one's own interests, is a greater 'equality among men, than that of strength'. (Ibid.) Equality of prudence results from the equal opportunity to learn from experience. 'For prudence is but experience; which equal time, equally bestows on all men, in those settings they equally apply themselves unto.' (Ibid.) Thus, like equality of strength, Hobbes does not claim that all people are equal in the amount of their prudence, but only that they are all equally capable of achieving a certain level of ability if they apply themselves. So not only are people relatively equal in strength, but they are also relatively equal in the ability of rationally pursuing their own interests. That people would pursue their own interests, over all else, in the state of nature seems to be largely based on the fear which equality of strength creates.

From this second equality a third develops, the equality of hope. This equality is simply a synthesis of the first two. When two people desire the same thing, neither one backs away; instead, the two become enemies in striving for it. They become enemies because they both perceive themselves as equal in strength and ability, and they thus come to have an equal hope of prevailing in any conflict. Such competition is rendered even more plausible by Hobbes' contention that it is also natural for individual persons to seek gain, safety and reputation, and that it is not uncommon for people to resort to violence to achieve these basic ends. (EW III 112; also see EW II 6n.) All of these natural psychological conditions lead to such a fear among persons as to transform the state of nature into a state of war, 'and such a war as is of every man against every other man'. (EW III 113.) This state of war is totally devoid of all the aspects of society and civilisation which we have come to accept as synonymous with human life itself. By so stating his case, Hobbes explicitly challenges the Aristotelian identification of human life with social life. (EW II 2–3.)

In this state of war, says Hobbes, the continual fear of our neighbours would make our lives reducible to a simple formula: 'solitary, poor, nasty, brutish and short'. (EW III 113.) It would be solitary because we have no reason to trust anyone else; poor because we have no possible benefit of commerce in such a war; nasty because we are continually threatened and fearful of one another; brutish because we only have time to act on our passions like our fellow animals; and short because the war of all against all results in many untimely and violent deaths. This incredibly pessimistic account of the nature of human life, Hobbes says, is borne out in part by the actions of all of us, when, without any provocation we arm ourselves and lock our doors.

Does [a person] not there as much accuse mankind by his actions as I do with my words? But neither of us accuse man's nature in it.

The desires and the other passions of man, are in themselves no sin. No more are the actions, that proceed from those passions, till they know a law that forbids them: which till laws be made they cannot know: nor can any law be made, till they have agreed upon the person to make it. (EW III 114)

The key to getting out of this miserable condition is the agreement, the contract, to allow for a common power which can make and enforce laws on us, thereby ending the natural war.

Hobbes singles out one particular consequence of the lack of law enforcement in the state of nature:

Where there is no common power, there is no law: where no law, no justice. . . . Justice, and injustice, are none of the faculties of body, nor mind. . . . They are qualities, that relate to men in society, not in solitude. (EW III 115)

This particular consequence is taken up at greater length subsequently in *Leviathan* in a general discussion of the relation between justice and law.

As a final note on this discussion of our natural self-interested dispositions, it is worth mentioning that Hobbes also identifies three passions which would incline individual persons to seek peace and therefore to seek some way out of the misery of the state of nature. These passions are: (1) 'fear of death'; (2) 'desire of such things as are necessary to commodious living'; and (3) 'hope by their industry to obtain them'.

These passions have the same basis as the threefold equality among persons: strength, prudence and hope. But now people have a strong reason 'which suggesteth convenient articles of peace, upon which men may be drawn to agreement. These articles are they which otherwise are called the Laws of Nature . . .' (EW III 116.) and Hobbes later equates the laws of nature with 'the true moral philosophy'. (EW III 146.) Hobbes' account of the general epistemic status of moral propositions, such as are embodied in the laws of nature, is the important part of his theory to which I now turn.

## MORAL EPISTEMOLOGY AND THE LAWS OF NATURE

For Hobbes, understanding is generally characterised as 'conception caused by speech'. One person is said to understand another's words when the one person has various thoughts caused by the hearing of the other's speech, *and* when these thoughts are those which the words of that speech were ordained to signify. (*Leviathan*, EW III 28.) But sometimes the equivocation of names makes

> it *difficult* to recover those conceptions for which the name was ordained and that not only in the language of other men . . . but also in our discourse, which being derived from the custom and common use of speech, representeth unto us not our own concep- tions. (Human Nature, EW IV 23)

The best example Hobbes offers of equivocation and inconsistency in the meaning assigned to names occurs in ethical discourse. In Chapter VI of *Leviathan*, Hobbes tells us that the names 'good' and 'evil' refer to objects of appetite and aversion respectively for the individuals who employ these terms, 'there being nothing simply and absolutely' good or evil. (EW III 41.) And in Chapter IV he says that all people are not 'like affected' and hence they call the same thing by different names. (EW III 28.) Specifically, with respect to the so-called virtues and vices, we find that

> one man calleth *wisdom* what another calleth *fear*; and one *cruelty*, what another *justice*; one *prodigality* what another *magnanimity*; and one *gravity* what another *stupidity*, &c. And therefore such names can never be true grounds of any ratiocination. (EW III 29)

Thus it would appear that a science of ethics which led to correct reasoning and understanding is blocked by the possible equivocation and relativity of ethical names, for terms like 'good' are 'relative to person, place and time'. (*De Homine*, Ch. 11, p. 47.)

But Hobbes also speaks of a kind of deductive knowledge in science, which is not linked to such an uncertain basis because it is *a priori*, not *a posteriori*. We can know various things to be true by right reasoning which proceeds from what we ourselves have made or generated; that is, it is possible to know that a figure will have a certain proportion because through geometry we have constructed that figure and its dimensions. Similarly, politics and ethics 'can be demonstrated *a priori*; because we ourselves make the principles— that is, the cause of justice (namely laws and covenants) . . .' (*De Homine*, Ch. 10, p. 42.) But such knowledge can only be achieved in civil society, because without a power to overawe us all and guarantee that these covenants will be kept, laws and covenants are not practical in the state of nature.[6]

Without such a power to guarantee a common basis for our various feelings of appetite and aversion, ethical propositions must only be contingently true. In Chapter VII of *Leviathan* Hobbes explains that all *a posteriori* reasoning of this type is conditional because it is not possible to know absolutely through discourse 'that this or that, is, has been, or will be'. (EW III 52.) In ethical discourse, the relativity of understanding is compounded by the fact that we must begin from the opinions we hold of what is conducive to our own pleasure, and we remain uncertain that we will continue to hold the same opinions later or that others will be of the same opinion about the causes of our own pleasures. Thus, for Hobbes, knowledge of what we ought to do remains uncertain and only contingently true. Hobbes' relativism makes it much harder, but not impossible, to generate a concept of obligation.

The notion of obligation in Hobbes' moral epistemology is stabilised by the idea that there are laws of nature or moral precepts found by reason alone. (EW III 116.) This position reflects, but only to a certain extent, the late medieval view that human reason could attain knowledge of the moral law. Aquinas had held this position also, but he contended that it was possible for only some humans to whom God had bestowed special powers. Hobbes is much more a forerunner of the Enlightenment moral philosophers than he is a follower in the Thomistic tradition. This is mainly due to the fact that Hobbes does not think that human reason needs to be aided in order to be able to come to a full knowledge of the moral law embodied in the laws in nature, and this is because both right and law of nature are derived from reasonable, prudential maxims known to all.[7] Here again we see that Hobbes is attempting to ground morality in strictly non-theological terms, although not necessarily in terms at odds with traditional natural law concerns.

In *Leviathan* Hobbes contrasts a law of nature with a right of nature. The latter is defined as

> the liberty each man hath to use his own power, as he will himself, for the preservation of his own nature; that is to say, of his own life; and consequently, of doing anything, which in his own judgement, and reason, he shall conceive to be the aptest means thereunto. (EW III 116)

And in the next paragraph he defines a law of nature to be:

a precept or general rule, found out by reason, by which a man is forbidden to do what is destructive of his life, or taketh away the means of preserving the same; and to omit that, by which he thinketh it may be best preserved. (EW III 116–17)

A right of nature and a law of nature, in one and the same matter, are inconsistent for Hobbes. A right 'consisteth in liberty to do or to forbear: whereas LAW, determineth and bindeth to one of them'. (Ibid.)

The conflict between right and law of nature is due to the particular conditions of lawlessness and insecurity in the state of war of all against all. In the state of nature 'every man has a right to every thing; even to another's body. And therefore as long as this natural right of every man to every thing endureth, there can be no security to any man.' (EW III 117.) People generally come to see that, in order to achieve security, they must not exercise their rights to all things, and from this understanding arise the laws of nature. From a self-generated desire for security, the first general rule of reason is derived:

that every man ought to endeavor peace as far as he has hope of obtaining it; and when he cannot obtain it, that he may seek, and use, all helps and advantages of war. (Ibid.)

Hobbes clearly uses the term 'ought' here. Furthermore, the rule of reason spoken of is the basis for the laws of nature which are said to be the very same as morality for Hobbes. It is thus quite plausible, I believe, to suggest that Hobbes has here set out a moral ought, that is, a precept stipulating a moral obligation, albeit one which is based largely on considerations of self-interest.

## CONSCIENCE, PROMISE AND CONTRACT

Even though Hobbes is generally a moral relativist, he does allow that there are certain laws or precepts which stipulate how human beings ought to act, and which thereby indicate our moral obligations. Because of the lack of external or authoritative moral pronouncement by others in the state of nature, morality under those conditions would be a matter between oneself and one's conscience. Yet Hobbes holds that laws which bind only *in foro interno* (in our consciences) are not laws properly so called. So in what sense are we bound or obligated by the precepts of reason and morality? It is to this central question in Hobbes' ethics that I now turn.

At the very end of Chapter 15 of *Leviathan* Hobbes clearly states what he believes to be the essence of the laws of nature. The laws of nature 'are but conclusions or theorems concerning what conduceth to the conservation and defense of themselves'. The laws of nature are thus merely 'dictates of reason' and not laws properly so called. For 'law, properly, is the word of him, that by right hath command over others'. (EW III 147.) The laws of nature bind the will and not the actions of a person because they tell only what is likely to produce the best results for individuals who follow them. Since each person, as a prudentially rational person, desires what is best, then each person desires what the laws of nature dictate. And while, in general, it would go against our own desires if we failed to conform to the laws of nature, such failure to conform to them may not go against our desires in certain circumstances, for example, if we had been condemned to death by the state. If violating the laws of nature does not always go against our prudentially rational desires, then it cannot be that we are obliged always to follow those laws. Hobbes' view of obligation is that we can only be bound by our own will. We are obliged to act only in those ways which are required so as not to contradict what we will to do. The paradigm case of obligation occurs when a person voluntarily agrees or promises to perform an action, thereby indicating both that he or she has a will so to act, and that not to act in this way would be to contradict the will.

In Chapter 15 of *Leviathan*, Hobbes contends that the 'laws of nature oblige *in foro interno*; that is to say, they bind to a desire they should take place: but *in foro externo*, that is, to the putting them in act not always'. (EW III 146.) The main reason offered for this claim is that no one can be bound to act contrary to that which grounds all of the laws of nature, namely self-preservation. Thus, when one of the laws of nature obliges a person to do that which would risk his or her life, the person's actions are not bound by that law of nature. The laws of nature bind only in the conscience, or as Hobbes also puts it 'they require nothing but endeavour, he that endeavoureth their performance, fulfilleth them'. (EW III 146–47.)[8]

At one crucial point in *Leviathan*, Hobbes constructs an analogy between being obliged to give the correct answer to a mathematical or logical problem, and being bound to follow the law of nature concerning the keeping of one's promises.

So that *injury*, or *injustice*, in the controversies of the world, is somewhat like to that, which in the disputations of scholars is called *absurdity*. For as it is there called an absurdity, to contradict what one maintained at the beginning: so in the world, it is called injustice, and injury, voluntarily to undo that, which from the beginning he had voluntarily done. (EW III 119)

In both cases, one is bound in the sense that one risks self-contradiction, that is, the rejection of what one has a will to do, if one does not assent to the correct answer or action. This doctrine not only creates a bridge between metaphysics and ethics, but it also creates a bridge between Hobbes' moral philosophy which places high priority on the natural law obligation to keep promises and his political philosophy which is based on the social contract. In logic and mathematics we assent to names and definitions, and are thus bound to accept valid conclusions which follow from these: in morality we assent to restrictions on our future conduct when we utter words which make promises, and we are thus bound to will to do the things we have committed ourselves to do; and in politics, we assent to be ruled by a sovereign through the social contract, and we are thus bound to endeavour to obey the laws propounded by that sovereign. In all three cases (logic, ethics and politics) we bind our wills by what we have previously assented to. In Chapter 16 of *Leviathan* Hobbes makes this explicit when he says that 'no man is obliged by a covenant, whereof he is not author; nor consequently by a covenant made against, or beside the authority he gave'. (EW III 149.)

In part II of his *Elements of Law (De Corpore Politico)* Hobbes explains that it is consistent with the dictates of conscience to obey the civil law, and even be forced to obey it.

For the conscience being nothing else but a man's settled judgment and opinion, when once he hath transferred his right of judging to another, that which shall be commanded is no less his judgment than the judgment of that other . . . according to his own conscience, but not his private conscience. (EW IV 186–87)

When we assent to be ruled by another, we authorise another person to issue commands to us, and we thereby give this person's commands the authority of our own consciences. As a result, it comes to be contrary to our own consciences to disobey the civil law. There is one exception here, namely, when our public conscience commands us to do something which is at odds with the dictates of our private conscience. As we will see later, there are relatively few cases which fit into this exceptional class, since in civil society most of one's private conscience has been voluntarily subjugated to the public conscience. Only those things which threaten self-preservation count as exceptions, since it is never rational voluntarily to give up one's right to self-preservation.

The obligation to obey the civil law is generated out of the moral obligation to obey that which we have agreed to do in our consciences. But this moral obligation is a defective type of obligation, since there may be self-interested reasons to disobey particular laws at particular times. The *might* of the sovereign is necessary to make conscience's dictates truly binding. In chapter 26 of *Leviathan* (EW III 253–54), Hobbes says:

> When a commonwealth is once settled, then are they [the laws of nature] actually laws, and not before; as being then the commands of the commonwealth; and therefore also civil laws: for it is the sovereign power that obliges men to obey them. For in the dif- ferences of private men, to declare, what is equity, what is justice, and what is moral virtue, and to make them binding, there is need for the ordinances of sovereign power, and punishments to be ordained for such as shall break them; which ordinances are therefore part of the civil law.

The sovereign power obliges us to obey the civil and also the natural law, Hobbes says, but of course this must be done by a sovereign who has indeed been duly authorised by us to speak in our names. Even so, the power of the sovereign does correct the deficiencies of mere private conscience by adding a layer of motivation to the binding quality of the laws of nature.

But why would anyone first agree to let another rule over one's own conscience? The rule which underlies the laws of nature, Hobbes tells us, has two corollaries:

> The first branch of which rule, containeth the first, and funda- mental law of nature; which is *to seek peace and follow it*. The second, the sum of the right of nature; which is *by all means we can to defend ourselves*. (EW III 117)

These corollaries point to the opposition of law and right in the state of nature. When reason shows that following the limitations of law will lead to insecurity and that it will threaten our self-preservation, then pure natural right resurfaces as the guiding rule of our actions. Since, in the state of nature, we are always insecure, we should only act to defend ourselves by exercising our right to all things. But this strategy, of course, will lead to insecurity and the perpetuation of the horrible conditions of the war of all. Such a situation is the lesser of two evils, but not the option which is preferable to us. We want to have the security of knowing that all of us will obey *the laws* of nature. Thus we come to seek a way out of the miserable condition called *the state* of nature by agreeing to transfer or relinquish our natural right to all, by a contract with our fellows.

The second law of nature states that rationale for the move out of the state of nature, where private conscience is the only moral authority. It holds that:

> a man be willing when others are so too, as far forth as for peace, and defence of himself he shall think it necessary, to lay down his right to all things; and be contented with so much liberty against all other men, as he would allow other men against himself. (EW III 117–18)

Once prudential reason has shown that we are better off seeking peace than continuing in the state of war, people begin to look for the conditions necessary to bring themselves out of the state of nature. The first thing that reason ascertains is that each person must give up the absolute right to all things. But to do so unilaterally would not be prudent, for there would be no assurance that one's neighbour would act likewise.[9] Without such an assurance, no one should initiate the move out of the state of nature, because of the vulnerability to attack that would result for each person from such a first step. Hobbes sets up the dilemma in this way:

> For as long as every man holdeth his right, of doing any thing he liketh, so long are all men in the condition of war. But if other men will not lay down their right, as well as he; then there is no reason for any one to divest himself of his; for that were to expose himself to prey, which no man is bound to do, rather than to dispose himself to peace. (EW III 118)

Before people will lay down their absolute rights, they seek some sign to show that their fellow neighbours, who also lay down their rights, will not reassert their absolute rights at the first opportunity of their own personal advantage. Seeking for a sign is the beginning of mutual promising. But such promising still results only in the defective form of obligation addressed above.[10]

> And the same are the bonds by which men are bound and obliged; bonds which have their strength not from their own nature, for nothing is more easily broken than a man's word, but from fear of some evil consequence upon the rupture. (EW III 119)

While laying down a right through mutual promising is formally irreversible, on pain of self-contradiction, it is more importantly not reversed for prudential reasons, namely, for fear of punishment at the hands of the sovereign. The motivator of our promise-keeping is the sovereign who is the third-party beneficiary of our acts of mutual promising to restrict our natural rights. We are formally bound or obliged by these promises because we have committed ourselves by our word and deed. But we actually follow through on these obligations because we fear what would happen if we did not.

For Hobbes, a person generally acts in order to achieve 'some good to himself'. In respect to laying down one's rights, this good can be of two sorts: 'it is either in consideration of some right reciprocally transferred to himself; or for some other good he hopeth for thereby'. (EW III 119–20.) People in the state of nature would not renounce their right to all things for altruistic reasons. They would only do so in expectation of some good to be received. Here Hobbes' egoistic psychology is at its peak, for he contends that

> the motive and end for which this renouncing, and transferring of right is introduced, is *nothing else* but the security of a man's person, in his life and in the means of so preserving life, as not to be weary of it. (EW III 120, my italics)

This egoism has another implication which is later developed into the only basis for moral rights in Hobbes' political philosophy. If people only act for their own advantage, then certain rights cannot be laid down. For instance, 'a man cannot lay down the right of resisting them, that assault him by force, to take away his life; because he cannot be understood to aim thereby, at any good to himself'. (Ibid.) As we will see later, even in civil society, morality remains firmly rooted in prudence.

## LAW AND MORALITY

From the account presented so far it should be clear that morality is a legally oriented concept for Hobbes. The natural laws, which encompass the precepts of morality, only achieve effective force when they are enforced by the sovereign through incorporation into the civil law. It is for this reason that Hobbes' detractors claimed that he had simply equated law and morality.[11] But this is not the case. There remained a significant, if limited, area of morality (or natural law) which did not overlap with civil law. In what follows I will argue that Hobbes' concept of law, while admittedly central to his views, did not overwhelm all aspects of his morality.

First, let us examine the definition and limitation of law for Hobbes. In the clearest formulation of his legal philosophy, the little noticed work *A Dialogue Between a Philosopher and a Student of the Common Laws of England*, Hobbes sets out four criteria of a valid law.

A valid law is:

(1) the command of him who has the sovereign power
(2) given to those that be his subjects
(3) declaring publicly
(4) what they must do and forbear to do. (EW VI 26.)

The first two criteria are fairly straightforward. Like Jean Bodin, Hobbes believes that sovereignty is key to proper law-making. And he also believes that laws are commands which bind only those who are properly subject to these commands. Interestingly, Hobbes thinks that this is also true of what he calls the moral law. 'Tis true that the Moral-law is always a Command or a Prohibition, or at least implieth it . . .' (EW VI 28.) So, one might think that all of the moral law is contained within the civil law, since the moral law which is outside of the civil law would not meet the requirement imposed by these first two conditions.

But, for any law to be binding two further conditions must be met. The law must be accessible to the people who are to be bound by it. This third criterion requires that the laws be publicly proclaimed so that it is possible for all subjects to know how they are bound. This ties into the fourth criterion, namely, that the law specify, in advance, what the people are to do and what they are not to do. These two requirements taken together form the foundation of various moral limitations on the law. This is first seen when it is realised that these two criteria impose the following procedural limitations on the sovereign: laws will not be legitimate if they cannot be found and

then understood by the people; laws will not be legitimate if they do
not clearly specify what actions lie under the domain of those laws;
and, laws will not be legitimate if they are claimed to be retroactively
binding. These limitations begin to resemble various constitutional
principles of more modern legal systems.

In *Leviathan* Hobbes develops this point further in discussing the
duties that the sovereign owes to the subjects in a given realm. The
social contract which gives rise to the law-making sovereign, as I
suggested above, is best seen as a third-party beneficiary contract, in
which the sovereign is not a party to the contract, and hence does
not have any specific duties to these subjects, but only rights
deriving from the contract. The contract is described by Hobbes as if
it were the result of an actual contracting between individuals in the
state of nature. Here is the way he characterises it:

> The only way to erect such a common power, as may be able to
> defend them . . . is to confer all their power and strength on one
> man, or upon one assembly of men, that may reduce all their
> wills, by plurality of voices, unto one will. . . . This is more than
> consent or concord; it is a real unity of that all in one and the same
> person, made by covenant of every man with every man, *I authorize
> and give up my right of governing myself, to this man, or assembly of
> men, on this condition, that thou give up thy right to him, and authorize
> all his actions in like manner.* (EW III 157–58)

As I mentioned at the outset, the idea of consenting to be governed
had traditionally been tied to the idea of an agreement between a
'people' as a whole and a ruler. But Hooker had set the stage for a
new view by proclaiming that there is a different kind of agreement
possible, namely, that made between each person, as an individual,
and God or the King. For Hobbes, the contracting parties also do not
constitute a people, since they approach the contract as discrete
individuals. But unlike Hooker, Hobbes claims that the contract is
between each person and each other person.

Hobbes' original contract is more than just a mere passive acceptance or consent by an individual to allow another person the right to
make laws. Rather, the original contract involves an act of trans-
ferring and simultaneously creating a party to be the beneficiary of
this transferred right. With the creation of this new party, the wills
of each party to the contract are united in the will of the new party.
This uniting of wills is not a loose association or federation which

can be broken up as easily as it was joined together. Instead, a bond is created which cannot be broken without self-contradiction of the individuals concerned.

Hooker rightly pointed out that what can be conferred can just as easily be taken back. For Hobbes, this was exactly what he did not want. In the state of nature a person can agree not to impede the power of another. Since a person's power is roughly equivalent to any other person's power, if someone agrees not to stand in the way of another person, there is a kind of warranting of the first person's exercise of power. But a person cannot technically transfer power to another person. For Hobbes transfer implies an irreversibility of action, in that what is transferred cannot be regained, without the consent of the person to whom it is transferred. Power and strength, though, must always remain within the individual person. Thus the collective power of the sovereign does not result from a transfer of power but from a transfer of right in which all persons in the state of nature agree not to impede the sovereign's exercise in power. The transfer of right is irreversible, not the conferring of power itself.

What all of this means is that the individual person retains certain powers which may be legitimately used if the transfer to the sovereign of the right to exercise various powers is somehow rendered void. Hobbes addresses this topic when he attempts to specify the duties of the sovereign. In *De Cive* he states this quite clearly: 'Now all the duties of the ruler are contained in this one sentence: the safety of the people is the supreme law.' (EW II 166.) And in *Leviathan* the safety of the people is said to involve 'public instruction, both of doctrine and example; and in making and executing good laws, to which individual persons may apply their own cases'. (EW III 323.) In general, if the sovereign does not provide for the safety of the people, then the social contract, which relied on the assurance of safety by the sovereign, is no longer in effect. And it is at this point that the people could legitimately use their own power which they had temporarily agreed not to use in certain matters.

Morality thus comes to limit the law-making functions of the sovereign in quite an unusual way for Hobbes. The limitation does not appear in the realm of justice, for justice is completely based on what the sovereign says it is. As Hobbes says, 'before the names just, and unjust can have place, there must be some coercive power'. (EW III 131.) In regard to justice, the sovereign appears to stand outside of morality. It is for this reason that Hobbes' sovereign is often regarded as being above moral criticism. In this respect, then, Hobbes does provide a basis for making the transfer of right to the sovereign something which cannot be easily taken back. For Hobbes, the sovereign as legitimate law-maker cannot be restricted merely because individuals happen to believe that this sovereign acts in a morally unjust way.

But the sovereign may attempt to exercise power in ways that are not legitimate, and it is at this point that morality re-enters as a limitation on law-making. For Hobbes there are moral categories other than justice which apply to the sovereign. Specifically there is the concept of equity which is closely related to the sovereign's duty to protect the safety of the people by providing 'good' laws. Equity dictates that the laws be made so that they are perceived to be fair by those who are subject to them. But, for Hobbes, even equity is grounded in prudence: the sovereign should not violate the principles of equity because to do so would risk the kind of open warfare which would jeopardise sovereignty by undermining the sovereign's ability to ensure the safety of the people. Unlike most other philosophical views of the moral limits on law-making, Hobbes held the all-or-nothing view that only when the immoral actions of the law-maker jeopardise that which grounds sovereignty are they limiting constraints on the law. Nonetheless, these are limits; it is, thus, inappropriate to characterise Hobbes as a defender of the kind of legal positivism which admits no moral limit whatsoever on the law-maker. To understand fully Hobbes' views about the moral limitations of sovereignty, we must understand the relation between prudence and morality, the final topic of this chapter.

## PRUDENCE AND MORALITY

Hobbes' original contribution to the history of ethics concerns the way in which he links the various components of morality together by reference to the concept of prudence. In exploring this point, I will contrast Hobbes' views with those of John Locke whose writings seem to be heavily based on Hobbes' conceptual scheme, but which ended in a more traditional conception of morality.

For Hobbes moral philosophy involved the study of what was good and the means to achieve the good. To understand the good, one needed first to understand what a person would call good in a situation where there was no society. Hobbes has a relatively easy time showing that self-preservation and self-interest will determine what is good for individuals in this pre-societal state, the state of nature. Thus, at least in the state of nature, prudence, which involves rational self-interested calculation, will be the basis of moral deliberations.

The social contract determines most of the domain of morality in civil society, but prudence still remains important at two levels. First, prudence is the vehicle by which persons decide to limit their natural passions and to establish the social contract. Here Hobbes is quite clear:

> if their actions be directed according to their particular judgments, and particular appetites, they can thereby expect no defence, nor protection, neither against a common enemy, nor against the injuries of one another. (EW III 155)

Second, it is prudence which determines when the contract has been rendered void. Each person continues to engage in prudential calculation concerning his or her putative obligations after civil society has been established. Indeed, even as Hobbes says that it is wrong to break the contract, he explains the wrongness by pointing out the likely harm to be done to individuals who break the contract, and who act in opposition to civil law and morality. Hobbes argues against those who, whenever it seems prudent, would break the contract in the following passages:

> The fool hath said . . . that every man's conservation, and contentment, being committed to his own care, there could be no reason, why every man might not do what he thought conduced thereunto: and therefore also to make, or not make; keep, or not keep covenants, was not against reason, when it conduceth to one's benefit. (EW III 132)

Hobbes responds that this 'specious reasoning is nevertheless false'. He agrees with the fool that what is reasonable is that which is shown to be beneficial or prudential. But he argues that the fool, through selective obedience to law, could not gain what is sought by all people, namely long-term security.[12]

> He therefore that breaketh his convenant and consequently declareth that he may with reason do so, cannot be received into any society, that unite themselves for peace and defence, but by the

error of them that receive him, nor when he is received in it, without seeing the danger of their error, which errors a man cannot reasonably reckon upon as the means of his security . . . (EW III 134)

The social contract, then, is itself justified in terms of prudence. And it serves as the basis of morality in civil society for Hobbes. But since it is never prudent to give up self-preservation, it may sometimes be right for the contract to be broken, especially in those situations where a sovereign power attempts to take the life of an individual. These cases are rare indeed and, as Hobbes says above, the advantages of civil society almost always outweigh whatever inconvenience there might be to an individual by keeping to the terms of the contract.

Hobbes' immediate successor, John Locke,[13] also held the social contract to be the chief determiner of what is morally right in civil society. But although Locke often speaks of what reason dictates in the state of nature, he does not justify either the legitimacy of the contract or the breaking of the contract in terms of prudence. Consider this central passage from Locke's *Second Treatise*.

The *State of Nature* has a Law of Nature to govern it, which obliges every one: And Reason, which is that Law, teaches all Mankind, who will but consult it, that being all equal and independent, no one ought to harm another in his Life, Health, Liberty, or Possessions. For men being all the Workmanship of one Omnipotent, and infinitely wise Maker . . . they are his Property, whose Workmanship they are, made to last during his, not one another's pleasure. (289)

Locke denies that reason is equivalent to pure self-interested calculation, and he does so for considerations of a theological nature, as the passage above indicates.

Locke also comes to the view that the state of nature is not a state of war, based on his belief that God has not placed us on this earth merely to look after ourselves, but to look after those who are innocent and incapable of defending themselves.

For *by the Fundamental Law of Nature, Man being to be preserved*, as much as possible, when all cannot be preserv'd, the safety of the Innocent is to be preferred. (297)

And here we have the plain *difference between the State of Nature, and the State of War*, which however some men have confounded, are as far distant, as a State of Peace, Good Will, Mutual Assistance, and Preservation, and a State of Enmity, Malice, Violence, and Mutual Destruction are from one another. (298)

While Locke agrees with Hobbes that self-preservation is important in the state of nature, he does not share Hobbes' bleak assessment of pre-social life and he therefore does not come to see prudence as the only basis for moral evaluation. As we see above, Locke believes that altruism, especially concerning the innocent, is also a proper basis for moral deliberation. When people leave the state of nature for civil society, Locke similarly does not place prudence as the overriding aspect of moral deliberation.

Locke may have toned his own views down, in part, because of the reaction to Hobbes' writings. Hobbes had been roundly criticised especially for failing to retain any of the traditional natural law considerations in his description of the state of nature, and hence in his account of human nature. Locke seems to have been greatly affected by the hostile reaction which Hobbes' writing received, especially from theologians in England. John Eachard, for example, claimed that Hobbes had not made out his case for thinking that 'Humane Nature (or reason) [is] so very vile and raskally, as he writes his own to be, nor his account of it altogether so demonstrative, as Euclid'.[14] In particular, Eachard says that Hobbes was too hasty in drawing the conclusion that prudence would be the most rational strategy to pursue in the state of nature.

Wherein he saies, that a great and necessary occasion of quarrelling and war is, that several men oftimes have a desire to the same thing; which thing if it happens not to be capable of being divided, or enjoyed in Common, they must needs draw and fight for't: Instead of which, he should have said; if these men be mad, or void of reason, it is possible they may fight for't: For being that every one of them have a equal right to this same, that is in controversie, they may either compound for it as to its value, or decide it by Lot, or some other way that reason may direct (which is the Law of *reason* and *humane Nature*, and not merely positive, because it is in *Law Books*). (p. 6)

This particular objection to Hobbes is voiced by Eachard on behalf of

Divine Providence, the Church and most especially the Clergy who have been 'so vilely aspersed and persecuted by our *Adversarie's* malicious suggestions'. (p. 1.)


## CONCLUSIONS

Hobbes was the first to attempt to ground the concept of moral obligation exclusively on rational self-interest. People are generally bound to do what they have stipulated that they have a will to do. The bindingness is based, in the first place, on the desire that all people have to avoid self-contradiction. Furthermore, in civil society, there is an additional motivation to our moral obligations. Our agreement, through the social contract, to be subject to the rule of the sovereign, further stipulates that we have a will to regard all laws as morally binding. Not only do we risk self-contradiction by failing to do what we are obligated to do, but we also risk the punishment of the sovereign. This fear of punishment is so strongly motivating that what was a defective, or merely self-enforced, sense of being bound becomes a properly binding (in terms of liberty constraining) sense of obligation.

Once civil society is in place, people are morally bound to follow all of the traditional dictates of the natural law, according to Hobbes. And this remains true as long as the sovereign is able to guarantee the safety of the people. If the sovereign indicates that such a guarantee is in jeopardy, then the sovereign's subjects are no longer properly obligated, although they remain obligated in conscience. The attempt to make sure that no one believes that the guarantee of safety is jeopardised, leads the sovereign also to feel obligated to make good laws and to treat the subjects equitably. These results of Hobbes' theory are again consistent with traditional natural law doctrine.

What marks Hobbes out as an extreme radical for his contemporary opponents is that he sought to equate reason and prudence, completely upsetting the tradition since Aquinas of seeing reason not as the servant of self-interest but of God's law. It seemed to matter little to his contemporaries that Hobbes did affirm the traditional virtues and found a strong basis for obligation in his conception of prudence. Hobbes' moral philosophy is unique in virtue of the central place that prudence takes in all of his deliberations. But it is important to note that Hobbes' positions on the great controversies of his day are not much at odds with those of his contemporaries.

Hobbes attempted to provide what the considered to be a less controversial and more reasonable basis for supporting the traditional
norms and virtues which, following Aquinas and his supporters in
the 17th century, were identified as constituting the substance of the
laws of nature. As a result, Hobbes can be seen as the first modern
moralist: the reasonable basis for natural law which he espoused did
not appeal to theological considerations, except as an afterthought
(in the final section of *Leviathan*). In a time of ferment, when the
authority of church and state was thrown into question, Hobbes felt
that only an appeal to non-theological considerations such as prudence could succeed. Hobbes was wrong about what would persuade
his contemporaries; but as writers like David Hume would well illustrate, he was right about what would be persuasive in the long run.

# Notes

1. Richard Hooker, *The Laws of Ecclesiastical Polity*, edited by R. A. Houk (New York: Columbia University Press, 1931), p. 176.
2. The English legal historians, Sir Frederick Pollock and Frederick William Maitland provide the best treatment of the history of contract law just prior to Hobbes' time. See their monumental study *The History of English Law Before the Time of Edward I*, 2nd ed., vol. 2 (Cambridge University Press, 1909).
3. The American jurist, Oliver Wendell Holmes, argues quite cogently for the historical thesis that assumpsit developed out of a need for contractual obligation that was not based on debt. See his book *The Common Law*, edited by Mark DeWolfe Howe (Boston: Little Brown, 1963) especially pp. 198–226.
4. Two other cases are important to consider as well. In *Provender v. Wood* (Hetley 31, 124 ER 318, 1631) the court ruled that 'the party to whom the benefit of a promise accrews, may bring his action'. And in *Starkey v. Mill* (Style 296, 82 ER 723, 1651), the principle articulated in *Provender* was applied to a commercial situation, and again the third party was said to have the right to sue.

   > Roll Chief Iustice held, that it is good as it is, for there is a plain contract because the goods were given for the benefit of the plaintiff, though the contract be not made between him and the defendant, and he may have an action upon the case for here is a promise in law made to the plaintiff, though there be not a promise in fact . . .

   For an analysis of these and related cases see G. W. F. Dold, *Stipulations for a Third Party* (London: Stevens and Sons, 1948).
5. *Leviathan*, EW III 114–15.
6. A number of commentators have written on the importance of the deductive method for Hobbes' philosophy. One of the most accessible of such commentaries was provided by J. W. N. Watkins, *Hobbes's System of Ideas* (London: Hutchinson & Co., 1965) chs. 2 and 3.
7. There is a significant group of interpreters of Hobbes who do not share my views on whether God is needed to aid us in knowing the laws of nature. A. E. Taylor, Howard Warrender and F. C. Hood have each advanced the thesis that God plays a central role in Hobbes' moral philosophy. Warrender presents the strongest argument against the interpretation I urge throughout my chapter. In *The Political Philosophy of Thomas Hobbes* (Oxford University Press, 1957) Warrender (p. 100) says:

   > In the present work, Hobbes's statements regarding the place of God will be taken as a necessary part of his theory, and it will be contended that this allows the most probable construction to be put upon his text. Thus it will be held that with regard to natural law, the ground of

obligation is always present as this derives from the commands of God in his natural kingdom, and does not depend in any way upon the covenant and consent of the individual or upon the command of the civil sovereign.

The bulk of my chapter can be construed as an attempt to defend the alternative interpretation of Hobbes, which Warrender calls the atheistical account of Hobbes.

8. J. W. N. Watkins argues quite cogently that the concept of endeavour is central to Hobbes' whole project of connecting natural philosophy with moral and political theory. See *Hobbes's System of Ideas*, op. cit., especially ch. 7.

9. Many contemporary philosophers trace the origin of decision theory, especially concerning the prisoner's dilemma, directly back to Hobbes. One of the chief defenders of this view is David P. Gauthier. See his important book, *The Logic of Leviathan* (Oxford University Press, 1969). Part II is of the most relevance to our concerns, and provides quite an interesting attempt to refute the views of Warrender.

10. Perhaps the most telling point in Warrender's favour is Hobbes' own claim that the laws of nature might not be a defective form of moral obligation in the state of nature. For this to be true, there would have to be some authority in the state of nature who issues moral commands. Warrender forcefully argues that God is the only entity that could fill this function (op. cit., p. 98). The chief passage from Leviathan that Warrender relies on is this:

> But yet if we consider the same theorems, as delivered in the word of God, that by right commandeth all things; then are [the laws of nature] properly called laws. (EW III 147)

As Warrender himself admits, this passage is conjectural and is thus subject to a number of interpretations. Since Hobbes has just said that the laws of nature are not properly called laws, the consequent clause must be something which Hobbes believes to be false. And by *modus tollens* Hobbes commits himself to believing that the antecedent clause is false also. It is for this reason that I hold that the laws of nature for Hobbes are a defective form of moral obligation.

11. John Eachard is one of the strongest defenders of the view that Hobbes conflated morality and legality. See the quotation from him which occurs near the end of the present chapter.

12. Hobbes's refutation of the fool has received very interesting commentary of late. A number of authors have reassessed Hobbes' attempt to answer the fool, as well as why Hobbes even mentions such a powerful objection to his own theory. Of special note are the following essays: Annette Baier, 'Secular Faith', *Canadian Journal of Philosophy*, 10/1 (1980); and David Gauthier, 'Three Against Justice: The Foole, The Sensible Knave, and the Lydian Shepherd', *Midwest Studies in Philosophy*, VII (1982).

13. John Locke (1632–1704) wrote two books in 1689 which are important in

the history of ethics. First, in his book *An Essay Concerning Human Understanding* he devotes parts of several chapters to the subject of ethical knowledge, arguing that such knowledge cannot be innate. Also, in his *Two Treatises of Government* Locke tries to blend concepts of natural right with the social contract theory Hobbes had developed a few years earlier.

14. *Mr. Hobbes's State of Nature Considered*, 1672, edited by Peter Ure (Liverpool University Press: English Reprint Series, 1958), p. 7.

# Bibliography

## WORKS BY HOBBES CITED

1. *The English Works of Thomas Hobbes of Malmesbury*, collected and edited by Sir William Molesworth (London: John Bohn, 1840; second reprint, Germany: Scientia Verlag, 1966) 11 volumes (cited as EW).
2. *De Homine*, translated by Charles T. Wood, T. S. K. Scott-Craig, and Bernard Gert, in *Man and Citizen*, edited by Bernard Gert (New York: Anchor Books, 1972).

## OTHER WORKS CITED AND/OR RECOMMENDED

1. Baier, Annette, 'Secular Faith', *Canadian Journal of Philosophy*, vol. 10, 1980, no. 1.
2. Barry, Brian, 'Warrender and His Critics', reprinted in *Hobbes and Rousseau*, edited by Maurice Cranston and R. S. Peters (Garden City, New York: Doubleday and Co., 1968).
3. Bodin, Jean, *The Six Bookes of a Commonwealle* (a facsimile reprint of the English translation of 1606), editor K. D. McRae (Cambridge, Mass.: Harvard University Press, 1962).
4. Bowle, John, *Hobbes and His Critics: A Study of Seventeenth Century Constitutionalism* (New York: Barnes and Noble, 1951).
5. Copp, David, 'Hobbes on Artificial Persons', *The Philosophical Review*, vol. 89, October 1980, no. 4.
6. Dold, G. W. F., *Stipulations for a Third Party* (London: Stevens & Sons, 1948).
7. Eachard, John, *Mr. Hobbs's State of Nature Considered: In a Dialogue between Philautus and Timothy*, edited by Peter Ure (Liverpool: The English Reprint Series of Liverpool University Press (1672) 1958).
8. Gauthier, David, *The Logic of Leviathan* (Oxford: Clarendon Press, 1969).
9. Gauthier, David, 'Three Against Justice: The Foole, The Sensible Knave and the Lydian Shepherd', *Midwest Studies in Philosophy*, vol. VII, 1982.
10. Gierke, Otto von, *The Development of Political Theory*, translated by Bernard Freyd (New York: W. W. Norton & Co., 1939).
11. Goldsmith, M. M., *Hobbes's Science of Politics* (New York: Columbia University Press, 1966).
12. Gough, J. W., *The Social Contract* (Oxford: Clarendon Press, 2nd ed., 1957).
13. Hampton, Jean, *Hobbes and the Social Contract Tradition* (Cambridge University Press, 1986).
14. Holmes, Oliver Wendell. *The Common Law*, edited by Mark DeWolfe Howe (Boston: Little Brown, 1963).
15. Hood, F. C., *The Divine Politics of Thomas Hobbes* (Oxford University Press, 1964).

16. Hooker, Richard, *The Laws of Ecclesiastical Polity*, edited by R. A. Houk (New York: Columbia University Press, 1931).
17. Kavka, Gregory, *Hobbesian Political and Moral Theory* (Princeton University Press, 1986).
18. Locke, John, *Two Treatises on Government*, edited by Peter Laslett (Cambridge University Press, 1967).
19. MacPherson, C. B., *The Political Theory of Possessive Individualism: Hobbes to Locke* (Oxford: 1962).
20. May, Larry, 'Hobbes's Contract Theory', *Journal of the History of Philosophy*, vol. 18, April 1980, no. 2.
21. May, Larry, 'Hobbes on Equity and Justice', in *Hobbes's Science of Natural Justice*, edited by Craig Walton and Paul Johnson (Dordrecht and Boston: Martinus Nijhoff, 1987).
22. Mintz, Samuel I., *The Hunting of Leviathan: Seventeenth-Century Reactions to the Materialism and Moral Philosophy of Thomas Hobbes* (Cambridge University Press, 1962).
23. Oakeshott, Michael, *Hobbes on Civil Association* (Berkeley and Los Angeles: University of California Press, 1975).
24. Pollock, Sir Frederick, and Frederick William Maitland, *The History of English Law Before the Time of Edward I*, 2nd ed. (Cambridge University Press, 1909) 2 vols.
25. Skinner, Quentin, 'Hobbes on Sovereignty: An Unknown Discussion', *Political Studies*, vol. 13, June 1965.
26. Taylor, A. E., *Thomas Hobbes* (London: Archibold Constable & Co., 1908) (facsimile reprint, New York: Kennikat Press, 1970).
27. Warrender, Howard, *The Political Philosophy of Thomas Hobbes: His Theory of Obligation* (Oxford: The Clarendon Press, 1957).
28. Watkins, J. W. N., *Hobbes's System of Ideas* (London: Hutchinson & Co., 1965).
29. Wolin, Sheldon, *Hobbes and the Epic Tradition of Political Theory* (Los Angeles: William A. Clark Memorial Library, 1970).
30. Yale, D. E. C., 'Hobbes and Hale on Law, Legislation and the Sovereign', *Cambridge Law Journal*, vol. 31, April 1972, no. 1.

# 6

# Hume*
## *David Fate Norton*

In the first book of David Hume's *A Treatise of Human Nature* and in his *Enquiry concerning Human Understanding* we see evidence of his deep interest in explaining certain of our basic beliefs about the world: the belief that there must be causes, that there are independent and abiding objects, and even that we each constitute, or are constituted by, an abiding and independent self. His writings on morals—the balance of the *Treatise*, the *Enquiry concerning the Principles of Morals*, and numerous shorter pieces—reveal an analogous concern to account for our substantive moral beliefs and related moral behaviour. More particularly, Hume wanted to account for the moral judgements we do in fact make, and he wished to do this in a manner that was descriptive or empirical, while yet recognising in these judgements an irreducible normative component. Taking it for granted that we express moral opinions that are informative, Hume attempted to provide an explanation of these expressions and an *anatomy* of morals itself.

The context in which Hume (1711–76) undertook this moral anatomy has both narrower philosophical and broader cultural aspects. Within the philosophical context, Hume's aims required him to address critically the principal moral theories that he found in the moral-theoretical world which he entered about 1725. These included a rationalist theory (represented by Ralph Cudworth and Samuel Clarke): the egoistical hedonism of Thomas Hobbes; and two schools of providential voluntarism, an egoist version (represented by Samuel Pufendorf), and a very different altruistic version (represented by Francis Hutcheson). Along the way he also found himself in partial disagreement with other important moral theorists (Hugo Grotius, Lord Shaftesbury, Bernard de Mandeville, and Joseph Butler, for example) who are perhaps not aptly grouped with any of those already mentioned.[1] Later I will return to Hume's

*Research for this chapter was supported by the Institute for Advanced Study, Princeton.

important objections to some of these predecessors, but for now I wish only to emphasise that he by no means flatly rejected everything found in these alternative 'moral systems', as he called them. On the contrary, although acutely critical when he thought criticism in order, Hume was prepared to borrow from his predecessors.

Equally important to an understanding of Hume's ethical theory is an appreciation of the broader cultural context in which he worked. Hume is unique among major philosophers in being also a historian of classical rank, and there are fundamental interconnections between his moral theory and his historical work.[2] Thus it is doubly instructive to rely on Hume's own views of the general historical setting of his work.

## HISTORICAL SETTING

Hume's very first utterance as a writer—a motto on the title pages of volumes one and two of his *Treatise*—may be taken as praise of the comparatively happy state of British intellectual affairs. Quoting the Roman historian Tacitus, he writes: *Rara temporum felicitas, ubi sentiri, quae velis; & quae sentias dicere licet.*[3] A survey of Hume's *History of England* and of his less explicitly historical works leads one to the conclusion that he traced this positive state of affairs in Britain to two long-lasting and not unrelated events. First, and doubtless surprisingly, the recovery of Roman law, and secondly, what he calls 'one of the greatest events in history', the Protestant Reformation.

Speaking in the most general terms, Hume suggests that ancient civilisation reached its high point at the time of Augustus, and then went into a long decline. The very size of Rome; the despotism and attendant destructiveness of its rulers; the rise of the barbarous nations; these things combined to overwhelm human knowledge and so 'men sunk every age deeper into ignorance, stupidity, and superstition; till the light of ancient science and history had very nearly suffered a total extinction in all the European nations'. Britain, an only partially developed outpost on the edge of classical civilisation, was itself 'very little advanced beyond the rude state of nature'.[4]

Christendom appears to have reached a natural end of its decline, Hume writes, at about the end of the 11th century. The northern barbarians had by then adopted a more settled form of life, while in southern Europe feudalism gave order, if not liberty and tranquillity.

'But', he goes on to say, 'perhaps there was no event which tended farther to the improvement of the state, than one which has not been much remarked, the accidental finding of a copy of Justinian's Pandects, about the year 1130, in the town of Amalfi in Italy'.

This recovery of the *Pandects* had, in Hume's view, both direct and indirect consequences. Directly, it led the clergy enthusiastically to adopt Roman jurisprudence, and to 'spread the knowledge of it throughout every part of Europe'. The English clergy, having large properties to protect from the aristocracy, saw that it was in their interest to establish the 'observance of general and equitable rules' from which they alone—as they alone were knowledgeable about these laws—could receive protection. Granted, Roman law never became the foundation of English jurisprudence, but English practice nonetheless altered under the influence of its recovery. As life throughout Europe gradually improved, British affairs 'took early a turn which was more favourable to justice and to liberty', and the study of law and civil employments came to be acceptable and even necessary to the landed class.

In the long run, then, the revival of ancient law contributed to the development of British liberty. Of course, as Hume makes perfectly clear, this was a very long run indeed, one leading first to the disorderly and licentious tyranny of the nobles, then the virtually absolutist tyranny of the Tudor dynasty, and finally the civil war, bloody, and no credit to either side. The English past offers only 'faint and disfigured originals' of present institutions, and so no sound appeals to this past are possible. Nevertheless, out of this mixture of accident tempered by an occasional bit of wisdom the English 'have happily established the most perfect and most accurate system of liberty that was ever found compatible with government'. (11a: XXIII.)

Indirectly, the recovery of the *Pandects* also contributed to a general revival of learning. They seemed central to Hume not merely because the clergy were stimulated to study Justinian's summary of Roman law, but because Roman law was, despite any use to which it was put by the church, essentially secular and necessarily civilising. He reports that law became so important to the landed classes that by the middle of the 15th century the Inns of Court housed 2000 lawyers. Doubtless so many lawyers constituted a plague of sorts, but at least many of these individuals would have had their attention firmly fixed on commercial affairs, and not on the relics or raids that Hume takes to characterise the concerns of, respectively, the clerics and the earlier aristocracy. Furthermore, the skills developed in such secular pursuits had other manifestations: as Hume notes, it was also in the mid-15th century that Lorenzo Valla was able to show that the Donation of Constantine, one of the false decretals ascribed to Pope Gregory IX, was a medieval forgery. (11a: XXIII; XII.)

Hume gives nothing like a detailed account of this revival of learning, but he makes perfectly clear his belief that the recovery of ancient literature was a necessary condition of the Reformation and, equally important, an indistinguishable beginning of what we now suppose to be a separate scientific revolution. This is by no means to suggest that Hume minimised the importance of the new natural philosophy. On the contrary, he saw himself as carrying out Newton's suggestion that the moral world should be dealt with in just the way that he had himself dealt with the natural world. Furthermore, Hume ranked Newton as perhaps the greatest genius in the history of the world, and gave Galileo, Kepler, Bacon and Boyle (in that order) rank in the same class. Hume's terminology and perspective are such that he can treat the new natural philosophy as an extension of the revival of learning; his 'science of human nature' was intended to be an experimentally-based humanism. (11a: LXXI; 1: xvii-xviii.)

There is a good deal of ambiguity in Hume's suggestion that the Reformation was one of the 'greatest events in history'. He obviously had no intention of suggesting that the rise of Protestantism constituted mankind's finest hour. However much Hume may have applauded the breakup of Roman Catholic religious hegemony, he found little to compliment in the behaviour of the reformers. He opens his discussion of the Reformation by taking note of the abuses which had finally made reform of the church inescapable, and goes on to say that the authority of the established church 'was ruined by the excess of its acquisitions, and by stretching its pretensions beyond what it was possible for any human principles . . . to sustain'. In the interim, however, he suggests that to understand the matter we need to consider why it is that 'there must be an ecclesiastical and a public establishment of religion in every civilized community'. This more general account is non-sectarian. (11a: XXIX; XXXI.)

Most of the trades and professions found in society, Hume argues, are such that they contribute to the interests of society at large as well as to those individuals who practise them. These, once established, the state wisely allows to direct themselves. On the other hand, there are certain professions (the judicial, military and administrative ones) that, although entirely necessary to society, are of no particular advantage to those who practise them. These professions the state must encourage, and this it does in a variety of ways, including the establishment of ranks and the giving of honours. Prima facie, it may appear that the clergy belong to the first group, and that religion, as much as medicine or law should be 'entrusted to the liberality of individuals' who, as members of the appropriate guild, will thereby be encouraged to vigilance and industry.

Not so. The 'interested diligence of the clergy is what every wise legislator will study to prevent', for such diligence is a pernicious influence, one that will pervert the truth by mixing it with 'superstition, folly and delusion' as each 'ghostly practitioner' makes himself appear more important, and his competitors more abhorrent. Free trade in religion results in disregard 'to truth, morals, and decency in the doctrines inculcated', as 'customers' are won by an industry that makes no scruple of appealing to credulity and the passions. Far better then for the state to bear the cost of an established church and to connive with the clergy to 'bribe their indolence' by making it superfluous for them to do more than 'prevent their flock from straying in quest of new pastures'.

A far cry from this, however, was the world in which the Roman church was the multi-national established church, for the very scope and constitution of this church made it comprehensively dangerous. True, it did on occasion check the despotic power of kings, and it probably facilitated the intercourse of Roman Catholic nations and encouraged the fine arts. But these were small compensations for the acceptance of an institution that encroached on every domain of political, social and intellectual life, and threatened to stifle mankind by the imposition of arbitrary and credulous limitations of enterprise and thought. (11a: XXIX.)

The Reformation may be judged, then, by the greatness of the evil to which the reformers responded. Martin Luther himself, although no less petty and dogmatic than the church he opposed, did nonetheless progress from what may well have been self-interested objections regarding what he saw to be abuses in the sale of indulgences, to objections against indulgences themselves, and from thence 'by the heat of the dispute' to doubts about the very authority of the Pope. Indeed, before they were done the reformers were to force debate on no less a question than that regarding the nature of the 'criterion' by which divine principles 'may be ascertained'. But so philosophical a consideration had little to do with the enthusiastic hearing Luther's opinions received. He in short order discovered himself the founder of a new sect and possessor of all 'the glory of dictating the religious faith and principles of mankind'. Clearly, his cause was aided by the then recent invention of printing and by the revival of learning, but Hume suggests that the rapid progress of the reform movement is itself enough to show that it was not reason and reflection that brought people to embrace the cause of reform: at the best of times argument and philosophy seem unable to free mankind from the bonds of superstition. It is not surprising then that Hume attributes Luther's success to essentially irrational factors— disgust with the established church, the political interests of such secular rulers as the Elector of Saxony, and the almost giddy response to the prospect of intellectual freedom implicit in the notion that each individual should pass a private judgement on matters of faith. Following Luther there was indeed a religious reformation, but this by no means substituted true religion for the previously prevailing false variety. (11a: XXIX; XXXVII.)

As befits his main subject, Hume is primarily interested in the Reformation in England. Notwithstanding the fact that the pre-Reformation church had been a bad bargain, the new English church, established and headed by Henry VIII, looked to be a worse one. Henry was nothing if not an impetuous, unbridled tyrant, and the break with Rome removed the only significant check on his will. The power of the nobles was broken, while Parliament, although represented by Hume's whiggish contemporaries as the always vigilant protector of English liberty, could scarcely have been more obsequious: the king was given the title of 'the only supreme *head* on earth of the church of England', and acknowledged to have the 'inherent power, "to visit, and repress, redress, reform, order, correct, restrain, or amend all errors, heresies, abuses, offences, contempts, and enormities, which fell under any spiritual authority, or jurisdiction"'. Nor did Parliament neglect to assign or confirm a like authority in secular matters. As a consequence, says Hume, no monarch in Europe had such absolute authority, while the English themselves 'were so thoroughly subdued, that like eastern slaves they were inclined to admire those acts of violence and tyranny which were exercised . . . at their own expence'. (11a: XXX; XXXIII.)

Hume does not soften his criticisms of Henry. The latter was a despot, and his despotic imposition of his erratic, inconsistent religious beliefs was the source of great injustice and suffering. But the canker of superstition required remedy, however painful. Uniting the spiritual and the civil domains, now that the King's supremacy in all matters was acknowledged, eliminated disputes regarding the limits of what had been contending domains. It was this supremely authoritarian arrangement that made it possible to check the excesses of superstition, to break 'those shackles by which all human reason, policy, and industry had so long been encumbered'. The King, although now head of the religious as well as the civil establishment, might well use the former for purely political purposes, but he had 'no interest, like the Roman pontiff, in nourishing its excessive growth'. This point was amply illustrated by Henry, who, though indistinguishable from the clergy in his zeal to maintain purity of belief (and thus to persecute those who disagreed with his beliefs), happily went about 'plundering the church'. Insofar as this resulted in the appropriation of monastic wealth and the closing of some 650 monasteries and convents, Hume expresses few regrets. Personal hardships resulted, but the best that can be said of these institutions is that they had helped to preserve and invent 'the dreaming and captious philosophy of the schools'. Far from producing useful, humane, or even elegant learning, they had perpetrated pious frauds and the factious quarrels of ignorance, and Henry's despoliation of them can be justified as a necessary step on the road to a freer society. (11a: XXXII; XXXI.)

The principal events of the Reformation occurred two centuries before Hume's birth, but its effects on him were far from remote. The Scottish Reformation, the English Civil War, the Commonwealth, the Glorious Revolution of 1688—these events were close to hand, as close as long Calvinistic sermons, the Act of Union, and the Jacobean uprisings of 1715 and 1745. In Hume's lifetime, Catholic supersitition and countervailing Protestant enthusiasm were factors of consequence, but he early in life concluded that no form of religion could provide a sound foundation for morality and society. The problem was that virtually none of his contemporaries saw things in this light. They still clung to the notion that morality and society rest on religious belief. Hume, using the methods and materials provided by the revival of learning—and his own good sense—set out to demonstrate that morality has a firm but entirely secular foundation.

## PHILOSOPHICAL SETTING

The narrower philosophical context of Hume's moral theory was itself shaped by the revival of learning and the Reformation. The new natural philosophy was particularly challenging to theoretical moralists, for, if correct in its general outlines, this new account of nature would require philosophers to formulate a corresponding account of value. This may not have been apparent to Copernicus when, early in the 16th century, he circulated in manuscript his theory that the sun, not the earth, was at the centre of the universe. Nor even to Tycho Brahe, whose discovery in 1574 of a new star in the Milky Way—of a change where, as he realised, no change should be—constituted perhaps the earliest confirmation of the Copernican theory. But to Galileo and many of his readers—by the early 17th century—it must have been obvious that the scholastic theory of value was inadequate.[5]

Copernicus had implicitly challenged the comforting anthropocentrism of the old cosmology. Galileo and the telescope established that the heavens are no more perfect than the earth: there are spots on the sun, craters on the moon. His reports on falling weights led him to the principle of inertia, or to the claim that for earthly bodies rest is no more natural than motion. In doing so he presented a fundamental challenge to the widely held belief that a hierarchy of values is intrinsic to the natural world itself, and that every part of nature has an intrinsic purpose (*telos*) and natural place. Galileo also argued that nature could be genuinely understood—its effects actually predicted—by eliciting its mathematical structure, and he went on to suggest that 'real' existence pertains only to qualities of a mathematical sort. The remaining 'qualities' (if that is what we should call them), he argued, are without such real existence; they are only affections—merely subjective responses to which we have given names that enable them to masquerade as real things. Consequently, those qualities that are of the greatest interest to moral philosophers, qualities such as goodness or virtue, evil or vice, were in effect banished from the real world. In the Scholastic scheme of things fact and value had been so interrelated that moral qualities seemed to be as objective and real as any others. In the reconstructed metaphysics of the new natural philosophy it looked as though such qualities could be only epiphenomenal, mere affections of the mind.

Those who found the new natural philosophy compelling could adopt one of several alternative moral theories. The rigorous natural-

ism of Hobbes was one such alternative. Hobbes rejected the Scholastic tendency to explain the natural world in the anthropomorphic
terms of human psychology and valuation (appetite and perfection,
for example). Instead, he explained the moral and human world in
terms of a revived atomism; man himself is simply another part of the
physical world, while the physical world itself is constituted by nothing
but bodies in motion. In no part of this extended natural world are
there any qualitative distinctions of real substance. Gone from Hobbes'
philosophy, then, is a distinctively moral domain. There is no
*summum bonum*, there is no realm of independent and intersubjective
values or ends, there is no disinterested desire for the good of
another, there is no free, immaterial soul to direct man's impulses.
Man is a part of nature, and nothing more. The physiocentrism of
Hobbes' position is complete, and by its completeness intrinsic moral
character is eliminated from man and the world. Granted, Hobbes
allows for the apparently moral (always at bottom, however, a form
of self-regard), and he can speak of 'natural right' (of each to all) and
of the 'natural law' (our obligation to preserve ourselves), but there
is here no relenting from the reduction of value to fact. Granted, he
allows for a fundamental human goal, but this is simply the desire to
be able to continue to desire and to satisfy desire.[6] What philosophers
call morality is a mere appearance, and nothing more. (48: 21–6.)

There were many who disagreed with Hobbes' moral conclusions,
and for many reasons. Virtually no one, it seems, accepted the view
that humans are essentially neutral particles, directed entirely by
external influences and a formless desire of self-preservation. For
example, Samuel von Pufendorf, one of the most influential moralists
of the period, pursued the more traditional Augustinian line. We
have indeed a 'deeply planted self-love that constrains us to look
after ourselves', but there is more to it than that: 'For man was not
born for himself alone, but equipped with such remarkable endowments by the Creator, that he may glorify Him, and become a fit
member of human society.' But, despite these innate endowments
and the end they entail, man, in his universally fallen state, is not
inclined to orderly, law-abiding behaviour. Consequently, his well-
being, even his safety, lies in the formation of societies firmly regu-
lated by law and the superior power required to produce an obligation to obey this law. (54: 28–19.)

In contrast to both Hobbes and Pufendorf, Lord Shaftesbury and
Francis Hutcheson represented man in a much more optimistic light.
Self-interested we may be, but our selfish side is tempered by a

natural, untaught concern for the welfare of others. The weakness of humans in their infancy shows how necessary sociability is to mankind, but if society is in this fundamental way necessary, and consequently universal, it is appropriate, surely, to say that it is natural. Less abstractly, we daily witness actions—our own behaviour and that of others—which can only be explained on the supposition that individual humans have genuinely altruistic motivations. It is only an obvious perversion of this evidence that gives Hobbes' egoistical theory any appearance of credibility, while the human behaviour we actually witness shows that his theory must be false.[7] In contrast to Hobbes and Pufendorf, then, Shaftesbury and Hutcheson argue that man has a moral sense: an active disposition to benevolence, and, moreover, a capacity to distinguish the morally good from that which is indifferent or morally evil.

Shaftesbury and Hutcheson are often linked together as the leading members of a moral sense school, but there is one very significant difference between them. Hutcheson, like Pufendorf, was a voluntarist. That is, he supposed that the universe and the form of the entities making it up are the result of a free act of creation on the part of the deity. As in Hutcheson's view the creator is first and foremost a benevolent being, it happens that he has endowed man well: our moral sense does in fact recognise and approve what is morally good, but the deity could in theory have made us to give our moral approval to that which we now suppose to be vicious or evil. Only the fact of God's benevolence guarantees that our responses are not uniformly altered in this way.

Shaftesbury, on the other hand, seems to have grafted his version of the moral sense onto the stock of the Cambridge Platonists, a group that had resisted all forms of voluntarism and Hobbes' conventionalism as well. Ralph Cudworth, for example, forthrightly embraced the findings of the new natural philosophy, but he rejected Hobbes' view that there are entities, particularly human entities, without natures.[8] In contrast, Cudworth insists that even moral good and evil are real and immutable aspects of reality, a conclusion that requires us to see that our minds are not mere blank tablets, lacking all 'innate furniture and activity', and that the 'first original and source of all things' cannot have been matter. Rather, the source of all things is to be found in an immutable, eternal deity who is not only omnipotent, but wise and rational beyond measure. (28: 640–45.) Thus while the power of the deity permits him to create whatever he will, this power operates only within the constraints of his own intellect. As a consequence, every created entity has a nature or a form that makes it what it is and not something else. Correlatively, man has a nature and, thereby, an intrinsic or innate purpose to his existence. Moreover, the good that he attains by fulfilling this purpose is itself an objective, independently existing entity of a determinate nature, a good that not even the deity himself can alter. There may well be things that are not (relatively speaking) good, but there is no power in heaven or earth—not even God's will—that can so change the nature of things as to cause the good and the not-good to be indistinguishable. (48: 27–33.)

There were, then, fundamental differences between those moral philosophers who resisted Hobbes. However, nearly every moralist of the period agreed that morality is absolutely dependent on the deity. Hugo Grotius did ever so tentatively suggest that there would still be laws of nature even if there is no God, or none who is concerned with human affairs—that there could be, in effect, a society of atheists—but this suggestion was repudiated often and with alarm. In this regard, Pufendorf was typical. As we have seen, he says that a concern for one's own preservation is natural, and he even grants that a law of nature of a certain kind, a dictate of reason, may be deduced from this fact. But 'to give these Dictates of Reason the Force and Authority of Laws, there is a Necessity of supposing that there is a God, and that his wise Providence oversees and governs the whole World, and in a particular Manner the Lives and Affairs of Mankind'. The 'wicked and absurd Hypothesis' of atheism, should it be accepted, would leave us without moral law, for the 'Edicts of Reason' cannot 'rise so high as to pass into a Condition of Laws; in as much as all Law supposes a superior Power'. Later in the same work he insists that there is no innocent form of atheism, and even the suggestion that it could arise from simple ignorance or imprudence is said to be 'most foul and scandalous', for, although one cannot say that every illiterate person is able to form or even to comprehend a 'philosophical Demonstration of God's Existence', this deficiency cannot be supposed a reason for doubting or denying this existence. On the other hand, nothing of value can be expected from those who deny either the existence of God, his concern with human affairs, or the immortality of the soul.[9] An atheist will be motivated by nothing but private interest and advantage, and, since he does not believe in the divine punishment of infidelities, the promises and covenants he makes are of no more worth than those of any common criminal. (53: 141–42; 254–55.)[10]

Cudworth, although not as strident as Pufendorf and others, was equally concerned about atheism, so much so that his lengthy *True Intellectual System of the Universe*, is largely devoted to confutations of the several kinds of atheism Cudworth recognised. Near the end of the final chapter Cudworth undertakes to 'Unravel and Confute, all the Atheistick Ethics and Politicks' by making it clear that the 'Artificial and Factitious Justice of the Atheist, is nothing but Will and Words', and that the atheist provides for civil authority no foundation except that of force. In contrast, Cudworth seeks to show that justice and obligation are 'not Made by Law and Commands, but in Nature; and [to] Prove This, together with Conscience and Religion, to be the onely Basis of Civil Authority. . .'. (27: 890–99.)

We see then that Pufendorf and Cudworth and other like-minded anti-atheistical moralists insisted that morality is dependent on a belief in the existence of a deity actively concerned with the affairs of the world. They claimed that, if there is no such deity then there will be no genuine morality and they challenged the atheist to prove them wrong. As Pufendorf so very explicitly puts it, those with the effrontery to doubt the existence and providence of the deity must not only show that their atheism is more reasonable than the contrary and all but universal belief in God. They must also show that the atheistic hypothesis will be of greater benefit to mankind than is theism, a task said to be manifestly impossible because atheists are completely unreliable. Hume responded to this challenge by arguing that religion, especially in its monotheistic form, is detrimental to society—and even if it were not such a negative influence it would still be, at a fundamental level, irrelevant to morality because moral merit is essentially different from religious merit. He met the full force of Pufendorf's challenge, and he did so without joining with Hobbes in the claim that there is no foundation for morality in nature. Not satisfied simply to show that religion provides no adequate basis for morals, Hume went on to show how moral values can be derived from nothing more than human nature and the circumstances in which humans find themselves.

## THE *TREATISE OF HUMAN NATURE*

David Hume was attracted to philosophy at a very early age. In a brief autobiography he says that *A Treatise of Human Nature*, his longest and most important philosophical work, was projected before he was 20; this work was in print before he was 30. According to its subtitle, the *Treatise* is an attempt 'to introduce the experimental method of reasoning into moral subjects'. How much first-hand knowledge of the new natural philosophy (*science*, as we now call it) Hume had is an actively debated topic, but he clearly appreciated the empirical method championed by Francis Bacon and put to use by Boyle, Newton and others.

It was through the use of this experimental method—gleaning 'experiments from a cautious observation of human life'—that the *Treatise* was to provide us with a science of human nature itself. (1: xix.) Hume begins with the human understanding, in which he finds a fair amount of built-in furniture in the form of instincts and propensities, innate dispositions, we might call them, but he finds that these fail to provide us with that clear, distinct, and certain knowledge of things claimed by so many philosophers. We can, however, see how it is that our mind or understanding works, and how it is that we come to have those fundamental *beliefs* about things and their relations (that there are enduring objects and causal relations, for example) that we do in fact have.[11]

In the second book of the *Treatise* Hume gives an account of the passions and of the will. Here it will be noticed that Hume's views of pride and humility are diametrically different from those found in many Christian writers. For Hume, pride is an affective response (one of the indirect passions) to one's own positive characteristics or qualities, whether these be possessions, mental or physical abilities, or virtues. There is no suggestion that pride is to be avoided because it is one of the seven deadly sins, or even a minor sin. Indeed, in its normal manifestations, pride is a desirable and necessary form of what we would now call self-respect. Nor is humility, the complement of pride, to be sought. Hume elsewhere says that his view of the virtues derived from classical, rather than Christian, sources; it is equally true that his view of the passions is unorthodox.

Book II is also important for the account it offers of the will and its direction. Hume is perhaps most famous for his analysis of our idea of necessary connection or the causal relation. He here sums up this important analysis by noting that he has shown that it is never possible, in any 'single instance', to discover 'the ultimate connexion of any objects . . . either by our senses or reason, and that we can never penetrate so far into the essence and construction of bodies as to perceive the principle, on which their mutual influence depends'. It is, rather, from the 'uniform and regular conjunction' of one object

with another that the ideas of cause and effect and of necessary connection arise. Furthermore, the 'necessity which enters into that
idea [of cause and effect], is nothing but a determination of the mind
to pass from one object to its usual attendant'. (1: 400.)

To make a long story as short as possible, Hume approaches the
debate over the freedom of the will with this previous finding firmly
in mind. By the term *will*, he says, 'I mean nothing but *the internal
impression we feel and are conscious of, when we knowingly give rise to any
new motion of our body, or new perception of our mind*'. From this starting
point he can easily argue that the will, no less than any physical
object, is subject to causal influences; that is, the will is itself an
effect, an internal impression, while effects are related to causes
only, so far as our experience goes, through constant conjunction.
Thus if Hume can show, (1) that in 'the common course of human
affairs' there is discernible 'the same uniformity and regular operation
of natural principles' that is found in the physical world, and (2) that
this uniformity also determines us to expect an event to follow from
its usual attendant (determines us to *infer*, for example, that a particular kind of action will follow from a particular kind of motive),
then he will have shown that there is no freedom of the will, or 'liberty
of indifference', as many philosophers, and especially theologians,
have claimed. (1: 399–407.)

It may seem that Hume's views regarding the will and liberty
are destructive of traditional morality, especially when he goes
on to argue that 'reason alone can never be a motive to any action
of the will . . . [nor] oppose passion in the direction of the will'.
He himself anticipated this objection, and countered by saying that
the kind of neccessity he has described is 'so essential to religion
and morality, that without it there must ensue an absolute sub-
version of both'. It is the alternative view, the supposition that there
is liberty of indifference, that is 'entirely destructive of all laws both
*divine* and *human*'. Such laws depend on rewards and punishments,
and they presuppose that the rewards and punishments they prescribe function as motives—that they 'have an influence on the
mind, and both produce the good and prevent the evil actions'.
Morality presupposes, in short, that motives are necessarily related
to actions, or that moral causes are necessarily related to moral
effects, and Hume believes that his theory explains this necessity
without putting human actions on 'the same footing with the
operations of senseless matter'. Instead, he says, 'I ascribe to matter,
that intelligible quality, call it necessity or not, which the most

rigorous orthodoxy does or must allow to belong to the will.' (1: 413, 410.)

When in the third and final book of the *Treatise* Hume turns at last to morals *per se*, he takes up first what appears to be an epistemological question, namely, is it by reason or by sense that we distinguish between virtue and vice? That the issue so raised is not merely epistemological is suggested, however, by the fact that the entire discussion takes place under the heading, 'Of virtue and vice in general'. Hume does argue that moral distinctions are not derived from reason alone, but one of his principal grounds for reaching this conclusion is the fact that human reason is not capable of grasping the allegedly eternal and immutable realities and relations which Cudworth and others claim to be the foundation of morality. Human experience simply does not enable us to speak with any authority about the moral nature or moral experience of the deity or other higher beings, nor does our experience include any relationships that are both unchanging and distinctly moral. Deference of offspring to parent, for example, may be morally obligatory in some instances, and not so in others, just as obedience to a sovereign may be obligatory or foolish, depending on the circumstances. Moreover, we do not discover the moral qualities of agents and acts by direct inspection. Vice, unlike shape or size, is not a fact we come to know by means of the understanding or the ordinary senses, even though it is by these faculties that we come to know that one human being has intentionally killed another. On the contrary, moral qualities, virtue and vice, are only perceivable if we attend to our own reactions in those circumstances in which we aptly assign *virtue* and *vice* as moral predicates.[12]

In the next section of the *Treatise* Hume argues that moral distinctions are derived from sentiment or a moral sense. Many commentators have suggested that this means that Hume was an ethical subjectivist—that he means to say that by remarks of the form 'Arthur is virtuous' (morally good) or 'Arthur is vicious' (morally evil) we are reporting only our approval or disapproval of Arthur or his behaviour. Hume may on occasion appear to say things which would lead the unwary to this conclusion, but his position is considerably more sophisticated than such an interpretation suggests.

Suppose that, as a result of witnessing Arthur's behaviour, I have uttered the remark, 'Arthur is virtuous'. Notice first that if this remark means only that I *approve* of the behaviour in question, so that the remark is adequately translated as 'I approve of Arthur's behaviour', or 'I have positive and pleasant feelings as a result of witnessing Arthur's behaviour', then my remark will be true just in the case that I have the feeling that I have in this indirect fashion reported myself to have. If 'Arthur is virtuous' means that I have a positive feeling about Arthur, then, if I have a negative feeling about him, 'Arthur is virtuous' would be false, and 'Arthur is vicious' would be true.[13] Some philosophers have held this view (it is Hobbes' view of the meaning of evaluative terms in the state of nature), and some may even yet hold it, but it is inconsistent with a great deal of what Hume has to say. He says of virtue and vice, for example, that 'it must be by means of some impression or sentiment they occasion that we are able to mark the difference betwixt them', and then goes on to add, 'We do not infer a character to be virtuous because it pleases: But in feeling that it pleases after such a particular manner, we in effect feel that it is virtuous'. The first of these remarks suggests that the sentiments *caused* by virtue differ from those *caused* by vice, while the second indicates that there are recognisably different kinds of approvals (pleasing sentiments), and that one 'particular' kind of pleasure is linked with virtue in such a way that this particular pleasure can be taken as a sign that a virtuous action (and by extension, a virtuous motive or character) has been experienced. (1: 470–71.) In short, much of what Hume has to say supports some form of objectivist reading of his position.[14]

We can best understand the positive theory of the *Treatise* by taking a different tack. Hume supposed that some of his predecessors had denied that there is in nature itself any foundation for the moral distinctions we appear to make. Others, he saw, had said essentially the same thing insofar as they claimed that the moral distinctions we make are arbitrarily imposed on ourselves and nature by a superior power outside nature. In the language of Hume and his contemporaries, these philosophers had raised doubts about the *reality* of moral distinctions and moral qualities; they had in effect raised the question, *Does the distinction we draw between virtue and vice have any objective foundation, or is it a merely arbitrary imposition on an otherwise undifferentiated reality?*

As we have seen, Hobbes had argued that there is no objective foundation for the moral distinctions we appear to draw because all actions are motivated by self-interest, and hence are all fundamentally alike—they are all selfish. In the *Treatise* Hume is prepared to accept one premise of Hobbes' argument, that concerning the pre-eminence of motive in the determination of virtue.[15] He rejects as ill-founded, however, the further claim that all our motives are self-interested. Experience shows that humans sometimes also act from motives that are other-interested, or benevolent. In that event, it can be said that the distinction between virtue and vice is a natural or real distinction. An individual is virtuous if he or she acts from an other-interested motive, and vicious if he or she acts only from motives of heedless self-interest.

Hume did not, as did Shaftesbury, suppose that there is in human nature a virtually unlimited disposition to benevolence, but he does in the *Treatise* claim that there are 'natural virtues' such as beneficence, generosity and clemency which, although limited in their effectiveness, do have a tendency to the good of others. This fact alone shows that Hobbes and the other egoists are mistaken. In a later work he is even clearer. Speaking of Hobbes and Locke, who had 'maintained the selfish system of morals', Hume says the most obvious objection to this theory is that it does not conform to the obvious facts. To even

the most careless observer there appear to be such dispositions as benevolence and generosity; such affections as love, friendship, compassion, gratitude. These sentiments have their causes, effects, objects, and operations, marked by common language and observation, and plainly distinguished from those of the selfish passions. . . . Many able philosophers have shown the insufficiency of these systems. And I shall take for granted what, I believe, the smallest reflection will make evident to every impartial enquirer. (5: 296, 298.)[16]

Insofar, then, as Hume supposes that our moral distinctions are founded on genuine differences of motive, he can be taken to suppose that the distinctions have, in one important sense, an objective foundation. It must be emphasised, however, that he rejected all suggestions that these distinctions are in any way dependent on *a priori* reason or any extrahuman component. (1: 619; 5: 298.)

As a corollary of this position Hume presents us with a causal theory of moral perception. This is a theory according to which our passions, and not our understanding, provide us with particular impressions by means of which we are able to gain an awareness of moral characteristics (other-interested motives, for example) that exist independently of our perception of them, or objectively.[17]

According to Hume, our moral sentiments are *impressions of reflection*, or a kind of *perception* whose causal origins can be traced beyond *impressions of sensation* to, first, actions, and then to the moral qualities of agents themselves.[18] The 'moral deformity' of a particular action, he says, is discovered 'by means of some sentiment, which the reflecting on such an action naturally occasions'. As we have already seen, the sentiments or 'distinguishing impressions by which moral good or evil is known' are specific, even unique, pains and pleasures. It is also important to notice that these unique moral sentiments have unique moral causes. The moral sentiments are not aroused by inanimate objects or by animate but non-human beings. They arise only when we observe the actions produced by particular motives or sets of motives (durable principles of mind), or when we observe actions which we assume to have been produced by such causes. (1: 466, 471, 581, 589.)

Our moral sentiments are, then, affective responses to specific motives that exist as durable principles of mind, and that 'must necessarily be plac'd either in ourselves or others'. (1: 473.) The feelings to which these durable principles give rise are the unique moral sentiments. Consequently (assuming the correctness of the theory Hume offers), the experience of a unique moral sentiment is direct evidence that there are in ourselves or others distinctive and causally effective characteristics. It is in this sense that Hume gives a positive response to the question, *Does the distinction we draw between virtue and vice have any objective foundation?* For Hume our moral distinctions do have an objective foundation. He did think Marcus Brutus was genuinely virtuous, and that Nero was genuinely vicious, and that the same distinctions mark, in greater or lesser degrees, other human beings. However, it is important to note that his explanation of this distinction eschews every trace of Platonism, rationalism, and supernaturalism. It is a part of the natural world itself, human nature and only human nature, that provides a foundation for such empirically respectable moral distinctions.[19]


## AN ENQUIRY CONCERNING THE PRINCIPLES OF MORALS

Hume was not satisfied with his performance in the *Treatise*, and some years later began, as he put it, to 'cast anew' the materials of the earlier work. In 1748 he published *Philosophical Essays concerning Human Understanding* (later retitled *An Enquiry concerning Human Understanding*). This was followed in 1751 by *An Enquiry concerning the Principles of Morals*. Between 1741 and 1757 Hume also published four volumes of moral, political and literary essays, the final volume of which included *A Dissertation on the Passions* and *The Natural History of Religion*. From 1754 to 1762 he published the six-volume *History of England* discussed above. Of all his writings Hume thought his second *Enquiry* 'incomparably the best'. It is reasonable then, that this work often serves as an introduction to his theory of morals, but as it is both shorter, and less abstract than Book 3 of the *Treatise*, some of the interesting discussions of the earlier work—most notably those concerning moral perception and the role of sympathy—are virtually omitted from the later one. (13: 3–4; 158.)

Hume begins the second *Enquiry* (as it is now commonly called) by remonstrating against those sceptical, or at least disingenuous, moralists who deny the reality of moral distinctions. It is even difficult to imagine, he suggests, a person so insensitive or benighted that he or she is unable to distinguish between right and wrong. There are differences between men that arise from nature, and further differences that arise from custom and education. No sceptic no matter how doubting, can sincerely maintain that there are absolutely no moral distinctions. Indeed, if we ignore these would-be sceptics, we find that they eventually give up their unconvincing claims and 'come over to the side of common sense and reason'. (5: 169–70.)[20]

There has been discussed of late, Hume goes on to say, an important question, that 'concerning the general foundation of Morals'. It has been argued—and Hume in the *Treatise* was obviously a party to this argument—that our moral distinctions derive either from reason or from sentiment. Here Hume suggests that there are sound arguments to support both positions, and thus that in the end we will find that reason and sentiment concur in most of our moral conclusions. Although he does not explicitly say so, it appears that Hume adopts this placating attitude because he thinks that the debate over reason and sentiment is at least partially misguided. The answer to the question regarding the general foundation or 'true origin of morals' is to be found by less abstract considerations, and when that answer has been found out the respective roles of reason and sentiment will be readily apparent. (5: 170–73.)

In the meantime Hume proposes to follow what he considers 'a very simple method'. He will 'analyze that complication of mental qualities, which form what, in common life, we call Personal Merit'. He will, that is, survey those mental qualities, the possession of which causes us to praise or blame the possessor. Such an analysis should be relatively easy to complete, for language itself 'guides us almost infallibly' in forming our judgements of the matter, as every language includes a set of terms by which we express such praise or blame. All that we need is to discover the circumstances which govern the use of these terms—to discover the common feature(s) of the qualities that are esteemed, on the one hand, or thought to be reproachable, on the other. 'As this is a question of fact, not of abstract sciences', success can be expected provided only that we follow the 'experimental method [of] deducing general maxims from a comparison of particular instances'. (5: 173–74.)

The particular instances on which Hume first focuses are those relating to two social virtues, benevolence and justice. It is obvious, he says, that our benevolent qualities are esteemed. To say of a person that he or she is *sociable, good-natured, humane, merciful, grateful, friendly, generous*, or the equivalent is to 'express the highest merit, which *human nature* is capable of attaining'. It is equally obvious, he suggests, that these qualities are esteemed because of 'their tendency to promote the interests of our species, and bestow happiness on human society'. The *usefulness* of these forms of benevolence is at least a necessary condition of the esteem we give to them, a conclusion that is confirmed by the fact that, once acts of a particular type cease to be useful, they cease to be esteemed. (5: 176–82.)

Hume's analysis of justice and four related virtues—allegiance, veracity, fidelity, and chastity—shows these to be slightly different from benevolence and its cognates. Justice and the virtues like it are not merely useful; their origin can be traced *entirely* to their general usefulness, and the praise we give them derives entirely from our recognition of their beneficial consequences.[21] These virtues depend for their existence on the particular circumstances of mankind. Alter these conditions—provide a profuse abundance of all we need, or make such items so scarce as to defy an adequate share to all who have need—and the foundation of justice would be wiped away. Had one of these conditions prevailed at the beginning of society, the rules for the distribution of property would never have arisen; should one prevail in the future, our present rules, proving useless, would atrophy, disappear. It is in this sense, then, that 'the necessity of justice to the support of society is the sole foundation of that virtue', and it is this 'circumstance of usefulness' that causes us to praise those actions and qualities that contribute to a well-ordered society. (5: 183–204.)

Why, Hume goes on to ask, does utility please—why is it that we esteem those qualities that are beneficial to society? Before answering the question he notes that it does not concern inanimate objects. We obviously find many such objects to be useful, but that is no reason to suppose that we are to call them *virtuous*, nor do we, except in odd, non-moral ways, attribute virtues to them: 'the sentiments, excited by utility, are, in the two cases, very different'. Those sentiments directed towards 'thinking rational beings' include esteem or approbation, while the sentiments directed towards mere things are clearly not the same. Our concern, then, is with our approbation of those distinctly human acts that benefit (or harm) man and society. (5: 213n.)

Hume supposes that two answers have been given to his question, Why does utility please? Some have said that acts useful to society receive our approbation because, and only because, we see them as benefiting ourselves personally. Others believe that these acts receive our approbation on some or even many occasions because, although they give us no personal benefit, they are recognised as beneficial to others. Hume again aligns himself with the second group. He grants that human nature is marked by a strong tendency towards self-interest, and that the claim that we support the principles of morality and social order out of self-love or private regard has creditable supporters, but he goes on to argue that the selfish theory is quite unable to account for crucial aspects of our experience, and hence cannot be correct. (5: 214–15.)

There is first the fact that we have and competently use moral language itself. Some of the moral sceptics have argued that our moral vocabulary owes its origin to skilful manipulators who, wanting to control the less sophisticated, invented a moral vocabulary and its use. According to this theory, while it is true that there are such terms as *virtue* and *vice*, *honour* and *dishonour*, *bravery* and *cowardice*, *chastity* and *infidelity*, these mark no real differences in things (actions or characters) themselves, and the use of the terms derives entirely from artifice and custom. Hume finds this claim less than credible, analogous, one might say, to the claim that, although there is absolutely no objective foundation for the discriminations of colour we do in fact make, one could nonetheless teach a race of sightless creatures to use, competently, the terms *blue*, *green*, *red*, *yellow*, *white*, *black*, and so on. Or, as he more directly puts it: 'Had nature made no such [moral] distinction, founded on the original constitution of the mind, the words, *honourable* and *shameful*, *lovely* and *odious*, *noble* and *despicable*, had never had place in any language; nor could politicians, had they invented these terms, ever have been able to render them intelligible, or make them convey any idea to the audience'. (5:214.)

The more common claim of the selfish theorists is that we approve the social virtues only because we ourselves are dependent on society, and thus have an interest in their promulgation and observance. Take away that interest, the theory runs, and you remove the support and the approbation given these virtues. Here Hume echoes Francis Hutcheson in arguing that the facts contradict the egoist's claim: We very often, he says, 'bestow praise on virtuous action, performed in very distant ages and remote countries', and by no stretch of the imagination can these approbations be accounted for by self-interest or be supposed to have any connection to our present well-being. By the same token, we may recognise as virtuous the act of an enemy despite the fact that this act is at the same time seen to be contrary to our interest. Private interest may often enough combine with public, and support the same ends and assessments, but there is more than that to the matter. Our approbation goes beyond our own interest to 'the interest of those, who are served by the character or action approved of', or to the interests of our fellow men, which, 'however remote, are not totally indifferent to us'. Hume supposes that he has here carried out a Baconian *experimentum crucis*, or an experiment that eliminates 'any doubt or ambiguity'. The selfish hypothesis maintains that public interest or benevolence can always be reduced to private interest. He believes that he has shown us 'instances, in which private interest was separate from public; in which it was even contrary', and yet those involved performed the *publicly* interested act. On other occasions, he finds, private and public interests concur, and thereby work together to produce a regard for virtue greater than that which would have been produced by self-interest alone. 'Compelled by these instances', he concludes, 'we must renounce the theory, which accounts for every moral sentiment by the principle of self-love.' (5: 215–19.)[22]

In the following sections of the *Enquiry* Hume focuses his attention on some of the non-social virtues, and thereby expands his account of the qualities that constitute personal merit in such a way that the claims of the selfish theory are further weakened. In Section VI he takes up those qualities which, while useful to their possessors, and approved of by those others who recognise them, are of no benefit to these approving non-possessors. Such qualities as discretion, industry, frugality, prudence, and discernment (the 'selfish virtues') tend only to the usefulness of their possessors, and yet we praise them and their possessors, a fact entirely inexplicable by the selfish hypothesis. Section VII treats of qualities immediately agreeable to ourselves, and Section VIII of those immediately agreeable to others. It is important to note that to each of these last two kinds of qualities our response is immediate. Thus, prior to any calculation regarding usefulness or useful tendencies, we praise such qualities as cheerfulness, greatness of mind, dignity and tranquillity, or wit, politeness, eloquence, decency and cleanliness. These qualities are approved of by those who observe them in others, and even those who only hear of a person endowed with such qualities find themselves responding with approbation. (5: 233–67.)

Although Hume suggests that these conclusions may have a certain *philosophical* novelty, it is difficult for him to resist the view that they are obvious and obviously correct. It is surely surprising, he says, that anyone would think it necessary to prove that 'Personal merit consists altogether in the possession of mental qualities, *useful* or *agreeable* to the *person himself* or to others'. Fortunately, although 'systems and hypotheses have perverted our natural understanding', or at least those of philosophers, ordinary individuals accept implicitly the view of merit that has been sketched. There is, however, a problem. It must be shown how this finding, obvious and important though it may be, provides us with a *foundation* for morality, assuming, as Hume himself appears to assume, that a further step must be taken to reach or understand this fundamental point. (5: 268–70.)

Hume's final point of departure in the *Enquiry* is the factual concomitant of the account of personal merit that he has completed. Humans are not entirely selfish creatures: 'there is some benevolence, however small, infused into our bosom; some spark of friendship for the human kind'. These altruistic or generous sentiments, however weak they may be, are at least sufficiently strong to lead us to prefer that which is 'useful and serviceable to mankind, above what is pernicious and dangerous'. (5: 271.) Moral distinctions are founded on this one fact, the fact that we have a sentiment of humanity, or that we desire, even weakly, what is beneficial for our fellow humans. The presence of this sentiment means that we respond with approval or disapproval to certain actions or qualities that we experience others to have. There are genuine and significant differences between characters and the actions resulting from them.

Some are beneficial to mankind, and some are pernicious. Witnessing these actions and characters, we respond with approbation or disapprobation, and in doing so we make *moral distinctions*, and call actions or characters resulting in public benefit *morally good*, and those intending injury *morally evil*.

This way of putting the matter is, Hume points out immediately, too general. It is not enough that we respond to the actions and characters of others with approval or disapproval. Some responses, those directed by the passions of avarice, ambition, vanity and the like, 'are here excluded from our theory concerning the origin of morals' because they 'have not a proper direction for that purpose'. The very idea of morality presupposes both a 'sentiment common to all mankind, which recommends the same object to general approbation', and a sentiment 'so universal and comprehensive' as to extend even to those persons the most remote from any given moral assessor. Hume's formulation of this point does not permit one to be sure that he means here to speak of two distinguishable sentiments, or merely of 'two requisite circumstances' that are specifically different. But whether we have sentiments of one kind or two, these sentiments derive from a single constitutive principle of human nature, or what Hume calls a 'universal principle of the human frame'. It is this *principle of humanity*, he says, that 'can alone be the foundation of morals', and he adds that the sentiments that derive from this principle: (1) are the same for all humans; (2) produce in each of us the same moral assessments; (3) have as their scope all humans; (4) produce moral assessments, in each of us, of all other humans. (5: 271–73.)[23]

If in all this Hume seems to presage the concern with universalisability that has been a prominent feature of ethics since Kant, he also seems to echo his own *Treatise*, where he insists that only the judicious or impartial observer can expect to experience *moral* sentiments, and also the writings of Shaftesbury, where one finds the suggestion that mankind is characterised by a *sensus communis* or sense of commonality and community. From each of these perspectives the second *Enquiry* is found to contain a positive, commonsensical theory of morals. It does seem, however, that Hume has significantly underestimated the difficulty we would have in isolating our precisely moral sentiments from those arising from self-interest, given what we can only suppose to be *our* more realistic and sophisticated understanding of the way that interest affects perception. Two centuries later we find it difficult to credit his claim that this distinction is 'so great and evident' that language itself is moulded by it, thus permitting us to 'express those universal sentiments of censure or approbation which arise from humanity' and for 'Virtue and Vice [to] become then known'. We are more likely to notice that the assurance Hume confessed to gave way to doubt. The natural philosophers, he notes, have measured the earth, accounted for the tides, ordered the heavens, and even calculated the infinite, and yet there is still dispute regarding the foundation of morals. 'When I reflect on this', he says, 'I fall back into diffidence and scepticism, and suspect that an hypothesis, so obvious, had it been a true one, would, long ere now, have been received by the unanimous suffrage and consent of mankind.' (5: 274–78.) It is surely relevant to remind ourselves, however, that Hume had enough confidence in his con-clusions to republish them regularly after 1751 until the time of his death, and that it was just before his death that he said that of all his works the *Enquiry concerning the Principles of Morals* seemed to him the best. This mixture of doubt and confidence is typical of Hume.

## THE NATURAL HISTORY OF RELIGION

Before sending his *Treatise of Human Nature* to press Hume syste-matically altered it so that it would 'give as little offense as possible' to the religiously orthodox. (13: 25, 34.) On this matter of prudence he was in one sense successful, for his most explicit expressions of *religious* scepticism are found only in his subsequent works. So far as Hume's ethical views are concerned, it is only in his *Natural History of Religion* that the full force of his response to the theistic moralists can be seen.

Pufendorf, Cudworth, and others, it will be recalled, had thoroughly denigrated the atheist, insisting that such an unbeliever was no better than a common thief, and that without the cement of religion society would be entirely impossible. Pierre Bayle (and, under Bayle's influence, Shaftesbury) responded to this view by suggesting that, although there seemed never to have been a society of atheists, such a society was possible.[24]

Hume, having reflected on the effects of religion on society, took a significantly more aggressive stance: there could be—indeed had been—societies of atheists, and these societies would have been—and were—*morally superior to Christian societies*. Religion is not the cement of social order, but the catalyst of social disorder. Furthermore, it is simply not the case that religion makes morality possible; on the contrary, religion, at least in its monotheistic form, makes morality impossible.

The *Natural History of Religion* (1757) was originally intended to appear in a volume entitled *Five Dissertations*, along with, most relevantly for this discussion, Hume's essays on the immortality of the soul and suicide. For reasons of prudence Hume withdrew the essays which suggested that we are, after all, only mortal, and that suicide is not immoral. But, although he modified slightly the *Natural History*, his critics were far from mollified, and criticised Hume for attempting 'to establish *naturalism*, a species of atheism, instead of religion'.[25]

Hume's concern in this work is with 'the origin of religion in human nature'. There seem to have been, he says, some nations or peoples who have 'entertained no sentiment of Religion', while among those who do have such sentiments there are very great differences of opinion: 'no two nations, and scarce any two men, have ever agreed precisely in the same [religious] sentiments'. Given these facts, it cannot be said that our religious conceptions are the effect of any 'original instinct or primary impression of nature'. They are not on a par with 'self-love, affection between the sexes, love of progeny, gratitude, [or] resentment', for the effects of these have been found to be 'absolutely universal in all nations and ages', and each such underlying instinct is seen to have 'always a precise determinate object, which it inflexibly pursues'. Religious belief must, therefore, derive from secondary principles, or principles of a sort that may be perverted or even altogether prevented by various accidents and causes. (9: 309–10.)

Polytheism or idolatry, Hume says, 'was, and necessarily must have been, the first and most ancient religion of mankind'. The historical facts support this contention, and so does the logic of development. We can as easily imagine that men lived in palaces before they occupied huts, as to believe that they first conceived of the deity as 'a pure spirit, omniscient, omnipotent, and omnipresent', before they took him to be 'a powerful, though limited being, with human passions and appetites, limbs and organs'. The human mind simply does not work in that way; rather, it rises gradually from the inferior to the superior. (9: 310–11.)

But what led men to frame any kind of religious hypothesis? It was not the contemplation of the works of nature as constituting a smoothly functioning whole in which every part is well-adjusted to contribute towards the completion of a well-designed plan. Primitive man did not see nature as such a whole. On the contrary, nature, if it was noticed at all, was seen as broken and mysterious, and the events of life and nature were viewed with puzzlement, with ignorance and with, most of all, fear. The seemingly inexplicable events of nature came to be understood as the province of some petty or awesome power(s), presumably intelligent, and able to be propitiated. The principles of human nature on which religion is founded are, then, the 'ordinary affections of human life; the anxious concern for happiness, the dread of future misery, the terror of death, the thirst of revenge, the appetite for food and other necessaries'. (9: 313–16.)

Man is perpetually suspended between 'life and death, health and sickness, plenty and want', conditions that are 'distributed amongst the human species by secret and unknown causes'. In this condition, we focus on these unknown causes, and while they are the object of our hopes and fears, while our passions keep us in a state of constant alarm, our imagination forms for us ideas of those powers on which our being seems to depend. These secret and unknown causes are personified—they are given 'thought and reason and passion, and sometimes even the limbs and figures of men'. Moreover, it was not only primitive man that was led to a belief in deities by the disorder of his circumstances. The same disorder underlies the beliefs in a supreme providence found among more civilised peoples. The religious opinions of modern man, like those of his ancestors, are based on 'irrational and superstitious principles', and it is these very same principles that have transformed polytheism into theism. (9: 316–17, 328–30.)

But, although the origin of theism can be traced to polytheism, it does not follow that there are no genuinely important differences between theism and polytheism. When Hume compares these two forms of religion, he finds that polytheism has the disadvantage of appearing so flexible in its tenets that there is no practice or opinion that it could not support; on the other hand it has the advantage that it is, by its very nature, highly tolerant of diversity. Theism has the contrary advantages and disadvantages, but appears to come off a poor second just because of its natural tendency towards intolerance. Theism might by some be expected to provide the finest examples of justice and benevolence, but in fact it is no example at all for its sects 'fall naturally into animosity, and mutually discharge on each other that sacred zeal and rancour, the most furious and implacable of all human passions'. Furthermore, because it represents the deity as infinitely superior to mankind, and is at the same time joined with 'superstitious terrors', theism debases mankind by representing 'the monkish virtues of mortification, penance, humility, and passive suffering, as the only qualities which are acceptable' to the deity. In contrast, the deities of polytheism are so very human themselves that they offer us the real possibility of emulating or even rivalling them. Consequently, polytheism encourages those genuine virtues that improve mankind, while theism is a danger to philosophy and learning, or to the liberalising arts. (9: 336–39.)

On each point of comparison, then, Hume finds polytheism superior to monotheism. In view of this finding, it is all the more significant that he has already argued that polytheism is, when all is said and done, *a form of atheism*. There is, Hume had argued, only an insignificant difference between the atheist who says there is no 'invisible, intelligent power in the world', and the polytheist who posits a bevy of deities practically indistinguishable from such quasi-material beings as elves and fairies. In contrast, the difference between the polytheist and the genuine theist is enormous, despite the fact that our language leads us to treat the two positions as similar. It is 'a fallacy', Hume writes, 'merely from the casual resemblance of names, without any conformity of meaning, to rank such opposite opinions under the same denomination'. And he goes on to conclude that 'These pretended religionists [the polytheists] are really a kind of superstitious atheists, and acknowledge no being, that corresponds to our idea of a deity. No first principle of mind or thought: No supreme government and administration: No divine contrivance or intention in the fabric of the world'. (9: 320.) In short, Hume finds that so far as several crucial social virtues are concerned, polytheism is demonstrably superior to monotheism, while in general the morals of polytheists are necessarily less corrupt that those of the theists.[26] But if polytheism is morally superior to monotheism, and yet polytheism and atheism are essentially one and the same, then one can equally well conclude *that atheism is morally superior to monotheism*.

Hume was not content, however, to argue the practical superiority of atheism over theism. He wanted also to complete a demonstration that would show that no form of theistic or transcendental ethics can be valid. To see how this is so we need to review briefly some of his other claims about religion or religious knowledge.

In Book 3 of the *Treatise*, it will be recalled, Hume argues that the rationalists' moral theory fails for want of the *possibility* of knowledge regarding the deity and the posited eternal and immutable relations. Those who maintain an abstract rational difference between moral good and evil, he writes, suppose not only that these relations are eternal and immutable, but also that their effects must necessarily be always the same, and thus that they 'have no less, or rather a greater, influence in directing the will of the deity, than in governing the rational and virtuous of our own species'. But, he goes on, it is one thing to know virtue, and quite another to conform the will to it. These are distinct particulars. Consequently, in order to prove, 'that the measures of right and wrong are eternal laws, *obligatory* on every rational mind' one would have to prove that the pretended connection between these (allegedly) eternal relations and the will is an absolutely invariable connection, or is 'so necessary, that in every well-disposed mind, it must take place and have its influence'. No such proof is possible. Our knowledge in the domain of morals is subject to the very limitations that mark the rest of our knowledge. No matter what our subject, we are unable to go beyond experience. Furthermore, just as our experience in natural philosophy and (as we now might say) philosophy of mind or psychology fails to provide knowledge of a deity whose operations solve metaphysical or epistemological problems, so does it fail in morals. In consequence, efforts to found morality on the abstract notions of the deity or a set of abstract relations are bound to fail. (1: 465–66.)[27]

Of course, many 18th-century philosophers and theologians were dissatisfied with abstract proofs of God's existence and providential concern. For these believers, proofs with greater empirical content were preferred, and seemed to be available. The order or design of the universe, for example, was taken to demonstrate that the universe has not merely a cause, but a cause possessed of the great intelligence and providential concern required to create so well-organised a product. On the other hand, the occurrence of miracles was thought to show that a divine and powerful Providence actively oversees the affairs of mankind.

Against these presumably empirical evidences of divine providence Hume levelled philosophically devastating attacks. The very concept of *miracle*, he pointed out, is incoherent when defined as a violation of a law of nature, for a law of nature is constituted of uniform experience. If there is a violation of that experience there is from that point no law. Further, had we ever a proof of a miracle as perfect as the proof of the law of nature allegedly violated, we would then at best have proof against proof, and be left without a foundation for belief. In fact, finally, the evidence for any given miracle can never amount to anything like a proof for such evidence is necessarily tainted. (5: 109–31 ['Of Miracles'].)

The argument from design is equally inadequate. The major premise of that argument alleges that the universe is wonderfully well designed. A second, less biased look, suggests that the universe includes a good deal of evil as well as of good, and thus taken as a whole, presents us with a mixed bag of evidence. The minor premise, that order can arise only from designing intelligence, is also suspect. But even granting these premises, the argument as presented must be rejected as invalid. A conclusion stating that the universe as experienced must have some cause or causes aptly called *intelligent* in some sense of that term, would follow from the premises. But the conclusion of the theist—that the universe is the work of a divinely perfect and providentially concerned Creator—does not follow. Neither the premises nor the facts justify a conclusion so pregnant with human significance. (5: 132–48; 12: *passim.*)

Step by step, then, Hume addressed himself to the possible religious foundations of morality. Rational theology, however elegant, has no foothold in reality. Empirical theology is either incoherent or inconclusive. Consequently, neither of these forms of theology can provide a sound foundation for morality. There is, however, a further religious alternative. There is revealed truth, the *ipse dixit* of the deity himself. That surely is beyond criticism. How could a mere philosopher cast doubt on truths imparted to us in this unique manner? What can a man say in response to the claim of divine revelation?

Directly, very little, Hume seems on occasion to grant.[28] But those theists who claim that *right* is right if and only if God says that it is, and because he says it is, and that *wrong* is wrong for the same reasons—who hold what is often called the divine command theory— put a different face on the matter and open their allegedly revealed truth to criticism. Nor is this criticism due simply to the fact that polytheists/atheists are morally superior to theists, or to the fact that what the deity does and commands often appears to us to be immoral. Rather, Hume rejects the divine command theory on the grounds that it is not, after all, a theory of *morality*. As a mere philosopher he is unable to prove the falsity of allegedly revealed truths, but he can show that these truths fail in one of the more important uses to which they are put, that of providing a foundation for morals.

Suppose, Hume says, someone founded a religion in which it were expressly declared that nothing but virtuous behaviour could gain the approbation of the deity, and even that this religion were served by an order of priests or clerics themselves entirely satisfied to do nothing more than to teach this opinion through daily sermons. So 'inveterate are the people's prejudices', he continues, 'that, for want of some other superstition, they would make the very attendance on these sermons the essentials of religion', thus substituting certain ritualistic acts for those of genuine virtue. The difficulty is, it seems, that men simply cannot bring themselves to accept that the best means of serving the deity is 'by promoting the happiness of his creatures'. On the contrary, because of the terrors with which they are haunted, men 'seek the divine favour, not by virtue and good morals, which alone can be acceptable to a perfect being, but either by frivolous observances, by intemperate zeal, by rapturous extasies or by the belief of mysterious and absurd opinions'. Religion thus leads mankind to eschew the practice of virtue, and to take up in its stead one or another practice 'which either serves to no purpose in life, or offers the strongest violence to [man's] natural inclinations'. Just because the practice is useless it is thought to be the 'more purely religious'. What, after all, could be a surer proof of devotion than to perform austere and bizarre acts that can have no purpose other than the expression of this very devotion? (9: 357–59.)

Two features of Hume's view emerge from his analysis. First, the *practice of religion* and the *practice of virtue* run along paths not merely separate, but entirely divergent. Religious acts are motivated by a kind of heedless self-interest and make no contribution to society or to individuals as members of society, and for that reason cannot be acts of virtue. Virtuous acts, on the other hand, are typically done from a regard for the interests of others, and do benefit society and its members. A man who courts divine favour in order to secure 'protection and safety in this world, and eternal happiness in the next', is not virtuous; he is simply selfish. Moreover, the practice of religion does itself lead men to neglect, even to repudiate, the practice of virtue. In his concern to distinguish himself before his deity, in his concern to focus the divine attention on himself, the religious man far too often succumbs to the temptation to commit what are nothing less than immoral acts: 'the greatest crimes have been found, in many instances, [to be] compatible with a superstitious piety and devotion: Hence, it is justly regarded as unsafe to draw any certain inference in favour of a man's morals, from the fervour or strictness of his religious exercises, even though he himself believe them sincere'. (9: 359; see also 12: 76.)

Hume amplifies his rejection of the claim that the fear of punishment and the hope of reward may be motives to virtue in two now predictable ways. First, he rejects the suggestion, found in Pufendorf and others, that we are motivated only by self-interest. In this respect Hume's criticisms of Hobbes, Locke and Mandeville serve a double role, as does his own (so he believed) fuller and more accurate account of human nature.

The overall effect is to show that fear is far from being the only passion capable of motivating us to action; that is, Hume surveys human nature and human behaviour and concludes that we are in fact motivated by a number of passions, including a limited but entirely natural (instinctive, uninstructed) generosity. Consequently, there is no reason to suppose that it is only by adding fear to the mixture that men can be motivated to keep rules or (what is *not* the same thing) to act virtuously. Even if, *contrary to fact*, virtue could be motivated by fear, it would not *necessarily* be motivated by fear. Because men are motivated by several passions other than fear, morality simply is not dependent on whatever it is that is said to be attained—a motivation or a sanction—by positing a divine and threatening lawgiver.

Secondly, if Hume's general account of the relationship between virtue and motivation is correct, it cannot ever be the case that it is *only* the fear of punishment or the hope of reward that motivates us to virtuous acts.[29] According to Hume, we assign moral blame to a person for not performing an action because we suppose that an individual in the circumstances this person was in 'shou'd be influenc'd by the proper motive of that action'. But if we then find that this proper motive was in fact present and operating, but that its influence was prevented by circumstances unknown to us, we withdraw our ascription of blame, and may even assign moral praise. This shows that 'all virtuous actions derive their merit only from virtuous motives, and are consider'd merely as signs of those motives'. And from this principle he concludes further that the virtuous motive from which an action derives its moral merit 'can never be a regard to the virtue of that action'. The action does not *become* virtuous (more accurately: the action cannot rightly be *called virtuous*) until it is desired for some reason that itself causes the action to be called virtuous in the first place. This other reason 'must be some other natural motive or principle', and this other motive or principle, Hume goes on to argue, can never be heedless self-interest. The persons we call virtuous are sometimes, and regularly at that, motivated by a concern for the interests of others. Pursuing one's self-interest may be a natural and even a reasonable thing to do, but in Hume's view the man who is motivated solely by self-interest is not a virtuous man. (1: 477–78.) The important point here, obviously, is that the divine command theory is shown to be incoherent. It claims to give an account of the origin and nature of morality, but fails in the attempt because it fails to distinguish what it can explain, namely, self-interested and necessarily non-moral religious motives, from those motives that clearly are moral, the other-interested motives.

## CONCLUSION

In the course of this review of Hume's moral theory we have seen that he was concerned with origins. In this regard Hume is by no means unique, or even unusual; a case could be made for saying that tracing phenomena to their origin is the commonest form of explanation. But Hume was unusual in his time because of the firmness of his commitment to the view that all genuinely helpful explanation by means of origins must be carried out within the limitations set by observation and experience, so that all authentic investigations into the origins of phenomena are of the same form. He called only one of his works a *natural history*, but all his published writings seem to incorporate the fundamentals of this loosely defined Baconian genre, and exhibit an obvious interest in explaining phenomena by following them to their ultimate natural origins.

We must not underestimate, however, the importance of the qualification inherent in the phrase, 'ultimate *natural* origins'. In the Introduction to the *Treatise of Human Nature* Hume tells us that the sciences—mathematics, natural philosophy, natural religion, logic, morals, criticism and politics are mentioned—are related to human nature, and so much so that there is one fundamental science on which all others depend, namely, the science of human nature. He then goes on to say that this fundamental science must itself be built on a foundation of 'experience and observation', or on the same foundation as the new natural philosophy that had had such unparalleled success in the preceding hundred years. It seems evident, he says, that it is impossible for any science to go beyond experience.

The 'essence of the mind' is as unknown as that of bodies. Consequently, we must approach the study of the mind in just the way
that bodies have been studied: by 'careful and exact experiments,
and the observation of those particular effects, which result from its
different circumstances and situations'. We may still attempt 'to
render all our principles as universal as possible, by tracing up our
experiments to the utmost, and explaining all effects from the
simplest and fewest causes', but experience always sets the limit,
and thus 'any hypothesis, that pretends to discover the ultimate
original qualities of human nature, ought at first to be rejected as
presumptuous and chimerical'. Those who are vain enough to think
they can ignore this counsel will only bring themselves and others to
despair. Those who accept it will find themselves satisfied to undertake no more than that which can be accomplished, and may
actually add to our knowledge of human nature. (1: xv–xviii.)

Hume made a genuine effort to follow this advice. To his argument showing that we are not motivated by self-interest alone he
adds a note in which he says that it is

> needless to push our researches so far as to ask, why we have
> humanity or a fellow-feeling with others. It is sufficient, that this
> is experienced to be a principle in human nature. We must stop
> somewhere in our examination of causes; and there are, in every
> science, some general principles, beyond which we cannot hope
> to find any principle more general.

It is possible, but unlikely, he adds, that the principles to which
he has been led will 'be resolved into principles more simple and
universal', but as these possibly more ultimate principles are not
relevant to the discussion of personal merit, 'we may here safely
consider' humanity and fellow-feeling as the 'original' principles
of morals. In an Appendix to the same work he suggests that the
'ultimate ends of human actions can never . . . be accounted for by
*reason*', but are determined by our affections or sentiments. To
support this claim he suggests that if we ask a man why he exercises,
he will say that he wishes to remain healthy. If we ask him why he
wishes to be healthy, he will say that it is because sickness is painful.
If we go on and ask him why he wishes to avoid pain, he will find it
impossible to give a further reason: 'This is an ultimate end, and is
never referred to any other object'. Should we by a different set of
questions bring this man to say that he does or desires something

because it gives pleasure, he will again have reached an end of reasoning. One cannot go on asking 'Why?' *in infinitum*. 'Something must be desirable on its own account, and because of its immediate accord or agreement with human sentiment and affection.' The lesson here is that virtue is such an end, something 'desirable on its own account . . . merely for the immediate satisfaction which it conveys'. For this to be the case, there must be in human nature some sentiment or feeling 'or whatever you please to call it' which virtuous acts arouse and which 'distinguishes moral good and evil, and which embraces the one and rejects the other'. (5: 219–20, 293–94.)

There is no point, then, in carrying our researches higher. We know nothing of higher principles from which morality could be derived. Such principles are mere phantoms, while the reality is less grandiose, but much closer to hand: we *feel* a distinctive sentiment of approbation when exposed to an action done with the intent to benefit another; we *feel* a contrasting sentiment of disapprobation in response to an action done with malicious intent. In addition to our feeling of natural obligation (a sense of self-interest), we *feel* a moral obligation to act in certain ways, to perform what we by nature take to be our moral duties, but this moral obligation is not something imposed by a superior being (neither the deity nor the state), nor is it derived from rational principles. Obligations are not deduced by reason. They are, like moral distinctions, felt.

Briefly stated then, morality and the obligations of morality are facts of the human experience, and facts that derive from nothing more than the interaction of human beings (as they happen to be structured) with the rest of the world, particularly the human world. However sceptical Hume may otherwise have been, he was mildly optimistic about what man could do for himself. He did not suppose mankind an entirely benevolent species. He did not suppose that a completely enlightened society was imminent, or even a long-range prospect. But he did see evidence of some generosity, of some virtuous motives, and of some significant ability to engage in practical reasoning. It was on this foundation in human nature that he thought man had built a workable system of morality, a system both distinctively moral and open to further development. To those who say that a morality based on experience alone is no morality at all, Hume's answer is straightforward: we have no evidence to support the claim that morality involves beings other than human ones, and no evidence that there are any supranatural beings, or extra-experiential principles, standing by to help us out. Morality for Hume has been, and must continue to be, built upon human nature itself, upon that part of our nature which enables us to establish humane and beneficial ways of guiding our conduct.

# Notes

1. Works by the writers mentioned here are included in the Bibliography of this chapter. Subsequent references found in the text of the chapter are keyed to this Bibliography.
2. For information about Hume as historian, see items 7, 8, 10, and 11 in the Bibliography.
3. 'The rare happiness of times when you may think what you wish and say what you think.'
4. According to Hume, Alfred the Great complained that on his accession (c. 875) 'he knew not one person, south of the Thames, who could so much as interpret the Latin service'. This ignorance was to some extent a British phenomenon, and corrected by Alfred's example as well as by the continental scholars he invited to Britain, but Hume was firmly convinced that there had been a Dark Age, and that the gradual revival of learning had been instrumental in freeing Europe from paralysing religious superstition. (11a: II.)
5. For works providing an introduction to the scientific revolution and its impact on early modern philosophy, see the Bibliography, items 20, 38, and 60.
6. '. . . the felicity of this life, consisteth not in the repose of a mind satisfied. For there is no such *finus ultimus*, utmost aim, nor *summum bonum*, greatest good, as is spoken of in the books of the old moral philosophers. Nor can a man any more live, whose desires are at an end, than he, whose senses and imaginations are at a stand. Felicity is a continual progress of the desire, from one object to another; the attaining of the former, being still but the way to the latter. The cause whereof is, that the object of man's desire, is not to enjoy once only, and for one instant of time; but to assure for ever, the way of his future desire.' (33: 63.)
7. Hobbes was widely taken to have argued that each individual desires only personal pleasure or the avoidance of personal pain, and this was taken to be perhaps the most fundamental maxim of what was called the 'selfish theory'. Hutcheson and Joseph Butler challenged this maxim by pointing out that individuals more typically desire particular objects or states of affairs (the thirsty man desires water, the miser desires money or wealth, the parent desires the comfort of the child). If the desired (or intentional) object is obtained, this achievement and the object may well together give rise to pleasure, but it seemed clear to Hutcheson and Butler (and has seemed clear to many philosophers since them) that the selfish theory as stated is contradicted by the facts of experience, and is therefore false.
8. Hobbes is one of those philosophers, Cudworth writes, who do not hesitate 'to shake the foundations of all things, and to deny that there was any immutable nature . . . of anything, and by consequence any absolute certainty of truth or knowledge; maintaining this strange paradox, that both all being and knowledge was fantastical and relative

only, and therefore that nothing was good or evil, just or unjust, true or false, white or black, absolutely and immutably, but relatively to every private person's humour or opinion'. (28: 540–41.)

9. An atheist was taken to be a person who doubted the truth on any one of these three beliefs, which were taken to be *practically* equivalent.

10. Pufendorf writes: 'For 'tis impossible, but that Men of these Principles [atheists] should measure all Right and all Justice by their own Profit and Convenience. Into the same Herd we may pack all those who practise some Villany or Vice for their set Trade and Employment; as Pirates, Thieves, Murtherers, Pimps, Courtesans, and other profligate Wretches who take Perjury for a Trifle, and make a jest of sacred *Obligations*.' (53: 276.)

11. Characteristically, in an Appendix to the *Treatise* Hume admits that his account of one such belief, that of our own personal identity over time, is defective.

12. Hume ends this section of the *Treatise* (1: 469–70) with a remark about the derivation of *ought*-statements from *is*-statements. Whatever may be the correct interpretation of these important remarks, they have received disproportionate attention, and have been too often isolated from the larger context the *Treatise* provides. Rather than offer what could only be another controversial interpretation of these remarks themselves, I shall simply note that one inference commonly drawn from them—that Hume insists that the domains of fact and value are entirely distinct—may be difficult to square with the moral theory found in the remainder of the *Treatise* and in Hume's later writings. For 50 years of commentary on the passage in question, see the Index entry, '*Is* and *Ought*' in item 34.

13. An alternative form of subjectivism would have it that 'Arthur is virtuous' is an indirect way of reporting that 'Most people approve of Arthur's behaviour', or variations on such a more generalised understanding of moral assessments.

14. This *objectivist* reading of Hume is confirmed when he goes on to say that:

(1) Moral pleasure and pain arise only from signs of mental qualities or character: 'an inanimate object, and the character or sentiments of any person may, both of them, give satisfaction; but as the satisfaction is different, this keeps our sentiments concerning them from being confounded, and makes us ascribe virtue to the one, and not to the other'. In the same manner, we can distinguish the different kinds of feelings aroused by the different mental qualities of a person. (1: 472.)
(2) Only those characters and actions which we regard disinterestedly can evoke the kind of sentiment that leads us to say that particular actions are morally good or evil. We may *sometimes* confuse an *interested* sentiment for a *moral* sentiment, but a 'man of temper and judgment' can and does make such discriminations. (1: 472.)
(3) We can distinguish between the intensity of our moral sentiments, and the degree of virtue or vice that occasions these sentiments. Corrections for time or distance are made to the reports of the moral

sense just as they are to the reports of our other senses. (1: 580–82; see also 48: 108–20.)

15. 1: 477; see also pp. 479, 575:

> 'Tis evident, that when we praise any actions, we regard only the motives that produced them, and consider the actions as signs or indications of certain principles in the mind and temper. The external performance has no merit. We must look within [the actor] to find the moral quality. This we cannot do directly; and therefore fix our attention on actions, as on external signs. But these actions are still considered as signs; and the ultimate object of our praise and approbation is the motive, that produc'd them.

16. For a somewhat more detailed discussion of Hume's views on the egoism of these writers see item 48: 43–8.
17. Presumably such moral qualities could be situated in the very person who experiences the sentiments to which these qualities give rise. But it is not clear whether or not it is Hume's view that one could overlook one's own moral qualities.
18. For Hume, *perception* is a generic term for (at least) all objects of thought: 'All the perceptions of the human mind resolve themselves into two distinct kinds . . . IMPRESSIONS and IDEAS'. *Impressions of sensation* are original perceptions from which *ideas of sensation* derive, while *impressions of reflection* are a species of secondary impression that derive from *impressions of sensation* directly, or indirectly, by means of ideas. (1: 1, 275–76.)
19. The *Treatise* includes further discussions of a number of important topics (the artificial virtues, the natural virtues, the principle of sympathy, for example) which must be passed over here. For Hume's own brief but clear summary of the distinction between natural and artificial virtues see 3: 354–55; for his views on sympathy and its operation, see 1: 317–20, 353–65, and 574–91. For commentary on these topics see items 15, 39, 51, and 58 of the Bibliography.
20. Hume does not follow his own advice about ignoring the sceptical moralists. See, for example, 5: 242–44 and 295–96.
21. In the *Treatise* Hume called justice and the virtues like it *artificial* virtues, but that terminology is generally dropped from the second *Enquiry*.
22. Those tempted to think that this argument is easily overturned should bear in mind that Hume needs only a single counter-example to show the falsity of the claim that *all public interest derives from private interest.* Thus, showing that in particular cases public interest could or even does derive from private interest will not overcome Hume's criticism; to do that one must show that public interest does and must necessarily always derive from private interest. Moreover, Hume's claim about our ability to use moral language appears to raise an entirely separate issue, and to require entirely separate refutation.
23. Hume then adds: 'And every quality or action, of every human being, must, by this means, be ranked under some class or denomination, ex-

pressive of general censure or applause'. And: 'Whatever conduct gains my approbation, by touching my humanity, procures also the applause of all mankind, by affecting the same principle in them; but what serves my avarice or ambition pleases these passions in me alone, and affects not the avarice and ambition of the rest of mankind. There is no circumstance of conduct in any man, provided it have a beneficial tendency, that is not agreeable to my humanity, however remote the person'. (5: 273–74.)

24. For a fuller account of this debate, and of the role Bayle appears to have played, see item 49 of the Bibliography.

25. For an account of these events and the changes made in the *Natural History of Religion*, see 9: 60–4 and 47: 319–27, 691.

26. Monotheism leads necessarily to greater corruption just because it achieves the higher and purer theory. While the supposed extent of the deity's 'science and authority' increases, so do our 'terrors naturally augment'; the 'higher the deity is exalted in power and knowledge, the lower of course is he depressed in goodness and benevolence; whatever epithets of praise may be bestowed on him by his amazed adorers'. It is this conflict, Hume goes on to suggest, which is responsible for the unhealthy mental state of many theists: their opinion itself, he says, 'contracts a kind of falsehood, and belies the inward sentiment. The heart secretly detests such measures of cruel and implacable vengeance; but the judgment dares not but pronounce them perfect and adorable. And the additional misery of this inward struggle aggravates all the other terrors, by which these unhappy victims to superstition are for ever haunted'. (9: 354–55.)

27. Hume's argument in the *Treatise* is generally supposed to be directed against the rationalists. He there mentions only William Wollaston but the second *Enquiry* indicates that he also had Nicolas Malebranche, Cudworth and Clarke in mind (5: 197). The argument bears equally against other ethical theories dependent on claims that neither have been nor can be confirmed by experience. If it is argued that the divine command theory is the contrary of that of Cudworth and the other rationalists—that it is voluntaristic and based on a revelation that does or may run contrary to reason—then one needs only to turn to 'Of Miracles' (4: 109–31) to determine how Hume would respond to an ethics that in this alternative manner takes us beyond experience. In general, Hume's view was that which he expressed to Hutcheson in 1740: 'Morality . . . regards only human Nature & human Life.' (13: I, 40.)

28. See, for example, the closing paragraph of the essay on miracles. (5: 131.)

29. Jean Barbeyrac, the editor of Pufendorf's *Law of Nature and Nations*, provides a clear statement of the view that Hume opposes:

> 'It is certain *that Morality is the Daughter of Religion, that they go hand in hand together; and that the Perfection of the latter, is the Standard of Perfection in the former.* . . . In fact, the fundamental Principles of Natural Religion, which must be the Basis of all other Religion; are

also the most firm, or rather only, Foundation of this Science of Morality. Without a Deity, *Duty, Obligation, Right,* are no more, to say the Truth, than fine Ideas; which may please the Mind, but can scarce touch the Heart; and which of themselves, cannot impose an indispensible Necessity to act or not to act, in such or such a certain manner. . . . But to give these Ideas their full Force and due measure of Efficacy; to make 'em strong enough to maintain their Ground against Passion and Self-interest; they will require a superiour Being; a Being superiour to us in Power and Might, who has subjected us to a strict Conformity therewith in our Conduct; who has bound us thereto . . . who has put us under an *Obligation,* properly so call'd . . . . This Fear of a Deity, who punishes Vice and rewards Virtue, has so great an Efficacy; that, altho' the fundamental Principles of Religion be much darken'd, by the Intermixture of Errour and Superstition; yet if they are not entirely corrupted and destroy'd, it will still continue to actuate, and have a considerable influence. . . . But shou'd you make the finest System in the World, if Religion has not its part in it, it will be little more than (as I may say) a speculative Morality; and you will be found to build on a sandy Foundation. (53: 14–15.)

# Bibliography

Throughout the text and footnotes of this chapter cited materials are referred to by number and page. The numbers used correspond to the entries in this Bibliography. Thus (1: 465–66) following a quotation means that the text cited is found on pp. 465–66 of item 1 below, which is a specific edition of Hume's *A Treatise of Human Nature*. For additional information about Hume's works see item 36 below; for references to discussions of Hume beyond those found in this selected bibliography, see item 32.

## HUME'S MAJOR WRITINGS IN CHRONOLOGICAL ORDER

Although Princeton University Press has announced plans to publish a critical edition of Hume's philosophical, political and literary works, there is as yet no standard, critical edition of any of Hume's philosophical or historical publications. Consequently, it is necessary to rely on a melange of editions in order to make use of the most complete and reliable texts.

1. *A Treatise of Human Nature: Being an Attempt to introduce the experimental Method of Reasoning into Moral Subjects*, 3 vols. (London: 1739–40). Citations here are to the edition of L. A. Selby-Bigge and P. H. Nidditch (Oxford University Press, 1978).
2. *An Abstract of . . . A Treatise of Human Nature . . .* (London: 1740). This work may be found in 1: 641–62.
3. *Essays Moral and Political*, 2 vols. (Edinburgh: 1741–42). The second volume of this work appeared at the same time as the second edition of volume one. Most of the essays in the two-volume work then appeared an additional ten times (1748, '53, '58, '60, '64, '67, '68, '70, '72, '77) under Hume's direction, although he died before the publication of the 1777 edition. Citations to these essays here are to vol. 3 of *David Hume: The Philosophical Works*, eds. T. H. Green and T. H. Grose (London: 1882; reprinted by Scientia Verlag Aalen, 1964).
4. *Philosophical Essays concerning Human Understanding* (London: 1748). A second edition appeared in 1750, a third in 1756, at which time the title was changed to that now in use, *An Enquiry concerning Human Understanding*. From 1756 on the work was available as part of a collection bearing the general title *Essays and Treatises on several Subjects*. This collection also included items 3, 5 and 6, and was republished at Hume's direction in 1758, '60, '64, '67, '68, '70, '72 and '77. Citations here are to the edition of L. A. Selby-Bigge and P. H. Nidditch, *Enquiries concerning Human Understanding and concerning the Principles of Morals* (Oxford University Press, 1975).
5. *An Enquiry concerning the Principles of Morals* (London: 1751). A second edition appeared in 1753, after which time the work was included in the collection *Essays and Treatises on Several Subjects*, which was republished

in the years mentioned in item 4. Citations here are to the edition of L. A. Selby-Bigge and P. H. Nidditch, *Enquiries concerning Human Understanding and concerning the Principles of Morals* (Oxford University Press, 1975).

6. *Political Discourses* (Edinburgh: 1752). A second edition was also published in 1752, and a third in 1754, at which time the work was included in the collection *Essays and Treatises on Several Subjects*, and republished, under Hume's direction in the years mentioned in item 4.

7. *The History of Great Britain. Vol. I. Containing the Reigns of James I and Charles I* (Edinburgh: 1754). See item 11a.

8. *The History of Great Britain. Vol. II. Containing the Commonwealth, and the Reigns of Charles II and James II* (London: 1757). See item 11a.

9. *Four Dissertations* (London: 1757). Includes *The Natural History of Religion*. This latter work is here cited from vol. 4 of *David Hume: The Philosophical Works*, ed. T. H. Green and T. H. Grose, 4 vols. (Darmstadt: Scientia Verlag Aalen, 1964; reprint of the edition of 1882).

10. *The History of England, under the House of Tudor. Comprehending the Reigns of K. Henry VII [through] Q. Elizabeth*, 2 vols. (London: 1759). See item 11a.

11. *The History of England, from the Invasion of Julius Caesar to the Accession of Henry VII*, 2 vols. (London: 1762).

11a. It will be seen that Hume wrote his history, in one sense of the word, backward—first covering the period 1603–88, then the period 1485–1603, and finally the period from roughly 50 BC to 1485. Following the publication of the last-written volumes, however, the work was re-pubished as a set, and with the materials in normal chronological order. Complete new editions, prepared for the press by Hume, were published in 1763, '67, '70, '72 and '78. From 1780 to c. 1900 the work was republished nearly two hundred times. In view of the fact that there are so many editions of this work I have here given references by chapters as these were numbered in the 1778 edition. A convenient modern version of this edition has recently been republished, ed. W. B. Todd, 6 vols. (Indianapolis: Liberty Press, 1983–85). For further details about the editions of the *History* see *David Hume: Philosophical Historian*, ed. D. F. Norton and R. H. Popkin (Indianapolis: Bobbs-Merrill, 1965).

12. *Dialogues concerning Natural Religion*, first published posthumously, as edited by Hume's nephew, David Hume the Younger, in 1778. Cited here from the edition published by Norman Kemp Smith in 1935 (reprinted Indianapolis: Bobbs-Merrill, 1947) and thereafter.

13. *The Letters of David Hume*, edited by J. Y. T. Greig, 2 vols. (Oxford: Clarendon Press, 1932; reprinted 1969, 1983). Hume's brief 'My Own Life' is included I, 1–7.

14. *New Letters of David Hume*, edited by R. Klibansky and E. C. Mossner (Oxford: Clarendon Press, 1954; reprinted 1970, 1983). Many additional letters of Hume have been published since 1954, in several different journals and books. For references to these see item 32 below.

STUDIES CITED AND RECOMMENDED READING

15. Árdal, Páll, S., *Passion and Value in Hume's Treatise* (Edinburgh University Press, 1966). A ground-breaking effort to explicate Hume's theories of the passions and morals.

16. Bayle, Pierre, *Le dictionnaire historique et critique*, 4 vols. (Rotterdam: 1697; 2nd ed. 1702). Cited here from *The Dictionary Historical and Critical of Mr Peter Bayle*, trans. P. DesMaizeaux, *et al.*, 5 vols., 2nd English edition (London, 1734–38). A convenient modern translation of selections from this work is *Historical and Critical Dictionary*, ed. and trans. R. H. Popkin (Indianapolis: Bobbs-Merrill, 1965).

17. ——, *Pensées diverses écrites à un Docteur de Sorbonne* (Rotterdam: 1682), and *Continuation des Pensées diverses.* . . . (Rotterdam: 1705). Cited here is the English translation of the first of these works, *Miscellaneous Reflections, Occasion'd by the Comet which appear'd in December 1680. Chiefly tending to explode Popular Superstitions*, 2 vols. (London: 1708).

18. Bentley, Richard, *The Folly of Atheism . . . A Sermon Preached in the Church of St. Martin in the Fields.* . . . (London: 1692; reprinted in *Eight Boyle Lectures on Atheism.* . . . New York: Garland, 1976). A clear, popular statement of the dependence of morality on God, his providence and a belief in both.

19. Berman, David, 'David Hume and the Suppression of "Atheism"', *Journal of the History of Philosophy* 21 (1983), 375–87.

20. Burtt, E. A., *The Metaphysical Foundations of Modern Physical Science* (London: Kegan, Paul, 1925; revised edition, 1932).

21. Butler, Joseph, *Sermons* (London: 1726; reprinted in whole or in part many times).

22. Chappell, V. C., ed., *Hume: A Collection of Critical Essays* (New York: Doubleday, 1966).

23. Cicero, Marcus Tullius, *De Officiis*. A discussion of morals by one of Hume's favourite classical authors. Many translations exist; that of Walter Miller, published in the Loeb Classical Library (1947), is printed alongside the Latin text.

24. Clarke, Samuel, *A Demonstration of the Being and Attributes of God* (London: 1705).

25. ——, *A Discourse concerning the Unchangeable Obligations of Natural Religion* (London: 1706). This and the preceding item are available in a facsimile edition of Clarke's *Works* (New York: Garland, 1978).

26. Colman, John, *John Locke's Moral Philosophy* (Edinburgh University Press, 1983).

27. Cudworth, Ralph, *The True Intellectual System of the Universe . . . wherein, all the Reason and Philosophy of Atheism is Confuted; and its Impossibility Demonstrated* (London, 1678; reprinted New York: Garland, 1978). Cited here from *The True Intellectual System of the Universe . . . with a Treatise concerning Eternal and Immutable Morality*, 3 vols. (London: 1845).

28. ——, *A Treatise concerning Eternal and Immutable Morality* (London: 1731; reprinted, New York: Garland, 1976). This work was published posthumously; cited here from the edition of 1845 (see previous entry).

29. Gaskin, John, *Hume's Philosophy of Religion* (London: Macmillan, 1978; 2nd ed. 1988).
30. Grotius, Hugo, *De jure belli ac pacis* (Paris: 1625). English translation, *The Rights of War and Peace*, trans. W. H. Kelsey, *et al.* (Oxford University Press, 1925).
31. Haakonssen, Knud, *The Science of the Legislator: The Natural Jurisprudence of David Hume and Adam Smith* (Cambridge University Press, 1981).
32. Hall, Roland, *Fifty years of Hume Scholarship: A Bibliographical Guide* (Edinburgh University Press, 1978). Supplements to this bibliography have been published annually in the journal *Hume Studies* for the past several years, and further annual instalments may appear in the same place. Less complete lists of work on Hume can be found in the quarterly and annual editions of *The Philosopher's Index*.
33. Hobbes, Thomas, *Leviathan* (London: 1651). Of the numerous modern editions that edited by M. Oakeshott (Oxford: Blackwell, 1947) is cited here.
34. Hutcheson, Francis, *An Essay on the Nature and Conduct of the Passions and Affections. With Illustrations on the Moral Sense* (London: 1728). Cited here from the 3rd edition, 1742; (reprinted Gainesville; Scholars' Facsimiles, 1969).
35. ——, *An Inquiry into the Original of our Ideas of Beauty and Virtue. . . .* (London: 1725). Cited here from the 4th edition, London, 1738; (reprinted Farnborough: Gregg International, 1969).
36. Jessop, T. E., *A Bibliography of David Hume and of Scottish Philosophy, from Francis Hutcheson to Lord Balfour* (London: Brown and Son, 1938; reprinted New York: Garland, 1983).
37. Jones, Peter, *Hume's Sentiments: Their Ciceronian and French Context* (Edinburgh University Press, 1982).
38. Kuhn, Thomas, *The Copernican Revolution* (Cambridge, Mass.: Harvard University Press, 1957).
39. Laird, John, *Hume's Philosophy of Human Nature* (London: Methuen, 1932).
40. Livingston, D. and King, J., eds., *Hume: A Re-evaluation* (New York: Fordham University Press, 1976).
41. Locke, John, *An Essay concerning Human Understanding*, ed. P. H. Nidditch (Oxford: Clarendon Press, 1979). First published in 1690.
42. ——, *The Second Treatise of Civil Government* and *A Letter Concerning Toleration*, ed. J. W. Gough (Oxford: Blackwell, 1948). These works were first published in, respectively, 1690 and 1689.
43. Mackie, J. L., *Hume's Moral Theory* (London: Routledge & Kegan Paul, 1980).
44. Mandeville, Bernard, *The Fable of the Bees: or, Private Vices, Publick Benefits*, ed. F. B. Kaye, 2 vols. (Oxford: Clarendon Press, 1957). The items making up this work were first published in the early decades of the 18th century.
45. Moore, James, 'The Social Background of Hume's Science of Human Nature'. In 50.
46. ——, 'Hume's Political Science and the Classical Republican Tradition'. *Canadian Journal of Political Science* 10, 809–39.

47. Mossner, Ernest Campbell, *The Life of David Hume* (Edinburgh: Thomas Nelson, 1954; 2nd edition, Oxford: Clarendon Press, 1980).

48. Norton, David Fate, *David Hume: Common Sense Moralist, Sceptical Metaphysician* (Princeton University Press, 1982; reprinted with corrections, 1985).

49. ——, 'Hume, Atheism, and the Autonomy of Morals', in *Hume's Philosophy of Religion*, ed. M. Hester (Winston-Salem: Wake Forest University Press, 1987).

50. Norton, D. F., *et al.*, eds., *McGill Hume Studies* (San Diego: Austin Hill Press, 1979).

51. Penelhum, Terence, *Hume* (London: Macmillan, 1975). A valuable general introduction to Hume's philosophy.

52. Price, Richard, *A Review of the Principal Questions in Morals*, ed. D. D. Raphael (Oxford: Clarendon Press, 1948). This work, which contains important discussions of 18th-century moral philosophy, was first published in 1757.

53. Pufendorf, Samuel, *De jure naturae et gentium libri octo* (Lund: 1672). Cited here from the English translation, *On the Law of Nature and Nations*, by Basil Kennet, *et al.*, with the notes of Jean Barbeyrac, London, 1729. Also available in the translation of C. H. and W. A. Oldfather (Oxford: Clarendon Press, 1934).

54. ——, Samuel, *De officio hominis et civis juxta legem naturalem libri duo* (Lund: 1673; English trans., *The Two Books on the Duty of Man and Citizen according to the natural Law*, by F. G. Moore (New York: Oxford University Press, 1927).

55. Raphael, D. D., ed., *British Moralists, 1650–1800*, 2 vols. (Oxford: Clarendon Press, 1969). See also 56.

56. Selby-Bigge, L. A., ed., *British Moralists*, 2 vols. (Oxford, 1897; reprinted, New York: Bobbs-Merrill, 1964). The editor's introduction provides a useful pre-20th-century perspective on British moral theory of the early modern period. See also 55.

57. Shaftesbury, (Anthony Ashley Cooper) The Third Earl of, *Characteristics of Men, Manners, Opinions, Times* (London: 1713). Cited here from the edition edited by J. M. Robertson, with an Introduction by S. Grean (New York: Bobbs-Merrill, 1964).

58. Smith, Norman Kemp, *The Philosophy of David Hume: A Critical Study of its Origins and Central Doctrines* (London and New York: Macmillan, 1941; reprinted 1964). The benchmark study in the literature on Hume.

59. Stewart, J. B., *The Moral and Political Philosophy of David Hume* (New York: Columbia University Press, 1963; reprinted 1973).

60. Westfall, Richard, *The Construction of Modern Science: Mechanism and Mechanics* (Cambridge University Press, 1977).

# 7

# Kant[1]
## *Christine Korsgaard*

. . . reason has no dictatorial authority; its verdict is always simply the agreement of free citizens, of whom each one must be permitted to express, without let or hindrance, his objections or even his veto. (C1 A738–739/B766–767)[2]

*Critique of Pure Reason*

For Immanuel Kant the death of speculative metaphysics and the birth of the rights of man were not independent events. Together they constitute the resolution of the Enlightenment debate about the scope and power of reason. In the *Critique of Pure Reason* Kant shows that theoretical reason is unable to answer the questions of speculative metaphysics: whether God exists, the soul is immortal, and the will is free. But this conclusion prepares the way for an extension in the power of practical reason.[3] Practical reason directs that every human being as a free and autonomous being must be regarded as unconditionally valuable. In his ethical writings Kant shows how this directive provides a rational foundation for morality, politics, and a religion of moral faith. Bringing reason to the world becomes the enterprise of morality rather than metaphysics, and the work as well as the hope of humanity.

## A CHILD OF THE ENLIGHTENMENT

Immanuel Kant was born in Königsberg, Prussia (now Kaliningrad, USSR), on 22 April 1724, into a devout Pietist family. His father was a harness-maker and the family was not well off. But Kant's mother recognised her son's intellectual gifts, and the patronage of the family pastor Franz Albert Schultz (1692–1763), a Pietist theology professor and preacher, enabled Kant to attend the Collegium Fridericianum and prepare for the university. He studied at the University of Königsberg from 1740–47, resisting pressure to choose one of the faculties and taking courses eclectically instead.[4] He was influenced by his teacher Martin Knutsen (1713–51), a Wolffian rationalist who taught philosophy and physics, and who took an interest in the developments of British philosophy and science. Knutsen introduced Kant to the works of Newton.

From 1747–55 Kant worked as a private tutor in the homes of various families near Königsberg, and pursued his interests in natural science. In 1755 he was granted the right to lecture as a *Privatdozent* (an unsalaried lecturer who is paid by lecture fees) at Königsberg. In order to earn a living Kant lectured on many subjects including logic, metaphysics, ethics, geography, anthropology, mathematics, the foundations of natural science and physics. We have testimonials to the power of Kant's lectures throughout his life: his audiences were large, and his ethics lectures are reported to have been especially moving.[5] In 1770 Kant was finally appointed to a regular professorship, the chair of logic and metaphysics at Königsberg. He lectured there until 1797. He died on 12 February 1804.

Kant never left the Königsberg area, but there are reports of his extraordinary ability to visualise, on the basis of written accounts, places and things he had never seen.[6] In a footnote to the preface of *Anthropology from a Pragmatic Point of View*, Kant complacently remarks:

> A city such as Königsberg on the River Pregel—a large city, the center of a state, the seat of the government's provincial councils, the site of a university (for cultivation of the sciences), a seaport connected by rivers with the interior of the country as well as with neighboring or remote countries having different languages and customs—is a suitable place for broadening one's knowledge of man and the world. In such a city, this knowledge can be acquired even without traveling. (ANTH 120n/4n)

Kant's parents died when he was young, and he had little contact with his family after that. He never married. The regularity of his habits, perhaps due to the poverty of his early life and to his poor health, is well-known. He only once got into trouble with the authorities. The events of his life were those of his intellectual life, and the political events in which he took such interest. His re-awakening to the problem set by the scepticism of Hume; his conversion to a morality based on the worth of humanity under the influence of Rousseau; and the American and French Revolutions formed the important episodes of his life.

In Enlightenment Germany the intellectual world was dominated by an extreme form of rationalism called the Leibniz-Wolffian philosophy. Christian Wolff (1679–1754) is generally considered one of the two founders of the German *Aufklärung*. Wolff constructed his philosophy from the ideas of Leibniz and Thomistic scholasticism. He took mathematics as a model, and believed that philosophy should be a universal deductive system, with every conclusion derived by syllogistic reasoning from necessary premises. Like Leibniz, Wolff based his system on the principles of contradiction and sufficient reason.[7] Wolff also believed that the principle of sufficient reason could be derived from the principle of contradiction, for there would be a contradiction in the insufficiently determined existence of a merely possible thing.[8] While human beings need to use empirical methods in our search for the reasons of things, in principle it should be possible to cast the sciences in a completely deductive form. The existence of God can be proved by ontological, cosmological and teleological arguments; and because we know that God exists we know that this is the Best of All Possible Worlds. The soul is simple and immortal, and, since actions other than those one performs are logically possible, the will is free.[9] Wolff's ethics is based on the idea that the will is necessarily motivated by the good—that is, by the perception of a perfection achievable by action. Wolff thought it contradictory to perceive a perfection and not desire it, so in Kantian terms we may say that he believed that the moral principle is analytic.[10] Seeking perfection will bring us happiness, and the perfection of each person harmonises with the perfection of every other. Immoral conduct is the result of confusion about what is good. Moral goodness is to be achieved through the clarification and correction of our ideas.

The influence of this system of dogmatic metaphysics on the thought of *Aufklärung* Germany can hardly be overestimated. Because he taught in the university, lectured in German, and wrote in German as well as Latin, Wolff had more direct influence than Leibniz himself. Wolff was the first philosopher to produce a full-fledged system in the German language, and he invented the technical philosophical vocabulary that was used by his successors.[11] Wolff's ideas were also presented in popular form in books written 'for the ladies', and spawned the Societies of the Friends of Truth, whose members pledged not to accept or reject beliefs except for sufficient reason.[12] Kant was educated in the Wolffian system, and long after he had rejected it he described Wolff as 'the greatest of all the dogmatic philosophers' (C1 B xxxvi/33). Wolff's students taught in universities all over Germany and wrote many of the textbooks that German professors were required to use in their courses. One of the most influential of them—Alexander Gottlieb Baumgarten (1714–62)—wrote the textbooks Kant used in his courses on meta-physics and ethics.

Of course this extreme rationalism did not go unchallenged. The followers of the other founder of the *Aufklärung*, Christian Thomasius (1655–1728), attacked the conception of philosophy embodied in the Leibniz-Wolffian system. Some were anti-metaphysical, and wanted philosophy to play a more popular, non-academic role. More impor-tant to the student of ethics is the fact that Thomasius himself, and others who opposed Wolffian rationalism, were associated with Pietism. Pietism, the religion of Kant's own family, emphasised inner religious experience, self-examination and morally good works; and Pietist theologians believed in a strong connection between morality and religion. When Wolff was appointed rector at the University of Halle, a Pietist centre, his inaugural lecture was 'On the Practical Philosophy of the Chinese'. Wolff claimed that the moral philosophy of Confucius shows that ethics is accessible to natural reason and independent of revelation. As a result, Wolff's Pietist enemies persuaded Frederick Wilhelm I to banish Wolff.

A later challenge to the Leibniz-Wolffian philosophy came when Germans began to study the British Empiricists, especially Hume. In Berlin after the middle of the century a movement called 'popular philosophy' flourished under the influence of Frederick the Great, overlapping in its membership with the Berlin Academy which Frederick had revitalised. Both groups were interested in the philo-sophical traditions of France and Britain, and the works of Locke, Berkeley, Shaftesbury, Hutcheson, Hume, Reid and Rousseau were translated. Moral sense theory was much admired, by Kant among others. Thus, rationalism in ethics was opposed both by the appeal to religion and the appeal to moral feeling and happiness. After the middle of the century rationalist metaphysics too came increasingly under attack.

And so in 1763 the Berlin Academy offered a prize for the best essay on the topic 'Whether metaphysical truths generally, and in particular the fundamental principles of natural theology and morals, are not capable of proofs as distinct as those of geometry; and if they are not, what is the true nature of their certainty, to what degree can this certainty be developed, and is this degree sufficient for conviction [of their truth]?'[13] One of the competitors was Kant, although he did not win the prize, which went to Moses Mendelssohn (1729–86). In his essay Kant denies that metaphysics has the same method as mathematics. The difficulty is that the concepts of metaphysics cannot be established synthetically the way the concepts of mathematics can. In mathematics the concepts create their objects, and we can be certain that they contain what we have put into them. Philosophy, on the other hand, has to analyze concepts which are given to it obscurely (PE 276–278/6–8; 283ff/14ff). Yet metaphysics is still seen to be possible and capable of a certainty sufficient for conviction: we must draw our inferences only from those predicates of a concept of which we are certain, and not jump to the conclusion that we have arrived at a complete definition (PE 292–293/25–26). Kant's ethical views in this essay display a curious combination of influences from Wolff and Hutcheson. The moral principles are the Wolffian 'do the most perfect possible by you' and 'do not do that which would hinder the greatest possible perfection realisable through you' (PE 299/32). Yet these principles are merely formal and so empty until we know what is perfect. For this reason ethics fails to have the requisite certainty. For, Kant says, a principle of obligation tells us that we ought to do something. Either we ought to do something as a means to an end, in which case we can prove the principle, but it is not a case of moral obligation; or we ought to do something as an end, in which case the principle is unprovable. Fortunately, Hutcheson has shown us that the subordinate principles that give ethics content are objects not of knowledge but of unanalyzable feeling (PE 299/33). It is yet to be determined whether the primary principles of obligation are based on the faculty of knowledge or of feeling (PE 300/34).[14] Kant's conclusions are in one sense the reverse of those he will ultimately reach: it is speculative metaphysics which will be left unfounded, and practical philosophy which will be set on a firm basis. Yet in the prize essay we see Kant set for himself the questions that will lead to his mature views: the question of the status of pure concepts, in metaphysics, and the question of rational determinability of ends and imperatives, in ethics.


## THE CRITICAL PHILOSOPHY

Throughout the 1760s and 1770s Kant was working out the views that would comprise the critical philosophy. Kant published little in

this period, but we know that he worked on ethics as well as metaphysics and decided against moral sense theory. In the Inaugural
Dissertation[15] of 1770 Kant says:

> So *moral philosophy*, in as much as it supplies the first *principles of
> critical judgement*, is only cognised by the pure intellect and itself
> belongs to pure philosophy. And the man who reduced its criteria
> to the sense of pleasure or pain, Epicurus, is very rightly blamed,
> together with certain moderns who have followed him to some
> extent from afar, such men as Shaftesbury and his supporters. (ID
> 395/59–60)

We also have the *Lectures on Ethics*, notes taken by Kant's students in
his ethics courses sometime in the years 1775–80, and the views in
these are close to Kant's critical views. And we have Kant's own
testimony, in a fragment written in the 1760s, of the profound influence exercised on his moral views by Rousseau, whose works he
was reading.[16]

Although Kant's moral views were developing, their articulation
had to await the working out of his conclusions about the status of
metaphysics. The first edition of the *Critique of Pure Reason* appeared
in 1781. Its conclusions overthrew the dogmatic metaphysics of the
Leibniz-Wolffian philosophy; Mendelssohn referred to its author as
'the all-destroying Kant'.[17] In fact, Kant's aim was not to destroy,
but to circumvent the scepticism of Hume. In the *Prolegomena to Any
Future Metaphysics*, Kant reports:

> I openly confess my recollection of David Hume was the very
> thing which many years ago first interrupted my dogmatic slumber
> and gave my investigations in the field of speculative philosophy
> a quite new direction. . . .
> I . . . first tried whether Hume's objection could not be put into
> a general form, and soon found that the concept of the connection
> of cause and effect was by no means the only concept by which the
> understanding thinks the connection of things *a priori*, but rather
> that metaphysics consists altogether of such concepts. I sought to
> ascertain their number; and when I had satisfactorily succeeded in
> this by starting from a single principle, I proceeded to the deduc-
> tion of these concepts, which I was now certain were not derived
> from experience, as Hume had attempted to derive them, but
> sprang from the pure understanding. (PFM 260/8)

Hume and Kant agree that metaphysical principles such as 'every event has a cause' are not analytic. In an analytic judgement the predicate is contained in the concept of the subject. A judgement that is not analytic is synthetic. If metaphysical principles are synthetic, we cannot lay them down as definitions and derive truths from them by the principle of contradiction. They must be demonstrated. But Hume showed that 'every event has a cause' could not be derived from experience. Although not analytic, the judgement must be *a priori*—knowable by pure reason. In the *Critique of Pure Reason*, Kant provides the needed demonstration—or 'deduction'—of the synthetic *a priori* principles of the understanding. 'Hitherto it has been assumed that all our knowledge must conform to objects.' Instead, we must suppose that objects must conform to our knowledge. For 'we can know *a priori* of things only what we ourselves put into them' (C1 Bxvi–Bxviii/22–23). But Kant's deduction only licenses our use of the principles of pure understanding for objects *as we experience them*, that is, as 'phenomena'. It does not provide us with a justification for applying them to things as they are in themselves—to 'noumena'.

In this way Kant rescues the metaphysical basis of natural science from Humean scepticism. But he does so at great cost to speculative metaphysics, for the traditional proofs of God, immortality and freedom are undermined. Kant has not shown that there is no God, immortality or freedom, but rather that these things are beyond the limits of theoretical understanding. Yet theoretical reason, in its search for the unconditioned—for the completeness of its account of things—compels us to ask whether these things are real. Human reason, the opening lines of the *Critique of Pure Reason* tell us, is compelled by its nature to ask questions it is unable to answer.

These conclusions set the problems for Kant's practical philosophy. First, the moral law itself must be a synthetic *a priori* principle (G 420/37–38). For, as Kant had already emphasised in the prize essay, 'The formula in which all obligation is expressed is: One *ought* to do this or that and leave the other' and 'every ought expresses a necessity of the action' (PE 298/31). But an ought statement cannot be derived from experience, which merely tells us how things are, and does not provide the required necessity. It must, therefore, be known *a priori*. But the moral ought cannot be established analytically. The argument for this in the Second Section of the *Foundations of the Metaphysics of Morals* (1785), picks up where the prize essay left off 22 years before. Hypothetical imperatives—principles which instruct us to do certain actions if we want certain ends—are analytic. While their material content comes from a law of nature telling us that a certain action is a means to a certain end, the necessity expressed in the 'ought' comes from a principle that is analytic for the will:

> Whoever wills the end, so far as reason has decisive influence on his actions, wills also the indispensably necessary means to it that lie in his power. This proposition, in what concerns the will, is analytical; for in willing an object as my effect, my causality as an acting cause, i.e. the use of the means, is already thought, and the imperative derives the concept of necessary actions to this end from the concept of willing this end. (G 417/34–35)

Willing something is determining yourself to be the cause of that thing, which means determining yourself to use the available causal connections—the means—to it. 'Willing the end' is already posited as the hypothesis, and we need only analyze it to arrive at willing the means. If you will to be able to play the piano, then you already will to practice, as that is the 'indispensably necessary means to it' that 'lie in your power'. But the moral ought is not expressed by a hypothetical imperative. Our duties hold for us regardless of what we want. A moral rule does not say 'do this if you want that' but simply 'do this'. It is expressed in a categorical imperative. For instance, the moral law says that you must respect the rights of others. Nothing is already posited, which can then be analyzed. In the prize essay Kant had thought that this meant that the moral principle could not be established. Now he concludes instead that the Categorical Imperative is synthetic *a priori*, and requires a 'deduction', like the deduction that established the principles of the pure understanding for the realm of experience.

The second result of the *Critique of Pure Reason* that bears on ethics concerns the issues of speculative metaphysics: God, freedom and immortality. As already noted, Kant concluded that these could not be objects of theoretical knowledge. In fact, the attempt to determine whether they are realities gives rise to antinomies: apparently equally good arguments on both sides of the question. The most important of these, concerning freedom, will serve as an example. Freedom, as Kant understands it, is a special kind of causality—first or spontaneous causality, unconditioned by any prior cause. One may argue that there can be no first cause, on the grounds that it would violate the rule that every event has a cause. On the other hand, one may argue that there must be a first cause, since the sufficient cause of anything must include all the causes that have led up to it, and there can be no sufficient cause if this is an infinite regress (A444–452 B472–480/409–415). Christian August Crusius (1715–75), a Pietist critic of Wolff whom Kant admired, had written about the antinomies, appealing to them as evidence of the limitations of human reason, and the need for reliance on faith and revelation.[18] Kant now resolves the antinomies by appeal to his distinction between noumena and phenomena. The antinomies show how important this distinction is, for without it reason must be seen as giving rise to contradictions and scepticism will be justified. In some cases, the antinomy is generated by a sort of equivocation—phenomena are treated as if they were noumena, and both of the arguments are false (A505–506 B533–534/448–449). In other cases, it turns out that one of the arguments is true of phenomena, while the other could be true—although we do not know that it is—of noumena. The antinomy of freedom takes the latter form. In the phenomenal world, because it is temporal and causality is temporal succession according to a rule, every event has a cause, and there can be no freedom. But the noumenal world does not exist in time and a spontaneous causality is possible, though not knowable, in it (A536–541 B564–569/466–469).

This leaves room for belief in the freedom of the will, which is the foundation of morality (A542–558 B570–586/469–479). As we will see, freedom of the will is important to Kant not merely for the familiar reason that we cannot be held accountable if we are not free, but because it provides both the content of morality and its motive. Kant will ask 'how would a free will with nothing constraining or guiding it determine its actions?' and he will argue that the answer is 'by the moral law' (C2 29/28–29). This solves the problem set by the antinomy, although only from a practical point of view. For reason says that there must be an uncaused cause in the noumenal world if an unconditional explanation of the phenomena can be given. Unless there is such a cause, the world is not, by the standards of human reason, intelligible. Speculative theoretical reason, however, cannot tell us what this cause would be. Practical reason, in providing us with the moral law, answers this question. This, according to Kant, provides us with a 'credential' for believing in the reality of the moral law, and so in the freedom of our own wills (C2 48/49). Once Kant discovers that there is a moral basis for belief in the freedom of the will, he uses the same method to show that there is a moral basis for belief in God and immortality.

## UNIVERSAL LAW AND HUMANITY

The views sketched above are not worked out until Kant writes the *Critique of Practical Reason* (1788). But first Kant produced a short book destined to become the main text for the study of his ethics, the *Foundations of the Metaphysics of Morals* (1785). The purpose of this work is 'the search for and establishment of the supreme principle of morality' (G 392/8). His plan was then to write a *Metaphysics of Morals*. In Kant's terminology, a 'critique' investigates the legitimacy of applying pure rational principles and their concepts to objects; while a 'metaphysics' sets forth those principles and their implications. The Third Section of the *Foundations* contains a deduction of the moral law and so is a critique of practical reason; at the time he wrote this work, he thought that that would be sufficient. Later he saw that the moral law could be validated in a different way, and the *Critique of Practical Reason* was the result.[19] But we must turn to the *Foundations* and the *Metaphysics of Morals* to get the substance of Kant's ethics, for in the second *Critique* the problem of validating the moral law and showing how it fits into his system supplants Kant's interest in its formulation and application.

Kant's method in the First Section of the *Foundations* is analytic: he uses examples in order to analyze our ordinary conception of a good will and to arrive at a formulation of the principle on which such a will acts. A good will is easily distinguished from one that acts from an indirect inclination, doing the right thing merely as a means to some ulterior end, a 'selfish purpose'. The difficult thing is to distinguish a good will from a will that has a 'direct inclination' to do something that is (as it happens) right (G 397ff/13ff). For instance, there are people 'so sympathetically constituted that without any motive of vanity or selfishness they find an inner satisfaction in spreading joy, and rejoice in the contentment of others which they have made possible' (G 398/14). Having a natural inclination to do what coincides with duty is not the same thing as acting from duty, so for clarity we must contrast this case with one where the duty is done without natural inclination. Take someone whose mind is 'clouded by a sorrow of his own which extinguished all sympathy with the lot of others' or one who is 'by temperament cold and indifferent to the sufferings of others' (G 398/14). If such a person is nevertheless beneficent, it must be from a good will. What is the principle on which he or she acts? We see, first, that such a person does his or her duty just because it is his or her duty. Furthermore, we see that what makes him or her do it—and so what makes it his or her duty—is not simply its purpose. For the naturally sympathetic person and the unsympathetic but beneficent person both have the same purpose, helping others, although one has this purpose because of a direct inclination and the other has it from duty. *Both* are contrasted with the selfish man who does the right thing for an ulterior purpose, such as fear of punishment or hope of reward.

Duty, then, is not a matter of having certain purposes. If we remove all purposes—all material—from the will, what is left is the formal principle of the will. The formal principle of duty is just that it is duty—that it is law. The essential character of law is universality. Therefore, the person who acts from duty attends to the universality of his/her principle. He or she only acts on a maxim that he or she could will to be a universal law (G 402/18). In this way Kant moves from the idea that a good will is one that acts from duty to a principle that can be used to tell us what our duties are.[20]

In the Second Section Kant reaches the same point by another route: the investigation of rational action. 'Everything in nature works according to laws. Only a rational being has the capacity of acting according to the conception of laws, that is, according to principles' (G 412/29). The principle that you give to yourself, that you act on, Kant calls a 'maxim'. Your maxim must contain your reason for action: it must say what you are going to do, and why. If your maxim is one that it is rational to act on, it meets certain tests, commands of reason expressed in imperatives. Your action must be a means to your end, and (unless it is morally required) your end must be consistent with your happiness. These tests are embodied in the two kinds of hypothetical imperatives, those of skill and prudence. But there is also an imperative that tells us what we must do, regardless of our private purposes. This is the moral or categorical imperative, and because it is independent of all material, we know that 'there is nothing remaining in it except the universality of law as such to which the maxim of the action should conform' (G 421/39). So from the very idea of a categorical imperative we can tell that it says: 'Act only according to that maxim by which you can at the same time will that it should become a universal law' (G 421/39; C2 27/26).

But how can you tell whether you are able to will your maxim as a universal law? On Kant's view, it is a matter of what you can will *without contradiction*. This is important, for it helps to secure the categorical character of the results—any agent who applies the contradiction test should get the same result, regardless of his/her private interests. To determine whether you can will your maxim at the same time as its universalisation without contradiction, you envision trying to will your maxim in a world in which the maxim is universalised—in which it is a law of nature. You are to 'Ask yourself whether, if the action which you propose should take place by a law of nature of which you yourself were a part, you could regard it as possible through your will' (C2 69/72). Contradiction may arise in two ways: if the maxim cannot even be *conceived* as a law of nature without contradiction, it is contrary to strict or perfect duty; if it can be conceived but could not be *willed* without contradiction, it is contrary to broad or imperfect duty (G 424/41–42).

The best example of the first sort of contradiction concerns a man whose maxim is to make a false promise in order to get some money, which he knows he will be unable to repay. To see whether this can be willed as a universal law, we imagine a world in which this is, so to speak, the standard procedure for getting ready money—it is a law of nature that anyone who needs money tries to get it this way. Then we imagine the agent trying to will to act on his maxim in that world. Kant tells us that this gives rise to a contradiction because such universalisation would make 'the promise itself and the end to be accomplished by it impossible; no one would believe what was promised to him but would only laugh at any such assertion as vain pretense' (G 422/40). It is important to notice the sense in which this is a contradiction. Kant's view, as we saw earlier, is that hypothetical imperatives are analytic, because they express a relation of conceptual containment. The negation of an analytic statement is a contradiction. The man in the example derives his maxim from a hypothetical imperative: 'If you want some ready money, you ought to make a false promise'. This imperative is derived from a causal 'law'—that false promising is a means to getting ready money—combined with the analytic principle that whoever wills the end wills the means. The causal 'law' in question, however, turns out to be no law at all, because false promising could not be the *universal* method of getting ready money. The efficacy of a lying promise depends on the fact that it is exceptional, for people believe promises only because they are normally made in good faith, and lend money on the basis of them only because they believe them. In willing the universalisation of his maxim, the deceitful promiser wills a world in which promises of this kind are not normally in good faith and therefore will not be accepted. This means that they will not be a means to getting ready money, and that the hypothetical imperative from which the deceitful promiser derives his own maxim will be falsified. This is where we get the contradiction: the lying promiser who attempts to will the universalisation of his maxim wills the denial of the analytical principle on which he himself proposes to act, and the denial of an analytical principle is a contradiction.[21] Later critics claim that undermining the efficacy of promises is only a contradiction if promises are themselves necessary. But Kant's point in the example is more modest than that; it is not intended to establish that promises are necessary. Promises are necessary for the man in the example, because *he* proposes to use a promise as the means to his own end.[22] This is why Kant says that he cannot will his maxim and its universalisation *at the same time*. Whenever you propose to perform an action whose efficacy depends on its exceptional character, you get a contradiction of this kind.

The other kind of contradiction arises when you attempt to will the universalisation of some policy which would undermine the will's efficacy more generally. For instance, if you try to will a universal policy of neglecting talents and powers, you contradict your will because these serve you for 'all sorts of possible purposes' (G 423/41). If you try to will a universal policy of not helping others, you contradict your will because you yourself, as a finite rational being, are often in need of assistance.[23] Kant is not offering an egoistic reason for an actual agreement here. Imagining yourself in a world without assistance is a thought experiment to determine whether you can will your maxim as a universal law. The duty of helping others holds even if you do not in fact get any assistance from anyone else, or have any real hope that you will.

At this point Kant has only told us what the categorical imperative is if there is one (G 425/43). But just as the laws of the understanding had to be established by a deduction showing that they apply to the world of experience, the categorical imperative must be established by showing that it actually applies to the human will. 'The possibility of reason thus determining conduct must now be investigated' (G 427/ 45). While this possibility cannot be established until the critical argument of the Third Section, the rest of the Second Section prepares the way.

Kant begins from his thesis that one always acts with some end in view. Ends may provide us with reasons positively, as purposes to be achieved, or negatively, as things we must not act against. If there is a categorical imperative, there must be an objective end, one determined by reason itself and so attributed to every rational will; when we act on the categorical imperative, this will be the end we have in view (G 427–428/45–46; MM 384–385/42–43). What would this end be? This kind of absolute value cannot be found in the objects of our desires, for they get their value from the fact that we desire them. Nor can it be found in our desires themselves, or in the various objects around us available for use as means. Rather, Kant says, 'man, and, in general, every rational being exists as an end in himself' (G 428/46).

This conclusion harks back to the claim with which the *Foundations* opens: the only thing which has unconditional value is a good will. A thing has conditional value if its value depends on whether certain conditions hold. For instance, the value of the means depends on the value of the end it serves; and the value of an object of desire depends on whether satisfying the desire will really contribute to the person's happiness. Even happiness is not valuable in all cases, and so is conditional. A thing has unconditional value if it has its value in itself and so has it under all conditions. Ultimately all value must spring from a source which is unconditionally valuable, for as long as we can question the value of something, we have not reached the end of its conditions. Kant's view is that only a good will has unconditional value of this kind. Since it is the objects of our own choices which we take to be good, and those objects do not have value in themselves, the source of value must be something that rests in us. It is not our needs and desires, for those are not always good. It must, therefore, be our humanity, our rational nature and capacity for rational choice. This is not different from saying it is a good will, for rational nature, in its perfect state, is a good will (G 428–429/46–47; C2 57–67/59–70; 87/90).

Kant says that the principle 'rational nature exists as an end in itself' is a subjective principle of human actions, but that since every rational being holds it, it must be taken to be objective as well (G 429/47). Because each of us holds his/her own ends to be good, each of us regards his/her own humanity as a *source of value*. In consistency, we must attribute the same kind of value to the humanity of others. These considerations establish humanity as the objective end needed for the determination of the will by a categorical imperative. It is a negative end, one that is not to be acted against, rather than a purpose to be achieved. This leads Kant to a new formulation of the imperative, the Formula of Humanity: 'Act so that you treat humanity, whether in your own person or in that of another, always as an end and never as a means only' (G 429/47).[24]

Kant then treats the same set of examples he used earlier, showing how the immoral maxims involve a violation of the unconditional value of humanity. Violations of perfect duty occur when the power of rational choice definitive of humanity is made subordinate to other, merely conditional goods. A suicide, for instance, treats his/her own humanity as something he/she can throw away for the sake of his/her comfort (G 429/47; MM 422–423/82–84). Anyone who uses deceptive or coercive methods to undermine the freedom of choice and action exercised by others also violates perfect duty. The lying promiser uses the lender as a mere means because he tricks him into giving away his money rather than allowing him to *choose* whether or not to do so. He thus treats his having the money, a conditional good, as if it were more important than the other's humanity. Coercion (except to protect rights) and deception are unjustifiable no matter what end they serve, for a good end is an object of every rational will, and reason is 'just the verdict of free citizens' (C2 62/64–65; C1 A739–740 B767/593).[25]

Although humanity is not a purpose to be achieved, we can act in a way that expresses a positive value for it, and imperfect duty is violated when we do not. We ought to realise our humanity by developing our talents and powers, our rational capacities. We ought to acknowledge that others are sources of value by treating their chosen ends as good, and pursuing their happiness as they see it (MM 388/46). All human activities and pursuits are to be regarded as good as long as everyone can in principle agree to them. 'This principle of humanity and of every rational creature as an end in itself is the supreme limiting condition on the freedom of the actions of each man' (G 430–431/49). The same idea is implicit in the Formula of Universal Law: for your reason to be sufficient, it need only be universalisable. Adoption of humanity as the unconditional end leads to the conduct which the Formula of Universal Law prescribes.

## CATEGORIES OF DUTY: THE METAPHYSICS OF MORALS

In the *Foundations*, a footnote to the first discussion of the four examples warns the reader that Kant will make his own division of duties when he writes the *Metaphysics of Morals*. He says that he has adopted the division normally in use by the schools, with one difference: he thinks that there are inner as well as outer perfect duties (G 421n/39n). When Kant did publish the *Metaphysics of Morals* (1797) he introduced a more rich and complicated classification of duties. Before moving to the question of how Kant establishes the validity of the moral law, I will describe the system of duties that Kant sets out in this later work.[26]

The *Metaphysics of Morals* is divided into two parts: the *Metaphysical Principles of Justice*, and the *Metaphysical Principles of Virtue*.[27] The *Metaphysical Principles of Justice* deals with *Recht*, right, and is concerned with the question how natural and acquired rights are possible, and how they give rise to political society. The duties it deals with are 'outer': the sense in which you 'have a duty' not to interfere with the freedom and property of another is that the other is authorised to use coercion against you if you do (MM 231/35–36). Rights arise from the Universal Principle of Justice: 'act externally in such a way that the free use of your will is compatible with the freedom of everyone according to a universal law' (MM 231/35). This principle is analytic, since one may arrive at it by analyzing the notion of external freedom (MM 231/35; 396/55). Freedom can only be limited by itself—your freedom is as extensive as possible consistent with the same freedom for others. Anything that prevents a hindrance to freedom is consistent with freedom. So, if someone tries to undermine your freedom and you use coercion against him/her, that is consistent with freedom—with universal freedom and so with *his* or *her* freedom. It follows by the law of contradiction that a right is united with the authorisation to use coercion against anyone who violates it (MM 231–233/35–37). We have an innate right to freedom, and we may acquire property rights. This is because of the Juridical Postulate of Practical Reason, according to which external objects may be property. Kant sees ownership as necessary for the use of objects as means. An object that cannot be owned cannot be effectively used, and so is, from a practical point of view, nothing at all. It would be inconsistent with freedom to limit it by nullifying the means it might use, so it follows that it must be possible for objects to be property (MM 246/52). A property right is correlated with an outer duty—a duty of justice. To say 'this is my book' means that the imperative 'you ought not to take this book' has acquired categorical or moral status. In this way outer duties—things that others may legitimately make us do or refrain from—are established. They are extensions of our innate right to freedom.

The *Metaphysical Principles of Virtue* deals with inner duties, duties of virtue. A duty of virtue differs from one of justice in several ways. First, a duty of virtue involves the free adoption of some end which pure practical reason directs. Duties of virtue arise from the Supreme Principle of the Doctrine of Virtue: 'Act according to a maxim whose ends are such that it can be a universal law that everyone have these ends' (MM 395/54).[28] Unlike the Universal Principle of Justice, this principle is synthetic: since it directs the adoption of ends and so concerns our motives, it must be established that it applies to the human will. It is deduced from the possibility of pure practical reason. It is a feature of human beings and probably all finite rational beings that we always act for an end (R 6n–8n/5n–7n; TP 279n–280n/65n). And, 'since sensible inclinations may misdirect us to ends (the matter of choice) which may be contrary to duty, legislative reason cannot guard against their influence other than, in turn, by means of an opposing moral end, which therefore must be given *a priori* independently of inclination' (MM 381/37–38). Practical reason is a faculty of ends, so if there is pure practical reason there must be necessary ends. This means that there are duties to have these ends, duties of virtue (MM 395/54–55).

The ends that reason sets are humanity in one's own person and that of every other, and, following from that, one's own perfection—moral and natural—and the happiness of others (MM 385–388/43–46). Virtue also encompasses the duties of justice: rights are sacred to a person who values humanity, and acts of justice are transformed into acts of virtue when done for this reason. To achieve virtue we must adopt these ends freely. We cannot be coerced to adopt them, in two senses: it is impossible in fact to force someone to adopt an end, and it would in any case be illegitimate to do so. My lacking a good moral disposition cannot hinder your freedom, but only my performing wrong actions (MM 381–382/38–39).

Duties of virtue are of broad obligation, while duties of justice are of strict obligation. Duties of justice require particular actions or omissions, and the obligation is strict because it can be discharged. If you perform a just action, it is not creditable, but just what you owe. If you do not, you have done something bad (MM 389–394/47–52; but see R 22n–23n/18n). Duties of virtue, by contrast, tell you to adopt and pursue certain ends. Such a duty cannot simply be discharged, for the ends in question cannot be completely achieved. So the obligation here is broad. To the extent that you pursue the end, as an end dictated by the law, you achieve moral worth. So, for example, the person who transgresses the rights of others is bad, the person who simply conforms to the law merely does what is owed, but the person who conforms to the law *because* he or she has made the rights of humanity his or her end is morally good (MM 390–391/48–49).

The distinction between strict and broad obligations is sometimes confused with the distinction between perfect and imperfect duties. Kant himself does not use the four terms in a perspicuous way.[29] Perfect duties require definite actions or omissions, while in the case of imperfect duties inclination is allowed to play a role in determining exactly what and how much we will do to carry them out. Duties of justice are all perfect, but there are both imperfect and perfect duties of virtue. We have an imperfect duty of virtue when there is a positive end to promote, but the law does not say exactly how. For instance, you ought to develop your talents and powers, but you may choose those that are suitable to your occupation and tastes (MM 392/50). You ought to promote the happiness of others, but you may concentrate your efforts on the happiness of your friends (MM 390/48). Perfect duties of virtue arise because we must refrain from particular actions *against* humanity in our own person or that of another. Suicide, physically destructive habits, and the failures of self-respect exhibited in self-deception and servility violate perfect duties to ourselves (MM 421–444/82–107). Failures of respect, such as calumny, mockery and pride, violate perfect duties to others (MM 462–468/127–133). And the general duty to *adopt* morally good ends—the duty of moral perfection—is perfect. Adopting an end is a definite, though internal, action. But making something your end and making that end the motive of your conduct is not something a human being can simply *decide* all at once to do. Our motives for the outward acts we do for these ends may be mixed with non-moral motives, and we cannot be certain that they are pure (MM 392–393/51; 441–442/103–104; see also R 29–30/24–26). For instance, you may resolve, when tempted, not to commit suicide not only because you value humanity in your own person but because you are afraid; or your beneficence may require the support of your natural sympathies. So Kant says of the duty of moral perfection that it is 'in quality strict and perfect, though in degree it is broad and imperfect' (MM 446/110). The internal actions that are required are definite, but they are not dischargeable. Valuing humanity in the proper way must be worked at: it is an internal labour with which we are never simply done. So the obligations of virtue are always broad.

So there are four categories of duties of virtue: (1) perfect duties to oneself, to preserve and respect the humanity in one's own person; (2) imperfect duties to oneself, to develop one's humanity, intellectually and physically; (3) duties of love for others, to promote their happiness; and (4) duties of respect for others, including respect for their rights. The degree of one's virtue is measured by the extent to which one succeeds in doing all of these duties from the pure moral motive of regard for humanity. Complete virtue is unattainable (in this life), so our duty to achieve it is itself of broad obligation: it is a duty to progress towards it (MM 409/69; C2 82–86/ 85–89; TP 284–285-69).

Kant explains all of our duties in terms of freedom. Duties of justice spring from the very idea of external freedom: a world in which everyone's rights are respected is a world in which complete external freedom is achieved. Virtue is the achievement of inner freedom, for the virtuous person acts from freely chosen ends rather than being governed by inclinations and desires. If both of these kinds of duties were universally practiced, human beings would be in every sense free.

## AUTONOMY AND THE KINGDOM OF ENDS

The next step in the *Foundations* argument is to relate the two formulas already given to one another and produce a third.

> Objectively the ground of all practical legislation lies (according to the first principle) in the rule and in the form of universality, which makes it capable of being a law . . . subjectively, it lies in the end. But the subject of all ends is every rational being as an end in itself (by the second principle); from this there follows the third practical principle of the will as the supreme condition of its harmony with universal practical reason, viz., the idea of the will of every rational being as making universal law. (G 431/49)

Rational beings are the determiners of ends—the ones who set value on things. So a rational being must value rational nature as an end in itself; and it is with this end in view that we act only on maxims which could be universal laws. Since we are the ones who make rational nature our end, we are the ones who give ourselves this law. We are autonomous.

There are two ways of being motivated, autonomously and heteronomously. When you are motivated autonomously, you act on a law that you give to yourself; when you act heteronomously, the law is imposed on you by means of a sanction—you are provided with an interest in acting on it. Take a simple example: you might obey some positive law—for instance, you might pay your taxes—because you are afraid of being punished if you do not. This is heteronomy: your interest in avoiding punishment binds you to the law. On the other hand, you might pay your taxes even if you believe that you could avoid it, either because you think everyone should pay their share, or because you think that people should obey laws made by popular legislation. These would be, in an ordinary sense, examples of autonomy—of giving the law to yourself because of some commitment to it or belief in it as a law.

From what I have said so far, it looks as if you could adopt any principle autonomously, and the idea of autonomy does not determine the content of the principle that is autonomously adopted. But Kant claims that it does, and that the categorical imperative is in a special way *the* principle of autonomy. Heteronomous motivation can only be associated with hypothetical imperatives, for the hypothesis expresses the interest that binds you to the law. The main problem with most ethical theorists before Kant is that they have failed to see that moral motivation cannot be heteronomous. Duty is supposed to obligate us unconditionally. Any theory that tries to explain obligation by offering us an interest of some kind in doing our duty provides us with a principle that commands hypothetically, not categorically. When the imperative is hypothetical, we always have an option: either perform the action, or give up the interest. To explain obligation, we need an imperative that binds us unconditionally. But this means that moral motivation, if it exists, must be autonomous. There can only be one reason why human beings must obey the moral law, and that is that we give that law to ourselves (G 432–433/51).

The human will must be seen as universally legislative. Each of us has a will that makes laws for itself as if for everyone. Since human beings together legislate the moral law, we form a moral community: a Kingdom of Ends. The Kingdom of Ends is an ideal. It is 'a systematic union of different rational beings through common laws', a republic of all rational beings. It is a community in which freedom is perfectly realised, for its citizens are free both in the sense that they have made their own laws and in the sense that the laws they have made are the laws of freedom—the juridical laws of external freedom and the ethical laws of internal freedom. The Kingdom of Ends is also 'a whole of rational beings as ends in themselves as well as of the particular ends which each may set for himself', a system of all good ends (G 433/51). Each citizen takes his own perfection and the happiness of others as an end and treats every other as an end in itself. It is a community engaged in the harmonious and cooperative pursuit of the good.

The Kingdom of Ends provides us with a way of representing the sense in which moral laws are laws of autonomy. Suppose all rational beings were really to form a Kingdom of Ends, and held a constitutional convention to make its laws. What laws would we choose? Each of us would be eager to preserve his or her own freedom, so we would have to choose laws that preserved the freedom of each according to a universal law. Since we would will a world in which the assistance of others and the resources of human talents were available for use as the means of action, we would will that each person contribute something to the obligatory ends. The laws we would choose to be under, if it were ours to choose, would be moral laws. When we do obey moral laws, then, we are autonomous and free.[30] It is only because we are imperfectly rational, and subject to the importunities of desire, that morality appears to us as constraint—as *duty* (G 397/13).

This gives Kant another way of formulating the categorical imperative. We are always to act as if we were legislating for the Kingdom of Ends (G 434/52). Of course, this ideal is not actually brought about by the individual's living up to it. The accidents of nature, and the actions of other people, may distort the results of morally good conduct, and lead to the unhappiness of the moral agent or others. But since the moral law commands categorically, we must nevertheless act as legislators in the Kingdom of Ends. Although this seems like a constraint when the results will be bad, there is a sense in which the agent's freedom is highlighted in such a case. The agent is not constrained by external forces to act against the rational ideal that is the object of his/her will.

## THE FOUNDATION OF MORALITY

If there is a categorical imperative, a law of pure reason applying to the will, then these three formulas tell us what it is. But to demonstrate that the categorical imperative is real, Kant needs to show something else—that the human will can be motivated by it. Otherwise morality is a 'mere phantom of the mind' (G 445/64), a dogma of rationalist metaphysics which does not apply to the world. To establish the moral law, we need a critique of practical reason.

The categorical imperative is synthetic. Morality is not contained in the concept of a rational will. When a proposition is synthetic, its two terms must be linked 'through their union with a third in which both of them are to be found': it must be deduced (G 447/65). Kant's view is that this third term is provided by the positive conception of the freedom of the will. His argument is that (1) a rational will must be regarded as a free will, and (2) a free will is a will under moral law. Therefore, a rational will is a will under moral law.

The second premise is proved first. The will is the causality of a rational being. If the will's actions—its choices and decisions—are determined by the laws of nature, it is not a free will. Suppose that all your choices could be traced to a psychological law of nature: say, 'a person's will is always determined by the strength of his/her desires'. Although you would always do what you 'want most', your will would not be free. A free will is one that is not determined by an external force, even your own desires. This is the negative conception of freedom. But we also require a positive conception of freedom. The will is a causality, and the concept of a causality entails laws: a causality which functions randomly is a contradiction. To put it another way, the will is practical reason, and we cannot conceive a practical reason that chooses and acts for no reason. Since reasons are derived from principles, the will must have a principle. A free will must therefore have its own law or principle, which it gives to itself. It must be an autonomous will. But the moral law is the law of an autonomous will. Kant concludes that 'a free will and a will under moral laws are identical' (G 447/65).[31]

Readers are often puzzled by this argument. If the will is free to choose its own principle, why should it be under the moral law? To se why, consider the problem from the perspective of a free rational will. Because it is a rational will, it must have a principle. Because it is free, it must choose this principle for itself. Nothing determines this choice: it is completely spontaneous. Since its principle determines what it counts as a reason, nothing yet counts as a reason for it. But if nothing yet counts as a reason for it, it appears to have no basis for choosing its principle. There is no constraint on its choice, except that it choose a law. But notice that this is just what the Formula of Universal Law says. The only constraint that it imposes on our choices is that they have the form of law. Nothing provides any content for that law; all that it has to be is a law. The moral law simply describes the position of a free will. When the will's choices are directed by the moral law, it expresses its spontaneity. The moral law is the law of spontaneity. The will that is governed by morality is free.

On the other hand, if the will allows its choices to be directed by an external force, it surrenders its freedom. In *Religion Within the Limits of Reason Alone*, Kant emphasises that this is a *Fall*, perverse and inexplicable (R 34–35/30, 41–44/36–39, 78–79/73). Since the free will is not moved by desire unless it chooses to be, the will's surrender of its freedom cannot be explained by the pressures of temptation. Susceptibility to temptation is itself the product of the will's perverse choice to allow incentives of inclination to outweigh moral incentives (R 23–24/19, 30/25, 36–37/31–32).

But why should we believe that the human will is free? In the *Foundations* Kant begins this part of the argument by observing that as rational beings we must act under the idea of freedom. When we make rational choices and decisions, we must think of ourselves as free. A being which must regard itself as free really is 'practically free' and so bound by the laws of freedom (G 448/66). But Kant then complains that this argument by itself is circular if offered as an account of how we can be morally motivated. A *purely* rational will is just a will under moral laws, but we are not purely rational. Morality demands we subordinate our happiness to our freedom. What is needed is an explanation of how we can be motivated to do this. This explanation is provided by the idea of the intelligible world.

Everyone, Kant claims, distinguishes between things as they appear and things as they are in themselves. And everyone can apply this distinction to himself as well as to other things. But in addition, human beings have reason, which is distinguished from everything else in that it is a pure spontaneous activity. Therefore, a human being must count himself as belonging to the intelligible world, as well as to the world of sense (G 450–453/69–71; A538–541; B 566–569/467–469). The intelligible world is the noumenal world, regarded as consisting of pure agencies which generate the world that appears to us. We know nothing of these agencies, except that we must think of them as the source of the appearances from which our knowledge is constructed. But our own capacity for pure activity places us among them. If we are among the intelligences, we are free and spontaneous, and so bound by morality.

In the *Critique of Practical Reason* the argument goes the other way.[32] The reality of moral obligation is known through what Kant calls a 'Fact of Reason' (C2 31/31). This fact is our consciousness of the moral law and its capacity to motivate us whenever we construct maxims. We are conscious of the law not only in the sense that it tells us what to do, but in the sense that we know we *can* do what it tells us, no matter how strong the opposing motives (C2 30/30). The fact that we are able to act against our strongest desires reveals to us that we are free, and so are members of the intelligible world.

The intelligible world plays two roles in Kant's argument. First, the distinction between the intelligible and sensible worlds removes the fatal difficulty for morality that would otherwise come from the universal determinism that holds in the phenomenal world (G 455–456/75–76). Just as importantly, the intelligible world explains 'the interest attaching to the ideas of morality' (G449/67). For we realise that '*The intelligible world contains the ground of the sensible world and so of its laws*' (G 453/72). The causal laws that determine everything that happens are part of the world of appearances, and are therefore part of what the intelligences produce. It is the intelligible world that generates the world as we know it. So if you are a member of the intelligible world, you are among the forces that make the world the way it is. If you will morally, you really are a co-legislator of the Kingdom of Ends. This is the motivating idea of morality.

> . . . the idea of a pure intelligible world as a whole of all intelligences to which we ourselves belong as rational beings . . . is always a useful and permissible idea for the purpose of rational faith. This is so even though all knowledge terminates at its boundary, for through the glorious ideal of a universal kingdom of ends in themselves (rational beings) a lively interest in the moral law can be awakened in us. (G 462/82)

## THE RELIGION OF REASON

The positive conception of freedom shows us how a metaphysical concept can be defined and supported by practical reason. The moral law defines spontaneous causality. 'In the entire faculty of reason only the practical can lift us above the world of sense and furnish cognitions of a supersensuous order . . .' (C2 106/110). In the Dialectic of the *Critique of Practical Reason* Kant extends this kind of account to the concepts of God and immortality. The moral law commits us to its complete object, the Highest Good: virtue and happiness proportional to it. Virtue is unconditionally good. But this does 'not imply that virtue is the entire and perfect good as the object of the faculty of desire of finite rational beings. For this, happiness is also required' (C2 110/114). The Highest Good is the systematic totality of good ends to which the moral law directs us. Morality demands that we make this our end, but it seems to be impossible to achieve. Complete virtue cannot be realised in this life, and virtue would have to be necessarily connected to happiness for the Highest Good to be realised.[33] But no such connection obtains, for virtue does not inevitably lead to happiness, nor morally good intentions to good results. In fact, an empirical causal connection would be insufficient to solve the problem, for it would have to be between good actions and happiness, yet good actions may be done without a good will (C2 125–129). This apparent impossibility gives rise to an antinomy. We know through the Fact of Reason that the moral law commands categorically. But we cannot be categorically commanded to seek an end that is impossible for us to achieve. 'If, therefore, the highest good is impossible according to practical rules, then the moral law which commands that it be furthered must be fantastic, directed to empty imaginary ends, and consequently inherently false' (C2 114/118).

It has seemed to critics that Kant here forsakes the purity of his position. The moral law is categorical and not conditioned by consistency with happiness. This criticism is a misunderstanding both of what Kant asserted earlier and what he claims here. As Kant himself points out in reply to criticisms by Christian Garve (1742–98), he never asserted, and nothing he says implies, that happiness is not of the utmost importance (TP 278–289/64–72). The unconditional character of morality means that the desire for your own happiness must not stop you from doing what is right; it does not mean that morality is the only good and important thing. Happiness is conditionally valuable, but when its condition is met, it is a genuine good. The moral law commits us to the realisation of the good things that rational beings place value on. A world in which good people are miserable is morally defective.

The threat posed by the impossibility of achieving the Highest Good is best understood by considering the way the moral motive functions. You view yourself as a member of the intelligible world and so as a possible co-legislator in a Kingdom of Ends. You are among the world's first causes. But there are other first causes: other persons, and whatever else is responsible for the way things appear to us and so of the material content of the laws of nature. In the phenomenal world the results of our actions are determined not just by our own intentions, but by the forces of nature and the actions of other persons. Our attempts to realise the good are often diverted by these other forces. It is this that gives rise to the antinomy. Kant's description of the problem in the *Critique of Judgement* is better:

> He [a righteous man] desires no advantage to himself from follow-ing [the moral law], either in this or in another world; he wishes, rather, disinterestedly to establish the good to which that holy law directs all his powers. But his effort is bounded; and from nature, although he may expect here and there a contingent accordance, he can never expect a regular harmony . . . with the purpose which he yet feels himself obliged and impelled to accomplish. Deceit, violence, and envy will always surround him, although he himself be honest, peaceable, and kindly; and the righteous men with whom he meets will, notwithstanding their worthiness of happiness, be yet subjected by nature, which regards not this, to all the evils of want, disease, and untimely death, just like the beasts of the earth. . . . The purpose, then, which this well-intentioned person had and ought to have before him in his pursuit of moral laws, he must certainly give up as impossible. (C3 452/303)

The motivating thought of morality is the thought that you can contribute to making the world a Kingdom of Ends. But if your attempts are always diverted by other forces, that thought is, as Kant says, false and fantastic.

The solution to this as to every antinomy is to appeal to the noumenal/phenomenal distinction. In the world of sense, there is no causal connection between a virtuous disposition and happiness, but there could be a connection between one's noumenal disposition and one's happiness in the world of sense. But this connection would be indirect: it would be mediated by an Author of Nature who had designed the laws of nature so that the connection holds (C2 114–115/119). In order to play the role envisaged, this Author would have to be omnipotent (to design the laws of nature), omniscient (to look into the hearts of rational beings and know their moral dispositions), and perfectly good. The Author of Nature would have the attributes traditionally ascribed to God (C2 140/145). If there were a God, then, the Highest Good would be possible, and morality would not direct us to impossible ends. Since we must obey the moral law, and therefore must adopt the Highest Good as our end, we need to believe that end is possible. So we need to believe in what will make it possible. This is not a contingent need, based on an arbitrary desire, but 'a need of pure reason'. This provides a pure practical reason for belief in God (C2 142–143/147–149).

A similar argument establishes the practical rationality of belief in immortality. The moral law commands you to seek your own moral perfection: the holiness of your will. This cannot be achieved in the course of your life, for no one with a sensuous as well as a rational nature has a morally perfect disposition. What a creature who exists in time, subject to causality and so to sensibility, can achieve is *progress* towards holiness of will. An endless progress is the same, in the eyes of God, as the achievement of holiness. 'The Infinite Being, to whom the temporal condition is nothing, sees in this series, which is for us without end, a whole conformable to the moral law' (C2 123/127).[34]

A faith in God and in immortality of the soul thus based on practical reason—'pure practical faith'—is not just wishful thinking, because it springs from a rational demand. As Kant strikingly puts it:

> Granted that the pure moral law inexorably binds every man as a command (not as a rule of prudence), the righteous man may say: I will that there be a God, that my existence in this world be also an existence in a pure world of the understanding, and finally that my duration be endless. (C2 143/148–149)

This does not mean that faith is commanded. The moral law demands that we think the highest good possible but 'the manner in which we are to think of it as possible is subject to our own choice' since 'reason cannot objectively decide whether it is by universal laws of nature without a wise Author presiding over nature or whether only on the assumption of such an Author' (C2 145/151). Faith springs from a need of the moral disposition and as such is voluntary. Salvation depends on moral character, not on what one believes.[35]

Our beliefs in God, immortality and freedom—that is, existence in an intelligible world—are 'postulates of practical reason'. A postulate of practical reason is theoretical in form, asserting something about what is the case, yet it cannot be shown theoretically to be either true or false. But we have an interest springing from the needs of morality in believing it.[36] Since practical reason supports belief in the postulates, its power is more extensive than that of theoretical reason. In establishing the postulates, practical reason takes up the metaphysical tasks that theoretical reason had to abandon. For if there is a God, who made the world in order to achieve the Highest Good, then the world does have an unconditionally good purpose. A teleological account of the sort that the metaphysician seeks—one according to which everything is made for the best in the Best of All Possible Worlds—would be true (C2 132–141/137–147).

But Kant insists that practical faith, although rational, does not in any way extend our *knowledge*. We cannot use the tenets of practical faith to explain the way things are, or for any theoretical purposes. This shows that our faculties are wisely adapted to our vocation. For the final purpose of the Best of All Possible Worlds is the achievement of moral goodness by human beings (C3 442–443/293). And if we had metaphysical knowledge:

> . . . God and eternity in their awful majesty would stand unceasingly before our eyes . . . Transgression of the law would indeed be shunned, and the commanded would be performed. But because the disposition from which actions should be done cannot be instilled by any command, and because the spur to action would in this case be always present and external, reason would have no need to endeavor to gather its strength to resist the inclination by a vivid idea of the dignity of the law. Thus most actions conforming to the law would be done from fear, few would be done from hope, none from duty. The moral worth of actions, on which alone the worth of the person and even of the world depends in the eyes of supreme wisdom, would not exist at all. (C2 147/152–153)

'I have therefore found it necessary to deny knowledge, in order to make room for faith' (C1 Bxxx/29).

## REVOLUTION AND WORLD PEACE

Kant was an ardent champion of the American and French Revolutions. His support for the latter won him a reputation as a Jacobin, and at one point there was a widespread rumour that he was going to Paris as an advisor to the new government.[37] Jachmann writes of Kant's impatience for news from France, and his obsession with the subject in conversation.[38] His enthusiasm for the Revolution was not as idealising as that of many of its admirers, and he did not turn against it when so many others did. According to one report 'he said all the horrors in France were unimportant compared with the chronic evil of despotism from which France had suffered, and the Jacobins were probably right in all they were doing'.[39] Given the high value he places on freedom and human rights, it is not surprising that he regards a republic as the ideal form of government. But it is surprising to find this enthusiasm for its ruthless establishment in a man who believed that we must always act as citizens in the Kingdom of Ends regardless of consequences, and have faith in God to set things right. What makes it even more surprising is that Kant himself wrote that revolution is always wrong, and that 'It is the people's duty to endure even the most intolerable abuse of supreme authority' (MM 320/86).[40]

Kant's political theory, like his ethics generally, owes a great deal to Rousseau. It is a social contract theory, in which people unite according to a General Will. I have explained above how property rights arise from the Juridical Postulate of Practical Reason. These rights exist in a state of nature, but they are 'provisional'. Since a right is an authorisation to use coercion, anyone may defend his right against another. Disputes will inevitably arise, and there is no way to settle them, except by violence. In this way we present a threat to one another in the state of nature. This licenses us to use coercion against one another to establish a juridical state of affairs— a state in which rights are guaranteed rather than provisional. So we have a right and, indeed, a duty to coerce others to enter into political society with us (MM 255–313/64–78).

The point of political society is to protect rights and freedom. The ideal state—indeed, the 'one and only legitimate constitution' (MM 340/112) is a republic (MM 340–342/112–114; PP 349–353/93–98). But as things stand we must take the existing government to represent the general will of the people, and, consequently, must obey it. Oddly, we must do this even if the existing government is the result of a recent revolution. The government itself has a duty to promote its own gradual evolution to a republican form. And there should be complete freedom of speech, so that the citizens can discuss these matters. But no citizen is in a legitimate position to force the transition (MM 318–323/84–89; 370–372/138–141; TP 297–306/79–87).

The argument that shows that individuals should enter into juridical relations with one another also shows that nations should do. Freedom will only be realised when there is a world community guaranteeing perpetual peace. Only a cosmopolitan union of all the states of the world under common law, on the model of the union of the American states, will guarantee peace. This being an unattainable ideal, there should at least be a Congress or League of Nations, and an observation of the Laws of Nations (MM 350–351/123–125; IUH 24ff/18ff; PP; TP 307–313/87–92). Important among these will be laws for the conduct of war, for wars should be conducted according to laws that will make possible the eventual achievement of peace. In the *Metaphysical Elements of Justice* (MM 343–351/114–125) and in *Perpetual Peace* (PP 343–360/85–105) Kant attempts to spell out in detail what these laws should be, and expresses a hope that rulers will attend to what he says (PP 368–369/115–116).[41]

Peace is important not only because it is the end of violence and injustice. Peace will bring with it the entire achievement of the Kingdom of Ends on earth. It goes hand in hand with the state of affairs in which every nation is a republic. When the people, not the rulers, decide whether to go to war, war will come to an end, for the people will not go to war for trivial reasons (PP 351/95). When there is less war, social institutions will improve, for as things now stand, they are mostly designed for the sake of war. Public funds will be channelled into education rather than war debts, and culture will be improved (IUH 26/21, 28/23; CB 121/66–67). Enlightenment—the condition in which people think for themselves (WE 35/3)—will be fostered by freedom of speech and discussion. And, finally, morality itself will be achieved, as the ultimate product of culture and enlightenment. For a 'good constitution is not to be expected from morality, but, conversely, a good moral condition of a people is to be expected only under a good constitution' (PP 366/113; OQ 92–93/152–153).

At the end of the *Metaphysical Elements of Justice* there is a suggestion that we may have an historical faith in the possibility of peace, on the same model as practical religious faith. No theoretical knowledge can be attained as to whether peace is possible or not. In such a case we may consider whether we have an interest in accepting the conjecture that it is. If the interest is based on morality—if the conjecture is one that must be true if moral ends are to be achieved—then we may accept it. 'Even if the realisation of this goal of abolishing war were always to remain just a pious wish, we still would not be deceiving ourselves by adopting the maxim of working for it with unrelenting perseverance' (MM 354/128). Indeed we have a duty to do this, and this gives rise to a need to believe it possible. The structure of the argument is exactly that of the argument for belief in God and immortality. Kant calls perpetual peace the 'highest political good'.

This faith in the possibility of peace is buttressed, in the historical writings, by a teleological interpretation of history in which nature is envisioned as working towards the moral condition of the human race, even using war and the selfishness of human nature as her tools. Every region of the globe supplies materials that humans can use to adapt to life there, and war has the function of ensuring that human beings eventually do spread everywhere. This brings about the cultivation and development of human powers and talents. As the populations of the various regions increase, these groups are again, inevitably, brought back into contact with one another. Differences of religion and language keep them at war for a time, but pressures to establish peace come from the need for commerce. Eventually this forces them to establish juridical relations with one another, and will lead to peace and justice all over the world.[42] This interpretation of history is offered, not as something knowable, and not as a reason for moral quiescence, but as a way those morally committed to peace can envision nature's cooperation with their efforts (PP 368/114).

This picture of history as leading to peace is strikingly deterministic. In it the moral disposition is seen as resulting from the republican constitutions and conditions of enlightenment that nature produces. Nature is seen as working through 'the mechanism of human passions' (PP 368/114), through competition, the love of luxury, and war; as using methods that would work on 'a race of devils' (PP 366/112). It is from a practical standpoint that we see ourselves as free; to the theorising mind, everything is explicable in terms of causes. While theoretical reason explains, practical reason is wholly normative: actual examples of moral conduct cannot be identified with certainty, nor are they necessary to support the moral law's claims on us (G 407–408/23–24).

And yet Kant believes that history *has* provided us with one piece of evidence that the moral disposition is real in the human race, and may yet prevail. This piece of evidence is the enthusiasm of the spectators of the French Revolution. The French Revolution aims at a republican constitution. It therefore aims at justice, and 'the condition whereby war (the source of all evil and corruption of morals) is deterred' (OQ 86/145). The enthusiasm of the spectators must be explained by the existence of a moral disposition, for 'genuine enthusiasm always moves only towards what is ideal and, indeed, to what is purely moral, such as the concept of right, and it cannot be grafted onto self-interest' (OQ 86/145). So Kant concludes:

> The revolution of a gifted people which we have seen unfolding in our day may succeed or miscarry; it may be filled with misery and atrocities to the point that a sensible man, were he boldly to hope to execute it successfully the second time, would never resolve to make the experiment at such cost—this revolution, I say, nonetheless finds in the hearts of all the spectators (who are not engaged in this game themselves) a wishful participation that borders closely on enthusiasm, the very expression of which is fraught with danger; this sympathy, therefore, can have no other cause than a moral predisposition in the human race. (OQ 85/144)

Kant began his critical work as the 'all-destroyer', toppling the edifice of the Leibniz-Wolffian philosophy, along with its optimism that God has chosen everything for the best in the Best of All Possible Worlds. In its place he put a faith in human freedom, as the source of purely rational morality and the cornerstone of a metaphysics of practical reason. This freedom is not an object of knowledge, but of a rational aspiration: something for human beings to achieve, and thereby to realise the ideals of reason in the world. The remarks on the French Revolution quoted above are from the essay 'On the Old Question: is the Human Race Constantly Progressing?' In the French Revolution Kant found evidence that freedom is real in human nature, and may yet become real in the world.

> I claim to be able to predict to the human race . . . I predict its progress towards the better . . . because it [the Revolution and its reception] has revealed a tendency and faculty in human nature for improvement . . . which nature and freedom alone, united in the human race in conformity with inner principles of right, could have promised. (OQ 88/147)

Optimism is restored, but it is an optimism based on a moral faith in humanity.

# Notes

1. I would like to thank Ted Cohen, Manley Thompson and the editors for comments on an earlier draft of this chapter.
2. Works by Kant are cited in the text, using the abbreviations below. Following standard practice, I have included a reference to the page number of the relevant volume of *Kants gesammelte Schriften* (published by the *Preussische Akademie der Wissenschaften*, Berlin) for all works except the *Critique of Pure Reason* and the *Lectures on Ethics*. The volume numbers are listed after the titles below. The second page number, following the slash, is that of the translation used. The *Critique of Pure Reason* is cited in the standard way, by the page numbers of the first (A) and second (B) editions. For further information see the Bibliography.

   PE:     *Enquiry concerning the clarity of the principles of natural theology and ethics* (the so-called 'Prize Essay') (II)
   ID:     *On the form and principles of the sensible and intelligible world* (Inaugural Dissertation) (II)
   LE:     *Lectures on Ethics*
   C1:     *Critique of Pure Reason*
   PFM:    *Prolegomena to Any Future Metaphysics* (IV)
   IUH:    'Idea for a Universal History from a Cosmopolitan Point of View' (VIII)
   WE:     'What is Enlightenment?' (VIII)
   G:      *Foundations of the Metaphysics of Morals* (IV)
   CB:     'Conjectural Beginning of Human History' (VIII)
   C2:     *Critique of Practical Reason* (V)
   C3:     *Critique of Judgement* (V)
   R:      *Religion within the Limits of Reason Alone* (VI)
   TP:     'On the Common Saying: "This may be True in Theory but it does not Apply in Practice"' (VIII)
   END:    'The End of All Things' (VIII)
   PP:     *Perpetual Peace* (VIII)
   MM:     *The Metaphysics of Morals* (VI)
   SRTL:   'On a Supposed Right to Lie from Altruistic Motives' (VIII)
   ANTH:   *Anthropology from a Pragmatic Point of View* (VII)
   OQ:     'An Old Question Raised Again: Is the Human Race Constantly Progressing?' from *The Conflict of the Faculties* (VII)

3. Just as reason provides principles that determine what, given our circumstances, we ought to believe, it can provide principles that determine what in our circumstances we ought to do. The latter is 'practical reason'. Some of the British Empiricists appear to have believed that practical reason is merely applied theoretical reason: for instance, instrumental practical reasoning is just 'applied' causal reasoning. See, for example, David Hume, *A Treatise of Human Nature* (ed. L. L. Selby-Bigge, London: Oxford, 1888) pp. 413–18. What this account leaves out is that if I am to act on the knowledge that something is a means to my

233

end, I must still have a distinctively *practical* rational capacity: that of being *motivated* to take the means to my ends. This distinctly practically rational capacity may also move us to govern our actions by principles of *pure* practical reason which are not applications but analogues of theoretical principles. For discussions of this point see Thomas Nagel, *The Possibility of Altruism* (Oxford: Clarendon Press, 1970; reprint Princeton: Princeton University Press, 1978) chapters V and VI: and my 'Skepticism about Practical Reason', *Journal of Philosophy*, vol. LXXXIII, no. 1 (January 1986) pp. 5–25.

4. Ernst Cassirer, *Kant's Life and Thought*, trans. James Haden (New Haven: Yale University Press, 1981) pp. 20–1.

5. Paul Schilpp, *Kant's Pre-Critical Ethics* (Chicago: Northwestern University Press, 1938; reprint New York: Garland, 1971) p. 6. See also the foreword to *Lectures on Ethics*, where Lewis White Beck quotes one of Kant's friends as saying:

> How often he moved us to tears, how often he agitated our hearts, how often he lifted our minds and feelings from the fetters of selfish eudaemonism to the high consciousness of freedom, to unconditional obedience to the law of reason, to the exhaltation of unselfish duty! The immortal philosopher seemed to us to be inspired with a heavenly power, and he inspired us, who listened to him in wonder. His hearers certainly never left a single lecture in his ethics without having become better men. (LE ix)

6. Cassirer, *Kant's Life and Thought*, p. 46.

7. That is, the principle that anything that exists or occurs must be explained by a reason which shows why the thing must exist or occur and cannot be otherwise than as it is.

8. Lewis White Beck, *Early German Philosophy: Kant and His Predecessors* (Cambridge, Mass.: Harvard University Press, 1969), p. 334.

9. Beck, *Early German Philosophy: Kant and His Predecessors*, p. 274.

10. See below, pp. 9–11.

11. Eric A. Blackall, *The Emergence of German as a Literary Language, 1700-1755* (Cambridge University Press: 1959) pp. 26–48.

12. Beck, *Early German Philosophy: Kant and His Predecessors*, p. 260.

13. Beck, *Early German Philosophy: Kant and His Predecessors*, pp. 441–42.

14. It is sometimes asserted that in his pre-critical period Kant was a moral sense theorist, or sentimentalist, but as the above discussion shows, he was at best an ambivalent one. (See also Schilpp, *Kant's Pre-Critical Ethics*, Chapter III.) Kant was a rationalist by training and perhaps by temperament, but there is no doubt he admired Francis Hutcheson (1694–1746) and Adam Smith (1723–90). Kant's admiration of Hutcheson is clear from the frequent (though critical) discussions of Hutcheson in his work. For Kant's admiration of Smith see D. D. Raphael and A. L. Macfie's Introduction to Smith's *The Theory of Moral Sentiments* (Indianapolis: Liberty Classics, 1982) p. 31. In this period among the British Moralists, the sentimentalists were incomparably better moral philosophers than rationalists such as Samuel Clarke (1675–1729) and his

followers. One may see Kant as trying to respond to two of the main objections which the sentimentalists levelled at ethical rationalism. First, the sentimentalists had a functional account of what reason is, which enabled them to deny that reason can give rise to *a priori* concepts such as the rationalists believed 'right' and 'good' to be. The early rationalists by contrast had no competing account of what reason is that they could use to support their position. Only with Richard Price (1723–91) do we find a British rationalist attacking this problem head-on. Second, the early rationalists insisted that reason can directly determine the will, but they did not have an account of *how* it does so. With his rich account of what reason is in hand, Kant attempts to construct a rationalist ethical theory which will solve these problems.

15. So called because it was publicly defended on the occasion of Kant's appointment to the Chair of Professor of Logic and Metaphysics at Königsberg.

16. In the mid-1760s Kant wrote:

> By inclination I am an inquirer. I feel a consuming thirst for knowledge, the unrest which goes with the desire to progress in it, and satisfaction at every advance in it. There was a time when I believed this constituted the honor of humanity, and I despised the people, who know nothing. Rousseau corrected me in this. . . . I learned to honor men, and I would find myself more useless than the common laborer if I did not believe that this view of mine can give a worth to all others in establishing the rights of humanity.

In rendering this passage I have drawn on the translations by Lewis White Beck in the introduction to *Immanuel Kant: Critique of Practical Reason and Other Writings in Moral Philosophy* (University of Chicago Press, 1949; reprint New York: Garland, 1976) p. 7; and by Paul Schilpp in *Kant's Pre-Critical Ethics*, p. 48.

17. Beck, *Early German Philosophy: Kant and His Predecessors*, p. 337.

18. Beck, *Early German Philosophy: Kant and His Predecessors*, p. 400.

19. Lewis White Beck, *A Commentary on Kant's Critique of Practical Reason* (University of Chicago Press, 1960) pp. 3–18. For further treatment see p. 223–4 and note 32 of this chapter.

20. Hume, in the *Treatise of Human Nature*, had argued that 'regard for the virtue of [an] action' cannot be 'the first virtuous motive, which bestows a merit on any action'. For, he says:

> Before we can have such a regard, the action must be really virtuous; and this virtue must be deriv'd from some virtuous motive: And consequently the virtuous motive must be different from regard to the virtue of the action. (p. 478)

This was, at the time, a potentially powerful point against his rationalist opponents. Because they argued that the sense of duty was the 'first' motive of moral conduct, Hume's argument forbids them to say that its motive is what makes an action a duty. It forces them to take an intuitionist view about the content of morality. But Kant overcomes Hume's objection by distinguishing between the formal and the material elements of motivation. If the 'first virtuous motive' does not have to be given materially, the objection does not hold. Nevertheless, an argument similar to Hume's is used by W. D. Ross 'against *any* theory which holds that motive of any kind is included in the content of duty'. Interestingly, Ross uses the argument in support of intuitionism, since he thinks that 'it would be paradoxical to hold that we ought to act from some other motive but never ought to act from a sense of duty, which is the highest motive'. See *The Right and the Good* (Oxford: Clarendon Press, 1930) pp. 5–6.

21. The reading of the contradiction test which I give here is not uncontroversial. There is disagreement both about Kant's intentions and about what form the contradiction test must take in order to work. For a defense of this interpretation against the major alternatives see my 'Kant's Formula of Universal Law', *Pacific Philosophical Quarterly*, vol. 66, nos. 1 and 2 (January/April 1985) pp. 24–47. As I point out there, my reading does not work for Kant's other example of this sort of contradiction, that of a man who considers suicide as an escape from future misery. I do not think that Kant was right in supposing that the duty not to commit suicide could be derived from the first contradiction test, for the universalisation of suicide as a method of escaping misery is not self-defeating, nor can I see that it is in any way self-contradictory. No reading that I know of successfully deals with all of Kant's examples, but this need not mean that the test cannot be constructed. It may mean that Kant chose his examples badly.

22. Kant's claim that his contradiction test can serve as a criterion for determining what our specific duties are has generated a vast literature of criticism and defense. The criticism I mention here, one of the most influential, was made by Hegel and the Idealists (see, for instance, Hegel, *Phenomenology of Spirit*, trans. A. V. Miller (Oxford University Press, 1977) p. 262 and *Philosophy of Right*, trans. T. M. Knox (Oxford University Press, 1952) p. 90). Idealists also claimed that the test forbids too much: Bradley, for instance, in 'Duty for Duty's Sake' in *Ethical Studies* (Oxford University Press, 1962) p. 155, claims that the test makes charity immoral, since universal charity would eliminate its objects. Both objections overlook the role of the agent's intentions and purposes in generating the contradiction. The first overlooks the fact that the agent intends to avail himself of the institution which the universalisation of his maxim would eliminate; for him, given his intentions, the institution is necessary. The second overlooks the fact that the agent's purpose in say, acts of charity, would be satisfied in a world where such were no longer called for. For a careful defense of Kant's view from these objections see Marcus Singer, *Generalization in Ethics* (New York: Atheneum, 1961) pp. 279–95.

23. For a helpful discussion of Kant's account of this duty see Barbara Herman, 'Mutual Aid and Respect for Persons,' *Ethics* 94 (July 1984) pp. 577–602.

24. For a more detailed explication of this argument, see my 'Kant's Formula of Humanity', *Kant-Studien*, Band 77, Heft 2 (April 1986) pp. 183–202.

25. On Kant's strictures against coercion and deception, see my 'The Right to Lie: Kant on Dealing with Evil', *Philosophy and Public Affairs*, vol. 15, no. 4 (Autumn 1986) pp. 325–49; and Onora O'Neill, 'Between Consenting Adults', *Philosophy and Public Affairs*, vol. 14, no. 3 (Summer 1985) pp. 252–77.

26. The *Metaphysics of Morals* has only recently received much attention in Anglo-American criticism. For treatments of this work and accounts of the division of duties, see Mary Gregor, *Laws of Freedom: A study of Kant's Method of applying the Categorical Imperative in the Metaphysik der Sitten* (Oxford: Basil Blackwell, 1963); Onora Nell (O'Neill), *Acting on Principle: An Essay on Kantian Ethics* (New York: Columbia University Press, 1975); and Bruce Aune, *Kant's Theory of Morals* (Princeton University Press, 1979).

27. *Metaphysische Anfangsgründe der Rechtslehre* and *Metaphysische Anfangs-gründe der Tugendlehre*. The English version of the former which I have used is translated under the title *Metaphysical Elements of Justice*, which unfortunately does not capture the symmetry.

28. In the *Foundations* Kant claims that in making moral decisions, the best formula to use is that of Universal Law (G 436–437/55). Interestingly, in the *Metaphysics of Morals* no direct use is made of the Formula of Universal Law: the Universal Principle of Justice and the Supreme Principle of Virtue are used instead. There are two possible reasons for this. One of course is that Kant changed his mind. A better reason is that the moral principles of the *Metaphysics of Morals* are at a general level, and Kant may still intend that one should use the universal law formulation at the level of particular decisions. The latter view has a certain plausibility, for the Formula of Universal Law is intended as a decision procedure. It is not a rule or a way of generating general rules, but a way of making decisions in concrete situations. This is why Kant holds the view, startling to many of his readers, that there can be no genuine conflicts of duty (MM 224/24). There is no room for conflict when decisions are made under the Formula of Universal Law, for the morally relevant features of the case are included in your maxim, and the maxim simply passes or fails the contradiction tests. Yet there are of course things to say about what in general our duties are, and this is the territory that the *Metaphysics of Morals* covers.

29. For a good account of this distinction see Onora Nell (O'Neill), *Acting on Principle*, pp. 43–58.

30. The idea of legislation in a Kingdom of Ends provides the most accessible link between Kant's own writings and those of his contem-porary 'contractualist' successors, for here we find the thought that we may be autonomously bound by the laws we would choose under ideal circumstances. For the most notable example see John Rawls, *A Theory of Justice* (Cambridge, Mass.: Harvard University Press, 1971).

31. This idea that freedom, autonomy and morality are the same is suggested by Rousseau in *The Social Contract*, trans. Maurice Cranston (Harmonds-worth: Penguin, 1968). Rousseau wrote: 'We might also add that man acquires with civil society, moral freedom, which alone makes man the master of himself; for to be governed by appetite alone is slavery, while

obedience to a law one prescribes to oneself is freedom' (p. 65). Possibly it was this suggestion that provided Kant with the solution to a problem he had worked on nearly all of his life—the problem of what freedom is.

32.  There is critical controversy over whether this resulted from a change in Kant's views. Kant did not say explicitly that it did; but in the *Foundations* he refers at the end of his argument to 'this deduction' (G 454/73), whereas in the *Critique of Practical Reason* he says that 'the reality of the moral law can be proved through no deduction' (C2 47/48). Additional external evidence is provided by the fact that writing the *Critique of Practical Reason* was a change of plan on Kant's part. (See Beck, *A Commentary on Kant's Critique of Practical Reason*, pp. 13–18.) For some recent discussions of this question, see Karl Ameriks, 'Kant's Deduction of Freedom and Morality' (*Journal of the History of Philosophy* 19 (January 1981) pp. 53–79) and Dieter Henrich, 'Die Deduktion des Sittengesetzes: Über die Gründe der Dunkelheit des letzten Abschnitte von Kants "Grundlegung zur Metaphysik der Sitten", in Alexander Schwan (ed.), *Denken in Schatten des Nihilismus* (Darmstadt: Wissenschaftliche Buchgesellschaft, 1975).

33.  It is not easy to understand why Kant holds that a perfect or holy will cannot be achieved in this life, either from what Kant says here or from the *Religion*, where he claims that there is 'radical evil in human nature'. In the *Religion* Kant squares the existence of evil with autonomy by showing how an evil will can be thought of as the result of our own choice. The incentives arising from our sensible nature do not compel us in any way: we act on them insofar as we make it our maxim to do so. But this makes it hard to understand why an imperfect will should be *inevitable* for a finite creature in the world of sense. Kant denies that the fact that we *have* non-moral incentives is an imperfection and, in any case, as he points out, the fact would not be imputable (R 28/23). For a discussion of this problem and of Kant's theory of moral faith generally, see Allen W. Wood, *Kant's Moral Religion* (Ithaca: Cornell University Press, 1970).

34.  It is not clear what exactly we are supposed to believe when we believe in immortality. Great difficulties lie here. If we are still to exist in time, the other life seems just to be a continuation of this one, perhaps with the same troubling conditions; if we are not, the notion of progress seems out of place. It also seems that it is in this other life that the virtuous are to be made happy. In fact in the earliest version of the theory, in the 'Canon' of the *Critique of Pure Reason*, this is the reason for belief in immortality (C1 A810–811 B838–839/639). Kant is aware of these difficulties, and takes them up in 'The End of All Things'. In fact, the case illustrates Kant's thesis, explained below, that the postulates of practical faith cannot be taken to extend our theoretical knowledge in any way (END 333–334/77). If we try to think of the other life, we necessarily think of something temporal; when we try to think of eternity, we find ourselves thinking of nature as petrified, or monotonous (END 334–335/78). This is a condition of the way we think.

35.  In *Religion Within the Limits of Reason Alone* (1793) Kant spells out in some detail what a religion based on moral faith would be, and offers reinterpretations of scripture and traditional Christian doctrines in terms of it.

This work got Kant into trouble with the authorities for the only time in his life. The liberal Frederick the Great died in 1786, and his more orthodox successor Friedrick Wilhelm II appointed Johann Christoff Wöllner as head of the state department of church and schools. Wöllner, a known opponent of the Enlightenment, began a campaign to stamp out religious enlightenment, and to enforce the authority of orthodox Protestant doctrine. Kant's prestige protected him from these repressive efforts for a time, but the *Religion* provoked Wöllner. Kant was forbidden to write on religious subjects by a direct order from the King, actually written by Wöllner. Notoriously, Kant complied 'as Your Majesty's most faithful subject', and took this phrase as license to publish his views about religion once again after Frederick Wilhelm's death. See Beck, *Early German Philosophy: Kant and His Predecessors*, p. 435.

36. The concept of property is also established by a postulate, the Juridical Postulate of Practical Reason, which says that external objects can be property (MM 246/52). One can see the similarity: it is theoretical in form, metaphysical in content (Kant carefully distinguishes 'property' properly speaking from mere empirical possession), and held valid because it is needed for the tasks of practical reason. Since the argument for the possibility of achieving world peace which has the same structure as his arguments for God and immortality, 'Peace can be achieved' is also a postulate of practical reason. See below, pp. 230–1.

37. G. P. Gooch, *Germany and the French Revolution* (New York: Russell & Russell, 1966) pp. 276–77.

38. Gooch, *Germany and the French Revolution*, p. 264.

39. Idem., p. 269.

40. See also the conclusion of Part II of 'On the Common Saying: "This may be true in Theory but it does not apply in Practice"', where Kant comes out strongly against revolution—to the relief, according to Gooch (*Germany and the French Revolution*, p. 269), of many of Kant's admirers who by then opposed the French Revolution. For discussions of the paradoxical character of Kant's attitude to the French Revolution see Lewis White Beck, 'Kant and the Right to Revolution', *Journal of the History of Ideas* 32 (1971), reprinted in Beck's *Essays on Kant and Hume* (New Haven: Yale University Press, 1978); and Hans Reiss, 'Kant and the Right of Rebellion', *Journal of the History of Ideas*, XVII, 2 (April 1956) pp. 179–92.

41. The League or Congress of Nations is only a 'negative surrogate' of a real World Republic, and the laws of war are in a sense only a negative surrogate of the laws of a world republic (PP 357/102). Instead of compelling us to act peacefully, they compel us to conduct ourselves in a way that will not make peace and international justice impossible (MM 347/119–120).

42. These remarks summarise things Kant says throughout his historical writings. See especially: *Idea for a Universal History from a Cosmopolitan Point of View; Conjectural Beginning of Human History;* and *Perpetual Peace,* First Supplement, 'Of the Guarantee for Perpetual Peace'.

# Bibliography

1. Ameriks, Karl, 'Kant's Deduction of Freedom and Morality', *Journal of the History of Philosophy* 19 (January 1981) pp. 53–79.
2. Aune, Bruce, *Kant's Theory of Morals* (Princeton University Press, 1979).
3. Beck, Lewis White, *A Commentary on Kant's Critique of Practical Reason* (University of Chicago Press, 1960).
4. ——, *Early German Philosophy: Kant and His Predecessors* (Cambridge, Mass.: Harvard University Press, 1969).
5. ——, Introduction to *Immanuel Kant: Critique of Practical Reason and Other Writings in Moral Philosophy* (University of Chicago Press, 1949: reprinted in New York: Garland, 1976).
6. ——, 'Kant and the Right to Revolution', *The Journal of the History of Ideas* 32 (1971) pp. 411–22. Reprinted in Beck's *Essays on Kant and Hume* (New Haven: Yale University Press, 1978).
7. Blackall, Eric A., *The Emergence of German as a Literary Language, 1700–1775* (Cambridge University Press, 1959).
8. Bradley, F. H., *Ethical Studies* (1876; 2nd ed., 1927: Oxford University Press Paperbacks, 1962).
9. Cassirer, Ernst, *Kants Leben und Lehre* (1918), trans. James Haden as *Kant's Life and Thought* (New Haven: Yale University Press, 1981).
10. Gooch, G. P., *Germany and the French Revolution* (New York: Russell & Russell, 1966).
11. Gregor, Mary J., *Laws of Freedom: A study of Kant's Method of applying the Categorical Imperative in the Metaphysik der Sitten* (Oxford: Basil Blackwell, 1963).
12. Hegel, G. W. F., *Phänomenologie des Geistes* (1807), trans. A. V. Miller as *Phenomenology of Spirit* (Oxford University Press, 1977).
13. ——, *Naturrecht und Staatswissenschaft im Grundrisse* (1821) 2nd ed.: *Grundlinien der Philosophie des Rechts* (1833), trans. T. M. Knox as *Philosophy of Right* (Oxford University Press, 1952).
14. Henrich, Dieter, 'Die Deduktion des Sittengesetzes: Über die Gründe der Dunkelheit des letzten Abschnittes von Kants *Grundlegung zur Metaphysik der Sitten*' in Alexander Schwan (ed.), *Denken in Schatten des Nihilismus* (Darmstadt: Wissenschaftliche Buchgesellschaft, 1975).
15. Herman, Barbara, 'Mutual Aid and Respect for Persons', *Ethics* 94 (July 1984) pp. 577–602.
16. Hume, David, *A Treatise of Human Nature*, L. A. Selby-Bigge (ed.) (Oxford University Press, 1888) 2nd ed. with additional editing by P. H. Nidditch (Oxford: Clarendon Press, 1978).
17. Hutcheson, Francis, *An inquiry into the Original of our Ideas of Beauty and Virtue* (London: 1725).
18. ——, *An Essay on the Nature and Conduct of the Passions and Affections. With Illustrations on the Moral Sense* (London: 1728).
19. Kant, Immanuel, *Untersuchung über die Deutlichkeit der Grundsätze der natürlichen Theologie und Moral* (1763), trans. G. B. Kerferd and

D. E. Walford as *Enquiry concerning the clarity of the principles of natural theology and ethics* in *Kant: Selected Pre-Critical Writings and Correspondence with Beck* (Manchester University Press and New York: Barnes & Noble, 1968).

20. ——, *De mundi sensibilis atque intelligibilis forma et Principiis* (1770) trans. G. B. Kerferd and D. E. Walford as *On the form and principles of the sensible and intelligible world* (Inaugural Dissertation) in *Kant: Selected Pre-Critical Writings and Correspondence with Beck* (Manchester University Press and New York: Barnes & Noble, 1968).

21. ——, *Eine Vorlesung Kant's über Ethik im Auftrage der Kantgesellschaft* (1775–80). Drawn from the lecture notes of Theodor Friedrich Brauer, Gottlieb Kutzner, and Chr. Mrongovious by Paul Menzer in 1924 and trans. Louis Infeld as *Lectures on Ethics* (London: Methuen, 1930; reprint Indianapolis: Hackett Publishing, 1980).

22. ——, *Kritik der reinen Vernunft* (1st ed. 1781, 2nd ed. 1787), trans. Norman Kemp Smith as *Immanuel Kant's Critique of Pure Reason* (New York: Macmillan, St. Martin's Press, 1965).

23. ——, *Prolegomena zu einer jeden künftigen Metaphysik* (1783), trans. P. Carus and revised by Lewis White Beck as *Prolegomena to any Future Metaphysics* (Indianapolis: Bobbs-Merrill Library of Liberal Arts, 1950).

24. ——, *Idee zu der einer allgemeinen Geschichte in weltbürgerlicher Absicht* (1784), trans. Lewis White Beck as 'Idea for a Universal History from a Cosmopolitan Point of View' in *Kant On History*, Lewis White Beck (ed.) (Indianapolis: Bobbs-Merrill Library of Liberal Arts, 1963).

25. ——, *Beantwortung der Frage: Was ist Aufklärung?* (1784), trans. as 'What is Enlightenment' by Lewis White Beck (ed.), in *Kant On History* (Indianapolis: Bobbs-Merrill Library of Liberal Arts, 1963).

26. ——, *Grundlegung zur Metaphysik der Sitten* (1785), trans. Lewis White Beck as *Foundations of the Metaphysics of Morals* (Indianapolis: Bobbs-Merrill Library of Liberal Arts, 1959).

27. ——, *Mutmasslicher Anfang der Menschen Geschichte* (1786), trans. Emil L. Fackenheim as 'Conjectural Beginning of Human History' in Lewis White Beck (ed.), *Kant On History* (Indianapolis: Bobbs-Merrill Library of Liberal Arts, 1963).

28. ——, *Kritik der praktischen Vernunft* (1788), trans. Lewis White Beck as *Critique of Practical Reason* (Indianapolis: Bobbs-Merrill Library of Liberal Arts, 1956).

29. ——, *Kritik der Urteilskraft* (1790), trans. J. H. Bernard as *Critique of Judgement* (New York: Hafner Library of Classics, 1951).

30. ——, *Religion innerhalb der Grenzen der blossen Vernunft* (1793), trans. Theodore M. Greene and Hoyt H. Hudson as *Religion within the Limits of Reason Alone* (La Salle, Illinois: Open Court, 1934; reprinted in New York: Harper Torchbooks, 1960).

31. ——, *Über den Gemeinspruch: Das mag in der Theorie richtig sein, taugt aber nicht für die Praxis* (1793), trans. H. B. Nisbet as 'On the Common Saying: "This may be True in Theory but it does not Apply in Practice" ' in Hans Reiss (ed.), *Kant's Political Writings* (Cambridge University Press, 1970).

32. ——, *Das Ende aller Dinge* (1794), trans. Robert E. Anchor as 'The End of

All Things' in Lewis White Beck (ed.), *Kant On History* (Indianapolis: Bobbs-Merrill Library of Liberal Arts, 1963).

33. ——, *Zum ewigen Frieden: Ein philosophischer Entwurf* (1795), trans. Lewis White Beck as 'Perpetual Peace, A Philosophical Sketch' in Lewis White Beck (ed.), *Kant On History* (Indianapolis: Bobbs-Merrill Library of Liberal Arts, 1963).

34. ——, *Metaphysik der Sitten* (1797) Part I, *Metaphysische Anfangsgründe der Rechtslehre*, trans. John Ladd as *The Metaphysical Elements of Justice, Part I of the Metaphysics of Morals* (Indianapolis: Bobbs-Merrill Library of Liberal Arts, 1965). General Introduction and Part II, *Metaphysische Anfangsgründe der Tugendlehre*, trans. James Ellington as *The Metaphysical Principles of Virtue* in *Immanuel Kant: Ethical Philosophy* (Indianapolis: Hackett Publishing, 1983).

35. ——, *Über ein vermeintes Recht, aus Menschenliebe zu lügen* (1797), trans. Lewis White Beck as 'On a Supposed Right to Lie from Altruistic Motives' in *Immanuel Kant: Critique of Practical Reason and Other Writings in Moral Philosophy* (University of Chicago Press, 1949; reprinted in New York: Garland, 1976).

36. ——, *Anthropologie in pragmatischer Hinsicht abegefasst* (1798), trans. Mary Gregor as *Anthropology from a Pragmatic Point of View* (The Hague: Martinus Nijhoff, 1974).

37. ——, *Der Streit der Facultäten* (1798), trans. as *The Conflict of the Faculties* by Mary J. Gregor (New York: Abaris Books, 1979). Part II, 'An Old Question Raised Again: Is the Human Race Constantly Progressing?' in Gregor's edition is a reprint of Robert Anchor's translation which appeared earlier in Lewis White Beck (ed.), *On History* (Indianapolis: Bobbs-Merrill Library of Liberal Arts, 1963).

38. Korsgaard, Christine M., 'Two Distinctions in Goodness', *The Philosophical Review*, vol. XCII, no. 2 (April 1983) pp. 169–95.

39. ——, 'Kant's Formula of Universal Law', *Pacific Philosophical Quarterly*, vol. 66, nos. 1 and 2 (January/April 1985) pp. 24–47.

40. ——, 'Skepticism about Practical Reason', *The Journal of Philosophy*, vol. LXXXIII, no. 1 (January 1986) pp. 5–25.

41. ——, 'Kant's Formula of Humanity', *Kant-Studien*, Band 77, Heft 2 (April 1986) pp. 183–202.

42. ——, 'The Right to Lie: Kant on Dealing with Evil', *Philosophy and Public Affairs*, vol. 15, no. 4 (Autumn 1986) pp. 325–49.

43. Leibniz, G. W., *Discours de métaphysique* (1686) and *Monadologie* (1714), trans. George R. Montgomery in *Leibniz: Discourse on Metaphysics/Correspondence with Arnauld/Monadology* (La Salle, Illinois: Open Court, 1973).

44. Nagel, Thomas, *The Possibility of Altruism* (Oxford: Clarendon Press, 1970; reprinted Princeton University Press, 1978).

45. Nell (O'Neill), Onora, *Acting on Principle: An Essay on Kantian Ethics* (New York: Columbia University Press, 1975).

46. O'Neill (Nell), Onora, 'Between Consenting Adults', *Philosophy and Public Affairs*, vol. 14, no. 3 (Summer 1985) pp. 252–77.

47. Paton, H. J., *The Categorical Imperative: a Study in Kant's Moral Philosophy* (London: Hutchinson's University Library, 1947; reprinted in Philadelphia: University of Pennsylvania Press, 1971).

48. Price, Richard, *A Review of the Principle Questions and Difficulties in Morals* (London: 1758).
49. Rawls, John, *A Theory of Justice* (Cambridge, Mass.: Harvard University Press, 1971).
50. Reiss, Hans, 'Kant and the Right of Rebellion' in *The Journal of the History of Ideas*, vol. XVII, no. 2 (April 1956) pp. 179–92.
51. ——, Introduction to *Kant's Political Writings* (Cambridge University Press, 1970).
52. Ross, W. D. (Sir David), *The Right and the Good* (Oxford: Clarendon Press, 1930).
53. Rousseau, J. J., *Du contrat social* (1762) trans. Maurice Cranston as *The Social Contract* (Harmondsworth: Penguin, 1968).
54. Schilpp, Paul, *Kant's Pre-Critical Ethics* (Chicago: Northwestern University Press, 1938; reprinted in New York: Garland, 1971).
55. Singer, Marcus, *Generalization in Ethics* (New York: Atheneum, 1961).
56. Smith, Adam, *The Theory of Moral Sentiments* (1759), D. D. Raphael and A. L. Macfie (eds) (Indianapolis: Liberty Classics, 1982).
57. Wolff, Christian, *Discursus Preliminaris de philosophia in genere* (1728), trans. Richard J. Blackwell as *Preliminary Discourse on Philosophy in General* (Indianapolis: Bobbs-Merrill Library of Liberal Arts, 1963).
58. Wolff, Robert Paul (ed.), *Kant: Foundations of the Metaphysics of Morals: Text and Critical Essays* (Indianapolis: Bobbs-Merrill Text and Commentary Series, 1969).
59. Wood, Allen, W., *Kant's Moral Religion* (Ithaca: Cornell University Press, 1970).

# 8

# Mill

## *John Lachs*

### LIFE AND WORKS

John Stuart Mill was born in 1806 in London. His father, James Mill, was a leading intellectual figure in the England of his day. James assumed direct responsibility for the education of his son; John Stuart grew into a widely read, well informed and inquisitive young person without ever having attended school. He studied the Classics in the original, mastered mathematics and logic, and spent considerable time acquainting himself with both the details of history and the results of the sciences. By the age of 15 he had become a vigorous participant in the social and political debates which occupied the reform-minded utilitarians who viewed Jeremy Bentham and James Mill as their leaders.

The intensity of this precocious intellectual development took its toll. At the age of 20 Mill sank into a deep depression which it took him years to overcome. In the process of doing so, he recognised that the cultivation of his feelings had not kept pace with the growth of his mind. He made determined efforts to round out his personality and to bring his thought in line with a broader, inclusive and constructive ideal of individual and social development. Although he never abandoned his commitment to the positive elements in Bentham's rationalistic approach to fulfillment, this experience of despair impressed on Mill the complexity and organic interconnectedness of the elements of human nature.

Mill accepted a position as clerk with the East India Company when he was 17. In his 25 years of service to this powerful organisation, which essentially ran India, Mill rose to a major administrative position. In 1831 he met Harriet Taylor, the brilliant wife of a financially successful but intellectually pedestrian merchant. They became constant companions and Mill credited her with being the prime inspiration and most helpful critic of his work. Because she was married to another man, their relation was considered scandalous and they were nearly ostracised from polite society. Some years after the death of Mrs Taylor's husband they were united in marriage. Their tender devotion to each other was exemplary during the relatively short years of their married life. Her untimely death on the occasion of a visit to France plunged him into deep grief. He bought a house in Avignon and resolved to spend a part of each year near her grave.

The capacity for such devotion, combined with Mill's brilliant mind, made him an exceptional individual. He was also remarkable for the clarity with which he understood that views about social reform require appropriate action on the part of those who hold them. Accordingly, many of his writings, though theoretical, were addressed to the generally educated public with the aim of persuading it of the truth of utilitarianism. And when the occasion arose, Mill himself was ready to stand for election to Parliament. He won and served a term as a member from Westminster, but his political skills did not prove equal to the force of his mind. He was defeated at the next election and returned, with some relief, to his intellectual pursuits.

Mill spent the last years of his life enjoying the fame and respect he so richly deserved. He died in 1873, at the age of 67. His literary heritage includes works on nearly the full spectrum of philosophical problems. He published *A System of Logic*, a study of reasoning peerless in his day and one of the best books on the subject ever written, in 1843. His systematic philosophical views are best expounded in *An Examination of Sir William Hamilton's Philosophy* (1865). The widely read monograph entitled *Utilitarianism* first appeared in *Frasers Magazine* in 1861 and has since become one of the most often quoted and reprinted works in moral philosophy. *On Liberty* (1859) is generally acknowledged as the most eloquent systematic defence of freedom ever written. *Three Essays on Religion*, published posthumously in 1874, details Mill's views on God and assesses the evidence for belief in His existence. *The Subjection of Women* (1869) is an impassioned plea for the equality of the sexes. In addition to these and other philosophical works, Mill also wrote on economics, sociology, political science, literature, law and psychology. The scope and power of his writings assure him a place among the major philosophers of the West and the finest intellects of the 19th century.

## INFLUENCES ON HIS THOUGHT

The predominant intellectual influence on Mill's ethical thought was the utilitarian tradition which had deep roots in England. He grew up in its daily presence because of his father's fervent commitment to it. Jeremy Bentham, its greatest, though by no means most subtle, advocate inspired the young Mill with a sense of the rational power and wholesome simplifying effect of his moral views. Although later reflections convinced Mill to reject Bentham's ideas on a number of important issues, he never abandoned either utilitarianism or his admiration for Bentham's commitment to put it into practice.

After his early depression Mill came in contact with the views of the French philosophers Comte and Saint-Simon. Their ideas about historical development sensitised him to the importance, both for understanding societies and for changing them, of tradition and social context. Adherence to British empiricism exercised a profound influence on Mill's ideas concerning how we come to have and to know values, and how we justify them. And the intellectual milieu in England, favouring individualism and viewing society as a structure created for the promotion of private ends, inclined Mill to champion the cause of liberty.

There was also a powerful silent, and for the most part unacknowledged, presence in Mill's moral philosophy. In spite of his open identification of happiness with pleasure, he also wrote of it as an activity which fulfills human existence. And although the natural stress of utilitarianism is on the assessment of the morality of individual actions, in *On Liberty* and elsewhere Mill showed surprising sensitivity to the central role in ethics of character and integrated personality. These tendencies, along with many of his views about human nature, show the abiding influence on him of the writings of Aristotle. Neither Mill nor his commentators have paid adequate attention to this debt.

Mill was convinced that the beliefs of people have a profound influence on what they do. The rational examination of opinions was for him, therefore, not of theoretical interest only; properly disseminated, its results could bring about significant social change. Accordingly, he endeavoured to write without excessive jargon and in a style accessible to the general reader. Although he also wrote for an audience of philosophers narrowly defined, many of his works were addressed to thoughtful laymen and dealt with topics of abiding personal, social and political concern.

The England of Mill's day was in a stage of painful transition. The Industrial Revolution had made such rapid improvements in the production of goods that Mill could write with confidence, in *Utili-*

*tarianism*, that 'most of the great positive evils of the world are in themselves removable, and will, if human affairs continue to improve, be in the end reduced within narrow limits'.[1] But there was no social mechanism in place for the rational distribution of this bounty. Private and class interests narrowly conceived stood in the way of improving the living conditions of all. While there was substantial sentiment for the liberalisation of society and for the elimination of blatant cruelty and injustice, the wheels of reform turned slowly. The gradual introduction of social change, achieved against reluctant segments of the community, tended, moreover, to concentrate growing power in the hands of government. And rapid industrialisation, with its pressure for uniformity, was widely perceived as a grave threat to the wholesome variety of opinions and types of personality in the moral world.

## UTILITARIANISM

Mill regarded his utilitarianism, to which he was wholeheartedly devoted, as the answer to these social and personal difficulties. He thought it provided a rational method for making decisions in matters of human concern. And this rationalisation was accomplished, he believed, without losing the wisdom of the ages, the important insights of the great moral and religious traditions. In his most sanguine moments Mill went so far, in fact, as to declare that many of the greatest moralists and religious reformers were utilitarians, even though in this matter they lacked clear self-understanding.

In its narrowest version, utilitarianism is a theory about what makes actions right. It holds that nothing we do is right in and of itself, nor is the intention that shaped it of significance in assessing its worth. Only the consequences of an action determine its moral value, for this value consists exclusively of its tendency to add to the sum total of good in the world. Mill himself did not take this minimalist view of utilitarianism; he thought of it instead in more cosmic terms as including, directly, a theory about what is of ultimate or intrinsic value and, derivatively, accounts of justice, virtue, liberty, good character and the good life, among others. He did not view these theories as tentative or experimental extensions of utilitarianism, but rather as integral parts of it, all of which together constituted a complete and adequate system of morality.

Mill's empiricism inclined him to think that only something experienced can be valuable as an end. He agreed with Bentham that our direct encounter with value occurs in the experience of pleasure. Delight or felt satisfaction was, according to his official view, the only thing desirable for its own sake; everything else was to be sought solely as means to this end. He made it perfectly clear that he meant by pleasure a state of feeling which, though it may be indefinable, is nevertheless well known and easily recognised by us.

Perhaps it was the evident identification, in ordinary language and thought, of feeling happy with being pleased that occasioned Mill to say that happiness is simply pleasure and the absence of pain.[2] However this may be, the identification had the powerful effect of enlisting the acknowledged and supposedly universal search for happiness as evidence for the truth of hedonism. Bentham adopted the bold view that hedonism was correct both in its psychological and in its ethical forms, viz. that pleasure was both the only object of human choice and the only worthy object. But Mill's generous sympathies and deeper insight into human nature did not let him rest with such a dogmatic and impoverished doctrine. He respected variety in motivations too much to believe that they could all be reduced to a single, simple one. And his most thoughtful account of happiness, in Section IV of *Utilitarianism*, shows clearly that this ultimate good is not simply identical with agreeable feeling.

## PLEASURE AND PAIN

Nevertheless, Mill's official view was that only pleasure is good as an end in itself and only pain evil. Nothing but states of feeling can have value and among these pain, considered in itself, independently of its effects, is unconditionally bad. Whatever else is evil, moreover, is so because it includes, involves or causes pain. Pleasure, on the other hand, no matter how harmful indulging in it may prove in the long run, is intrinsically good. And whatever else is good is so because it gives pleasure or has pleasure as one of its ingredients.

This is an indefensible, even absurd, position if we take a narrow view of the nature of pleasure and pain. But Mill avoided this pitfall: he included under the general category of pain not only physical sensations but also anguish, suffering, all manner of experienced misery and even mild forms of disagreeable feeling. And while the notion of pleasure encompassed, for him, the orgiastic and the physical, it also included the delight we take in something beautiful, the feeling of rational self-contentment, and agreeable states of consciousness of any kind.

This expansion of the ideas of pleasure and pain had already been present in the work of Bentham, who did not hesitate to speak of the feelings which attend our contemplation of future possibilities (such as heavenly rewards and eternal punishments) as pleasures and pains. Mill, accordingly, left the matter largely without comment: it seemed to him evident that hedonism had to be understood in its richest and most inclusive sense. He also treated Bentham's hedonistic calculus with silent approval. The calculus constituted a systematic attempt to make our choices, the assessment of actions in terms of their expected agreeable and disagreeable consequences, rational. Mill believed in the value of the growth of such rationality no less fervently than did others in the 19th century, but his enthusiasm was never as simple-minded as theirs: his hopes for and efforts on behalf of enlightenment were qualified by a profound understanding of the ambiguities of human nature.

It is not that proponents of the hedonistic calculus supposed that the principles of choice could ever be made completely scientific. Their primary agenda was to expand the moral imagination by stressing the importance of long-range consequences and of the welfare of everyone capable of pleasure and pain. Accordingly, they insisted that considering the intensity, duration, nearness and certainty of the pleasure an action promises was only the first step in our calculations. Next we must attend to the fecundity of the act, or its tendency to produce pleasure beyond its initial result as far into the future as it is possible to predict. This fertility must, moreover, be balanced against the potential impurity of the act, that is, its propensity to yield in the long run not only pleasures but pains as well. Careful consideration of fecundity and purity tends to make intense, immediate pleasures less alluring: it reveals that instant gratification of selfish or orgiastic cravings often leads to later pains and regret. Our ability to restrain the power of impulse constitutes the foundation of civilised life. Systematic attention to the eventual outcome of what we do, to the totality of benefits and costs accrued through time, helps us achieve control over the immediate by counterbalancing its pull with constant reminders of the havoc it may wreak.

The civilising influence of the calculus was greatly bolstered, in the opinion of its advocates, by its insistence on the widest possible distribution of pleasure. This is what Bentham called the 'extent' of the agreeable feeling generated by an action, that is, the number of people affected by it. Ethical hedonism destroys the legitimacy of selfishness: if pleasure is the only good, it cannot matter whether you have it or I. The only important question is how to maximise it in the world, and it is immediately clear that we cannot do that by leaving any being capable of feeling out of consideration. We thus get the striking consequence that in determining the rightness of an act we must take into account its impact on every sentient creature it is likely to affect. This is the idea which came to be expressed as 'Each is to count for one, and no one for more than one', a principle to which utilitarians since Bentham have shown uncompromising devotion.

This remarkable principle embodies the most generous, enlightened and humane tendencies of utilitarianism. It stresses the importance of each individual and insists that in making decisions no one affected can be excluded as unworthy and nobody's welfare can be overlooked. But even though the maxim is democratic in intent, it is not egalitarian: while the pleasure and pain of everyone is to be taken into account, the weight given to each is a function of the intensity and quantity of his or her satisfactions. If some action were to affect only three people, for example, two of whom would suffer pain while the third enjoyed exquisite delights, the principle does not commit us to favouring the majority. The feelings of each must, of course, be considered, but since the job of the moral agent is to maximise satisfaction, if the pleasure of one exceeds the pain of the others, we must prefer the act that favours the former.

Looking at matters in this light may help the advocates of the calculus deal with the problem of the pain of animals. If pleasure is the only good and pain the only ultimate evil, each sentient creature must be an object of our concern. This puts the feelings of animals at least nominally on a par with those of human beings. Appropriate as this may be because it mandates the humane treatment of animals and could well serve as the foundation of an ecologically sophisticated ethics, it nevertheless raises the question if we are ever right in giving precedence to human satisfactions over those of the far more numerous bugs and beasts. We clearly think that we are and many utilitarians appear, at least by their silence, to agree with this opinion.

When marginal human pleasure is measured against significant animal pain, we must forbear and do without. But is there any rational justification for our readiness to kill animals for food and to use them for experimentation while we steadfastly refuse to allow the same to be done to us? Bentham's only sensible answer would have to be based on the plea that humans have a greater capacity for delight and suffering than our sentient cousins. For this reason, though each of them is to be considered in our deliberations about what to do, the intensity and quantity of their feelings places animals at a disadvantage against humankind. It is important to remark that this defence of our practices rests on an empirical premise concerning the sensitivity of animals. If that assumption happens to be false, the hedonistic calculus would lead to revolutionary changes in our relations to the rest of animate nature.

## QUALITY OF PLEASURES

Mill's approach to this problem, as to many others, was considerably more sophisticated. His endorsement of the long-range rationality and altruism promoted by the calculus did not stop him from making a profoundly important change in Bentham's position. Traditional hedonists tend not to distinguish between higher and lower pleasures: for purposes of rational calculation, the only relevant feature of our pleasures, they believe, is their quantity. This judgement appears to be reinforced by the argument that if pleasure is the only good, nothing but *more of it* can make one pleasure better than another. Mill rejected this reasoning and sided with the commonsense view that some forms of agreeable feeling are intrinsically of a higher quality than others, even though they may not be as long lasting or as intense. The intellectual enjoyments of Socrates, he said, though less orgiastic, are nevertheless of a higher grade than the pleasures of an animal or a fool. The refined delights of a sensitive and sophisticated human being are clearly preferable to the raucous satisfactions of tavern and bed.

The introduction of qualitative differences among feelings easily disposes of the question of why human satisfactions should be preferred over the pleasures of animals. It also provided an answer, Mill thought, to the critics who viewed utilitarianism as 'a doctrine worthy only of swine'.[3] The commitment to a hierarchy of enjoyments capped by those the exercise of intellect, imagination and the moral sentiments makes possible, enables the utilitarian to adopt Christian and even Stoic virtues without denying that pleasure is the only good. The view is decidedly highbrow and shows the assurance of a cultivated mind and of a self-possessed age about having discovered what is permanently valuable in human life.

In developing the theory of the qualities of pleasure, Mill remained faithful to his empiricism. The evidence that refined enjoyments are better than gross physical ones must come from a study of actual human choices. People in whom mental life has not reached a high level cannot, of course, be supposed to have expressed a preference: unless we experience both the higher and the lower pleasures, we cannot choose between them. Our study must, therefore, focus on those who have had a taste of both. These, Mill found, tended almost without exception to favour the mental and the cultivated.

The argument is a brilliant way of making the opinions of the seriously outnumbered philosophers and holy men carry the day. But it lacks sympathy with the intellectual dropout, the men and women who tested the higher pleasures and opted for wine. For each Plato there may be many an Aristippus who, though taught by the same Socrates, chooses a life of intense, immediate physical satisfactions. Of course, such people tend not to make a mark in the world of mind. But if we want to know what those who have experienced both the finer and the baser pleasures are inclined to choose, we cannot leave their lives out of account.

## ACTIONS AND AGENTS

The ideal of utilitarians is to develop a method according to which we can determine the rightness and wrongness of actions by reference to their consequences alone. Mill was particularly careful to distinguish the morality of actions from the morality of the agents whose actions they are. Not only can moral persons perform immoral acts and immoral agents moral ones, the facts we adduce to determine the ethical standing of the two are different. If actions lead, on balance, to good consequences, they are right. If agents tend, on the whole, to have good intentions, then they are moral. Mill wanted the distinction to be absolute: our intentions add nothing to the morality of what we do, while the outcome of our acts is irrelevant to what manner of persons we are.

The rigid line of demarcation suggests that utilitarianism has no concern with what sorts of people inhabit the world so long as their actions produce more pleasure than pain. While this is correct about the view taken narrowly as a theory about the rightness of actions, it is certainly false if we regard it, as Mill often but not always did, as a more cosmic approach to the moral life. Utilitarians have typically taken an interest not only in what makes actions right, but also in how we can get people to do the right thing. And this naturally led them to deal with virtue and its conditions, that is, with the way education and the rules of social interaction foster the development of responsible individuals.

The idea that pleasures differ in quality introduces individuality into the utilitarian calculus in a novel way. The ability to enjoy pleasures is a natural endowment of all, requiring no special cultivation of character. What we as a society must do to enhance the probability that people act for the common good even at personal cost may be seen to involve education. But, as Bentham clearly grasped, this need not come to more than the shaping of behaviour by externally imposed sanctions or threats of punishment.[4] For utilitarians before Mill, it indeed had not mattered what manner of people we were, so long as we behaved correctly. With the view that the best pleasures, the highest values, are accessible only to the cultivated person, however, the internal qualities of individuals assume central importance in the primary task of moral life, namely, the maximisation of the good in the world. Motive and character, the private features of subjective life, become in this way the key to the value of our pleasures and the guide to which and whose enjoyments we should promote.

It would be quite wrong to suppose that Mill had a clear understanding of the radical nature of his view of the qualities of pleasure. He is sometimes charged with inconsistently maintaining both that pleasure is the only good and that there is something in certain enjoyments which makes them intrinsically better than others. This problem, which has occupied commentators for over a hundred years,[5] was not fully appreciated by Mill. At the very least, he never offered a convincing response to the charge.

Mill also failed to see a tension or inconsistency between the stress on pleasurable results however and by whomever achieved, and devotion to the importance of cultivated individuals. Mill had the twin strengths of good judgement and intellectual honesty. The former enabled him to recognise views which were sensible, important and in all probability true. The latter made it impossible for him to reject ideas which were probably true solely on the basis of their failure to harmonise with his other opinions. The drive for system was never so strong in his soul as to make him forsake his first allegiance to truth. Moreover, in the justly famous Section II of *On*

*Liberty*, he himself indicated that most of our treasured dogmas are probably no better than half-truths. These, he said, even if contradictory, must be affirmed and defended with rigour in every society in order to keep them alive for future choice and adjudication. Given the imperfect state of our knowledge, we cannot blame Mill for having done his share to keep some important views, which are probably true and possibly incompatible, as live intellectual options for his age.

The point is that Mill saw the value of a world in which pain is minimised and in which intense, enduring satisfaction is the birth-right of all. At the same time he was convinced that some enjoyments are vastly better than others and these are accessible only to people who reject lesser pleasures and thoughtfully control their desires and their deeds. The two ideals, that of maximised pleasure, espoused in *Utilitarianism*, and that of cultivated and free persons, eloquently expressed in *On Liberty*, are not only logically distinct but also, at least in some of their practical applications, incompatible. From the standpoint of ethical theory, the good is either pleasure or it is developed personality—it cannot be both. We shall see later that Mill's attempts to make peace between the two views inevitably led to the quiet surrender of hedonism.

## CONSCIENCE

Mill's account of conscience provides further illustration of his interest in the internal life. Bentham cynically believed that by nature humans always acted selfishly. There were, he maintained, four great sources of external pressure in response to which, in an almost mechanical way, we tended to modify our narrowly self-seeking behaviour. The laws of the physical world teach the glutton to curb her overeating. The pointed comments of people and their desire to avoid him indicate to the unkempt man that it is time to bathe. The possibility that God may punish them keeps gossips from spreading vicious rumours. And laws, jails and the police may be enough to dissuade at least some would-be criminals from mayhem and plunder. To these four external sanctions or motivating forces Mill adds a most important fifth, that of conscience. This internal voice or feeling may well be seen as the difference between the crude, natural man-animal and the human being who lives and thrives in society. Accordingly, conscience is a human, though not for that reason unnatural, creation; it is a result of that refinement of character which endows us with moral sentiments and renders us fit for social life.

The force of conscience derives from the 'mass of feeling which must be broken through in order to do what violates our standard of right'.[6] These sentiments—of sympathy for others, concern for their welfare and pain at harming them—are fostered by living in co-operative communities where the interests of divergent individuals become identical or inseparable. The external sanctions themselves can function well only by adding to this stock of feelings. They cannot succeed in socialising behaviour without changing the tastes and perspectives of the inner person. The solution to the perennial problem of moral philosophy of how to reconcile the good of self-interested individuals with that of the community lies, therefore, in the development of morally sensitive, cultivated persons. The interests of such people are intertwined with those of their fellows, their intelligence enables them to recognise this connection and their conscience makes them act on it. In the typically optimistic fashion of the 19th century, Mill thought that each generation brings us closer to a society consisting mainly or exclusively of such morally cultured individuals.

## TWO VIEWS OF HAPPINESS

Mill frequently referred to utilitarianism as 'the greatest happiness principle'. The centrality of the notion of happiness for his ethics made it imperative for him to articulate a careful and defensible theory of it. Yet his initial account, which is generally taken as his official view, is simple and undeveloped. On inspiration clearly derived from Bentham, he declared that 'by happiness is intended pleasure, and the absence of pain; by unhappiness, pain, and the privation of pleasure'.[7] The identification of pleasure with happiness has a certain plausibility if we focus primarily on the feeling tone of our better moments. At such times, delight or satisfaction suffuses our consciousness and we can appropriately say that we feel happy. It is a characteristic claim of hedonists that there is no difference to be drawn between being happy and feeling happy, and in his official view Mill appears to subscribe to this position without qualification.

The simplicity of this theory and the confirmation it seems to receive from everyday experience make it powerfully attractive. But it quickly foundered on the rock of Mill's honesty. In discussing what is desired for its own sake and not for any ulterior result, Mill could not make himself deny the obvious fact that power, money, fame, music and even virtue function as such ends for many people. Frequently they are desired, he noted, not for the pleasure they give but as things worth having for their own intrinsic qualities. He could also not close his eyes to the additional fact that people tend to want such ends-in-themselves in the context of pursuing happiness: they often see love and health and beauty as parts or elements of their well-being. But if all of this is true, happiness cannot be identical with enjoyment. Pleasure is a feeling or a sensation which, in its simplicity, does not have parts. Least of all can it have as elements such physical objects as money or such complex social relations as power. Happiness must, then, be something far broader and more encompassing than feeling good. It is 'a concrete whole'[8] consisting of a variety of ingredients which it takes time to acquire or achieve and to enjoy.

This discussion in *Utilitarianism*, when conjoined with some comments on individuality in *On Liberty*, points to a second, more interesting, but by Mill unelaborated, theory of the nature of happiness. The second view is reminiscent of Aristotle in presenting happiness as characterising not moments of consciousness but whole lives or significant portions of them. Though enjoyments play a role in such lives, happiness is much more closely connected with our activities than with our feelings. A satisfying existence is one in which we can do a wide variety of things and in which these activities form a meaningful and concrete whole. The purpose structuring this totality[9] needs to be freely chosen: in this way one's life pattern can express one's personality and can, concurrently, help to shape it. Happiness, therefore, is in the end the outcome of the 'interplay of person and action',[10] of the fashion in which the individual self, its beliefs and its activities harmonise or form a unity.

The second theory has several great advantages over the first. It distinguishes the longer-term condition of persons, to which we refer by saying that they *are* happy, from their passing affective states, which we indicate when we remark that they *feel* happy. It also shows, far more convincingly than Mill's official view, the importance of free choice or liberty for happiness. Finally, it connects the issue of increasing human well-being with the problem of how to enhance the autonomy and deepen the culture of individuals. Mill gave no explicit sign of having been aware that he held two views concerning the nature of happiness. Yet there is little doubt that he did, his hedonist background inclining him to the first position, while his later reflections and his devotion to human self-development made him favour the second view.

## THE PROOF OF UTILITARIANISM

The detailed developments and technical difficulties which have occupied utilitarians in our own day were of little concern to Mill. He did not worry, for example, about the precise weight we should give to the interests of unborn generations. Even the distinction between act and rule utilitarianism, which has since become a commonplace, failed to receive explicit articulation in his work.[11] The reason for this is both obvious and adequate. Utilitarianism was, for Mill, not a clever or sophisticated professional position, but an intellectual vantage point which anchored his hope for the rational reform of much of moral, social and political life. Accordingly, the details of greatest interest to the professional philosopher held, in this field, relatively little fascination for him; he was an advocate, not a student, of the utilitarian calculus. If we insisted on determining whether he was an act or a rule utilitarian,[12] we would have to conclude that he was both: on the one hand, he spoke of the rules of social life and of secondary principles, yet on the other, his desire to enhance individual responsibility made him suggest that the morality of each act be judged by its specific consequences.

Mill's lack of interest in the technical refinements of utilitarianism may appear to be at odds with his concerted attempt to prove its truth. Yet even this proof had a primarily practical purpose: demonstration of first principles, he pointed out, can amount to no more than the provision of reasons to incline the mind to belief.[13] The aim, then, was to convince people, in a rational way of course, that the greatest happiness principle constituted the proper foundation of morality. Mill has endured nearly endless abuse for the allegedly fallacious way in which he did this, though none worse than that heaped on him by a scornful G. E. Moore.[14] It is not that this proof, developed in Section IV of *Utilitarianism*, is a model of reasoning. Nor is it, however, the tissue of fallacies critics have attempted to make it out to be. A fair assessment would display it as an interesting and imaginative, but only partially successful, attempt to support a fundamental moral principle on an empiricist basis. Much of the misunderstanding of Mill's argument derives from his critics' inability to see or unwillingness to accept this empiricist starting-point.

The unstated premise of the proof is the rejection of any intuitive, transcendent or supernatural foundation for ethics. Moral knowledge must have the same ground as knowledge of any other kind: it must be justified by reference to ordinary experience. To say that an end is good is to affirm its desirability; accordingly, we must look for the experiential base of value in the desires of individuals. It is simply senseless to speak of the worth of any object or end independently of the tendency of humans to prize it: the value of anything is a relational affair involving not only its qualities, but also the needs and inclinations of the people who encounter it. If we tend, on the whole, to recognise the colour of things, there is no reason to suppose that we do worse with those features of objects relevant to the purposes of life. That an object is desirable can, therefore, be reasonably inferred from the fact that it is generally desired, and this does not commit Mill to the view that anything desired by anyone is, for that reason, good.

The empiricist principle which would have us seek evidence for the value of things in affective and conative experience enabled Mill to sidestep the charge that he confused two different meanings of the word 'desirable'. It is of course true that 'desirable' means both 'able to be desired' and 'worthy of being desired'. But we have nowhere to go other than human experience if we wish to determine what constitutes, for us, an appropriate object of pursuit. Anything large numbers of people have prized generation after generation has a high probability of being good. It is extremely unlikely that the bread we have eaten for thousands of years will turn out, on close examination, to be not food but poison. The empiricist (and naturalist) proposition with which Mill began is, to be sure, open to question. Critics may argue that adopting it is ill-advised; that, however, is a charge less serious and more difficult to substantiate than extravagant claims of blatant fallacy.

The reason Mill wanted to establish the legitimacy of arguing from widespread human desires to the desirability of their object was his interest in showing that the general happiness was the only or the greatest good. Since happiness is a common and persistent object of pursuit, the connection between desire and desirability entitled him to say that it is a major and enduring value. Next he needed to prove that nothing but happiness is ever sought as an end and that, therefore, it is the only good. It is to Mill's credit that he chose not to try to do this by means of the tired argument that we want things only on account of the pleasure they bring. Instead, he invented a new approach, reasoning that anything we desire as an end is wanted as a part of happiness. His associationist psychology enabled him to explain how, for example, love and power, which may initially have been desired only as means to happiness, can come to be sought for their own sake and thus become indispensable elements in human well-being. This account required, as we saw earlier, a conception of happiness different from his official view. If, in accordance with this second theory of happiness, each individual's well-being is a whole consisting of a variety of elements, we can plausibly maintain that it represents, as far as that person is concerned, the only end desired.

The third and final part of the argument is the least successful. It is compressed into a single sentence which reads: 'Each person's happiness is a good to that person, and the general happiness, therefore, a good to the aggregate of all persons'.[15] This takes Mill from individual well-being to the happiness of the community, closing the gap that usually exists between narrowly conceived private and broadly inclusive public benefits. The problem is that, by Mill's own admission, the evidence for the goodness of anything consists in its broad-based pursuit. Now even if each person fervently desires his or her own happiness, we have no reason to conclude that anyone cares about the general good. On the contrary, we tend to seek our happiness independently, and sometimes at the expense, of the well-being of others. Moreover, the general happiness is not simply the sum of the well-being of each member of the community; in the current imperfect state of the world, goods are often incompatible and we must sacrifice the interests of some in order to secure the happiness of the greatest possible number. Who could desire this abstract maximisation, given that no individual can be sure that his or her happiness will always be a part of the public good? Evidently only the public itself, or 'the aggregate of all persons'. Unfortunately, however, the sum total of persons is not an additional individual endowed with consciousness; it can, for this reason, neither desire nor pursue anything.

Mill's attempt to prove the greatest happiness principle was cleverly designed to yield a sweeping ethical hedonism on the basis of a weak form of psychological hedonism and an ethical altruism grounded in psychological egoism. The first deduction, though it is both subtle and novel, succeeds only at the price of abandoning a pleasure-based account of happiness and thus falls short of demonstrating that enjoyment is the only good. The second inference fails altogether; there is simply not enough evidence that people desire the public good. Perhaps cultured individuals who understand their enlightened self-interest would. But persons of such mental development are made, not found, which suggests that what Mill optimistically took to be data for philosophy constitute instead only a task for education.

The fact that Mill did not succeed in proving utilitarianism even in his own sense of offering reasons adequate to induce belief, should not be taken as a crippling argument against it. No ethical theory has ever received conclusive proof or even convincing confirmation. We must, accordingly, choose among them on the basis of spotty evidence and of their ability to accommodate and systematise in a single edifice of thought the insights, interests and lasting commitments of human life. Judged by these standards, Mill's ethics is in a much stronger position than the vast majority of its rivals.

## JUSTICE

If we now look to see how utilitarianism can incorporate the most firmly held of our values, we can find no better test case than that of justice. For the dictates of fairness are often conceived as absolute and altogether independent of any considerations of what promotes the general happiness. Mill himself acknowledged this and devoted the disproportionately long and detailed last chapter of *Utilitarianism* to an analysis and discussion of it. His approach shows his characteristic respect for facts, his empiricist strategy and the fertile inventiveness of his mind.

The essence of justice, he argued, consists in the protection of rights both in the sense of freedoms and in the sense of entitlements. We can also put the matter negatively, as he frequently did, by saying that justice is the violation of the right of any specific person when that is conjoined with a call for punishment. An urgency and imperiousness attend both the safeguarding of rights and the punishment of offenders against them; we feel that justice must be done whatever the cost. Now Mill's strategy, reminiscent of Hume's in his analysis of causation, is to liberate the intellectual content of the idea of justice from the subjective and emotional elements which encrust it in the public mind. Getting clear on the notion of justice should enable us to determine if it is compatible with utility. How we *feel* when we demand that the principles of justice be obeyed, on the other hand, is important only for the motivating power of these principles; it is irrelevant to their moral force and justification.

The rights in whose protection justice consists constitute the central interests of human beings. Without physical safety and security in our possessions 'nothing but the gratification of the instant could be of any worth to us', for we could then 'be deprived of everything the next instant by whoever was momentarily stronger than ourselves'.[16] It is, therefore, of the greatest significance for the advancement of the general happiness to nurture and protect these security-interests. The principles of justice are thus not only compatible with utilitarianism, but are actually derivable from it. If we were completely rational and always acted to further the greatest good of the greatest number, considerations of fairness and equity would never be far from the centre of our attention.

But, it may be objected, even if in a utilitarian calculus the benefits of defending rights tend to outweigh its costs, this does not confer on the demands of justice the unconditionality they enjoy in experience. Mill's reply was that this absoluteness is appearance only, created by the strength of the feelings which surround and support such vital interests. In fact, the maxims of justice in their application frequently conflict and require adjudication by reference to some broader principle. And we would all agree that any given claim of equity can be legitimately overruled if the human cost of securing it becomes intolerable. So in actual moral practice, the requirements of justice do not carry absolute weight: they must contend against conflicting claims of a variety of sorts. Because they represent such central human interests, however, they are frequently accorded moral supremacy, though never without an assessment of the likely consequences of acting on them instead of on a rival principle.

The apparent absoluteness of the call of justice is, then, fully derivable from the feelings which accompany it. Mill focused on three which together compose the sentiment of justice. The experienced impulse of self-defence is generalised by the feeling of sympathy, particularly as this is fostered by social life, to the point where a wrong against virtually any other human being evokes the same revulsion and resistance as does an attack on oneself. But the greatest source of the sense of sweeping unconditionality is the animal feeling of retaliation for injury. The desire for revenge mobilises the entire organism, conveying a sense of absolute need for action. Social sympathy harnesses this emotion as well, until it ceases to attend personal injuries unless they are also detrimental to the common good. In this way, our impulses and emotions become incorporated in our moral life and provide important support for socially beneficial behaviour. It is unfortunate that this process has misled philosophers into supposing that there are standards of conduct independent of the calculation of utility.

## LAW AND MORALITY

His focal emphasis on the social good enabled Mill to provide a single criterion for the justification of both laws and morality. The edicts of the legal system, when properly constituted, are in fact simply those central demands of morality concerning which there is general agreement. The criminal law, for example, protects the most vital interests of human beings; in abiding by it, our actions are not only legally but also morally right. But the sphere of morality, of concern for the welfare of all, is broader than anything that can be codified and universally enforced. Accordingly, the utilitarian calculus provides both the justification of law and a standard on the basis of which legislation, when it goes astray, may be criticised. The question that needs to be asked about every statute is the same we must answer about each significant individual action: is it likely to yield at the least cost in pain the greatest amount of happiness possible for the largest number of the people it affects? If the response is negative, neither law nor personal action enjoys the approval of morality.

But laws cannot fulfill their function of reducing the incidence of antisocial behaviour so long as they remain merely external constaints on conduct. Legislation must be conceived as a primary means of educating the public, and education consists, first and foremost, of the expansion of the moral imagination and the improvement of character. Mill viewed mankind as 'a progressive race' and thought that the deliberate attempt to create better people through sound social policies and rational legislation constitutes perhaps the main engine of this advancement. Social life itself tends to expand our sympathies; if government and our other institutions give intelligent support to the socialising forces naturally at work, we can reasonably anticipate the emergence of ever greater numbers of sensitive, responsible and generous human beings.

This optimistic assessment of the future may appear to minimise the role of self-improvement and cede unchecked reign to legislation. The appearance, however, is deceptive. All of *On Liberty* is magnificent testimony to Mill's belief in the possibility of individuals shaping and bettering their lives, in the importance of autonomy for such achievements and in the need for limiting the sphere of law to safeguard autonomy. The fundamental assumption of the book is that human beings are independent agents capable of pursuing their good without assistance. It is not that contact with our fellows fails to enrich us or even that life outside of the human community is possible. But, in the end, all actions in these communities are the actions of individuals, and all the happiness and suffering affect living, feeling persons only. Accordingly, these centres of sentience and agency must, in some spheres, be left alone to make their own decisions and to engage in the activities which please them. Only in this way can the general good be maximised, for feeling and self-determining persons are the bearers of all value and even 'the worth of a State, in the long run, is the worth of the individuals composing it'.[17]

Although Mill did not subscribe to the fiction of a social contract in order to conceptualise the proper relation of the individual to the organised community, he agreed with the advocates of that view that the authority of the state must be both justified and limited. The primary function of political power is to protect us from each other, that is, to safeguard our fundamental security-interests against external threat. It is not the role of the state, however, to shield me from myself, even if there is reason to believe that my actions are foolish or may hurt me. The justification for state authority, then, is self-protection and its limit is the autonomous person when he or she engages in self-regarding actions. This means that both genetically and morally, the individual has primacy over social structures and institutions. On the one hand, the commonwealth is created and sustained by private persons. On the other, its aim is to supply but one condition of their welfare, which makes its power over them and its claim on their resources sharply limited. 'Over himself, over his own body and mind, the individual is sovereign'.[18]

## LIBERTY

By 'liberty' Mill understood the ability of persons to follow their inclinations. It naturally involves individual differences in what we desire and inequalities in what we can accomplish on our own. But the differences are, if anything, to be celebrated, and the inequalities never warrant official efforts to eliminate them. Although he offers a utilitarian justification of the claim that we have a right to liberty, our immunity from interference by others is due to what or who we are, namely, individual persons, and in that respect resembles a natural right. Neither the state nor informal groups of citizens must violate this right by coercing us to do otherwise than we desire. Such exercise of power over us is, however, the only form of intervention proscribed; we can plead, exhort, inform and reason with people in order to win them over to our beliefs or to our way of behaving.

The scope of liberty extends to all 'self-regarding' actions. Under this category Mill included everything a person might do, so long as its consequences affect the interests of the agent alone. Concerning such activities, which range in dignity from religious observances to masturbation, it is simply inappropriate to pass legislation. It is equally unjustified for the state to interfere with what informed, consenting adults wish to do, if their activities affect the interests of no one beyond themselves. With these declarations Mill challenged the tendency of the British government of his day to use the force of law to universalise the presumed preferences of society. If liberty were taken seriously, there would be no laws against prostitution, homosexuality and the other activities we have come to call 'victimless crimes'. Most important, there should be no central control over what we think or say, what sorts of persons we choose to be and the life-plans we create for ourselves.

In just the same way as Mill's initial focus shifted in *Utilitarianism* from the rightness of actions to the quality of persons, so in *On Liberty* his interest turned from the liberty to act to free individuals. Our ability to conduct our lives as we see fit, to pursue the values we choose and, through the directed exercise of our faculties, to fashion our own character constitutes the heart of what freedom yields for us. The growth of persons is as organic and internally generated as that of trees;[19] a climate of repression stunts their development and restricts their rich, natural variety. Since we know neither the finest form of character nor the best life, it is wise to permit open experimentation with both. The object is to leave free play to the spontaneity of individuals: it is only through this creative power that the greatest achievement, human self-creation, can take place. 'Among the works of man', Mill remarked, 'the first in importance surely is man himself'.[20]

It may appear that this view, according to which human character constitutes the greatest good, is at odds with Mill's earlier claim that happiness is the only value. This is certainly true if happiness is identified, along the lines of Mill's first theory, with pleasure. But the second theory, interpreting happiness as a quality of structured, meaningful lives, eliminates the incompatibility. For life-plans cannot have meaning unless they are freely chosen. Now 'he who chooses his plan for himself, employs all his faculties',[21] and in doing so inevitably creates his own character. Action and happiness, on the one hand, and character-formation, on the other, are in this way connected through choice. It thus becomes irrelevant whether we speak of happy lives or self-formed character as the final good: each is but an inseparable aspect of a larger whole.

This perspective on the connection of happiness and human self-creation discloses the reason for the centrality of freedom in our lives. A scientific dictatorship could guarantee us pleasures beyond our wildest dreams. There is no reason to believe, therefore, that liberty is a condition of obtaining maximum enjoyment. On the contrary, because the right to choose is at once the right to make mistakes, it is probable that freedom will always be the soil of perversity, of error and of pain. But it is also an indispensable prerequisite of human development: of the growth of cultured, self-determining persons and the unfolding of their satisfied lives. And this, in turn, helps us discern the ultimate utilitarian defence of free societies. The greatest good of the greatest number must not be conceived in a lowly, narrow or exclusive way. We should think of it as the greatest good of which humans are capable, that is, as a perfection in accordance with 'the permanent interests of man as a progressive being'.[22] This can mean nothing less than a happy life 'in the higher meaning', a life 'human beings with highly developed faculties can care to have'.[23]

It is interesting to note that this deepest, classical justification of freedom plays only a minor role in *On Liberty*. Instead, much of the argument hinges on modern, sceptical premises. Freedom of thought and speech are vindicated on the assumption that no one is likely to know the truth, and conflicting ideas must always be on hand to continue the inquiry. Freedom to choose the means to happiness receives support, at least in part, through the principle that no one knows better what pleases me than I. And the freedom to embrace whatever plan of life I wish is defended on the basis that we lack certain information about which modes of existence are genuinely satisfying. It is probable that Mill relied heavily on these arguments because of his desire to address and convince his readers independently of their attitude towards utilitarianism. Much as he was anxious to persuade people of the truth of the greatest happiness principle, he must have thought it even more important to support the cause of liberty. Given his view of the central significance of freedom for human fulfillment, his strategy was not only understandable but wise.

## ASSESSMENT

In an unfortunate passage, Mill restricted freedom to 'human beings in the maturity of their faculties'.[24] Children and young people, he asserted, have to be protected against themselves, and it is legitimate to impose a despotic rule on barbarians, so long as we make a sincere attempt to educate them for liberty. The readiness to exercise freedom is measured by our ability to profit from discussion; only this opens the road to rapid self-improvement through rational persuasion.

Now it is perfectly understandable that Mill should have taken this view: he did, after all, hold a deep belief in the progress of mankind, culminating in the emergence of cultured, eloquent and urbane individuals. But advocates of liberty must display the broadest sympathies and affirm the legitimacy of self-directed experimental life-patterns of every sort. This suggests that total devotion to freedom is not easily reconciled with a hierarchy of values or with belief in historical development in a single direction. There is no reason to deny liberty to people who value self-determination as much as we do, but who happen to be obstinate and taciturn. There are alien but magnificent, perhaps spiritual, forms of individuality which may flourish in other societies, even 'backward' ones. And it is certainly impossible to raise children to appreciate and to be able to utilise freedom without conferring it on them, in every area of choice where we can avoid disaster, as early in their growth as possible.

We have every reason to believe that Mill was a true lover of liberty. In many of the most important areas of belief, he transcended the intellectual limits of his age: his arguments for the equality of women have never been surpassed. It is regrettable that his profound insight into the need for freedom did not lead him to a deeper appreciation of all forms of life.

There is another area in which Mill could not fully follow out the implications of his view that neither God nor the state is in charge of our lives because, in the end, we own ourselves. The principle of liberty permits the unhindered performance of any action which affects, even if it harms, the agent alone. Freedom would be severely restricted if the hurt could be only insignificant or slight: if a slow form of suicide, such as that through smoking, is allowed, there is no basis for gainsaying the pill or gun. Yet Mill endorsed the old, worn view that we are not free to surrender our freedom. We cannot sell ourselves into slavery and, presumably, cannot terminate our lives, because doing so would erase the only reason, namely, our liberty, which we can give others to respect our choice.[25]

The issue is not, of course, whether it is at any point wise to become a slave or to commit suicide. The question relates only to our right to choose such possibly quite wrong-headed actions. And on this count Mill's argument appears to be simply mistaken. The reason we must refrain from interfering with a person's self-regarding actions is not concern for future, but respect for present liberty. Each promise we make diminishes our future liberty; if we wanted to keep tomorrow fully open for choice, we should ban marriage and the appointment calendar. Liberty of action is focused in the now; maximisation of it in a person's whole life is not a concern of freedom but of welfare or happiness.

In any final assessment of Mill's moral philosophy, such problems and errors must be judged small clouds in an otherwise sunny sky. It is not, of course, that he has succeeded in proving utilitarianism right or in persuading people who had favoured a rival view. But he established the greatest happiness principle as a permanently attractive and influential position in ethics and made it one of the two or three truly major alternatives. His account of the power of reason to order life and to render it better provides both hope and method for our self-improvement. His insistence on the importance of empirical knowledge for moral judgement and of human desires for the moral life constitutes a much-needed counterweight to the removed and often unrealistic speculations of ethicists. His clear analyses of many of our thorniest permanent concerns restores our faith in the contribution philosophy can make to the resolution of problems in our personal lives as well as in social policy.

At at time when individuality is on the wane and when its advocates are denounced as anti-social, it is of the greatest moment to read a defence of its utility. Mill's own sentiments constitute the best refutation of those who think that individual self-creation is somehow at odds with social justice or the common good. For while exhorting us to private choice and to the development of a distinctive personality, he could also write:

> The entire history of social improvement has been a series of transitions, by which one custom or institution after another, from being a supposed primary necessity of social existence, has passed into the rank of an universally stigmatised injustice and tyranny. So it has been with the distinctions of slaves and free-men, nobles and serfs, patricians and plebeians; and so it will be, and in part already is, with the aristocracies of colour, race, and sex.[26]

A philosophy which can provide practical advice in the affairs of life and at the same time inspire such elevated sentiments deserves continuing attention and respect.

# Notes

1. John Stuart Mill, *Utilitarianism*, in *Collected Works* X (Toronto: University of Toronto Press, 1969) p. 216.
2. Ibid., p. 210.
3. Ibid.
4. Jeremy Bentham, *Introduction to the Principles of Morals and Legislation*, *The Works of Jeremy Bentham*, vol. I (New York: Russell & Russell, 1962) pp. 14–15.
5. For the fullest discussion of this issue, see Rem B. Edwards, *Pleasures and Pains* (Ithaca: Cornell University Press, 1979).
6. *Utilitarianism*, p. 229.
7. Ibid., p. 210.
8. Ibid., p. 236.
9. John Stuart Mill, *Autobiography*, in *Collected Works* I (Toronto: University of Toronto Press, 1981).
10. John Lachs, 'Two Views of Happiness in Mill', *The Mill News Letter* IX, 1 (1973) p. 19.
11. For the distinction between act and rule utilitarianism see, for instance, Chapter 3 in William Frankena, *Ethics* (Englewood Cliffs, NJ: Prentice Hall, 1973).
12. For discussion of this issue, see J. O. Urmson, 'The Interpretation of the Moral Philosophy of J. S. Mill', and Maurice Mandelbaum, 'Two Moot Issues in Mill's *Utilitarianism*', both in *Mill: A Collection of Critical Essays*, J. B. Schneewind, ed. (Notre Dame, Ind.: University of Notre Dame Press, 1969).
13. *Utilitarianism*, p. 208.
14. G. E. Moore, *Principia Ethica* (Cambridge: Cambridge University Press, 1954). See esp. chapter III.
15. *Utilitarianism*, p. 234.
16. Ibid., p. 251.
17. John Stuart Mill, *On Liberty*, in *Collected Works* XVIII (Toronto: University of Toronto Press, 1977) p. 310.
18. Ibid., p. 224.
19. Ibid., p. 263.
20. Ibid.
21. Ibid., p. 262.
22. Ibid., p. 224.
23. John Stuart Mill, *A System of Logic*, in *Collected Works* VIII (Toronto: University of Toronto Press, 1974) p. 952.
24. *On Liberty*, p. 224.
25. Ibid., p. 299.
26. *Utilitarianism*, p. 259.

# Bibliography

## PRIMARY SOURCES

1. *Autobiography* (New York: Columbia University Press, 1924).
2. *Collected Works of John Stuart Mill* (Toronto: University of Toronto Press, 1963-   ), 21 vols.
3. *On Liberty* (Indianapolis: Hackett, 1978).
4. *The Subjection of Women* (New York: Longmans, Green & Co., 1906).
5. *A System of Logic* (London: Longmans, Green & Co., 1959).
6. *Utilitarianism* (Indianapolis: Hackett, 1979).

## SECONDARY SOURCES

7. Berger, Fred R., *Happiness, Justice, and Freedom: The Moral and Political Philosophy of John Stuart Mill* (Berkeley: University of California Press, 1984).
8. Cowling, M., *Mill and Liberalism* (Cambridge University Press, 1963).
9. Cranston, Maurice H., *John Stuart Mill* (New York: Longmans, Green & Co., 1958).
10. Duncan, G. C., *Marx and Mill: Two Views of Social Conflict and Social Harmony* (Cambridge University Press, 1973).
11. McCloskey, H. J., *John Stuart Mill: A Critical Study* (London: Macmillan, 1971).
12. Packe, Michael St John, *The Life of John Stuart Mill* (New York: Macmillan, 1954).
13. Plamenatz, J., *The English Utilitarians* (Oxford University Press, 1949).
14. Schneewind, J. B. (ed.), *Mill: A Collection of Critical Essays* (Garden City, New York: Doubleday, 1968).
15. Smith, James M. and Sosa, Ernest (eds), *Mill's Utilitarianism* (Belmont, CA: Wadsworth, 1969).
16. Stephen, Sir Leslie, *The English Utilitarians* (London: London School of Economics, 1950) vol. 3.
17. Thomas, William, *Mill* (Oxford University Press, 1985).

# 9

# Nietzsche
## *Richard Schacht*

*Morality in Europe today is herd animal morality*—in other words, as we understand it, merely *one* type of morality beside which, before which, and after which many other types, above all *higher* moralities, are, or ought to be, possible.

*Beyond Good and Evil*, 202[1]

In *Ecce Homo* Nietzsche (1844–1900), termed himself an 'immoralist' (EH IV:2); and in a great many of his writings he is harshly critical of what he often simply calls 'morality'. Yet he was preoccupied with moral matters throughout the whole of his philosophical life. One of his primary concerns was to effect a radical transformation in our entire approach to and assessment of morality, preparing the way for a new understanding of its place in human life and for the possibility of 'higher moralities' contrasting significantly with those which have prevailed throughout most of human history, both past and present. Nietzsche's efforts along these lines belie the simplistic caricatures of his views with respect to morality so often attributed to him by both his critics and his admirers. Indeed, they constitute an impressive and important moral philosophy (at least in the sense of a philosophical examination of morality), entitling him to a prominent place in the history of ethics—and in contemporary moral-philosophical inquiry as well. Moreover, his hostility to what he frequently simply calls 'morality' is actually directed only against the sway and consequences of certain types of morality, and against certain ways of conceiving of it. There is much more than this to his thinking with respect to it, and his treatment of it is far more complex, subtle and ultimately constructive than is generally recognised.

## LIFE, WORKS AND RECEPTION

Friedrich Wilhelm Nietzsche was born on 15 October 1844, in Saxony (then a province of Prussia). His all too short productive adult life ended with his collapse in early 1889, although he lived until 1900. He began his brief but remarkable career as a classical philologist, called to a professorship at Basel (Switzerland) at the astonishingly early age of 24. He taught at Basel from 1869 until 1879, when he retired owing to the deterioration of his health, and in order to be able to devote himself to the increasingly philosophical concerns which had come to preoccupy him. His writings during this period, from *The Birth of Tragedy* (1872) to *Human, All-Too-Human* (1878–79), reflect the early influence of Schopenhauer on him. More importantly, they reveal a sensitivity to worrisome tendencies in the cultural and intellectual life of his time, and a conviction of the importance of discovering some way to counter Schopenhauerian pessimism and to respond to the looming crisis he felt our civilisation faced, which he subsequently diagnosed in terms of 'the death of God', 'the advent of nihilism', and 'decadence'. In these writings he made his first attempts to comprehend and come to terms with these problems, and began to develop what eventually became his own quite distinctive philosophical idiom and method.

Nietzsche's subsequent response to this crisis, during the final decade of his productive life, was literary as well as philosophical. In *Thus Spoke Zarathustra* (1883–85) and other efforts of a literary nature, he attempted to give expression to aspects of his emerging reinterpretation and revaluation of human life and possibility in a more evocative manner than prosaic writing would permit. Most of his writings during this phenomenally productive decade, however, took the form of reflections of a critical and philosophical nature, beginning with *Daybreak* (1881) and *The Gay Science* (1882), continuing with *Beyond Good and Evil* (1886) and *On The Genealogy of Morals* (1887), and concluding with *Twilight of the Idols*, *The Antichrist* and *Ecce Homo* (all written in 1888 but published some years later). During this period he also filled numerous notebooks with further reflections of a similar nature, a substantial selection of which was published posthumously under the title *The Will to Power*.

Following his final burst of activity in 1888, Nietzsche suffered a complete mental and physical collapse in January of 1889, and remained a partially paralysed invalid for the rest of his life, never regaining his health or sanity. (This probably was the consequence of his having contracted syphilis many years earlier.) In subsequent decades his reputation suffered greatly through the manipulation of his literary estate by his sister, which contributed to his lamentable appropriation by ideologists of the extreme right and the travesty of his celebration as the philosophical inspiration of National Socialism. A further obstacle to his philosophical reception was created by his attainment of the status of a cult hero in certain literary and popular circles in Germany in the early decades of this century.[2]

Nietzsche's style and manner of writing were partly responsible for both the enthusiasm and the disdain which his writings inspired in different quarters. Unlike most philosophers, he generally did not set out his views systematically, in clearly discernable lines of argument cast in dry and measured prose. His works for the most part consist in series of short paragraphs and sets of aphorisms, often only loosely if at all connected. Many deal with philosophical topics, but in very unconventional ways; and because his many remarks about these topics are scattered through a large number of different works, they are all too easily taken in isolation and mis-understood. His language, furthermore, is by turns coolly analytical, heatedly polemical, sharply critical and highly metaphorical; and he seldom indicates at all clearly the scope of his claims, and what he means by the terms he uses. It is not surprising, therefore, that many philosophers have found it difficult to know what to make of him and to take him seriously; and that he has been and continues to be interpreted in a great many different ways, and to be claimed as a kindred spirit by representatives of the most diverse orientations.

## BASIC CONCERNS AND VIEWS

The early Nietzsche was greatly concerned with basic problems he discerned in contemporary western culture and society, which he believed were becoming increasingly acute, and for which he con-sidered it imperative to try to find new solutions. He sought to diagnose these ills, convinced that Schopenhauer's bleak picture of the world and the human condition was fundamentally sound, and yet also determined to discover some way of avoiding Schopenhauer's pessimistic conclusions.[3] Traditional religious and philosophical thought, he felt, far from providing what was needed, were deeply flawed, and in any event were on the wane; and modern science held no greater promise, being incapable either of yielding genuine knowl-edge or of showing the way to cultural renewal. In *The Birth of Tragedy* he looked to the ancient Greeks for clues and to Wagner for in-spiration, believing that their art held the key to human flourishing in this Schopenhauerian world. In his subsequent series of *Untimely*

*Meditations* he expanded on his theme of the need to reorient human thought and endeavour in a manner more conducive to the creativity and vitality of human life, and criticised a variety of tendencies detrimental to them which he discerned among his contemporaries.

These essays were followed by a number of books consisting of large collections of aphorisms, in which Nietzsche refined, sharpened and extended his analytical and critical assessment of various human tendencies and social cultural phenomena, among which prevailing forms of morality came to figure prominently. During this period his thinking became much more sophisticated, psychologically and sociologically and also philosophically; and he developed the distinctive philosophical style and concerns which found mature expression in the writings of the last half-dozen years of his productive life. In the early 1880s, when he conceived and wrote *Thus Spoke Zarathustra*, he also arrived at a conception of human life and possibility—and with it, of value and meaning—which he believed could serve to fill the void left by the collapse of traditional modes of interpretation, and to overcome the nihilism attendant on their collapse.

Nietzsche may have prophesied the advent of a period of nihilism, as traditional modes of interpretation and valuation were abandoned, with 'the death of God' and the demise of metaphysics, and the discovery of the inability of science to yield anything like absolute knowledge; but this prospect deeply distressed him. He was firmly convinced of the untenability of the 'God-hypothesis' and associated religious interpretations of the world and our existence, and similarly of their metaphysical variants. Having also become persuaded of the fundamentally non-rational character of the world, life and history, he took the basic challenge of philosophy to be that of overcoming both these ways of thinking and the nihilism resulting from their abandonment. This led him to undertake to reinterpret life and the world along lines which would be more tenable, and would also enable us to find a new 'centre of gravity' by means of which we might live.[4]

What Nietzsche called 'the death of God' was both a cultural event—the waning and impending demise of the 'Christian-moral' interpretation of life and the world—and also a philosophical development: the abandonment of the 'God-hypothesis' as a notion deserving to be taken seriously. As a cultural event it was a phenomenon to be reckoned with, and a source of profound concern, since he feared the 'nihilistic rebound' he suspected would follow in its wake and worried about the consequences for human life and culture if no counter-movement to it were forthcoming. As a philosophical development, on the other hand, it was his point of departure, which he took to call for a radical reconsideration of the nature of everything from life and the world and human existence and knowledge to value and morality. The 'de-deification of nature', the 'translation of man back into nature', the 'revaluation of values', the tracing of the 'genealogy of morals' and their critique, and the elaboration of 'naturalistic' accounts of knowledge, value, morality and our entire 'spiritual' nature thus came to be among the main tasks with which he took himself and the 'new philosophers' he called for to be confronted. He did not carry out these tasks at all completely, and did not even approach them systematically; but in his published and unpublished writings he offered a wealth of remarks, observations and suggestions pertaining to them which collectively contribute substantially to their treatment.

Nietzsche emphatically rejected not only the 'God-hypothesis' (as a notion utterly without warrant, owing its acceptance only to naïvety, error, need or ulterior motivation), but also any metaphysical postulation of a 'true world of "being"' transcending the world of life and experience. With them, moreover, he also rejected the related 'soul-' and 'thing-hypotheses', taking both notions to be ontological fictions reflecting our artificial (though convenient) conceptual shorthand for products and processes. In place of this cluster of traditional ontological categories and interpretations, he conceived of the world in terms of an interplay of forces without any inherent structure or final end, ceaselessly organising and reorganising itself as the fundamental disposition he called 'will to power' and attributed to all dynamic quanta of force giving rise to successive arrays of power-relationships among them. 'This world is the will to power— and nothing besides', he wrote; 'and you yourselves are also this will to power—and nothing besides!' (WP 1067). His idea of the 'eternal recurrence' underscores this conception of a world without beginning or end, in which the pattern of organisation and disintegration and reorganisation is endlessly repeated, and things ever happen in the same manner as they always have. Its primary significance for Nietzsche, however, was not as a cosmological doctrine to be literally construed, but rather as a picture intended to test one's ability to affirm life and the world as they are, and to focus one's attention on them.

Nietzsche thus construed our human nature and existence *natural-*

*istically*, in terms of 'will to power' and its ramifications in the establishment and expression of the complex systems of dynamic quanta we fundamentally are. 'The soul is only a word for something about the body', he has Zarathustra say (Z I:4); and the body is fundamentally an arrangement of natural forces and processes. At the same time, however, he insisted on the importance of social arrangements and interactions in the development of human forms of awareness and activity, and moreover on the possibility of the emergence of exceptional human beings capable of an independence and creativity elevating them above the generality of mankind. So he stressed the difference between 'higher men' and 'the herd', and through Zarathustra proclaimed the 'overman' (*Übermensch*) to be 'the meaning of the earth' (Z P:3), representing the overcoming of the 'all-too-human' and the attainment of the fullest possible 'enhancement of life'. Far from seeking to diminish our humanity by stressing our animality, he sought to direct our attention and efforts to the emergence of a 'higher humanity' capable of endowing existence with a human redemption and justification.

Notwithstanding his frequent characterisation as a nihilist, therefore, Nietzsche in fact sought to counter and overcome the nihilism he expected to become prevalent in the aftermath of the collapse and abandonment of traditional religious and metaphysical modes of interpretation and evaluation. While he was very critical of the latter, it was not his intention merely to oppose and subvert them, and to deny the possibility of putting anything in their place that would compare favourably to them in soundness. So he attempted to make out the possibility of forms of truth and knowledge to which philosophical interpreters of life and the world might after all aspire, and espoused a 'Dionysian value-standard' in terms of which his project of a 'revaluation of values' might be carried out.

As has been indicated, Nietzsche proposed that life and the world be interpreted in terms of his conception of 'will to power'; and he framed his 'Dionysian value-standard' and his 'revaluation of values' in terms of this interpretation as well. The only positive and tenable value-scheme possible, he maintained, must be based on a recognition and affirmation of the world's fundamental character, and so must posit as a general standard the attainment of a kind of life in which the 'will to power' as the creative transformation of existence is present in its highest intensity and quality. This in turn led him to take the 'enhancement of life' and creativity to be the guiding ideas of his 'revaluation of values' and development of a naturalistic value-theory.

The strongly creative flavour of Nietzsche's notions of such a 'higher humanity' and associated 'higher morality' reflects his linkage of both to his conception of *art*, to which he attached great importance. Art, for Nietzsche, is a fundamentally creative (rather than cognitive) affair, serving to prepare the way for the emergence of a sensibility and manner of life reflecting the highest potentiality human beings may possess. Art, as the creative transformation of the world as we find it (and of ourselves thereby) on a small scale and in particular media, affords us a glimpse of the possibility of a kind of life that would be lived more fully in this manner, and constitutes a step in the direction of its emergence.[5] In this way, Nietzsche's mature thought thus expands on the idea of the basic connection between art and the justification of life which was his general theme in his first major work, *The Birth of Tragedy*.

## APPROACHING MORALITY

Well before Nietzsche wrote *Beyond Good and Evil* and *On the Genealogy of Morals*, in which (as these titles indicate) morality came to be one of his primary concerns, he had begun to suspect that the entire domain of morality was far more problematical than had previously been recognised, and that a radical reassessment of it was required. His reassessment began in such relatively early works as *Human, All-Too-Human* and *Daybreak*, with tentative probings and reflections on the nature and functions of various forms of morality past and present; and in his writings during the last half-dozen years of his productive life, it became one of the principal instances of his 're-valuation of values', carried out with increasing thoroughness and emphasis.

Nietzsche is best known in moral philosophy for his emphatic rejection of a variety of claims long made for and about morality, concerning its status and claims on us. While his position is indeed a radical one, however, it is often misunderstood; for what emerges from his reassessment of morality is not its complete condemnation or repudiation, but rather a moral philosophy attentive to the complexity of morality in human life, sensitive to the variety of its forms and their differing significance in this context, and ultimately constructive rather than merely critical in import.

Nietzsche notoriously makes much of the point that 'there are no absolute morals' (D 139); indeed that 'moral judgement' is an 'illusion', and that *'there are altogether no moral facts'* (TI VII:1); he states that 'my chief proposition' is that *'there are no moral phenomena'*, but rather only 'a moral interpretation' of certain phenomena which 'itself is of extra-moral origin' (WP 258). On the other hand, however, he allows that there can and do exist various moralities, devoting a great deal of attention to them; and he grants and makes much of the fact that they have long played a very significant role in human affairs and the course of human development. Indeed, he is prepared to go further still, holding that once morality is 'naturalised', restored to its proper role as a 'means of life' and of 'the enhancement of life' (WP 298), and adjusted to take account of the differing 'conditions of preservation and development' of different types of human beings, it ceases to be a harmful 'lie' and dangerous 'illusion', and acquires legitimacy and positive significance.

The reconciliation of his remarks along the lines first mentioned with the admissions he makes and claims he advances of the latter sorts may seem to pose problems. These problems, however, are not as serious as they might appear to be; for his contentions of the former sort do not actually conflict with the latter. These contentions are not intended to have the force of a denial of the reality of moralities as features of human life, or even of the possibility of justifying all forms of morality. Rather, they are meant as rejections of claims for moral principles and values of a different kind, to the effect that they possess unconditional validity in their own right and are binding independently of any and all extra-moral circumstances and considerations. Nietzsche's basic point here is that all moralities are of extra-moral origin, and derive whatever force and standing they may have from factors and considerations which themselves are quite other than 'moral' in nature; that no actual or possible morality is 'absolute', none being anything more than a contingent, conditioned set of rules of limited applicability; and that there are no *underivatively* 'moral' values, and no *intrinsically* 'moral' phenomena.

Nietzsche prides himself on being an exception to the rule among his philosophical predecessors and contemporaries, in recognising how very problematic past and present moralities actually are in a variety of basic respects. He considers himself to differ from them in taking morality to *be* a 'problem' to be critically investigated, rather than something to be embraced and vindicated more or less as it is received. 'To see and to demonstrate the problem of morality', he writes, 'that seems to me the new principal task. I deny that it has been done in previous moral philosophy' (WP 263). Philosophers, of

course, have long concerned themselves with morality very extensively, and in some cases have even made bold to undertake to
establish a 'science of morals'. On Nietzsche's view, however, what
they in the main have wanted basically to do was 'to supply a
*rational foundation* for morality'. Thus, he observes,

> They never laid eyes on the real problems of morality; for these
> emerge only when we compare many moralities. In all 'science
> of morals' so far one thing was *lacking*, strange as it may sound:
> the problem of morality itself; what was lacking was any suspicion
> that there was something problematic here. (BGE 186)

Speaking very generally, Nietzsche's preliminary aim is to arrive
at a knowledge of the nature of morality in its various actual and
possible forms that will prepare the way for an adequate appraisal of
it (and them) along the lines of his larger project of a 'revaluation of
values'. His larger aim, however, is not only the criticism and overcoming of all 'merely moral' modes of thought and evaluation, but
moreover a subsequent reorientation and new grounding of normative thinking. In this connection, he maintains that philosophers
must restrain their impatience to establish anything as grandiose as
a 'science of morals', let alone something along the lines of 'a
rational foundation of morality', and must first of all direct their
attention to 'the facts of morality' to be found in human history and
present-day life, with all the care, detachment and descriptive and
analytical acumen they can muster. 'What is still necessary here', he
writes, is 'to collect material, to conceptualise and arrange a vast
realm of subtle feelings of value and differences of value which are
alive, grow, beget, and perish . . .—all to prepare a typology of
morals' (BGE 186).
   While he might easily have done so, however, Nietzsche did not
lose himself in the preliminary tasks of description and genealogy,
nor confine himself entirely to the subsequent but nonetheless still
only intermediary tasks of interpretation and critical and revaluative
analysis. He came to believe that he had done enough along these
lines to place him in a position to begin to develop a new form of
normative theory, centring on what he takes to be his 'fundamental
innovation' of a 'naturalisation of morality' (WP 462). In what
follows, I shall briefly examine each of these aspects of his moral
philosophy, which reduces to no one of them, but rather consists in
all of them taken together.

## THE SOCIAL NATURE OF MORALITY

Nietzsche's point of departure is the observation that throughout human history, what he calls 'moral prejudices' of one sort or another have prevailed, finding expression in 'sentiments', 'valuations', 'attitudes', 'beliefs', 'convictions' and the disposition to pass 'judgements' concerning various qualities, tendencies, actions and intentions. He has a special interest in what he often refers to as 'our morality' (and 'our moral prejudices'); but he holds that one cannot even begin to achieve an adequate understanding and fair assessment of it unless one broadens one's view to include others, both independent of and ancestral to it. The moral philosopher's first order of business, therefore, is the task of description, both cross-cultural and historical; for, as has been seen, he holds that it is 'only when we compare *many* moralities' that 'the real problems of morality emerge' (BGE 186). It is a further task to determine the sorts of social functions various moralities perform and social requirements or needs to which they answer. It is yet another, moreover, to uncover the psychological factors at work in the motivation of individuals to embrace or reject different forms of morality. In short:

> Anyone who now wishes to make a study of moral matters opens up for himself an immense field of work. All kinds of individual passions have to be thought through and pursued through different ages, peoples, and great and small individuals; all their reason and all their evaluations and perspectives on things have to be brought into the light. . . . It would require whole generations, and generations of scholars who would collaborate systematically, to exhaust the points of view and the material. The same applies to the demonstration of the reasons for the differences between moral climates. (GS 7)

The fundamental step which must be taken if one is ever to arrive at a sound understanding of morality, for Nietzsche, involves viewing moralities from *without* (GS 380)—and more specifically, recognising them to be devices whereby modifications of the attitudes and actions of human beings living together are brought about. These modifications may be of diverse kinds; but he contends that they generally are related to the establishment or maintenance of *advantages* of some sort (accruing either to certain segments of the populations of various societies or to these societies themselves as ongoing enterprises), and have the basic character of *direction*, which in most cases reduces to that of *control*.

'Advantages' must not be taken too narrowly here; it is to be understood as embracing a broad range of respects in which the position of such groups in relation to others and to other forms of life may be secured and enhanced. In the first instance they pertain to the preservation of the group. Thus Nietzsche contends that an analysis of various moralities reveals that 'their erection was the erection of the conditions—often erroneous—of existence of a limited group—for its preservation' (WP 260). They generally perform the function of strengthening the hand of the groups which develop them in their dealings with others, or at least of heightening their sense of their superiority in relation to others.

The notion of 'direction' similarly is to be understood rather broadly in this connection. What moralities fundamentally convey, on Nietzsche's view, are norms of human life. They distinguish among purported human possibilities, identifying certain ways one might be or act as better or worse than others, and endowing these discriminations with normative force. They thus perform a directive role, encouraging or discouraging ways of living, thinking and choosing to which those concerned may or may not have any prior inclination. In the latter case they may at least initially bear the aspect of constraint, while in the former they serve more to refine and intensify; but in both they educate and transform the consciousness and conduct of those who come under their influence.

Moralities generally thus are taken by Nietzsche to be fundamentally (although by no means purely) *social* phenomena. In making this observation he means more than merely that they pertain chiefly to interpersonal relationships. His larger point is that moralities as a rule are primarily the moralities of certain societies, peoples or groups, and are only secondarily the moralities of individuals. So, for example, he remarks that we should not be misled by the 'refined' character of our modern 'sense of morality'. We must recognise that, fundamentally considered, morality (*Sittlichkeit*) 'is nothing other (and thus in particular *nothing more*) than obedience to customs, of whatever kind these may be; customs, however, are but the *traditional* ways of acting and esteeming' (D 9). In short, it is 'society', on Nietzsche's view, which is the source of 'all morality and all celebration of moral action' (WS 40). This early insight is reflected in one of his best-known (but frequently misunderstood) observations: 'Wandering through the many subtler and coarser moralities which have so far been prevalent on earth', he writes, 'I finally discovered two basic types and one basic difference'. The two types are '*master morality* and *slave morality*'—and, he continues, 'I add immediately that in all the higher and more mixed cultures there also appear attempts at mediation between these two moralities' (BGE 260).

All such moralities for Nietzsche are to be regarded as social formations, and referred to the character of the social groups, structures and processes of which they are the issue. The moral sensibilities of individuals (the moral views of philosophers most definitely included) are not to be thought of as somehow originating and developing within each of them independently of these social formations, any more than their religious beliefs may be supposed to take shape throught their autonomous employment of their own intellectual and spiritual resources. Rather, they are primarily the effects of the internalisation of initially external social norms, together with the operation of a variety of psychological factors rooted in the individual's particular constitution and history. Both of the two basic types of moralities Nietzsche discerns ('master' or 'noble' moralities and 'slave' or 'herd' moralities), along with their various historical admixtures, are in this respect fundamentally akin to the very ancient phenomenon he calls the 'morality of mores' (D 9).

Nietzsche places considerable emphasis on the point, however, that such moralities may be and have been of significantly different sorts and origins. In particular, they can have the character of an aristocratic code, embodying 'aristocratic value judgements' reflecting the self-affirming self-consciousness of 'the noble', powerful, high-stationed and high-minded, who felt and established themselves and their actions as good, that is, of the first rank, in contradistinction to all the low, low-minded, common and plebian'. On the other hand, they may have the character of the expression of the 'herd instinct' of the latter, which 'at last gets its word (and its *words*) in', proscribing what the 'herd' finds threatening and prescribing what seems advantageous to it (GM I:2). Or, somewhat differently, they can take shape in more direct and insidious reaction to the former, 'when *ressentiment* itself becomes creative and gives birth to values' and to opposing conceptions of 'good' and 'evil' (GM I:10).

## 'HERD' and 'SLAVE' MORALITIES

While Nietzsche considers it important to bear in mind that moralities other than those he terms 'herd' and 'slave' moralities have on

occasion prevailed and remain possible, much of what he has to say
pertains to these types. He focuses his attention on them not only
because he takes them long to have been the rule in most human
societies, but also because he regards modern-day western morality
as a late and dangerous case in point. They (and 'our morality' along
with them) most emphatically are not *his* sort of morality—'morality
as constantly practised self-control and self-overcoming in the greatest
and smallest matters' (WS 45), a morality 'which desires to train men
for the heights' and so promotes 'the elevation of the type man' (WP
957). He readily allows, however, that they are prominent features
of human life past and present, which require to be reckoned with in
any treatment of morality.

Reflecting on 'the oldest moral judgements', Nietzsche suggests
that they had their origin in the tendency to suppose that ' "whatever
harms me is something evil . . . , whatever benefits me is something
good" ' (D 102), and in the subsequent shift of the frame of reference
from the individual to the group. Thus he observes that 'preserving
the community generally and protecting it from destruction' was its
primary emphasis, and after that 'preserving the community on
a certain level' (WS 44). These circumstances are reflected in the
fact that 'the person whose conduct is sympathetic, disinterested,
commonly useful, and social is now regarded as the *moral* one' (D
132). Nietzsche allows this to be a *fait accompli*, but contends that,

> Behind the basic principle of current moral fashion: 'moral actions
> are actions of sympathy for others,' I see a social impulse of fear-
> fulness at work, which dresses itself up intellectually in this way.
> This impulse has as its highest, most important and immediate
> aim the removal from life of everything *dangerous* which was
> earlier associated with it, to which end *everyone* is supposed to
> contribute and make every effort: consequently only actions con-
> ducive to the common security and feeling of security are permitted
> to be accorded the predicate 'good'! (D 174)

The type of morality which emerges may be dressed up and presented as a 'morality of "neighbour love" '; but Nietzsche contends
that 'here, too, fear is again the mother of morals' (BGE 201). 'Herd
morality' may thus be seen to be 'malice spiritualized', the subtle
and 'favourite revenge of the spiritually limited against those less
limited' (BGE 219). It is diagnosed as the expression of a general
tendency the formula for which is that '*the more dangerous a quality*

*seems to the herd, the more thoroughly it is proscribed'* (WP 276). Its positive side, on the other hand, is the expression of 'all the herd thinks desirable', combining the celebration of the very qualities constitutive of its 'mediocrity' with the promotion of conditions conducive to its 'comfort' (WP 957). So he remarks that 'the herd animal thus glorifies the herd nature', and 'with fair words' masks its 'judgement of comfort'—and 'thus "morality" arises' (WP 285).

It is worth noting that a morality suited to the convenience, limitations and conceit of the 'herd' need not be a 'slave morality', for Nietzsche, since it may or may not be the case that the 'mediocre' and 'ill-constituted' find themselves in circumstances to which 'slave morality' is a response. 'Thus in the history of morality', he writes, 'a will to power finds expression, through which now the slaves and oppressed, now the ill-constituted and those who suffer from themselves, now the mediocre attempt to make those value judgements prevail that are favourable to *them*' (WP 400). It may be that these 'value judgements' exhibit strong affinities, as indeed he would appear to suppose. But this does not mean that there are no differences among the forms of morality associated with them.

So, for example, Nietzsche remarks that 'the weakness of the herd animal produces a morality very similar to that produced by the weakness of the decadent' (WP 281). Yet he also allows for the possibility of an at least marginally healthy and flourishing type of 'herd animal' with a morality well suited to its needs, urging that 'two types of morality must not be confused: the morality with which the healthy instinct defends itself against incipient decadence—and another morality with which this very decadence defines and justifies itself and leads downwards' (WP 268). Indeed, he actually considers even more fine-grained discriminations within this 'basic type' of morality to be required. Thus he enumerates and distinguishes the following four possibilities, under the heading of morality's 'usefulness for life':

(1) Morality as the principle that preserves the general whole, as a limitation on its members: 'the *instrument*'.
(2) Morality as the principle that preserves man from the inner peril of his passions: 'the *mediocre*'.
(3) Morality as the principle that preserves man from the life-destroying effects of profound misery and atrophy: 'the *suffering*'.
(4) Morality as the principle that opposes the fearful outbursts of the powerful: 'the *lowly*' (WP 266).

It is the last-mentioned of these possibilities to which his notion of 'slave morality' specifically refers. What gives 'slave morality' proper its distinctive flavour and orientation, however, is taken by Nietzsche to be its reactive character in relation to the qualities possessed by those to whom the population among whom it originates are in thrall, which appear to the latter to be linked to the ascendance of the former over them and so to threaten them. And this means that it is at least initially bound up with the obtaining of a rather specific sort of *social situation*. This situation is one in which there is 'a ruling group' and a 'ruled group', and in which the former, moreover, is both strikingly different from and quite indifferent to the latter. It blithely exploits the latter as it pursues its own course and celebrates, cultivates and gives expression to 'everything it knows as part of itself' that sets it apart from and enables it to dominate the population over which it holds sway (BGE 260).

These might seem to be rather special circumstances; but Nietzsche would appear to think they once rather widely obtained. In any event, the phenomenon he calls 'slave morality' is the mode of moral value- and norm-determination with which he suggests such a subjugated population might respond to its plight. 'Suppose the violated, oppressed, suffering, unfree, who are uncertain of themselves and weary, moralise', he writes; 'what will their moral valuations have in common?' His answer is that they are likely to take a dim view of 'the whole condition of man' (BGE 260). Their valuations will tend generally to reflect unfavourably on the basic character of human nature and human existence, and so to express what Nietzsche terms a fundamental 'hostility to life'.

It is this sort of morality he has in mind when he links it with 'pessimism' and contends that 'insofar as we believe in morality we pass sentence on existence' (WP 6); when he holds it to be 'detrimental to life'—to the 'enjoyment' and also the 'beautifying and ennobling of life', and further 'to the development of life', in that 'it sought to set the highest phenomena of life at variance with life itself' (WP 266); and when he speaks of 'morality as the instinct to deny life', owing to its hostility to 'all the forces and drives by virtue of which life and growth exist' (WP 343). It constitutes one of the fateful 'metamorphoses of slavery', the 'transfiguration through morality' which has the effect of elevating the slave's distorted perspective to the status of the last and highest word with respect to human life and conduct (WP 357). And this is something to which Nietzsche objects in the strongest possible terms.

## CRITICAL CONSIDERATIONS

There are, however, a variety of human (and all-too-human) needs, vulnerabilities, limitations, drives and dispositions to which moralities may answer, on Nietzsche's view; and he suggests that the remedies moralities provide and the satisfactions they afford in relation to them may or may not be adequate to them, and also may be more or less costly in the toll they exact. All, he contends, are of extramoral and indeed extra-rational origin, and maintain and extend their sway by extra-moral and extra-rational means. All admit of some sort of explanation in terms of one or more of the sorts of factors just indicated—which explanation, while not amounting to a vindication, does at least confer on them a kind of understand-ability, and even a measure of appropriateness, in relation to the human situations in question. This is what he means when he speaks of 'morality as the work of immorality', and contends that 'the origin of moral values is the work of immoral affects and considerations' (WP 266).

This is an important part of what Nietzsche terms 'moralistic naturalism: the tracing back of apparently emancipated, supra-natural moral values to their "nature": that is, to natural immorality, to natural "utility", and so on (WP 299). There is nothing intrinsically 'moral', he argues, about the ends moralities serve and the func-tions they perform. The establishment of conditions conducive to preservation and growth, the allaying of dangers from without and within, the attainment of mastery over nature, others and oneself, the achievement of self-esteem and the obtaining of revenge, are the sorts of purposes in terms of which he contends that the emergence of various moralities are to be understood. And there is quite evidently nothing inherently 'moral' about them. Indeed, in the per-spective of the most commonly prevalent of these moralities, many of them are positively 'immoral'.

Seizing on this point, Nietzsche proceeds to employ it to mount what he takes to be an internal argument against certain claims commonly made for such moralities, and in particular against 'the assertion that moral values are the supreme values'. For he holds that 'the supremacy of moral valuations would be refuted if it could be shown to be the consequence of an immoral valuation', and thus 'a special case of immorality' (WP 583). 'To abolish the supreme value hitherto, morality', he maintains, 'it suffices to demonstrate that even morality is immoral, in the sense in which immorality has always been condemned' (WP 461). For if (or to the extent that) moralities legislate against the very conditions of their own establish-ment, the legitimacy of such proscriptions is subverted by insight into the nature of the phenomenon of moral valuation itself. Where this is so, morality in effect 'contradicts itself' (WP 266), and thus falls by its own hand. And Nietzsche considers this to apply to many 'apparently emancipated, supranatural moral values', which more or less explicitly condemn much of what is 'natural' to human life and involved in their emergence within it (WP 299).

This argument, however, does not go nearly far enough, or apply broadly enough. Morality in its supposedly more sophisticated as well as cruder forms further is held by Nietzsche to be 'the work of error' (WP 266), and so in another and deeper sense to be ironically subverted by one of its own principal demands—namely, that of truthfulness or honesty. 'But among the forces cultivated by morality was *truthfulness*: this eventually turned against morality' (WP 5), with consequences now proving fatal to this original source. For Nietzsche contends that, 'As the will to truth thus gains self-consciousness—there can be no doubt of that—morality will gradually perish now', at least as it has long been construed (GM III:27). The critique he develops, which leads him to this conclusion, focuses on what he takes to be the presuppositions of moralities of a non-'naturalistic' character, and on the implications for the latter of the untenability of these presuppositions. 'This is *my* point of view', he writes: 'I deny morality as I deny alchemy—that is to say, I deny its presuppositions; but *not* that there have been alchemists, who believed in these presuppositions and acted on them' (D 103).

What Nietzsche has in mind here, in the first instance, is that the situation of such moralities with respect to their justifiability is hopeless. They cannot stand in the absence of an other-worldly, religious or metaphysical grounding and sanctioning; but they also cannot be defended *by reference to* any such set of beliefs, since the latter do not survive critical examination. Thus he maintains that 'the whole of our European morality' is a part of 'what must now collapse', with the recognition that 'the belief in the Christian God' is 'unbelievable' and requires to be abandoned; for this morality 'was built on this faith' and 'propped up by it' (GS 343). 'When one gives up the Christian faith, one pulls the right to Christian morality out from under one's feet', he writes: 'it stands and falls with faith in God'. For it fundamentally has the status of 'a command' which 'has truth only if God is the truth' (TI IX:5).

A morality of this sort 'no longer has any sanction after it has tried to escape into some beyond', and this 'beyond' is discovered to be a fiction (WP 1). Once the erroneousness of supposing any such 'other world' to exist is recognised, no morality of this sort can be saved. One may embrace it without any explicit awareness that one is presupposing anything along these lines, and even without being at all prepared to affirm anything of the sort. One's 'right to it', how-ever, on examination turns out to be dependent on the soundness of positing some such higher reality to which it can be referred; and consequently, Nietzsche holds, it cannot be sustained.

He further observes that 'when the English actually believe that they know "intuitively" what is good and evil', and 'therefore suppose that they no longer require Christianity as the guarantee of morality', they err and deceive themselves. For they thereby take as an intuitive apprehension of moral truths what is merely the experience of senti-ments which are among 'the *effects* of the Christian value judgement and an expression of the strength and depth of this dominion' (TI IX:5). He similarly denies that any other morality can be legitimately deemed self-evident, or considered to require no justification beyond one's moral intuitions or the deliverances of one's conscience; for he holds that an understanding of the manner in which such 'subjective value feelings' are shaped and acquired should undermine any confidence one might have been inclined to repose in them (GS 335). If a morality has nothing more going for it than certain 'intuitions' and deliverances of conscience on the part of its adherents, there-fore, it has no claim to tenability.

The erroneous interpretations of such 'subjective value feelings' as the immediate apprehension of 'moral truths' is not the only thing Nietzsche has in mind when he contends that morality up to now has rested on a 'dreadful *forgery of the psychology of man*' (WP 786). What he terms 'the erroneousness of . . . the whole nature of moral judgements to date' (GS 7) is also held to be related to a further set of mistaken suppositions pertaining to human actions. 'The error of free will' (TI VI:7) is one; and the myth of the possibility of genuine 'altruism' is another. Nietzsche sees 'a tremendous rat's tail of errors' here (WP 705), and holds that their exposure leaves little of morality as it has for the most part been understood still standing. There are actions to which the predicates 'moral' and 'immoral' are commonly applied; but he maintains that as these notions are conceived, in point of fact *'there are neither moral nor immoral actions'*.

This entire distinction 'moral' and 'immoral' proceeds from the idea that moral as well as immoral actions are acts arising from free spontaneity—in short, that such a spontaneity exists, or in other words: that moral judgements in general relate only to one species of intuitions and actions, those that are *free*. But this whole species of intentions and actions is purely imaginary. (WP 786).

In sum: 'If only those actions are moral . . . which are performed out of freedom of will, then there are no moral actions' (D 148). For the doctrine that each human being possesses a 'free will' is an 'error', motivated by a desire to be able 'to impute guilt', justify punishment, and influence behaviour (TI VI:7).

Nietzsche further maintains that those who are commonly deemed 'moral men' are no more truly 'moral' than the rest of mankind in their basic manner of conduct. What he here has in mind is *altruism*, the reality and indeed the very possibility of which he disputes, even while conceding the important influence which the idea and ideal of altruism have had in human affairs. He does not consider 'our morality' to be confined to the celebration and advocacy of altruism; but he does suppose the latter to be so central to the former that its abandonment would in effect spell the end of morality as we know it. And he contends that 'the antithetical concepts "moral" and "immoral"' are rooted in the 'psychological error' which consists in the interpretation of certain human actions and motives as '"selfless", "unegoistic", "self-denying"—all unreal, imaginary' (WP 786).

Nietzsche by no means thinks that human beings never do anything that is not in their own interest. On the contrary, he recognises and indeed makes much of the fact that they can be and often are induced to act in ways which are at variance with it. Even when acting contrary to their own actual best interest, however, he argues that people do so in direct or indirect consequence of the operation of motivating forces geared to the securing of advantages and the avoidance of disadvantages. If anything like a disposition to benefit others is exhibited by some, he maintains, it is only a derivative one, in the formation of which self-interested motives have been enlisted and are covertly operative.

Thus if 'moral actions' are construed as actions *serving* primarily to benefit others (either individually or generally), then of course *there are* such actions. But if it is further laid down that actions of this sort qualify as 'moral' only if their determining ground is a 'moral will' existing and operating independently of all forms and manifestations of self-interest, and having the good of others as its inherent object, Nietzsche takes objection to the supposition that anything human beings ever do answers to this description. He finds it quite understandable that actions benefitting others, and those who perform them to their own disadvantage, should be *praised*; but he contends that 'this praise certainly was not born from the spirit of selflessness', and 'has always been far from "selfless", far from "unegoistic"', since it is fundamentally tied to estimations of the 'probable consequences' of such actions 'for us and society'. Acting in a 'selfless' and 'self-sacrificial' manner earns praise *'because it brings advantages'* (GS 21). Nietzsche allows that human beings respond to such praise and encouragement, as well as to the prospect of the imposition of negative sanctions if they fail to act in the prescribed manner, and thus may gradually come to be disposed to do so. But while such influences may join with their basic susceptibilities to create the semblance of a 'moral will', it is in terms of them rather than the possession of any such faculty operating independently of them that the phenomena variously described in terms of 'selflessness', 'benevolence' and "altruism" are to be understood.

If 'the spirit of selflessness' is conceived essentially as the outcome of the process which 'trains the individual to be a function of the herd', therefore, and altruism is construed as 'herd instinct in the individual' (GS 116), their possibility and reality may readily be granted, and the morality centring on them may be allowed to play a significant role in human life and have a genuine basis in fact. But if larger claims are made for them, and they are taken to involve the radical transcendence of all more mundane elements of human nature and conditions of human existence, they turn out to be among the grand illusions and errors by means of which human life has been sustained and transformed, but which cannot be philosophically countenanced. Once one discerns the 'psychological error' it involves, 'one grasps that altruistic actions are only a species of egoistic actions' (WP 786).

## REVALUATION OF MORAL VALUES

It bears repeating, however, that their erroneousness notwithstanding, Nietzsche does not deny to moralities the power to exert a significant influence on the course and character of human life. He considers them not only to be symptomatic of the affective constitutions of those who embrace them, and expressive of the conditions of the preservation and flourishing of the human communities in which they appear, but also to promote the adoption of certain valuations by those whose lives they touch. Under the spell of such 'moral values', people come to live differently than they otherwise would or might, were they to come to adopt differing sets of values. What Nietzsche takes to be the dominant morality of the present time is marked by a number of these value-determinations. And his most fundamental objections to it concern the detrimental impact he considers them to have on the quality of human life.

'Even if a morality has grown out of an error', he writes, 'the realisation of this fact would not as much as touch the problem of its value' (GS 345). The latter, in his view, ultimately comes down to its 'value for life'; and when assessed in this light, he argues that present-day morality—a 'herd-animal morality' aiming at the happiness and well-being of all and championing selflessness, 'equal rights' and 'sympathy with all that suffers' (WP 957)—fares very badly indeed. His opposition to it derives from his conviction that 'a tendency hostile to life'—to its enhancement, if not to its mere preservation—is 'characteristic of morality' of this sort. 'Whoever reflects on the way in which the type man can be raised to his greatest splendour and power', he contends, and on the other hand considers the nature of this morality and the consequences of its ascendency, must recognise that 'morality has been essentially directed to the opposite end: to obstruct or destroy that splendid evolution wherever it has been going on' (WP 987). A new and different sort of look at 'moral values' is called for; and the 'standard by which the value of moral evaluations is to be determined' is that of 'the elevation and strengthening of the type man' (WP 391).

Nietzsche arrived at this position after having earlier considered, and dismissed, the idea that these 'evaluations' and the precepts deriving from them might be justified by reference to considerations pertaining to the 'greatest happiness'. In the first place, he observes that it is not clear whether this is supposed to mean 'the greatest amount that particular individuals might eventually achieve, or an ultimately achievable (but in no way calculable) average-happiness of all' (D 106). And he then suggests that the desired justification is not forthcoming in either case. For, with respect to the former, he contends that 'the precepts one calls "moral" are in truth directed against individuals and by no means promote their happiness'—

except, perhaps, in the event that they have been so thoroughly schooled by morality that they know no greater form of felicity than that which they derive from adherence to it. And with respect to the latter, he reflects: 'These precepts have equally little relation to the "happiness and well-being of mankind"—which words cannot even be given any strict meaning, much less be used as guiding stars on the dark ocean of moral endeavour' (D 108).

In the second place, and more fundamentally, Nietzsche takes a very dim view of the preoccupation with 'happiness' which under-lies this entire approach to morality. Thus he derides 'the indefati-gable, inevitable British utilitarians', who promote '*English* morality' with great zeal, out of the conviction that 'it serves humanity best, or "the general utility", or "the happiness of the greatest number"— no, the happiness of *England*'. For in addition to being afflicted with this odd enthusiasm, he holds that 'none of these ponderous herd animals' recognises 'that "the general welfare" is no ideal, no goal, no remotely intelligible concept, but only an emetic' (BGE 228). And he further suggests that their 'morality of utility' reflects the stunted aspirations of 'the violated, oppressed, suffering, unfree, who are uncertain of themselves and weary' and are preoccupied with merely 'enduring the pressure of existence' (BGE 260), knowing nothing of 'creative powers and an artistic conscience' (BGE 225).

Nietzsche takes an equally dim view of that seemingly more re-fined variant of 'herd morality' which celebrates 'selflessness' as a basic ideal and principle of moral worth. The idealisation of selfless-ness, he contends, has the fundamental significance of a reaction to (and defensive strategy directed against) those in whom basic human 'drives' are strongest and therefore most threatening, on the part of those in whom they are relatively weak and the capacity to assert themselves directly is wanting. It is the culmination of a development involving the denigration of 'everything that elevates an individual above the herd and intimidates the neighbour', while only the 'modest, submissive, conforming mentality, the *mediocrity* of desires attains moral designation and honours' (BGE 201). This development may be understandable; but in his view it also poses a danger, since the strongest of the 'forces and drives by virtue of which life and growth exist' are thus given a negative valuation, and those who possess them are given a bad conscience with respect to them. And to the extent that the latter are induced by an altruistic morality to make that sort of self-sacrifice on behalf of others which consists in checking and repressing these 'forces and drives' in order not to risk harming or offending them, human life is diminished both in vigour and in quality.

The self-assertiveness against which Nietzsche takes the valuation of selflessness to be detrimentally directed, however, should not be confused with the mere selfishness and impulsive self-indulgence of which everyone is capable. Indeed, where the latter are concerned, he is more than willing to concede value to self-control and self-denial, not only for the 'herd' but for all. For he regards such 'self-overcoming' not only as a means to the harmonisation of ordinary social relations, but moreover as indispensable to the achievement of significant forms of self-assertion on the part of those who have it in them to rise to them. In this context he thus takes the morality of selflessness to have something to be said for it, notwithstanding its underlying twofold connection with 'weakness'. As a *general rule* he considers it to be preferable to an 'egoistic' morality or to mere egoism; and the exceptions to it, on the desirability and importance of which he lays great stress, are better handled by being allowed for *beyond* it, on his view, rather than by being generally prescribed in place of it or incorporated into it.

Nietzsche's revaluation of this 'moral value' thus does not stop with the critique which reveals it to be a 'false valuation', nor with a 'genealogical' and psychological analysis which renders it even less palatable (although more understandable). It also extends beyond a reflection on the nature of life and what is conducive to the enhancement of life which leads to his judgement that, its erstwhile and general utility notwithstanding, it is 'a burden which may become a fatality' (WP 404). For it involves its additional subjection to a differentiating assessment in various more specific human contexts, in the light of the 'order of rank' applying to them and their place in the larger economy of human life and development.

Thus Nietzsche would by no means have everyone abandon the 'herd morality' he so frequently excoriates, despite his low assessment of its basic values of harmlessness, happiness and selflessness. On the contrary, he considers it to be entirely fitting, and hardly capable of being improved on (at least in its milder, non-ascetic form) where all those who do not have it in them to be *more* than the 'herd type' of human being are concerned. What he objects to is rather its inculcation in the potential exceptions to the human rule. 'The ideas of the herd', he writes, 'should rule in the herd—but not reach out beyond it' (WP 287). His critique of the 'evaluations' he takes to be central to this type of morality thus must be understood as subject to these qualifications if its force and its limits are to be properly understood.


## A 'NATURALISTIC' CONCEPTION OF MORALITY

This sort of assessment of moral values might appear to be the culmination of Nietzsche's thinking with respect to morality. And in a sense it is, at least where moralities past and present are concerned. In another sense, however, what he has to say along these lines is but the conclusion of an investigation that is merely a long preliminary in relation to a further part of his treatment of morality. For he is concerned not merely to come to terms with such moralities, but to look beyond them, and to achieve a reorientation of the manner in which morality is understood that would serve to place it on a new footing and enable it to acquire new meaning and significance.

Here as so often elsewhere, Nietzsche is not content to allow the notion to remain the exclusive possession of those whose construal and application of it draw his fire on it, and to disassociate himself from it as completely as he repudiates their views. Rather, he proceeds to appropriate it and recast it along lines he considers more tenable, thereby giving it a new lease on life and a positive role in his own thinking. Moral philosophy takes (or should take) a new turn, in his view, and is provided with new tasks, when its subservience to prevailing modes of moral interpretation is ended. It is one of his main purposes to set it on this different course.

Thus Nietzsche seeks to revolutionise moral thinking, and to help usher in a new 'period which should be designated negatively, to begin with, as *extra-moral*', but which also may no less appropriately be thought of as involving the *reformation* of morality, and thus a new chapter in its (as well as mankind's) history. 'The overcoming of morality'—that is, morality in the traditional sense—may be the initial task confronting 'the finest and most sharply honed . . . consciences of today' (BGE 32). But with the accomplishment of this preliminary task another takes its place, in which 'morals' or moral theory is transformed into the elaboration of 'the doctrine of the relations of supremacy under which the phenomenon of "life" comes to be', and may flourish and admit of enhancement (BGE 19).

This, at any rate, is the perspective in which Nietzsche proposes to reinterpret and resurrect the notion of morality, thereby abolishing the longstanding opposition between the 'moral' and 'natural'. His formula for this is the 'naturalisation of morality'. By this he means not only the establishment of the status of all putatively 'moral phenomena' as 'natural phenomena', but also the recasting of morality along 'naturalistic lines', with 'purely naturalistic values' replacing distinctively and irreducibly 'moral values' as its basic principles. This he proclaims to be one of his 'fundamental innovations' (WP 462). He insists that it is not his intention to 'promote any morality' (GS 292); for in his view there is no *one* morality which alone is appropriate for all human beings under any and all circumstances. So, for example, as has been seen, he contends that 'herd animal morality' is at once well suited to the conditions of existence and constitutions of many human beings, and also highly detrimental to others. If, as he urges, 'moralities must be forced to bow first of all before the order of rank' (BGE 221) in consequence of the recognition that 'the demand of one morality for all is detrimental for the higher man (BGE 228), he also holds that 'the order of rank between man and man' mandates the establishment of comparably differing moralities adjusted to their divergent requirements and capabilities.

'Every naturalism in morality—that is, every healthy morality— is dominated by an instinct of life; some commandment of life is fulfilled by a determinate canon of "shalt" and "shalt not".' (TI V:4). Owing to the constitutional differences among human beings, how- ever, different manners of life are properly prescribable for various human 'types', in the form of differing moralities. For if these con- stitutional differences translate into different 'conditions of life', and if one thinks of a 'morality' as 'a system of evaluations that partially coincides with the conditions of a creature's life' (WP 256), as Nietzsche proposes to do, the result is a form of moral pluralism when this general conception of morality is applied more concretely to human life, according to which different moralities are warranted in dif- ferent human contexts, while being undesirable in others.

While this moral pluralism may be regarded as a kind of relativism, it is not a *cultural* relativism, let alone a subjective one. It does not involve the denial that there are any objective considerations tran- scending cultural formations or subjective determinations by refer- ence to which particular moralities may be justified and assessed, even though it does deny unconditional validity to any of them. It links them to the contingent and varying but nonetheless definite psycho-physiologically grounded 'conditions of life' of human beings. None is or can be absolute; but moralities answering to this descrip- tion are not merely conventional either, and clearly cannot be considered arbitrary. They are indeed 'relative'; but what they are relative *to* are circumstances pertaining to the actual constitutions of human beings of different sorts. Nietzsche's 'naturalisation of morality' thus involves the incorporation of moral theory into philosophical anthropology, in the context of which it loses its autonomy but acquires legitimacy.

Nietzsche's meta-level 'morality of development', however, reflects his conviction of the possibility of carrying the matter a step further. It represents a broadening of the context in which moral theory is situated, through the introduction of considerations deriving from his more comprehensive interpretation of 'life' and his associated general theory of value. Moralities, in his naturalistic perspective, when they are what they should be, are 'means' serving 'the aim of enhancing life' (WP 298); and for him this is not simply a matter of enabling each particular form of life, as it is, to flourish. He requires more of moralities than that they answer to the 'conditions of life' of various types of human beings, and thus within such contexts may be deemed 'healthy'. Rather, it is to 'life' more generally that they require to be referred—human life as a broader phenomenon, the strengthening and enhancement of which they are to serve, indirectly if not directly.

It is not primarily because of its benefits for the general run of mankind, for example, that Nietzsche would have 'herd animal morality' cultivated among them. His reason is rather that the attainment of 'a high culture', and thus of an enhanced form of human life, is possible 'only on a broad base, on a strong and healthily consolidated mediocrity' (WP 864). And it is similarly not owing to its advantages for exceptional individuals *themselves* that he considers a strongly self-assertive and rather 'egoistic' morality to be warranted in their case; nor yet again because he takes such a morality to *be* what the 'morality of development' of which he speaks comes down to in concrete terms. Rather, his advocacy of the former in their case derives from his conviction that, in the long run (though by no means in each instance and directly), the prospects for the enhancement of life will thereby be brightened, and will otherwise be virtually nil.

Both kinds of morality thus have the status of means to the same larger end; but they are no more than means. And they are means of very different sorts, adapted to the differing roles human beings endowed with varying capacities are suited to play in the attainment of this end. His 'morality of development' is a meta-level morality, in the sense that it is not a morality for everyone or anyone to live by, but rather a higher-order principle of moral theory by reference to which particular types of moralities may be identified and endowed with significance. It derives its meaning from his interpretation of 'life' in terms of 'will to power' and its transformations, and its force from the standard of value he extracts therefrom. And its implications vary with the human contexts and possibilities obtaining at different junctures in human history and in the cases of different human types.

Moral philosophy for Nietzsche thus is ultimately a strongly normative as well as analytical and critical affair, notwithstanding his insistence on the necessity of 'naturalising' moral theory. It must take account of the links between moralities and the affective phenomena and social circumstances which tend to shape them and impose constraints on their modifiability; yet it should also be sensitive to the extent to which they nonetheless admit of modification, and be concerned with the respects in which this may be desirable. It further must be appreciative of the fact that human beings differ in respects which are relevant to the determination of the sorts of morality appropriate for them. It therefore must deal with the possibility and desirability of differing moralities in different human contexts; and, recognising that the morality prevailing 'in Europe today' is 'merely *one* type of human morality beside which . . . many other types, above all *higher* moralities, are, or ought to be, possible' (BGE 202), it should proceed from an examination of the former to the exploration and elaboration of the latter.

## NIETZSCHE'S 'HIGHER MORALITY'

In speaking here and elsewhere of possible 'higher moralities' and contrasting them with 'herd animal morality', Nietzsche does not merely have in mind the sort of thing he takes to have been its most notable historical rival, which he terms 'noble' or 'master morality'. He does indeed regard the latter as a type of 'higher morality' in relation to the former. The kind of higher morality with the possibility of which he is above all concerned, however, and for the preferability of which he argues in the case of the potentially 'higher man', is by no means simply 'master morality' resurrected. It may be akin to the latter in certain respects; but it differs importantly from this general type in its more basic forms as well, reflecting the fact that Nietzsche takes the 'higher humanity' which this exceptional sort of human being is capable of attaining, to differ markedly from the sort of existence he supposes to have been characteristic of these 'master races'.

While he considers the *kind* of morality he has in mind to be appropriate for 'higher men' generally, he does not conceive of it as having the same specific content for them all. By its very nature it requires to be supplied with content reflecting not only the exceptional resources and abilities with which he takes potentially higher men generally to be endowed, but also the specific directions they may come to be given in particular cases. Thus he urges that, in place of seeking to establish some 'universal law' or 'categorical imperative', we 'limit ourselves' to something quite different, at once less 'selfish' and more important: 'to the *creation of our own new tables of what is good*', as 'human beings who are new, unique, incomparable, who give themselves laws, who create themselves', and so '*become those we are*' (GS 335). The 'laws' potentially higher men are here spoken of as giving to themselves, and the 'tables of what is good' they are depicted as creating for themselves, are to be thought of as the concrete realisations of the 'higher morality' by means of which the higher humanity they have it in them to attain can be developed.

Nietzsche often stresses the function of this kind of morality as a form of *discipline* indispensable to the potentially higher man's realisation of his potential. Thus he speaks of it as serving 'to train men for the heights' (WP 957), and to enable one to 'transfigure himself and place himself way up, at a distance', in contrast to others which answer to various all-too-human desires and interests (BGE 187). And in the same vein he writes:

> All those who do not have themselves well under control, and do not know morality as self-mastery and self-overcoming constantly practised in the greatest and smallest matters, come naturally to exalt the good, sympathetic, benevolent sentiments of that instinctive morality which has no head, but rather seems simply to be all heart and helping hands. (WS 45)

A morality of 'self-mastery and self-overcoming' involves restraint, resistance to impulse, negation and proscription no less than do other forms of morality. Moralities of this type too have their 'shall nots' as well as their 'shalls', as does 'every healthy morality' along with all 'anti-natural morality' (TI V:4). If anything they are even more severely opposed to the principle of *laisser aller* ('everything is permitted', or: do whatever you please) than are other forms of morality. The restrictions and prohibitions they impose, however, have the significance of conditions of the possibility of attainment of states representing an enriched, strengthened, refined and more creative form of life.

While morality in its more commonplace forms is to be super-seded, therefore, Nietzsche holds that if their supersession is not accompanied by the adoption of something along these lines, nothing on the order of an enhancement of life can be expected to result. And it too may also be considered a 'morality', at least in an extended sense of the term. Nietzsche suggests that what is required is 'to *give* oneself a goal', and to work out the means whereby it may be attained; and in this connection he calls for 'an *experimental morality* (WP 260). The 'laws of life and action' appropriate to the attaining of a goal one has fixed on are what one's particular morality here would consist in; and they may be said to have an 'experimental' character, in that they require to be worked out through the explora-tion of alternative ways of pursuing it.

This is the context in which this notion of a higher sort of morality appropriate to higher men is to be viewed. Broadly conceived, it has the basic general character of a dual demand. It requires of those capable of doing so that they strive at once to achieve a radical 'self-overcoming' with respect to all those 'all-too-human' tendencies which would weaken them and dissipate their energies, and also to engage in the most intensive possible cultivation and exercise of their creative powers, thereby attaining those 'higher, rarer, more remote, further-stretching, more comprehensive states' with which he associates 'the enhancement of the type "man"' (BGE 257).

Self-overcoming, self-mastery, self-cultivation and self-direction in the employment of one's powers, along with the '*loftiness* of soul' they make possible, thus characterise both Nietzsche's higher type of human being and his higher type of morality. Here 'the greater, more manifold, more comprehensive life transcends and *lives beyond* the old morality; the "individual" appears, obliged to give himself laws and to develop his own arts and wiles for self-preservation, self-enhancement, self-redemption' (BGE 262). With respect to content, therefore, this higher morality would inevitably take on a multiplicity of specific forms, to which there is in principle no limit. Thus in a section entitled 'On the Way of the Creator', he has Zarathustra ask:

'Can you give yourself your own evil and your own good and hang your own will over yourself as a law?' (Z I:17).

Whether this sort of law is one to which the term 'morality' may be considered legitimately applicable is in the end of little consequence to Nietzsche. What matters to him is that one see what is meant, rather than what one chooses to call it. Concern for others and their well-being admittedly does not figure directly in it (although the same applies with respect to concern for one's own preservation and well-being); and some may take this consideration alone to weigh against the employment of the term in this connection. To Nietzsche's way of thinking, however, that would be a mere prejudice, even if one deeply entrenched in popular and philosophical usage. He would frankly concede that he is simply breaking with the traditional way of conceiving of morality in this respect, in the interest of giving the notion a new use which acquires great importance in the aftermath of the collapse of traditional modes of interpretation and evaluation, and in the light of those he proposes in place of them.

Notice remains to be taken of but one further aspect of Nietzsche's higher type of morality. It is relatively concrete, but does not relate directly to the specific 'laws of life and action' associated with particular tasks exceptional human beings might set for themselves. It pertains rather to the general manner in which he supposes they would be prompted to live their lives by that sensibility engendered through their attainment and appreciation of their own high spirituality and spiritual superiority, which are of the essence of his 'new nobility'. He gives expression to it most fully in a passage in the last part of *Beyond Good and Evil*, which deals with 'What is Noble'. There he writes:

> To live with tremendous and proud composure; always beyond—. To have and not to have one's affects, one's pro and con, at will; to condescend to them, for a few hours; to seat oneself on them as on a horse, often as on an ass—for one must know how to make use of their stupidity as much as of their fire. To reserve one's three hundred foregrounds; also the dark glasses; for there are cases when nobody may look into our eyes, still less into our 'grounds'. And to choose for company that impish and cheerful vice, courtesy. And to remain master of one's four virtues: of courage, insight, sympathy and solitude. (BGE 284)

In a sense this is intended as description rather than prescription; for Nietzsche takes himself here and in other such passages to be laying down or articulating no 'law', either for all human beings or even for any particular set or type of them, but rather to be characterising a certain distinctive manner of existence, which some may be or become capable of attaining and sustaining. This is a kind of description, however, which is intended to have normative import, for some if not for all. It expresses features associated with that 'higher humanity' which he considers not merely to be a human possibility, but moreover to be highly estimable and superior to any other; and it sets forth a standard pre-eminently worthy of adoption by those who have it in them to measure up to it. The higher morality with which it is associated may be no morality for everyman, and no morality of any conventional sort; but Nietzsche never pretended or supposed that it is. Whether one chooses to call it a morality of a different kind or something else altogether, it is what he would have both exclude *laisser aller* and supplant all more commonplace moralities among those capable of doing without them. It may be 'beyond good and evil'; but it amply warrants his insistence that 'at least this does *not* mean "beyond good and bad" ' (GM I:17).[6]

# Notes

1. In all citations of (or references to) Nietzsche's texts, I shall follow the custom of identifying the passages indicated by the use of the arabic numbers with which the sections of his works are numbered, and the works themselves by acronyms for their titles in English translation. In the cases of a few of his works, the section numberings begin anew in each part of the work. In such cases the arabic section number will be preceded by a roman numeral identifying the part of the work in which the indicated section appears. These roman numerals are not generally supplied by Nietzsche himself; but they follow the order of the parts of the works in a manner that will be clear to any reader who consults their contents. Acronyms of works cited in this essay and the English titles from which they derive are the following:

    A = *The Antichrist*
    BGE = *Beyond Good and Evil*
    BT = *The Birth of Tragedy*
    D = *Daybreak* (or *Dawn of Day*)
    EH = *Ecce Homo*
    GS = *The Gay Science* (or *Joyful Wisdom*)
    GM = *On the Genealogy of Morals*
    HH = *Human, All Too Human*
    TI = *Twilight of the Idols*
    WP = *The Will to Power*
    WS = *The Wanderer and His Shadow*
    Z = *Thus Spoke Zarathustra*

    Citations from D, HH and WS are my own translations, following the Colli-Montinari *Kritische Gesamtausgabe*. Citations from other works follow Walter Kaufmann's renderings in his translations of these works.
2. For a fuller discussion of Nietzsche's life, intellectual development and career, and of his reception and uses and abuses following his collapse, see Walter Kaufmann, *Nietzsche: Philosopher, Psychologist and Antichrist*, 4th ed. (Princeton University Press, 1974).
3. For an excellent study of Schopenhauer's philosophical thought, see Patrick Gardiner, *Schopenhauer* (Baltimore: Penguin, 1963).
4. On these points, see my *Nietzsche* (London: Routledge & Kegan Paul, 1983), chapters I–VI. What follows is a brief summary of the account of Nietzsche's thought on these matters that is elaborated there.
5. See my *Nietzsche*, chapter VIII.
6. This essay derives in part from my entry on 'Nietzsche' in *The Encyclopedia of Religion* (New York: Macmillan, 1986), and in part from my *Nietzsche*, ch. VII.

# Bibliography

## SOME EDITIONS OF NIETZSCHE'S COLLECTED WORKS

1. *Werke: Kritische Gesamtausgabe*, Giorgio Colli and Mazzino Montinari, 30 vols (Berlin: de Gruyter, 1967–78).
2. *Werke: Musarionausgabe*, 23 vols (Munich: Musarion, 1920–29).
3. *Werke in drei Banden*, Karl Schlechta (ed.), 3 vols (Munich: Carl Hanser, 1954–56); with an Index in a fourth volume (1965).
4. *The Complete Works of Friedrich Nietzsche*, Oscar Levy (ed.), 18 vols (New York: Macmillan, 1909–11; reissued New York, Russell & Russell, 1964).


## SOME ENGLISH TRANSLATIONS OF SPECIFIC WORKS

Some of Nietzsche's works and writings are available in English only in the Levy *Complete Works*. The best translations are those made by Walter Kaufmann and by R. J. Hollingdale (in several instances in collaboration). The translations listed below are theirs or else those made by others in the cases of works they have not translated.

5. *The Birth of Tragedy* (1872), trans. Kaufmann, with *The Case of Wagner* (New York: Vintage, 1966).
6. *Philosophy in the Tragic Age of the Greeks* (1870–73), trans. Marianne Cowan (South Bend, Ind.: Gateway, 1962).
7. *On the Use and Abuse of History* (1873), trans. Adrian Collins (New York: Bobbs-Merrill, 1957).
8. *Schopenhauer as Educator* (1874), trans. J. W. Hillesheim and Malcolm R. Simpson (South Bend, Ind.: Gateway, 1965).
9. *Untimely Meditations* (1873–76), trans. R. J. Hollingdale (London: Cambridge University Press, 1983). Includes the essays *David Strauss, Confessor and Writer* (1873) and *Richard Wagner in Bayreuth* (1876) as well as *On the Use and Abuse of History* and *Schopenhauer as Educator*.
10. *Human, All Too Human* (1878–80), trans. R. J. Hollingdale (London: Cambridge University Press, 1986). Includes the original vol. I (1878) and subsequently added two parts of vol. II: *Assorted Opinions and Maxims* (1879), and *The Wanderer and His Shadow* (1880).
11. *Daybreak* (1881), trans. R. J. Hollingdale (London: Cambridge University Press, 1982).
12. *The Gay Science* (1882), trans. Kaufmann (New York: Vintage, 1974).
13. *Thus Spoke Zarathustra* (1883–85), trans. Kaufmann (New York: Viking, 1966); also in *The Portable Nietzsche* (New York: Viking, 1954); trans. Hollingdale (Harmondsworth and Baltimore: Penguin, 1967).
14. *Beyond Good and Evil* (1886), trans. Kaufmann (New York: Vintage, 1966); trans. Hollingdale (Harmondsworth and Baltimore: Penguin, 1973).

15. *On the Genealogy of Morals* (1887), trans. Kaufmann and Hollingdale, with *Ecce Homo* (New York: Vintage, 1968).
16. *The Case of Wagner* (1888); see *The Birth of Tragedy*.
17. *Twilight of the Idols* (1888), trans. Kaufmann, in *The Portable Nietzsche* (New York: Viking, 1954); trans. Hollingdale, with *Antichrist* (Harmondsworth and Baltimore: Penguin, 1968).
18. *The Antichrist* (1888), trans. Kaufmann, in *The Portable Nietzsche* (New York: Viking, 1954); trans. Hollingdale, with *Twilight* (Harmondsworth and Baltimore: Penguin, 1968).
19. *Nietzsche contra Wagner* (1888), trans. Kaufmann, in *The Portable Nietzsche* (New York: Viking, 1954).
20. *Ecce Homo* (1888), trans. Kaufmann, with *Genealogy* (New York: Vintage, 1968); trans. Hollingdale (Harmondsworth and Baltimore: Penguin, 1979).
21. *The Will to Power* (1883–88), trans. Kaufmann and Hollingdale (New York: Vintage, 1968).
22. *Selected Letters of Friedrich Nietzsche*, trans. and ed. Christopher Middleton (University of Chicago Press, 1969).
23. *Nietzsche: A Self-Portrait from His Letters*, trans. and ed. Peter Fuss and Henry Shapiro (Cambridge, Mass.: Harvard University Press, 1971).


SELECTED STUDIES OF NIETZSCHE IN ENGLISH

24. Alderman, Harold G., *Nietzsche's Gift* (Colombus, Ohio: Ohio University Press, 1977).
25. Allison, David B. (ed.), *The New Nietzsche: Contemporary Styles of Interpretation* (New York: Dell, 1977).
26. Copleston, Frederick, *Friedrich Nietzsche: Philosopher of Culture* (London: Burns, Oates & Washburn, 1942).
27. Danto, Arthur C., *Nietzsche as Philosopher* (New York: Macmillan, 1965).
28. Deleuze, Gilles, *Nietzsche and Philosophy*, trans. Hugh Tomlinson (London: Athlone Press, 1983).
29. Derrida, Jacques, *The Question of Style* (Venice: Corbo e Fiore, 1976).
30. Hayman, Ronald, *Nietzsche: A Critical Life* (New York: Oxford University Press, 1980).
31. Heidegger, Martin, *Nietzsche*, 4 vols., trans. David Krell, Joan Stambaugh and Frank Capuzzi (New York: Harper & Row, Vol. I, 1979, Vol. II, 1984, Vol. III, 1987, Vol. IV, 1982).
32. Higgins, Kathleen, *Nietzsche's 'Zarathustra'* (Philadelphia: Temple University Press, 1987).
33. Hollingdale, R. J., *Nietzsche* (London: Routledge & Kegan Paul, 1973).
34. Hollingdale, R. J., *Nietzsche: The Man and His Philosophy* (Baton Rouge, La.: Louisiana State University Press, 1965).
35. Jaspers, Karl, *Nietzsche: An Introduction to the Understanding of His Philosophical Activity*, trans. Charles F. Wallraff and Frederick J. Schmitz (Chicago: Regnery, 1965).
36. Jaspers, Karl, *Nietzsche and Christianity*, trans. E. B. Ashton (Chicago: Regnery, 1961).

37. Kaufmann, Walter, *Nietzsche: Philosopher, Psychologist, Antichrist*, 4th edn (Princeton University Press, 1974).
38. Love, Frederick, *The Young Nietzsche and the Wagnerian Experience* (Chapel Hill: University of North Carolina Press, 1963).
39. Magnus, Bernd, *Nietzsche's Existential Imperative* (Bloomington, Ind.: Indiana University Press, 1978).
40. Morgan, George A., Jr., *What Nietzsche Means* (Cambridge, Mass.: Harvard University Press, 1941; New York: Harper & Row, 1965).
41. Nehamas, Alexander, *Nietzsche: Life as Literature* (Cambridge, Mass.: Harvard University Press, 1985).
42. Schacht, Richard, *Nietzsche* (London: Routledge & Kegan Paul, 1983).
43. Solomon, Robert C. (ed.), *Nietzsche: A Collection of Critical Essays* (Garden City, New York: Doubleday Anchor, 1973).
44. Stambaugh, Joan, *Nietzsche's Thought of Eternal Return* (Baltimore: Johns Hopkins University Press, 1972).
45. Stern, J. P., *A Study of Nietzsche* (London: Cambridge University Press, 1979).
46. Strong, Tracy, *Friedrich Nietzsche and the Politics of Transfiguration* (Berkeley: University of California Press, 1975).
47. Wilcox, John T., *Truth and Value in Nietzsche* (Ann Arbor, Mich.: University of Michigan Press, 1974).

# 10

# Dewey
## *James Gouinlock*

We have advanced far enough to say that democracy is a way of
life. We have yet to realize that it is a way of personal life and one
which provides a moral standard for personal conduct.[1]

Dewey's ethical theory is not only situated historically within both a
philosophical and a cultural context, but it has a history of its own.
His first writings on moral subjects were those of an absolute idealist,
dating from 1887. His last writings occurred more than 60 years
later, and they were cast within the framework of his own naturalism
and instrumentalism. This period of about six decades was marked
by continual creative change in his thought. Dewey's philosophy is
always in the making—never finished, never particularly polished,
and always hurrying beyond the status of the moment.[2]

## CULTURAL AND INTELLECTUAL CONTEXT
## OF DEWEY'S PHILOSOPHY

Dewey was famous for making such remarks as the following:
'Philosophy recovers itself when it ceases to be a device for dealing
with the problems of philosophers and becomes a method, cultivated
by philosophers, for dealing with the problems of men'.[3] Accordingly, his ethical theory was a deliberate response to what he took to
be the great moral perplexities and challenges of his own time; and
his analyses of alternative philosophical ideas were addressed not
only to their coherence, their compatibility with experience and
with science, but also to their bearings on the moral life as it elapsed
in the conditions of the 20th century.

At the time of Dewey's birth in 1859 America was an agrarian
nation; only about 15 per cent of the population lived in urban areas.
The total population numbered slightly more than 30 million. Just
the number of immigrants would exceed that figure during Dewey's

306

lifetime. Thomas Jefferson had been dead less than 35 years; there were 33 states in the union, the western territories were wide open, and the Civil War had not yet begun. The radio and the telephone— to say nothing of the electric light and a functional internal combustion engine—had not yet been invented.

By the time of his death in 1952 the majority of the population was massed in cities. Due to the growing waves of immigration and to the heterogeneous conditions of life, the nation's population was increasingly pluralistic in composition. The US had become in- dustrialised; and traditional forms of association had been trans- formed by the seeming imperatives of economic life. The forces that shape the life of communities had become so many, so complex, and so powerful as to seem incomprehensible and uncontrollable. Two world wars had been fought and nuclear weapons introduced; and under these unprecedented stresses Americans were striving to maintain and improve democratic institutions.

The period of Dewey's lifetime was swarming with changes in our systems of belief, and these changes had a great effect on his philosophy. His first religious convictions, which he received from his mother, were a form of protestant fundamentalism. But he arrived in the same year as Darwin's *Origin of Species*, which challenged the prevailing conceptions of man and his status in the universe as no other work since the time of Descartes. Einstein's equation of matter and energy replaced Newton's conception of atomic sub- stances. Dewey took special note of the ever-growing profusion of technological applications of science, which demonstrated to him the astounding power of experimental method. Not only biology and physics, but anthropology, sociology and psychology under- went extraordinary transformation during Dewey's life. He paid close attention to these movements and made every effort to utilise them. The prevailing philosophies during Dewey's formative years were variations of idealism, and the most sophisticated form of empiricism was that of John Stuart Mill.

In briefest outline, such were the practical and intellectual environ- ments within which Dewey lived and thought, and he devoted his life to the coordinate tasks of reconstructing them. Indeed, his philo- sophic work was not an activity apart from his practical aims, as a chronicle of his beliefs and achievements illustrates. Dewey stated that he always felt a craving for unity in his own person and in his relations to the world. This craving was thwarted by the religion of his childhood, which taught that man is inherently sinful and the natural world a scene of no intrinsic worth. At the University of Vermont he was introduced to biology and the much debated theory of biological evolution. Dewey warmly embraced the truth of the Darwinian point of view, for it denied that living beings are separate substances with self-contained essences. Rather, it regarded the nature and behaviour of biological life as functions of processes inclusive of organism and environment. Hence the notion of fixed and inherent qualities in human beings (such as sinfulness) must be rejected; and nature must be regarded as possessing traits supportive of human existence. The precious values of experience must similarly be understood as functions of natural processes. In his graduate studies at Johns Hopkins he was introduced to Hegel's philosophy and its legacy. Hegel's denials of the dualisms of thought and being, of individual and society, and of nature and the divine were eagerly adopted by Dewey. In time, for both moral and technical reasons, he abandoned an explicitly Hegelian position; but he always retained the notion of organic continuities between man and nature. While in his 30s he abandoned the notion that religious claims have cognitive validity.

Dewey's philosophical anthropology was deeply indebted to William James's revolutionary work, *The Principles of Psychology*, which incorporated Darwinian assumptions into the analysis of human nature. Inspired by James's suggestions, Dewey understood human thought and conduct in terms of a live creature participating in and contending with the environment's ongoing processes hurrying to uncertain outcomes. Intelligent conduct consists in understanding and directing such processes in a manner to unite the powers of the individual with those of the environment in consummatory experience. The most important feature of one's environment is other persons, and hence proper education emphasises formation of the virtues that permit individuals to function together in a manner that is at once cooperative and fulfilling. Dewey was always fundamentally concerned with education, and his philosophy thereof focused on the means of developing emotional and intellectual habits in children that will facilitate intelligent conduct across the whole range of human behaviour. While head of the Department of Philosophy, Psychology and Pedagogy at the University of Chicago, Dewey founded and directed the University Elementary School (better known as the Laboratory School or the Dewey School), where his developing pedagogical principles were put into practice. The first principle of education in democracy, as he conceived it, is to extend the means of intelligent conduct to all people, regardless of their wealth, creed, sex, race or social position.

Most of his academic career was spent at Columbia, where he wrote all of his mature philosophy; and during this time he was extremely active in public affairs, always in an effort to extend and enrich democratic life. He was, for example, a founder and the first President of the American Association of University Professors, whose principal aims he envisaged as the advancement of academic freedom and promoting high standards of education. He was also active in the New York Teachers' Union. He helped to found the American Civil Liberties Union; he served a term as President of the People's Lobby, a political action group devoted to a fuller democratisation of American life. He also served a term as President of the League for Industrial Democracy. He was the first Chairman of the Committee for Cultural Freedom, which was established to promote uninhibited intellectual inquiry and to identify institutions that would hinder or prevent it. He was the first President of the League for Independent Political Action, whose intent was to give Americans an alternative to the stereotypes of the existing political parties by forming a third party. He travelled extensively—to Japan and China, Mexico, Turkey and Russia, where he engaged in teaching and learning, observing educational and political practices, and incorporating what he learned and observed into his philosophic reflections. At the age of 78 Dewey responded courageously to an extraordinary challenge. He accepted the chairmanship of the Commission of Inquiry to examine the validity of the charges made by Josef Stalin against Leon Trotsky. At issue was not just the guilt or innocence of Trotsky, but the matter of whether Stalin's Russia was brutally oppressive or a fledgling democratic paradise. Dewey presided at the hearings, which were held in Mexico City in April of 1937. For this he was reviled by the host of left-wing intellectuals sympathetic to Stalin's regime. Dewey and the Commission found Trotsky not guilty of the charges.[4]

During his time in New York Dewey wrote extensively in journals of opinion, such as the *Nation, Commentary, Christian Century,* and— above all—the *New Republic.*[5] In all these activities, as well as many others, he endeavoured to refine, extend, and share his ideas, and put them to work for the sake of human freedom and happiness. He was always at the centre of major public policy debates; and the distinguished historian Henry Steele Commager wrote of him: 'So faithfully did Dewey live up to his own philosophic creed that he became the guide, the mentor, and the conscience of the American people: it is scarcely an exaggeration to say that for a generation no major issue was clarified until Dewey had spoken'.[6]

The attempt to understand Dewey's philosophy apart from these concerns must have rather anemic issue. He thought of himself as addressing, by actions as well as by means of philosophical analysis, the problems of democracy in 20th-century America. He directed his attention especially to democracy as a way of life, which is a notably more generic condition than that of political democracy. There is a sense in which his moral concerns were broader still. He was personally identified with human welfare, with the sufferings and strivings of ordinary people. He was concerned to identify the values that are resident in mortal existence, to understand them as functions of inclusive natural processes, and to formulate distinctions and methods that will be effective in criticising, securing, enriching and extending these values. This effort culminates in the philosophy of democracy or—as Dewey sometimes called it—social intelligence.[7]

In addressing his philosophy to problems of men, Dewey had already made some basic moral commitments. For example, he appears never to have seriously questioned that we should be impartial—that we should treat each other as moral equals. While he devotes considerable attention to what these notions might mean and how we might act in order to treat others as moral equals, he provides rather little argument in favour of this position.[8] Many readers, accordingly, will find that Dewey is often moralising rather than philosophising; and they will judge that there are important questions that he neglects.[9] But Dewey is much more concerned to see how we can explicate and implement the moral life than to demonstrate to wicked persons that their behaviour is morally wrong. He is also vehemently opposed to prescribing a definite list of rights, duties or ends. His aim, rather, is to provide the assumptions and instruments with which individuals can richly and freely conduct their lives together. It is liberative, not prescriptive.

> Philosophic discourse partakes both of scientific and literary discourse. Like literature, it is a comment on nature and life in the interest of a more intense and just appreciation of the meanings present in experience. . . . Its primary concern is to clarify, liberate, and extend the goods which inhere in the naturally generated functions of experience.[10]

Readers will understand and appreciate Dewey more fully if they study him in light of this statement.

## CRITIQUE OF THE CLASSIC TRADITION IN PHILOSOPHY

The exposition of his views can begin with his critique of what he called the classic tradition in philosophy. According to the classic tradition in its various forms, the nature of being is essentially changeless. Plato, the principal progenitor of the tradition, argued that there is a realm of ideas, or forms, that is to be radically distinguished from the world of change and experience. The forms alone are really real; change is an inferior grade of being—somehow unreal, or mere appearance. The forms are perfect, eternal and unchanging; and they are (when known) infallible standards for evaluation and knowledge. Self-realisation of the person consists of that condition wherein the individual soul achieves an order replicating the divine order, the order of the forms. The soul of the philosopher who knows the forms will by nature assume the perfect harmony and order of the divine realm. Likewise, the good of the earthly society is to conform to the same order of perfection. The realm of change, as such, can yield neither truth nor goodness. Confined to the world of becoming, we stumble blindly and helplessly.

The Platonic view is repeated with variations in all those philosophies that suppose there is an order of being radically distinguished from the world of experience. It occurs in natural law theories, theologies, Cartesianism, theories of social contract and Kantianism. Dewey found it also in modern liberalism in its view that *laissez-faire* economic institutions represent the 'true' order of nature. It is found in Marxism in the assumption of an invariant dialectic of class struggle. It is in philosophic idealism as the doctrine of a fixed essence of the absolute, manifesting itself historically, where the individual must conform to the existing order as the divine order. In all such philosophies the pattern to which conduct ought to conform is fixed and given by an invariant order. In such systems the logic of moral reasoning is, in effect, deductive: one must classify events of on-going life as belonging or not to the antecedently given scheme of things.

Dewey found such notions of being indefensible. They were, he judged, little more than blind dogmas—which is not to say that he failed to analyze them in detail. To the contrary. He wrote repeatedly and extensively on what he took to be the fundamental errors of the classic tradition, and he advanced an alternative view of nature in its stead. The first point to be noted is that he insisted on the reality of change. There are no fixed essences; all beings undergo variations in the processes constituting their nature. The fault in the classic tradition is not one of harmless philosophic speculation. The assumption of a changeless condition to which we must conform is, in effect, a demand that individuals and institutions reckon their behaviour by what is, after all, the prejudice of a given individual or group in a given time and place, set forth as an eternal verity. (The truth of Dewey's critique is supported not least of all by the wondrous variety and multiplicity of counsels of perfection, each of which claims to be final.) The classic tradition authorises fixed and rigid rules and/or ends of action. Hence it is stultifying; it prohibits experimentation, variety—the creative search for more agreeable and fulfilling forms of life.

There is a logic and theory of knowledge organic to the generic notion of change. Where the classic theory typically incorporates the notion of mind directly grasping the essence of things, Dewey's instrumentalism, following the pragmatism of Peirce and James, holds that knowledge of an object consists in knowing how that object functions in relation to other events. In determining the conditions of its occurrence and the variations it undergoes in relation to other things, we know it. Knowledge is not of essences, but of the correlation between processes of change. Accordingly, active experimental manipulation of events is substituted for contemplation. Following Dewey, the individual does not strive to intuit a perfect form and somehow assimilate himself to it; he tries to determine the way his behaviour might vary in relation to deliberately managed processes of change. According to Dewey's pragmatic conception, ideas are instruments for the deliberate reconstruction of present circumstances for the sake of producing desired outcomes. An experimental hypothesis prescribes definite actions to be performed in order to achieve a definite end; that is, it predicts that the introduction of specified conditions will produce certain consequences. Creative intelligence is the prescription of novel relationships as means to reorder a disintegrated situation.

There is an important sense in which the epistemology of the classic tradition is individualistic. Knowledge is an achievement of the individual mind, acting with its inherent resources. Again following Peirce, Dewey stressed that inquiry is a social process and knowledge a social product. One of the crucial features of experimental method is that it is inherently the work of a community of inquirers. As we shall see later on, Dewey's philosophy of social intelligence adapts the notion of the social nature of scientific inquiry to moral deliberation. Just as individual mind does not make an unaided grasp of truth, the unaided individual does not have access to some kind of universal moral principle. In science and morals alike, intersubjective agreement is most apt to result from a deliberately social process.

A fuller account of Dewey's analysis of the classic tradition would include his critique of the notion of experience as constituted of subjective and intrinsically unrelated atoms of sensation[11]; but this section will be concluded by reference to a closely related notion: that human nature is self-complete, self-enclosed and essentially changeless. This is the idea of human nature as substance, given classic formulation by Descartes and with few exceptions held as an axiomatic assumption until Hegel and even beyond. Thus we have the philosophic rationale for a fixed and changeless human nature. Insofar as Dewey is correct in assuming that human nature is an outcome of the interaction of the biological individual with the natural—above all, social—environment, then we can learn how variations in the environment determine variations in character and conduct.[12] It would be hard to underestimate the importance to Dewey of an experimental science of human nature. Such a science would be a great instrumentality in the assessment and formation of human practices with regard to the alleviation of human ills and the enrichment of human goods. 'Our science of human nature in comparison with physical sciences is rudimentary, and morals which are concerned with the health, efficiency, and happiness of a development of human nature are correspondingly elementary.'[13]

The absolutist character of the values embedded in the classic tradition was attacked by Dewey at every opportunity. His critique was anything but nihilistic. Dewey was in fact extremely sensitive to the profuse and precious values that nature affords. The classic tradition had functioned to obscure our awareness of these values and the means of identifying and securing them. The various forms of the tradition can be understood, indeed, as seizing on one or a few values and absolutising them: taking them to be fixed and unchanging, and excluding from consideration the plurality of values not falling within the ambit of their particular principles. Hence it is this tradition, and not Dewey, that would impoverish the possibilities

of joy and delight and of human association. True, the denial of
moral absolutes makes moral decision much more demanding; and
many people suppose that such denial makes intersubjective moral
agreement impossible. The notion of moral agreement will receive
extended attention later. For the moment let it be stated that a moral
absolute makes agreement easy only if there are no competing
absolutes. It is appropriate to examine three features of Dewey's
ethical theory: its scientific character, its pluralism regarding evaluative criteria, and its democratic character.

## ETHICAL DISCOURSE AS SCIENTIFIC

There are two clichés about Dewey as a moral philosopher. First,
he wanted to introduce scientific method into ethics: he wanted
to make moral deliberation in some sense scientific. Second, he
wanted to reconstruct and enrich our notions of democracy; he is the
philosopher of democracy. Both these clichés are true, but neither is
well understood. Indeed, the organic unity of the scientific Dewey
and the democratic Dewey is hardly recognised; but this connection
must be grasped if we are to appreciate his philosophy. When these
two dimensions of his thought are united with the philosophic
Dewey that was outlined in the preceding section and will be further
explored in the next section, a significant portion of his contribution
to the theory of the moral life will be available to us.

What it means to be scientific in the moral life is really quite simple,
but many followers and critics of Dewey have made the crucial
mistake of assuming that the scientific dimension is exhaustive of all
moral reflection and discourse.[14] To be scientific means, first, that
one exercises creative intelligence in the manner that was indicated
in the above section. Valued events are properties of objective
relationships. Hence, like any other event in nature, they are subject
to prediction and control. More importantly, values, or goods, can
be deliberately constructed; that is, we may formulate hypotheses
that propose specific reconstructions of a given situation. If the
hypothesis is more or less accurate, and if we introduce the conditions prescribed by it, then we will transform the situation from
problematic to consummatory. This, and only this, is what Dewey
means when he speaks of ideas directing conduct. He has no thought
of resurrecting a demonstrative process—whether of particular
imperatives deduced from generic principles or evaluative state-

ments derived from descriptive. Such reasoning would be precisely to disinter the absolutist logic of the classic tradition.

A second feature of the scientific character of moral discourse would be to make it deliberately public and collaborative—an explicitly social process modelled in part after the community of inquirers in experimental investigations. This feature can be most fully understood in connection with democratic procedures of moral communication; so it will be examined in the section on 'Ethical Discourse as Democratic', below.

The final point to be made here about being scientific refers to the habits, or virtues, of the scientific intellect: one who is properly experimental tries to be well informed about the constituent variables of the problematic situations he addresses. He is not gullible, does not rely on prejudice or dogma and does not accept any assumptions to be beyond revision. He is inquiring and open-minded equally in respect to both his own convictions and those of others. These qualities, too, will be more fully addressed below under 'Ethical Discourse as Democratic'.

The complex and far-reaching situations with which we contend as human beings and as democratic citizens require extensive inquiry to determine their constituent functions, and they similarly require creative hypotheses as essential conditions for their resolution. Dewey's contributions to the great national debates of his day are exemplary of such discourse; but his intent was not to dictate solutions to these problems. Rather, he wanted all persons to be sufficiently educated in the means of intelligent conduct to participate in such discourse with each other.

He was deeply impressed by the manifest powers of science to discover and harness natural processes, and he sometimes spoke rhapsodically about the possibilities of utilising the same methods for addressing the conditions of human misery and happiness. Moral knowledge, in Dewey's idiosyncratic usage, is not the cognitive grasp of statements like 'One ought to tell the truth', or 'Kindness is good'. It is knowledge of those actual and potential relationships in nature that can be deliberately utilised in the construction of goods. To quote from the *Ethics* of 1932:

The need for constant revision and expansion of moral knowledge is one great reason why there is no gulf dividing non-moral knowledge from that which is truly moral. At any moment conceptions which once seemed to belong exclusively to the biological or physical realm may assume moral import. This will happen whenever they are discovered to have a bearing on the common good. When knowledge of bacteria and germs and their relation to the spread of disease was achieved, sanitation, public and private, took on a moral significance it did not have before. For they were seen to affect the health and well-being of the community. . . . The list of examples might be extended indefinitely. The important point is that any restriction of moral knowledge and judgments to a definite realm necessarily limits our perception of moral significance. . . . Probably the great need of the present time is that the traditional barriers between scientific and moral knowledge be broken down, so that there will be organized and consecutive endeavor to use all the available scientific knowledge for humane and social ends.[15]

Once again we see Dewey's confidence in science; but at the same time we see that his intentions for it have nothing to do with demonstrating moral principles.

## THE IRREDUCIBLE PLURALITY OF MORAL CRITERIA

One might agree with Dewey about the usefulness of science in resolving problematic situations, but he might protest that we need something more: a criterion for deciding what is a *correct* resolution of the situation. This is a question of fundamental importance, and it must be addressed; but one meaning of the question must first be dismissed. If an inherently satisfying situation is produced—if the agents find it fulfills the complex of needs and interests that were operative in its reconstruction (and if they are not doing injury to their character), then there is no need to introduce some further norm that presumably justifies this fulfillment. Human nature is capable of an indefinite plurality of rich and inherently satisfying experiences. Each situation provides its own intrinsic rewards, and Dewey saw no need to justify such values at large.

Tormenting moral problems occur, however, when the particular reconstruction preferred by one individual or group is more or less resisted, or violently opposed, by other individuals or groups. What does Dewey say about problems of this sort? He attends at length to the question of moral criteria for resolving problematic situations.

In the *Ethics* of 1932 Dewey distinguishes three generic classes of moral value: ends, the right, and standards. The first category is that in which good or goods are distinguished, and wisdom is the name given to the power of discriminating goods. The second class of moral value is that in which generalised demands or claims on human behaviour are made. Here we speak of rights, duties, obligations. The third generic classification pertains to that form of evaluation in which we make immediate approvals and disapprovals of conduct. Under the influence of experience and reflection, these direct and spontaneous valuations yield general standards of approbation and disapprobation, which constitute, according to this analysis, measure of virtue and vice.

In these discussions Dewey is not first of all engaged in prescribing what our goods, duties and virtues ought to be. He is bent primarily on distinguishing types of moral evaluation. He argues that these three types are irreducible: they do not collapse into a single form or criterion of evaluation. Each type has its own characteristic demand on conduct. Accordingly, there can be fundamental conflicts of, for example, the right and the good. Dewey devotes his attention to discerning how these three 'independent variables'[16] can be adjusted to one another, and he believes a substantial degree of reconciliation can be accomplished. Nevertheless, as he argued in a paper in 1930 that served as a prelude to the *Ethics*, the lesson of this analysis is that we must be sensitive in any moral situation to the distinctive demands made by these 'independent factors', as he also calls them. To quote from this paper:

In the face of the role played by the real conflict of forces in moral situations and the manifest uncertainty about which side [among these forces] to take, I am inclined to think that one of the causes of the inefficiency of moral theories resides in their attachment to the unitary concept, which has led them to simplify moral life excessively. The result is an abyss between the involved realities of practice and the abstract forms of the system. A moral philosophy which frankly recognizes the impossibility of reducing all the elements of moral situations to one single principle, one which would admit that every human being can only do his best to shift for himself among the disparate forces, would throw light on our real difficulties and would help us to make a more accurate estimate of competing factors. It would be necessary to sacrifice the idea that there exists, theoretically and beforehand, a unique and ideally correct solution for every difficulty into which a person will be thrown.[17]

These analyses of irreducible features of moral situations are intended as explications of moral experience. Such analyses are desirable precisely because moral theories characteristically neglect one or more traits of moral experience, and they consequently formulate an ethical theory that would function at the expense of the moral life.[18]

In many of his discussions Dewey sounds much like a utilitarian. In an approving tone he writes,

> But the utilitarian theory, in addition to its insistence upon taking into consideration the widest, most general range of consequences, insists that in estimating consequences in the way of help and harm, pleasure and suffering, each one shall count as one, irrespective of distinctions of birth, sex, race, social status, economic and political position.[19]

It would be a serious mistake, however, to reduce Dewey's position to that of the utilitarians. There is no evidence that he would endorse their principle unconditionally. Utilitarians are guilty of a form of reductionism, in that their criterion for moral judgement is exclusively that of utility. Dewey distinguished what he called three independent factors in morals, but utilitarians heed only one of them.[20]

If anything can be said with confidence of Dewey as a philosopher it is that he was extremely sensitive to and respectful of the varieties of human experience, including moral experience. One of his most common objections to philosophical theories is their disregard for the salient phenomena of life activity. Accordingly, he would never dismiss out of hand any moral claim just for the sake of preserving the uniformity of antecedent theory. To Dewey, an honest philosophy must respect genuine pluralism in the moral life. In the article 'Philosophy', written in 1934, he argued that philosophies necessarily have roots in certain historically conditioned moral interests. 'Each system has of necessity an exclusive aspect, often expressing itself in a controversial way, because it is, implicitly, a recommendation of certain types of value as normative in the direction of human conduct. . . .' He continues,

The connection of philosophy with conflicts of ends and values
serves to explain . . . criticisms frequently brought against the
enterprise of philosophy. One of them points to the diverging and
controversial character of philosophy in contrast with the definite
trend toward unity in the sciences. If, however, valuation enters
into philosophy, divergence is inevitable. It could not be eliminated
except by attainment of a complete consensus as to universal ends
and methods. If those who hold up different values as the
directive aims of life were to agree with one another in their interpretations of existence, it would be a sure sign of insincerity.[21]

Neither a utilitarian nor any absolutistic moral thinker could write,
as Dewey did,

> Realization that the need for reflective morality and moral theory
> grows out of the conflict between ends, responsibilities, rights,
> and duties defines the service which moral theory may render,
> and also protects the student from false conceptions of its nature.
> The difference between customary and reflective morality is
> precisely that definite precepts, rules, definitive injunctions and
> prohibitions issue from the former, while they cannot proceed
> from the latter. Confusion ensues when appeal to rational principles
> is treated as if it were merely a substitute for custom, transferring
> the authority of moral commands from one source to another. . . .
> Moral theory does not offer a table of commandments in a catechism
> in which answers are as definite as are the questions which are
> asked. It can render personal choice more intelligent, but it cannot
> take the place of personal decision, which must be made in every
> case of moral perplexity.[22]

Much of the genius of Dewey as a moral philosopher lies in his
recognition of the plurality of humane moral positions that can be
taken by rational persons, and in his consequent plea that none of
these positions should be absolutised. Rather, if we seek concord
and happiness in human conduct, the method that suggests itself is
that of democracy. Indeed, Dewey's philosophy of democracy con-
summates his ethical theory. We shall see that the persons engaged
in social intelligence would possess certain habits, or virtues; but
they would not cling for dear life to some invariant principle of moral
judgement. Their decisions would reflect genuine and impartial
concern for the welfare of others, and this concern would extend to

the plurality of serious moral convictions that are effective in the moral life. A genuinely democratic method would not be devoted to just a single moral criterion. The impartial concern for everyone's well-being would tend to the general welfare, but not exclusively so, because we would also have regard for values that are not distinctly utilitarian.

It was remarked early in this chapter that Dewey devotes little in the way of systematic argument to support the assumption of moral equality, moral impartiality. Clearly, he vigorously subscribed to some sense of democratic equality, which he regarded as the fundamental American project; and he was above all concerned to see how it might be interpreted and implemented. All the same, there are arguments of some consequence that Dewey mentions in defence of democratic equality. One of these is the rejection of the notion of a hierarchy of beings. 'Now whatever the idea of equality means for democracy, it means, I take it, that the world is not to be construed as a fixed order of species, grades or degrees. It means that every existence deserving the name of existence has something unique and irreplaceable about it, that it does not exist to illustrate a principle, to realize a universal or to embody a kind or class.'[23] In addition to his repudiation of arguments for a hierarchy of being with a corresponding hierarchy of human status, he urged that the isolation of various groups from the life of community is injurious not only to those groups, but to the rest of the society as well, for the latter are deprived of the stimulus and enrichment that the excluded groups can contribute. Another sort of comment that we find is familiar: just belonging to a certain sex, race, religion, or social class is not an adequate test for exclusion from the economic, political and social life of a community.

But even when the grosser forms of discrimination are exposed, moral problems do not vanish. Well meaning people honour principles that are sometimes incompatible with those of other persons, and they seek incompatible ends. I stated earlier that in ethical theory there is a scientific Dewey and a democratic Dewey. Are these two different persons? Is the experimental moral life to be distinguished from the democratic way of life, or do they consitute some kind of unity? The answer, of course, is the latter.

## ETHICAL DISCOURSE AS DEMOCRATIC

'We lie, as Emerson said, in the lap of an immense intelligence. But that intelligence is dormant and its communications are broken, inarticulate and faint until it possesses the local community as its medium.'[24] Unlike any philosopher in history, Dewey locates *communication* at the very heart of the moral life. 'Apart from conversation from discourse and communication, there is no thought and no meaning, only just events, dumb, preposterous, destructive.'[25] It had to be so. He was deeply impressed by the social nature of scientific discourse. To Dewey, moreover, respect and regard for other persons implies that they be consulted whenever one's own conduct engages theirs. He knew that no person should be regarded as a final repository of moral wisdom. He knew that no prescription for behaviour could be regarded as immune from criticism. He knew that the moral life is marked by competing and changing demands. It was obvious to him that free individuals cannot regulate their lives together except by the deliberate, open and experimental coordination of their efforts. He believed that political democracy is hopeless unless we would be democratic in all personal relations. He also believed that democracy as a way of life would be the most fulfilling and satisfying mode of existence for human beings.

The idea that a person could determine morally what to do in his relations to other persons without directly consulting them and without being prepared to revise his intentions in light of their shared discourse, without being willing to formulate a course of action in concert with others—all this is unthinkable for Dewey. In the end, of course, they are real historical persons who must judge and act; so Dewey's procedure would not bring an end to disagreement and discord; but it might reduce them more than any of the other methods hitherto undertaken. It remains to analyse democracy as moral method more fully.

In a characteristic remark, Dewey says, 'The keynote of democracy as a way of life may be expressed, it seems to me, as the necessity for the participation of every mature human being in formation of the values that regulate the living of men together. . .'[26] The values that regulate the living of men together are, of course, moral values. They are not fixed and immutable, but are subject to formation. In addition to its being an intrinsic end, democracy as a way of life is a means for the formation of these values.

Conceived just as a method of addressing moral dilemmas, it proceeds something like this: some kind of social conflict or crisis—great or small—develops, and a way is sought to adjust and unite the various interests. Rather than follow the traditional methods of deferring to power or authority, the parties implicated share in the process of analyzing the problem and in formulating and implementing a plan of action. Neither does each individual trust in the infallibility of his own intuitions or the finality of his own ethical theory. There is consultation and communication; all sides are heard and considered. Novel alternatives are proposed, examined, revised, abandoned, and so forth. When (and if) a plan for reconstructing the problematic situation is adopted, it is not taken as absolute. It is put to the test and is subject to revision in light of further experience.

The process is not only social, but intelligent, in the manner suggested above in 'Ethical Discourse as Scientific'. The participants have to be well informed or willing to be well informed. This is no small matter. Dewey judged it of incalculable importance to discover the nature and effects of the multitude of forces that determine our shared life. If we are deliberately to reconstruct our problematic situations, we must know their constituent functions. The process is also scientific in that hypotheses must be proposed for sometimes complex transformations of existing conditions; and such hypotheses will be worthless and even pernicious if their predictions are based on false or inadequate assumptions. Consider the dismaying variety of hypotheses offered as means of transforming our economic predicaments. In brief, we will have a serious misunderstanding of moral disagreements if we assume that they are reducible exclusively to questions of moral principle.

It is hard to underestimate the importance of being scientific; but social intelligence is not reducible to science either. In problematic situations great and small we are dealing with a variety of human values—the things we distinguish with such names as goods, rights and obligations—all of them necessary for social intercourse. Social intelligence does not produce moral norms *a priori*. The occasion for democratic procedures is in many cases precisely a moral conflict. The problem is to address these antecedently existing and conflicting moral commitments. Even when individuals are agreed on the facts of a case, they do not necessarily have the same evaluation of them. Dewey had an exaggerated confidence in the moral efficacy of shared information, but he never supposed that evaluation is reducible to cognition. To put it over-simply: our evaluations are responses to our cognitions; they are not deduced from them. Accordingly, agreement about what is at issue in a given situation is not tantamount to agreement about what to do about it.

How is scientific intelligence a mechanism for dealing with such an impasse? Scientific knowledge does more than prescribe how events can be directed to certain outcomes. It also qualifies, or modifies, antecedently existing evaluations. Dewey seems never to tire of pointing out that when we acquire a different understanding of the meaning of events, our assessment of them tends to change as well. If, for example, one believes that the current regime is oppressive, and if he also believes in the irreconcilability of class antagonisms, he is more apt to have a favourable estimate of revolution; but if he believes there are other ways to deal with conflict, his admiration for revolution is apt to dwindle. In the democratic approach to morally problematic situations, various knowledge claims are advanced and evidence for them is adduced and examined; and this sharing of reliable information will be of great help in prompting a convergence of evaluations. Of still more help, Dewey believes, is the cooperative formation of novel plans of action. Creative intelligence tends to convergence in action by contriving plans of action that would incorporate and expand hitherto disparate interests in a reconstruction of ongoing events.

However useful all such procedures might be, we cannot assume that their exercise will cause divergence in moral convictions to vanish. But science is not the only resource in social intelligence. Of at least equal importance, Dewey recognised, is the nature of the parties sharing in the deliberative process. He thrust into prominence the requirement that individuals possess certain traits of mind and character. We must 'realize in thought and act that democracy is a *personal* way of individual life; that it signifies the possession and continual use of certain attitudes, forming personal character and determining desire and purpose in all the relations of life'.[27] Without the appropriate moral qualities, the users of experimental method could be extremely threatening to human welfare; and without scientific intelligence, democratically-minded persons would be largely impotent to achieve their aims.

Dewey wrote of the virtues of the democratic individual almost from the beginning of his career. It is the focus of his many writings on education. In the classic *Democracy and Education* he characterised education as 'the process of forming fundamental dispositions, emotional and intellectual, toward nature and fellow-men'.[28] Although he wrote with insight on the subject of virtues as habits, his references to them are somewhat snarled. At times one would think that all virtue is summed up in the norms and procedures of experimental science: intelligence encompasses all virtue. In various writings, however, we find commended and analyzed such traits as impartiality, conscientiousness, sympathy, effective regard for others, kindliness, courage, tolerance, flexibility, creativity, imaginativeness, whole-heartedness, faithfulness, thoughtfulness, wisdom, independence, insight, integrity, sincerity, fairness and initiative. No doubt there are others; but as the preceding list suggests, these discussions were never distilled into systematic form. But it is not necessary for a fundamental understanding of Dewey's ethical theory that they should be. Certainly there are the habits of experimental inquiry. 'Some of its obvious elements,' Dewey says,

> are willingness to hold belief in suspense, ability to doubt until evidence is obtained; willingness to go where evidence points instead of putting first a personally preferred conclusion; ability to hold ideas in solution and use them as hypotheses to be tested instead of as dogmas to be asserted; and (possibly the most distinctive of all) enjoyment of new fields for inquiry and of new problems.[29]

There are distinctly moral virtues as well. In regard to the latter, Dewey's spirit is well conveyed in the following remarks from 'Creative Democracy—the Task Before Us'. Faith in democracy, he writes,

> may be enacted in statutes, but it is only on paper unless it is put in force in the attitudes which human beings display to one another in all the incidents and relations of daily life. To denounce Naziism for intolerance, cruelty, and stimulation of hatred amounts to fostering insincerity if in our . . . relations to other persons, . . . we are moved by racial, color, or . . . class prejudice. . . . Intolerance, abuse, calling of names because of differences of opinion about religion or politics or business, as well as because of differences of race, color, wealth, or degree of culture, are treason to the democratic way of life. . . . Merely legal guarantees of the civil liberties of free belief, free expression, free assembly are of little avail if in daily life freedom of communication, the give and take of ideas, facts, experiences, is choked by mutual suspicion, by abuse, by fear and hatred.
> . . . Democracy is the belief that even when needs and ends . . . are different for each individual, the habit of amicable cooperation . . . is itself a priceless addition to life. To take as far as possible every conflict which arises . . . out of the atmosphere and medium

of force . . . into that of discussion and of intelligence, is to treat those who disagree . . . with us as those from whom we may learn, and in so far, as friends.[30]

If we were to analyze these remarks systematically, we would find a full catalogue of personal qualities essential to carrying on fruitful moral discourse. Clearly, democratic habits incorporate much more than scientific habits. The participants in social intelligence must be informed and have scientific habits of inquiry. They would not be dogmatists and absolutists. They would welcome innovative proposals for shared action. They would enter the process of social intelligence with many convictions, of course; but they would not assume that those who disagree with them are knaves or fools.

There are additional personal qualities of consequence. The parties in social intelligence do not take an inherently prejudicial view of the opinions of others. Presumably, all views are sympathetically and impartially heard. The situation is not one of intransigent partisanship; it is not conceived as a system of adversary relations. A plurality of moral positions might be found to be worthy of respect, and there is an even-handed search for cooperative solutions.

It is important to recognise that the theory of democratic moral discourse is not morally neutral. It is a method in which a kind of moral equality and impartiality is presupposed.[31] There is mutual respect and willingness to learn; and there is respect for the virtues of experimental inquiry. Dewey, then, advances certain norms for sharing in the democratic formation of values. Certain moral and intellectual virtues must be lodged in those who participate in the process. This conception of social intelligence is far removed from the simplistic notion of democracy as counting heads—no matter how wicked, stubborn, or ill-informed they might be.

With such a medium of discourse many of our problems would be more manageable. They tend to become intractable because they are struggles of unyielding and intolerant partisanship. They are more in the nature of a power struggle than a dialogue. If social intelligence were actualised, there would still be disagreements, of course; but Dewey believed they would be more amenable to adjustments, reconciliations and creative unifications.

Dewey proposes these normative procedures as ideal limits, to which mortals can approximate in varying measures but cannot fully satisfy. The sharers in this process are natural and historical beings. Social intelligence is a means for such beings to utilise the resources of experience to contend with the characteristic hopes and vexations of the moral life. Given these realistic assumptions, the moral norms built into the method would be imperfectly observed even under the best of circumstances. Even were they perfectly observed, they could not be unfailing instruments for solving problems to everyone's satisfaction. The values at stake in a specific situation are always to some extent diverse and incompatible, and no two people are likely to weigh them in precisely the same way, regardless of how conscientious they are. Democracy is a method for respecting, criticising, arbitrating and enlarging the plurality of values in social life.[32]

To understand Dewey's philosophy, it is essential to recognise that he does not resort to postulations that would provide timeless and allegedly perfect moral principles. Such devices have been the stock in trade of the classic tradition, against which, as we have seen, Dewey set himself. The postulate of a 'perfectly rational' moral agent, or 'ideal' choice conditions, from the nature of which eternal and unchanging principles are deduced, is exactly the sort of philosophical conceit from which Dewey wished to rescue us. As the renewed proliferation of absolutist, non-historical, moral theories attests, one person's conception of perfection is not another's; nor is one person's ideal another's. Such notions are philosophically disguised prejudices, to which the philosopher wishes to subject us. In abjuring such ambitions, Dewey's ethical theory might accomplish more in the way of actual human satisfaction in the moral life. *Just because* we live in societies where there are divergent moral claims, each wanting to be satisfied, and *just because* there are irreducibly divergent ethical theories, each claiming priority, the virtues of democracy as a way of life present themselves as the best means so far conceived for approaching to concord in moral affairs. As a necessary prelude to such a condition, philosophers and laymen alike must recognise the intellectual bankruptcy of absolutist pretensions. (Similarly they must recognise the practical futility of various subjectivisms.)

Dewey was well aware that the personal habits of the democratic life are difficult to attain, but he was confident that they are attainable in significant measure. Inspired by Darwinian biology and James's *Principles of Psychology*, he argued that human nature is a function of the *inter*action of the biological organism and its environment. There are native impulses and capacities to be sure, but these become specific forms of conduct only as functions of interactions—above all, social interactions. Accordingly, virtues and vices are learned behaviour; and they are acquired more in social practice than by deliberate instruction. As human nature develops in and through the characteristic routines of a given culture, the individual becomes submissive, authoritarian, cooperative, inflexible, experimental, dogmatic, open-minded, sympathetic, intolerant or whatever as he learns from the peculiarities of his own environment. Hence Dewey's complaint,

> The real trouble is that there is an intrinsic split in our habitual attitudes when we profess to depend upon discussion and persuasion in politics and then systematically depend upon other methods in reaching conclusions in matters of morals and religion, or in anything where we depend upon a person or group possessed of "authority". We do not have to go to theological matters to find examples. In homes and schools, the places where the essentials of character are supposed to be formed, the usual procedure is settlement of issues, intellectual and moral, by appeal to the "authority" of parent, teacher, or textbook. Dispositions formed under such conditions are so inconsistent with the democratic method that in a crisis they may be aroused to act in positively anti-democratic ways for anti-democratic ends. . . .[33]

At bottom, then, the problem of achieving democratic attitudes is educational and cultural. This is by no means to say that the achievement of the democratic way of life is easy; it is to locate the problem and identify its nature.

## DEWEY AND DEMOCRATIC CULTURE

In what sense is Dewey's ethical theory successful? There are many individuals whose personal attitudes and conduct, and world-view as well, have been profoundly directed by the ideas they have discovered in Dewey's writings; and this alone is a great tribute to the force of his thought. Such persons do not take Dewey's ideas to be final, of course, but as vital for further growth and refinement. To be convincing in theory was hardly his principal goal, however. In light of his own aims, we must judge by a different measure. Dewey would consider his philosophy successful insofar as it became embodied in social life and institutions, in personal relations, public discourse and policy-making. The changes he would look for would not be so much in the nature of specific policies as in the habits of life that determine the formation of policies and all human relations.

Regarding our public life, the most obvious phase of experience where Dewey's influence has been felt is in education. The efficacy of his proposals for education is difficult to weigh: it is often a matter of controversy to decide whether a given educational experiment is genuinely of the sort he recommended; and the fruitfulness of various forms of educating is often difficult to gauge. It is safe to conclude, nevertheless, that there have been many constructive changes in education for which Dewey is more responsible than any other theorist; and it is also safe to conclude that we are better prepared to participate in social intelligence as a consequence of such changes.

He always stressed that deliberate improvements in such matters as education—or in any social practice—must rely on effective social science. Only by the use of such discipline can we reliably determine how variations in behaviour are correlated with changes in policy and institutional practice. Dewey had very high hopes for the social sciences in this regard. Therefore he would be most disappointed by their rather meagre results.

Minorities and women are able to play a much fuller role in American life than they did even a generation ago. This is not due in large measure to Dewey's particular influence; but the democratisation of our shared life is surely a realisation of his vision. On the other hand, our discourse remains shrill and strident—perhaps in this regard it is even deteriorating. There is intolerance, inflexibility and abusive language on all sides, including that of intellectuals; and the spirit of inquiry and cooperative search for solutions is hardly to be found.

A strong case can be made that Dewey succeeds in articulating the meaning and ideals of the western democratic tradition more fully than any other thinker. Social intelligence seems such a sane and promising procedure. Yet philosophers continue to vacillate between their futile absolutisms and their futile subjectivisms. It may well be, of course, that the instruments of moral life that Dewey distinguished are beyond our competence. Even if we cannot master these instruments to the extent that he hoped, an approximation to them might still be our greatest resource.

# Notes

The complete works of John Dewey are being published by Southern Illinois University Press, Carbondale, Illinois. *John Dewey: The Early Works, 1882–1898*, have been published in five volumes (1961–71). *John Dewey: The Middle Works, 1899–1924*, have been published in 15 volumes (1971–83). *John Dewey: The Later Works, 1925–1953* (to be 16 volumes) are not yet completed, but the first 10 volumes and the 12th have been published (1981–87), and they include all writings from 1925 to 1935 and *Logic: The Theory of Inquiry* from 1938. All volumes in the series are edited by Jo Ann Boydston.

1. John Dewey, *Freedom and Culture* (New York: G. P. Putnam's Sons, 1939) p. 130.
2. To follow and analyze these developments would require extensive scholarship. In this paper I can try to identify only the late or mature Dewey. Even here I must be both selective and interpretive, leaving out of consideration, for example, his treatment of freedom and responsibility, egoism and altruism, and his theory of judgement. I also omit to point out the uneven quality of much of his writing, his lapses into obscurity and even bombast.
3. Dewey, 'The Need for a Recovery of Philosophy' (*Middle Works*, vol. 10 [1917]) p. 46.
4. For a wealth of detailed information about Dewey's life, see George Dykhuizen, *The Life and Mind of John Dewey* (Carbondale, Illinois: Southern Illinois University Press, 1973).
5. For an account of Dewey's political views as expressed primarily in such journals, see Gary Bullert, *The Politics of John Dewey* (Buffalo, New York: Prometheus Books, 1983).
6. Henry Steele Commager, *The American Mind: An Interpretation of American Thought and Character since the 1880's* (New Haven: Yale University Press, 1950) p. 100. During his career Dewey gave the Gifford Lectures, William James Lectures, Paul Carus Lectures and Terry Lectures, among others. He received honorary degrees from many universities, including Columbia, Harvard, Yale, the University of Pennsylvania and the University of Paris.
7. One might object that the subject matter I have been talking about is social and political philosophy, not ethics. Such a rigid separation of inquiries, however, is just the sort of intellectual gulf that Dewey protested against all his life. Contrived intellectual divisions presuppose contrived ontological divisions, such as that between the individual and society. The ethical life *is* a social life.
8. But see above, p. 319–20, for mention of the sort of arguments that Dewey does employ on occasion.
9. Although it is controversial as to what constitutes an important question, there is doubtless merit in such a charge. Dewey himself is overflowing with good will, and his moral philosophy is largely addressed to individuals who, if not saintly, are morally earnest.

10. Dewey, *Experience and Nature* (*Later Works*, vol. 1 [1925]) pp. 304–5.

11. This notion by itself guarantees a dualism of man and nature, and it means that nothing that occurs in experience can be regarded as a function of variations in the natural world. Experience for Dewey is a natural function, indicative of relations between natural events. The continuity of experience and nature is a theme of many works, principally *Experience and Nature*.

12. The notion of human nature as substance is also convenient for the formulation of moral philosophies in complete estrangement from the changing conditions of nature and history, such as social contract theories. As we have seen earlier in this section, there are additional assumptions supporting timeless moral theories; but Dewey's critique of this conception of human nature tends to undermine the notion that moral philosophy can assume an ahistorical character.

13. Dewey, *Human Nature and Conduct* (*Middle Works*, vol. 14 [1922]) p. 5.

14. The most systematic misunderstanding of the scientific dimension in Dewey's ethical theory has been given in two highly influential writings by Morton White: 'Value and Obligation in Dewey and Lewis', *The Philosophical Review*, LVIII, no. 4 (July 1949) pp. 321–30 and chapter 13 of his *Social Thought in America* (New York: Viking Press, 1949). My reply to White is 'Dewey's Theory of Moral Deliberation', *Ethics*, 88, no. 3 (April 1978) pp. 218–28. My *Excellence in Public Discourse: John Stuart Mill, John Dewey, and Social Intelligence* (New York: Teachers College Press, 1986) covers many of the issues in the present article in more detail. Dewey's metaphysical studies are treated in my *John Dewey's Philosophy of Value* (New York: Humanities Press, 1972).

15. Dewey and James H. Tufts, *Ethics* (*Later Works*, vol. 7 [1932]) pp. 282–83. Note: All quotations from *Ethics* in the text are from portions written by Dewey.

16. Ibid., p. 235.

17. Dewey, 'Three Independent Factors in Morals' (*Later Works*, vol. 5 [1930]) pp. 287–88.

18. Dewey also argues that these modes of evaluation are social functions. By contrast, ethical theories that treat, say, duties and rights as possessing pre-social status are prone to neglect the irreducibly social functions of these relations in the formation and securing of actual human values. Theories claiming a direct intuition of moral goods similarly inhibit the analysis of moral relations in their actual tendencies.

19. Dewey and Tufts, *Ethics*, p. 239.

20. Dewey also sharply distinguishes his position from features historically associated with utilitarianism, such as the hedonistic psychology and the felicific calculus. (See note 32, below, for his objection to the latter.)

21. Dewey 'Philosophy' (*Later Works*, vol. 8 [1933]) p. 27.

22. Dewey and Tufts, *Ethics*, pp. 165–66.

23. Dewey, 'Philosophy and Democracy' (*Middle Works*, vol. 11 [1919]) p. 52.

24. Dewey, *The Public and Its Problems* (*Later Works*, vol. 2 [1927]) p. 372.

25. Dewey, 'Events and Meanings' (*Middle Works*, vol. 13 [1922]) p. 280.

26. Dewey, 'Democracy and Educational Administration', *School and Society*, XLV (1937) p. 457.

27. Dewey, 'Creative Democracy—The Task Before Us', *The Philosopher of the Common Man: Essays in Honor of John Dewey to Celebrate his Eightieth Birthday*, Sidney Ratner (ed.) (New York: G. P. Putnam's Sons, 1940) p. 222.
28. Dewey, *Democracy and Education* (*Middle Works*, vol. 9 [1916]) p. 328.
29. Dewey, *Freedom and Culture*, p. 145.
30. Dewey, 'Creative Democracy—The Task Before Us,' pp. 223–26.
31. Dewey asks for more than this. Ideally, each member of a democratic community has positive concern for the welfare of others and identifies his own good as an organic part of the inclusive good of the community. Simple impartiality would be a minimal condition of effective discourse.
32. There has been an obstacle to recognising at once that Dewey's ethical theory is consummated in the philosophy of social intelligence. Dewey has two discussions of moral deliberation that make the process sound remarkably individualistic, rather than democratic. When describing deliberation in the *Ethics* of 1932, Dewey writes: 'Deliberation is actually an imaginative rehearsal of various courses of conduct. We give way, *in our mind*, to some impulse; we try, *in our mind*, some plan. Following its career through various steps, we find ourselves in imagination in the presence of consequences that would follow; and as we then like and approve, or dislike and disapprove, these consequences, we find the original impulse or plan good or bad. Deliberation is dramatic and active, not mathematical and impersonal; and hence it has the intuitive, the direct factor in it' (*Ethics*, p. 275). A similar statement is made in the chapter 'The Nature of Deliberation' in *Human Nature and Conduct*. Such statements prompted Charles Stevenson to accuse Dewey of being preoccupied with personal decision to the neglect of interpersonal problems (Charles L. Stevenson, *Facts and Values* [New Haven: Yale University Press, 1963] p. 115). Dewey's remarks sound individualistic indeed; and if one had no wider acquaintance with his thought, it would be easy to understand Stevenson's complaint.

    It is worth noting the context of the apparently individualistic discussions of deliberation. In each case, he is attending to a *psychological* issue. In *Human Nature and Conduct*, for example, he is putting his position in contrast to utilitarian calculation. The utilitarians had claimed that decision-making is a matter of addition and subtraction, followed by adoption of the plan with the highest arithmetical sum of pleasures. In contrast to the bookkeeping account, Dewey described the actual process of deliberation as that of being directly moved by the appealing and repulsive qualities of events as immediately experienced and as foreseen and imagined. As a matter of psychological fact, he contends, we do not add up predicted pleasures indifferently and then take the plan promising the highest sum. The termination of deliberation consists just in being moved to action. The agent deliberates in a particular problematic situation, looking for a solution to it. In the end, that plan of action which stimulates the strongest response in the agent is the plan that is followed. The plan that is literally most attractive is the one that is chosen. 'What then is choice?' Dewey asks. 'Simply hitting in imagination upon an object which furnishes an adequate stimulus to the recovery of overt action' (*Human Nature and Conduct*, p. 134).

Why does Dewey contend with the utilitarians about this point? If, psychologically, choice takes place in the manner described, then the quality of one's choice is determined by one's character. To use Aristotelian terminology, quality of choice is a function of the moral and intellectual virtues possessed by the agent. Immediately following his treatment of choice, Dewey launches on an analysis of appropriate personal habits—their nature and conditions. He urges that formation of character is the only guarantee of moral behaviour.

The point to fix on here is this: Dewey's study of deliberation in this context is addressed exclusively to its psychological nature. He does not take up in these passages the topic of deliberation as social method. But what he writes of the motive powers of deliberation applies *a fortiori* to situations in which the values at issue are presented not just imaginatively but directly in communication by the persons who are their advocates. Especially in *The Public and Its Problems*, Dewey emphasises the vital force of face-to-face communication. Democracy, he says, 'is a name for a life of free and enriching communion. . . . It will have its consummation when free social inquiry is wedded to the art of full and moving communication' (*The Public and Its Problems*, p. 350). Accordingly, one cannot conclude from such passages as those cited in *Human Nature and Conduct* that Dewey's theory of moral deliberation is individualistic.

Similarly in regard to the passage quoted above from the *Ethics*. Again the psychology of deliberation is at issue, and again Dewey concludes: 'It is this direct sense of value, not the consciousness of general rules or ultimate goals, which finally determines the worth of the act to the agent' (*Ethics*, pp. 274–75). Here he is contending not only with the felicific calculus. He is also trying to give due weight to the various 'moral sense' schools, which claim an intuitive recognition of value. This 'intuition', however, is the product of habit and experience; and it should not be regarded as morally authoritative in and of itself. 'Here is the inexpugnable element of truth in the intuitional theory. Its error lies in conceiving this immediate response of appreciation as if it excluded reflection instead of following directly upon its heels' (ibid., p. 275).

33. Dewey, *Freedom and Culture*, p. 129.

# Bibliography

## WORKS CITED

### Books

1. Bullert, Gary, *The Politics of John Dewey* (Buffalo, New York: Prometheus Books, 1983).
2. Commager, Henry Steele, *The American Mind: An Interpretation of American Thought and Character since the 1880s* (New Haven: Yale University Press, 1950).
3. Dewey, John, *Democracy and Education. Middle Works*, vol. 9 (1916). (See statement regarding the collected works of John Dewey at the heading of Notes.)
4. ——, *Reconstruction in Philosophy. Middle Works*, vol. 12 (1920).
5. ——, *Human Nature and Conduct. Middle Works*, vol. 14 (1922).
6. ——, *Experience and Nature. Later Works*, vol. 1 (1925).
7. ——, *The Public and Its Problems. Later Works*, vol. 2 (1927).
8. —— and James H. Tufts, *Ethics. Later Works*, vol. 7 (1932).
9. ——, *Freedom and Culture* (New York: G. P. Putnam's Sons, 1939).
10. Dykhuizen, George, *The Life and Mind of John Dewey* (Carbondale, Illinois: Southern Illinois University Press, 1973).
11. Gouinlock, James, *John Dewey's Philosophy of Value* (New York: Humanities Press, 1972).
12. ——, *Excellence in Public Discourse: John Stuart Mill, John Dewey, and Social Intelligence* (New York: Teachers College Press, 1986).
13. James, William, *The Principles of Psychology* (1890), 3 vols. (Cambridge, Mass.: Harvard University Press, 1981).
14. Stevenson, Charles L., *Facts and Values* (New Haven: Yale University Press, 1963).
15. White, Morton, *Social Thought in America* (New York: Viking Press, 1949).

### Articles and Contributions to Books

16. Dewey, John, 'The Need for a Recovery of Philosophy', *Middle Works*, vol. 10 (1917) pp. 3–48. (See statement regarding the collected works of John Dewey at the heading of Notes.)
17. ——, 'Philosophy and Democracy', *Middle Works*, vol. 11 (1919) pp. 41–53.
18. ——, 'Events and Meanings', *Middle Works*, vol. 13 (1922) pp. 276–80.
19. ——, 'Three Independent Factors in Morals', *Later Works*, vol. 5 (1930) pp. 279–88.
20. ——, 'Philosophy', *Later Works*, vol. 8 (1933) pp. 19–39.
21. ——, 'Democracy and Educational Administration', *School and Society* XLV (1937) pp. 457–62.
22. ——, 'Creative Democracy—The Task Before Us', *The Philosopher of the*

*Common Man: Essays in Honor of John Dewey to Celebrate his Eightieth Birth-day*, S. Ratner (ed.) (New York: G. P. Putnam's Sons, 1940).

23. Gouinlock, James, 'Dewey's Theory of Moral Deliberation', *Ethics*, vol. 88 (1978) no. 3, pp. 218–28.

24. White, Morton, 'Value and Obligation in Dewey and Lewis', *Philosophical Review* 58, (1949) no. 4, pp. 321–30.

## FURTHER SCHOLARLY RESOURCES

A large commentary on Dewey's philosophy has accumulated, including many studies of various aspects of his moral philosophy. Surprisingly, there has been as yet no full-scale treatment focused on his ethical theory. The best bibliography of writings both by and about Dewey is *John Dewey: A Centennial Bibliography*, by Milton Halsey Thomas (Chicago: University of Chicago Press, 1962).

Also useful to scholars and students is *Guide to the Works of John Dewey*, edited by Dr Jo Ann Boydston (Carbondale: Southern Illinois University Press, 1970). This volume addresses various areas of Dewey's philosophy, including his moral philosophy. In each instance an essay and a relevant bibliography is provided by a distinguished scholar.

The Dewey archives are located in the Morris Library at Southern Illinois University. The Center for Dewey Studies, where the complete works are edited, is also at Southern Illinois University. Dr Jo Ann Boydston is Director.

Readers interested to begin study of Dewey's philosophy at first hand will find a relevant selection of writings in *The Moral Writings of John Dewey*, edited and with an Introduction by James Gouinlock (New York: Hafner Press, 1976).

# 11

# Sartre
## *Hazel E. Barnes*

## SARTRE-IN-THE-WORLD

The individual, Sartre declared, is a 'singular universal'. He or she is a unique exemplification of the total culture, the 'objective mind' of a period but not a passive product of it. Each one, from a particular position within a given society, totalises his/her experience and in doing so acts so as to modify the world. It is not only the actions of the famous but the innumerable choices of the 'nameless dead' that have made a historical era what we now assert that it was. Sartre was acutely aware of himself as a singular universal. It would be impossible for us to dissociate his philosophy from the history of Europe in this century. One is tempted to say that the reverse is also true.

Even in his student days in Paris at the Ecole Normale Supérieure Sartre (1905–80) recognised in himself an impulse *vers le concret*. He resisted equally the belief that human behaviour can be understood scientifically as if like other natural phenomena and the notion that consciousness implies a hidden subjectivity isolated from the rest of the universe. A little later he embraced with alacrity Heidegger's statement that consciousness is always outside, there in the world, that the focus of philosophy and psychology alike must be on man-in-the-world. This conviction led Sartre ultimately to engage himself politically both as person and as philosopher, but it took a long time.

Paradoxically, the man who has been called 'the conscience of our time' and who in the last decade of his life was a militant activist, at least insofar as his physical condition allowed it, remained apolitical until well into his 30s. He began by viewing philosophy as ancillary to his literary aspirations; he saw art as a corrective to life and a means to personal salvation.

Thirteen-years-old at the end of World War I, Sartre, in the period between the wars, showed neither deep concern nor political acumen in response to such major events as the Great Depression and the rise of Hitler. In attitude (one could hardly call it theory) he favoured some sort of socialism, not Communism but something vaguely resembling Trotsky's ideal of permanent revolution. Stendhal and Dos Passos alike helped to form his self-image as a rebel in search of authentic independence. More bohemian than political, he despised the stuffy hypocritical Establishment while availing himself of all the privileges of a bourgeois intellectual. He refrained from voting on the grounds that all candidates were corrupt or incompetent. The only positive social action of Sartre's which Simone de Beauvoir has recorded is his contribution of some money, as much as he could afford, to a group of strikers.[1]

In September 1938, after Hitler's attack on Poland, Sartre went with Beauvoir on a vacation to Avignon. He remarked to her that he thought it 'possible to live in great tranquillity even at a time when your life is hedged about with danger'.[2] In his *War Diaries*, which date from the period of the 'Phony War', he inclines to the belief that the imperialistic powers will refuse finally to resort to full-scale military engagement.[3] Like much of the rest of the non-German world, he wondered if war was not in process of being proved out-moded. Yet it was during this same period that Sartre awoke to the realisation that his personal life could not be kept inviolate and apart from that of the collectivity. In February 1940 he argued on the basis of an 'ethics of authenticity',[4] that while our freedom allows us to transcend any situation by transforming it in a personal project, an individual is responsible for whatever happens in that he must take it to his own account and adopt a decisive form of action with regard to it. (As he was to express it later in *Being and Nothingness*, the war that comes is my war insofar as I do not act to prevent it.) In this same year he said that he intended to go into politics when the war ended.[5] Sartre said that it was during his brief sojourn in a German camp for war prisoners that he first felt a sense of solidarity with his fellow beings. He wrote there, in the guise of a Christmas play, his first piece of engaged literature, *Bariona*, portraying Jews in Palestine who resolve to fight to the death against their Roman rulers in revolt against Herod's proclamation of the 'murder of the innocents'.[6]

Back in Paris, after securing his release by means of forged papers, Sartre joined with other intellectuals in backing the Resistance movement, even travelling secretly into Free France in a futile effort to enlist the active support of Gide and Malraux. He himself has said that the concept of radical freedom which dominates *Being and Nothingness* and the novels and plays that he wrote in the early 1940s reflects the ideal of individual heroism appropriate to the Resistance fighter, who worked for the sake of others but who most often had to act alone.

> The secret of a man is not his Oedipus complex or his inferiority complex: it is the limit of his own freedom, his capacity for resisting torture and death. . . . Yet, in the depth of their solitude, it was the others that they were protecting, all the others, all their comrades in the Resistance. Total responsibility in total solitude— is this not the very definition of our freedom? This being stripped of all, this solitude, this tremendous danger, were the same for all . . . Each of them, standing against the oppressors, undertook to be himself, freely and irrevocably. And by choosing for himself in freedom, he chose the freedom of all.[7]

The notion of a solitary freedom virtually without limits gradually gave way in Sartre's work to concern with the way in which a person's free action is deviated, 'stolen from him by the world'. He relates the change directly to his own experiences and observation in post-war political developments. While he never sought political office, Sartre carried through on his promise of going into politics. Although a fully adequate chronicle of his political activities would constitute a lengthy biography and a detailed account of 40 years of world history, we may, for the general purposes of a history of ethics, divide Sartre's career into three periods. The divisions can be marked by what Sartre has referred to as 'conversions'.

The first of these was the resolution to engage himself actively in the reshaping of France after liberation. The years immediately following World War II, the years of the Cold War (1945–52), saw Sartre active on two fronts. As the author of best-selling fiction he espoused the cause of 'engaged' or committed literature, not only condemning the ideal of *ars gratia artis*, but arguing that the non-committed writer was *ipso facto* the supporter of the status quo. 'Not to choose is already to have chosen.' In more direct action Sartre helped to establish and became Editor of *Les Temps Modernes* (1944), a leftist journal which addressed itself directly to current issues. In 1948 he and a few others founded a new political party, Rassemblement Démocratique Révolutionnaire, an ill-fated attempt to bring together Communists and other socialistically inclined groups in an effective coalition. Although he was frequently the object of vituperation from the Communists (including outright slander and the false accusation that he had been a Nazi collaborator), Sartre increasingly allied himself with the Soviet side, holding United States imperialism to be the greater threat. He quarrelled with Merleau-Ponty, who objected to Sartre's initial reluctance to publish information concerning forced labour camps in the Soviet Union. He became gradually estranged from Camus, whose book *The Rebel* Sartre denounced as offering a philosophy of retreat from the realities of history and as playing into the hands of the forces of reaction.

The second stage began in 1952, the year marked by Sartre's final break with Camus. He now concluded that literature was not privileged, that it was not enough to engage himself as a writer, that he must work more directly and more realistically with what he considered to be the liberating forces for a social revolution. Ironically, this date marked the beginning of his close cooperation with the Communists. Yet he never actually became a member of the Party. In a radio speech that year he declared that anyone who expressed the wish to work with the Communists without being willing to become a member and submit to party discipline was 'a slimy rat'. Sartre added that he knew whereof he spoke since he himself was one.[8] During the years that followed, Sartre made several trips to the Soviet Union for conferences, literary or more overtly political. Simone de Beauvoir records as one instance of his positive influence, the fact that he was instrumental in getting the Soviet authorities to allow translations of Kafka to circulate. Always an uneasy fellow-traveller, Sartre finally broke with the Communists completely on the occasion of the Soviet intervention in Hungary in 1956. He continued, however, to support those countries and causes which were Marxist oriented, making semi-official visits to China, to Yugoslavia (he particularly admired Tito), and to Cuba. Rather typically, Sartre at first bestowed almost extravagant praise on Castro in the first years of his regime, then later criticised him severely for his action against dissident writers. At home Sartre opposed the policy of the French government in Algeria and was one of 122 persons to sign a manifesto against that war. In consequence of this action, he narrowly escaped legal prosecution, and his apartment was bombed. Sympathetic to the aspirations of the Third World, Sartre nevertheless refused to side with the Arabs against Israel. Instead he held talks with leaders on both sides in a futile endeavour to establish peace between them. In 1966–67 he participated in the Russell Tribunal. Reluctant at first, he finally joined in the judgement that the United

States had pursued a policy of genocide in Vietnam. One other event of this decade had political overtones, Sartre's rejection of the Nobel prize, which would have been awarded to him in 1964. His refusal was due in part to his objection on principle to prizes and awards that did not come as payment for specific work and to his dislike of the prospect of being canonised as a member of the Establishment. But another reason was his belief that the Nobel Prize Committee was using the prize for political purposes as shown, in Sartre's mind, by its previous award to Pasternak.

Sartre's final conversion occurred at the time of the student revolt in France in 1968. He saw in the short-lived collaboration of students and workers a sign that the true revolution was beginning. The Communists' disavowal of the movement put the final touch to his disillusion with all party politics. Henceforth his activities were specifically 'issue oriented', and they were many. Declaring that any intellectual who truly believed in the cause of revolution would devote himself wholly to supporting it, Sartre proceeded to lend his name to any leftist group that kept the notion of radical social change alive. He became the titular editor of *La Cause du Peuple* and distributed copies of it on the street when it was officially banned. He joined in all sorts of demonstrations, legal and otherwise, and once even succeeded in getting himself arrested.

Despite growing blindness and impaired health, Sartre devoted the last decade of his life to activities of this sort, signing manifestoes and giving interviews when he was no longer able to move about freely. His last intellectual efforts took the form of taping conversations with young Maoists with whose collaboration he tried to reconcile the claims of personal freedom and of communal society.[9] A spontaneous gathering of 50 000 people witnessed his burial. For some months afterwards the numerous encomia and the vitriolic attacks that appeared in French journals attested alike to Sartre's ability to 'speak to our condition'.

## THE PHILOSOPHICAL MILIEU

Anchored firmly in the phenomenological stream of Continental philosophy, Sartre so completely ignored the Anglo-American analytic tradition that one cannot even read his work as a reaction against it.[10] He first became interested in philosophy when as a student he studied Bergson.[11] A more lasting influence was Hegel, to whom Sartre was introduced by Alexandre Kojève. Like other existentialist thinkers, Sartre revolted against Hegel's idealism, but he retained a good deal of it as well. Sartre's description of psychological conflict between two persons owes much to Hegel's description of the battle for dominance between master and slave. In his later work the search for a totalising view of history is more Hegelian than even he seems to have realised. Sartre himself never acknowledged any debt to Nietzsche and indeed criticised him adversely on several occasions, but his influence on the early work of Sartre seems obvious. Oreste, who in *The Flies* strongly recalls the Nietzschean superman as forlorn and solitary, proceeds to create a new world in the wake of 'God is dead'.[12] The hero of Sartre's novel *Nausea* reflects *The Birth of Tragedy*, both in his Dionysian vision of the nauseating absurdity of reality and in his conclusion that existence can be justified only by art. Perhaps the most significant parallel (one would be rash to call it a direct consequence) is Sartre's implicit assumption of Nietzsche's claim that ethical systems are but the sign languages of emotions. Sartre puts the idea more positively. Any chosen ethics must of necessity be without external foundation. But inasmuch as it is human consciousness which brings meaning into the world, everyone creates his/her own values and, whether in good faith or bad, acts by an ethics which reflects and supports those values.

Husserl and Heidegger contributed most to the formation of Sartre's philosophy. Much of the language of *Being and Nothingness* and many of its ideas wear a familiar look to anyone who has read *Being and Time* even though Heidegger's 'Dasein' and Sartre's 'human reality' are strikingly different in their being-in-the-world.[13] It was Heidegger who explicitly dissociated himself from Sartre (and from all other existentialists) by stating that his intention was not after all to give precedence to existence but rather the reverse.[14] The writings of the later Heidegger with their all but mystic emphasis on the necessity of listening to Being and on such concepts as Holiness are even further removed from Sartre. And of course the political commitments of the two men were diametrically opposed. From Husserl Sartre adopted *in toto* the descriptive method of phenomenology and the centrality of the intentionality of consciousness, but it was his sharp break with Husserl apropos of the transcendental ego that led him to his own highly original view of consciousness.[15] In describing consciousness as pure, self-reflecting activity, neither substance nor personal subject, Sartre simultaneously built on the work of his German predecessors and offered a more philosophical formulation of the idea independently arrived at and expressed by Sartre when he was 18 years old—that consciousness was 'a void in being'.[16] We shall see that Sartrean ethics is inextricably intertwined with his position on what consciousness is and is not.

Sartre's work could not have existed in anything like its present form had it not been for his knowledge of two other men outside the existentialist-phenomenological tradition—Freud and, later, Marx. While acknowledging a great indebtedness to Freud (he applied the term 'existential psychoanalysis' to his own approach to the study of human behaviour), Sartre challenged both the essential biological conditioning of sexuality in Freudian theory and the even more fundamental concept of the Unconscious.[17] His substitution of bad faith, or the lie to oneself, for the Freudian explanation of repression had the effect of replacing psychological determinism with moral judgement. The influence of Marx became dominant only gradually during the 1950s. With Sartre it was his attempt to cope with problems in an idealogically split world that led him to the serious study of Marx and not the reverse. As with his other predecessors, Sartre transformed what he borrowed. *Critique of Dialectical Reason*, which attempted to reinsert the individual project into the heart of Marxism, to make it once again a living movement and not a dogma, received its most adverse criticism from Marxist reviewers.[18]

## SARTREAN ETHICS

Sartre concluded *Being and Nothingness* with the statement that he planned to write a book which would discuss such ethical questions as naturally derived from the ontology presented in the preceding volume. The posthumously published *Cahiers pour une morale*[19] contains his notes for this ethics, which Sartre never completed.[20] In part this material offers a kind of postscript to *Being and Nothingness*, emphasising particularly the positive possibilities of empathic comprehension of others' projects, reciprocity, and the recognition of freedom as a value to be universally fostered. The bulk of the book, however, anticipates what Sartre will do later in *Critique of Dialectical Reason*. In the mid-1960s Sartre again began to make notes for an ethics, this time for one more relevant to his neo-Marxist orientation, but he put the project aside in favour of his study of Flaubert, *The Family Idiot*. It would be a mistake to conclude from this record either that his philosophy allowed no room for an ethics or that ethical questions were secondary for Sartre. The truth is that the notion of human freedom and consequent moral responsibility dominates everything that Sartre has written.

Also pervasive in all of Sartre's writing is his atheistic humanism. Having declared for himself in his 12th year that God does not exist, Sartre does not attempt to prove the point but takes it for granted.[21] He claims, however, that his is the most thoroughgoing atheism that the world has known insofar as it rejects not only the notion of a personal creator but of any underlying cosmic purpose or rational order. Even the idea of a given human nature he would remove as offering any universal support for our belief as to what the human individual ought to be or do. Whether we are speaking of an individual life or of society, there is no objective pattern to which we may turn for guide or model or guarantee. From one point of view, Sartrean ethics must be seen as not only humanistic but individualistic, for there is no reality such as group mind or hyperorganism or merging of consciousness. In another sense nobody is ever alone. We are in fact together-in-the-world; it is through the other's responses that I get a sense of the quality of my own being; moreover, in carrying out my own projects, I inevitably impinge on the world of others. Some such idea must be behind the rather puzzling statement by Sartre in a popular lecture on Existentialism—that in choosing for myself I choose for humanity.[22] Consistent with what he has said elsewhere, the sentence seems to mean two things: first, since humanity has not been predefined, my own choice and action contribute to defining it, both in the sense that my choice expresses what I find appropriate for a human being and that the accumulation of human behaviour will in fact constitute what humanity will have been—at that point when, as William James put it, the last man has had his last say. Second, my choice will in at least some small degree be helping to construct the world in which future persons will make their own free choices. One other aspect of Sartre's humanism should be noted. This is the extent to which his thought reflected the Judaeo-Christian tradition, despite his rejection of it. Such phenomena as bad faith, original sin, transubstantiation still find their place in a purely human context; the desire to achieve the kind of existence traditionally ascribed to God remains a central motif of Sartre's ontology; and psychology.[23]

It is convenient to divide Sartre's work into two periods in which he was concerned respectively with first the individual and then the collective structures of groups and society. From this point of view the works of the early Sartre point to or derive from the principles laid down in *Being and Nothingness*; those of the later Sartre are centred on *Critique of Dialectical Reason*. This procedure is entirely appropriate so long as we recognise that the later theory, too, is grounded in the ontology of *Being and Nothingness*.

To get to the foundation of Sartre's thought, we must start with the theory of consciousness outlined in *The Transcendence of the Ego* and developed in *Being and Nothingness*. The title of the latter refers to the two regions of reality which Sartre terms respectively Being-in-itself and Being-for-itself; the former is the designation of all that is not consciousness and the latter of individual consciousness, which in humans, at least, is always self-consciousness.[24] Consciousness, for Sartre, exists only as the activity of intending objects other than itself while implicitly aware of itself as not being those objects. As intentional activity, consciousness makes itself be by its choice of action in the world. The self is essentially engaged in the world and responsible for what both itself and the world become.

Consequential for ethics are two corollary concepts of Sartre's ontology. The first grows out of his analysis of being-for-itself and bears most importantly on individual ethics. The second concerns his understanding of being-in-itself and takes on its true significance in the social sphere.

The first of these corollaries is bad faith (*la mauvaise foi*), a basic form of self-deception all too familiar to us, which is possible, Sartre says, only because our being is characterised by a split or lack. A person cannot be in the way that a thing or animal is. For example, we cannot correctly say of a man that he is a coward in the same way that we can say he is six feet tall. The same is true with respect to his profession or social status. Sartre has provided an example from everyday life of how making ourselves be is an active project and at the same time a kind of game.

> Let us consider this waiter in the café. His movement is quick and forward, a little too precise, a little too rapid. He comes toward the patrons with a step a little too quick. He bends forward a little too eagerly; his voice, his eyes express an interest a little too solicitous for the customer's order. Finally there he returns, trying to imitate in his walk the inflexible stiffness of some kind of automaton while carrying his tray with the recklessness of a tight-rope-walker by putting it in a perpetually unstable, perpetually broken

equilibrium which he perpetually reestablishes by a light movement of the arm and hand. All his behaviour seems to us a game.
He applies himself to chaining his movements as if they were
mechanisms, the one regulating the other; his gestures and even
his voice seem to be mechanisms; he gives himself the quickness
and pitiless rapidity of things. He is playing.[25]

If, as Sartre claims, the waiter can never be a waiter 'in the sense
that this inkwell *is* an inkwell or the glass *is* a glass', this is because
the human individual exists simultaneously in two different ways.
He/she *is* as a 'facticity'. The waiter is a waiter and is not a policeman.
He cannot truthfully say simply, 'I am not a waiter'. But he is also a
'transcendence'. He is a waiter only insofar as he chooses to continue
playing the role of waiter. And although, as Sartre points out, society
has many devices by which it attempts to imprison a person in a
role, human consciousness always overflows its immediate activity.
Sartre's waiter is not an example of a man in bad faith, but he
shows us how he or anyone else could be.[26] Bad faith is the illicit,
exclusive affirmation of either transcendence or facticity at the
expense of the other. Most often it vacillates between them. It plays
with the ambivalent nature of the verb to be. Lying to oneself, in bad
faith one either refuses to acknowledge responsibility for one's
actions and the motives behind them (facticity) or denies that one
can become other than what one has been or do other than what
one does (transcendence). Sartre's example of the homosexual is
illuminating. The man who has internalised society's attitude that to
be a homosexual is shameful may tell himself that he is not really a
homosexual by counting every instance of his sexual relations as
somehow exceptional, as not making him a homosexual.[27] He is
equally in bad faith, however, if he insists that he does not want to be a
homosexual but is so constituted that he cannot behave otherwise.
Good faith, or authenticity, for Sartre would simultaneously
acknowledge responsibility for what one has objectively done and
for what one has made of oneself while recognising that one is free
to change the pattern.[28]
For the early Sartre the ethical thrust of this position was to
provide a better explanation of what we commonly call rationalisa-
tions or Freudian defence mechanisms and to demonstrate that as
free and responsible beings we are called on to create and to live
authentically. We are, each one, as it were, a plan aware of itself.[29]
Obviously a certain pluralism is allowed here, but the central

premise that everyone equally is a free self-creating process must be kept central.

At first Sartre's primary concern was with the individual's efforts to achieve and sustain this kind of authenticity for himself or herself, but the question of ethical responsibility with regard to others followed swiftly on the recognition that in acting on the world one inevitably changes it for others as well as for oneself. Before looking directly at the question of human relations, let us consider the second corollary of Sartre's ontology: the part assigned to the in-itself, a certain materiality.

In *Being and Nothingness* Sartre wished chiefly to show that a person is always free to bestow a new ordering and meaning on his own materialised past and that he still chooses whatever situation he finds himself in. We are free even under the sadist's knife.[30] The freedom in *Being and Nothingness* is a freedom for heroes; bad faith is cowardice. Nine years later in *Saint Genet, Actor and Martyr*,[31] Sartre had modified his radical position on freedom commensurately with his recognition that the laws and dominant attitudes of a society so circumscribe the field of choices for any person that in the case of the oppressed and the outcast even the inner life is as if 'possessed'. For the individual labelled subhuman or anti-human only desperate solutions were possible. In Jean Genet Sartre found another kind of existentialist hero and formulated with reference to him a new view of freedom in a world structured by the bad faith of others.

> In the end one is always responsible for what is made of one. Even if one can do nothing else besides assume this responsibility. For I believe that a man can always make something out of what is made of him. This is the limit I would today accord to freedom: the small movement which makes of a totally conditioned social being someone who does not render back completely what his conditioning has given him. Which makes of Genet a poet when he had been rigorously conditioned to be a thief.[32]

Here the conditioning is the result of the conflict among freedoms. In *Critique of Dialectical Reason* Sartre went still further in stressing the restrictions consequent on any action in the world. By our acts we imprison ourselves as our inscriptions in matter are turned back against us. Our self-objectification becomes reification. In *Being and Nothingness* freedom was absolute; in *Saint Genet, Actor and Martyr* it was conditioned; *Critique of Dialectical Reason* shows us the processes whereby freedom is alienated.[33]

What nobody has ever tried to do is to study the type of passive action that materiality as such exerts on men and their history by returning to them a stolen *praxis* in the form of a counter-finality. . . . Man has to struggle not only against nature and against the social environment which has produced him and against other men, but also against his own action as it becomes other.[34]

At least two comprehensive notions are involved in this passage: materiality, which was implicitly present even in *Being and Nothingness*, and counter-finality, a new and dominant motif in *Critique of Dialectical Reason*. Sartre's view of materiality has been greatly expanded in the later work. Although he still insists that self-awareness sets us as a species apart from the rest of nature, he recognises nevertheless that we and other organisms, as well as inanimate things, are all made of molecules. 'We will accept the idea that man is one material being among others and that as such he does not enjoy a privileged status.'[35] But by a kind of transubstantiation, Sartre says, the human being becomes a thing to the exact extent that the thing becomes human. Pure matter we never encounter except abstractly.[36] It is worked matter which fixes meanings, transfers them from one generation to the next and thus becomes the driving force of history.[37] I carve out my individual being by my actions in the world. To see what I have been is to look at what I have done.

Unfortunately objectification *may* become a reification which 'steals my action from me'. We now confront counter-finality, the unexpected result of a deliberate act. Sartre claims that there is no significant human action that does not to some slight degree produce a counter-finality, at least to the extent of introducing at some point in the future a new possibility that the agent had not anticipated. The simplest and most obvious example of a counter-finality occurs when the physical world itself turns one's action against one. Sartre gives the example of peasants who clear a wooded hillside to provide more farmland only to find themselves with less cultivable land as the result of erosion and floods.[38] More complex counter-finalities involve the interaction of human activities; for example, well-intentioned efforts to restore a failing economy by curbing inflation may produce a depression. Or, what especially interested Sartre, the steps taken by a revolutionary group to ensure its survival have usually resulted in a new form of tyranny against its own members.

The 'practico-inert' is Sartre's term for the world of worked matter in which and by means of which humans make their history. In the context of the passage quoted Sartre is concerned primarily with social movements and the counter-finalities unwittingly effected by groups in their conflict with natural forces and with other groups. Yet the statement that man must struggle 'against his own action as it becomes other', that is, as it is externalised, objectified in the world, might be taken to refer also to individuals' relations to themselves and to particular others. There is more than a close parallel, there is a definite interaction between 'the type of passive action that materiality as such exerts on man' and the interplay of subjects and objects in the sphere of human relations. The tendency for human self-objectification to become reified is manifest in the realm of individual psychology as well as in the social field. Human history and the individual life story follow the same lines—in the way that ontogeny repeats phylogeny.

We may best begin, as Sartre did, with the individual, prereflective consciousness.[39] An individual consciousness is a wellspring of freedom that takes on the form of a 'fundamental project', a specific, chosen orientation towards the world, a way of being. The fundamental project itself stands as a particular vantage point from which the view is necessarily partial. Sartre claims that at certain instants, which may be experienced as either threatening or liberating, we are overwhelmed by the revelatory comprehension that all could have been different, that the world could be viewed otherwise, that even now we could be radically other than we are.[40]

But to live wholly reflectively, to weigh every decision by reference to a carefully thought through system of values is to predetermine all future experience, to put oneself into a carapace. The alternative, to respond spontaneously and non-reflectively to whatever is immediate, is to be a weathervane. Thus, even for the most liberated of authentic consciousness there is a dilemma. Is to be true to oneself to be true to a free, untrammelled consciousness or to the ego constructed by that consciousness?[41]

Most people are content to live within the shelter of a fixed self-image and an unchanging value system; this is because the ego is felt to be less a prison than a bulwark of protection. Sartre says that the ego serves to shield from us the terrifying unknown regions to which our free consciousness might lead us. We take refuge in the notion of being a definite self that can be counted on. The structures and content of the ego, in contrast to basic consciousness, have the weight of psychic being, a materiality. Our memories, our habits, our self-image, like all other self-objectifications, the actions and events of our lives, function as the material continuity of the history of our consciousness. Without them we would not *be*. Yet the relation between a consciousness and its ego varies from person to person. Some are like spiders, moving freely in space as they attach themselves to the world by filaments of their own making. Others, like certain marine creatures, creep along with the weight of their shells on their back. Perhaps most, like hermit crabs, move within the confines of the cast-off shells of others. Only the first is meeting the challenge to live ethically, in Sartrean terms.

We will turn now to the subject of our relations with other individuals. Sartre's negative picture of human relations as they are usually lived is encapsulated in his play *No Exit* with the climactic line, 'Hell is others'. If Hell is others, it is because of the tyranny of the look by which one person turns the other into an object. This language is not entirely metaphorical. I *am* an object, though not exclusively so. In extreme cases my body may be literally manipulated or treated as a thing (as in the hands of cannibals or of the agents of the Holocaust). To know that I am looked at is to realise that I have an object side. My self for others is what I *am*. What I do or say may be used against me. My words and actions are judged and categorised by a subject I do not control. The components of my idea of the kind of person I am cannot exclude my awareness of the self, or selves, I have been for others.

Most of the time, for most people, according to Sartre, human relations are a fluctuating battle of subjects and objects which nobody finally wins. Psychologically the goal is to secure one's own being, and one can try to achieve it by assuming the role of tyrant or tyrannised. The one who cherishes the illusion of being only subject may seem to be protected against any look of judgement deriving from an alien value system. But to the extent that the illusion can be maintained, there is no possibility of growth from one's contact with others, and there is always the risk that the other will suddenly look back. The one who chooses to be object may seem to escape from the burdensome and risky task of perpetual self-creation, but it is at the expense of denying the freedom that one actually is. The variations on this theme are infinite, but all prove ultimately to be unsatisfactory since they are based on an untruth. We are all both subjects and objects. As consciousness we are pure subjectivity (though not in the personalised sense of 'I' or ego). Yet we know others and are known by them as objects. There is no merging of consciousnesses. I cannot know the other's interiority.

Is there after all no exit? I think that Sartre has allowed for one and that we may discover it in the metaphor of the look.[42] Even literally, a look does not need to be a hostile stare of judgement; it is not necessarily petrifying like the look of Medusa. There is the look as exchange, which is the equivalent of a mutual pledge and invitation, an assurance that, insofar as it is possible, each will try to understand and will respect the structures of the other's private world and will put up no barriers before his or her own. It is possible also for two people to look-together-at-the-world; in other words, to be joined in a common project. Sartre reminds us, however, that an outsider, a hostile Third, may bring to bear an objectifying look on the original pair, making of them an us-object, an idea that is the source of the shifting of the unstable relationships in *No Exit*.

In *Being and Nothingness* Sartre's brief discussion of the wider social sphere does not move significantly beyond the conflict of subjects and objects. The destructive look is manifest wherever there is a class structure. Us-objects, persons designated as subhumans, are established by the look of colonialists, racists, sexists. So long as the Other's look is internalised and its judgement accepted as indicating what the looked-at are in their being, no revolt is possible; us-objects do not act. At this stage Sartre could not see any corresponding union of subjects in the oppressing class. It was not until *Critique of Dialectical Reason*, published 17 years later, that he described the emergence of the group-in-fusion, the revolutionary group, in connection with which he analyzed the nature of a new 'We'.

Historically, Sartre claims, human groups have struggled against one another, driven by need in a world characterised by scarcity.[43] When unified groups have emerged, it has always been under the necessity of opposing a hostile Other. Once the enemy has been overcome, the group disintegrates or is reified in the form of an oppressive institution. In the pre-revolutionary stage oppressors and oppressed alike are united only in collectives; relations are those of the series. All alike feel powerless, caught in the depersonalised structures of the practico-inert.

Sartre's simplest example of collectives and the series is the queue waiting for a bus.[44] The only unity here is the spatial organisation of the city and the impersonal bus route (the collective). By convention nobody looks at anybody else, except perhaps for a surreptitious appraising glance. I am differentiated from others only by my position in the line.

Series may become groups when their members realise that they are all equally vulnerable to an outside threat which only an action supported by all can oppose with any chance of success.[45] The precipitating cause will be an act performed by the oppressive government, employer, or outside aggressor, a step that proves to be a counter-finality from the point of view of the agent. Faced with extermination or enslavement, the group-in-fusion is formed in the white heat of action that has to be taken in the face of common danger. In describing the emergent 'We', Sartre makes use of two ideas. First, this 'We' is neither a collective consciousness nor a hyperorganism (consciousnesses do not merge). Its unity is out there in the world; a common praxis is inscribed in the practico-inert. The 'We' of the group is a multiple looking-together-at-the-world. Second, there is the importance of 'the Third'. Sartre brings in the Third in two ways. The old hostile Third is still there in the guise of the threatening oppressor or aggressor, but this time the threat becomes itself the unifying object of common action. In addition Sartre introduces a totally new kind of Third—a Third who mediates, not as the detached arbitrator between individuals or groups but as an involved member of the group. Each member of the group, instead of being either subject or object to the others, makes himself a third person. The group is a union of Thirds. Sartre's odd use of this term expresses not only the idea that nobody is either a subject or an object to anybody else (the objectifying look has disappeared) but that nobody is other. Everyone is the same, the group is a collection of 'myselfs'. We are all one common project. It does not matter who shouts a command nor who performs a particular act. Everyone is a regulating Third. Now at last number brings power. *We* are a hundred strong. Each is the hundredth to the other 99.

Once the group-in-fusion has achieved its goal, the question is how to maintain itself as a fused group when the unifying threat of the external other is removed or remote. Ironically, the absence of the immediate threat of the hostile Third tends to disintegrate the group as its presence precipitated the group's formation. The problem is not crucial if the common project has been in response to a specific natural disaster such as a tornado or a flood, though even then persons often feel nostalgic regret when the experience of human solidarity has ended. But if the group has come into being as a genuinely revolutionary and liberating movement, the threat of exploitation and alienation can never be removed once and for all. There is still need for the group to exist. Only its constant vigilance can prevent the return of seriality and impotence in the face of the paralysing practico-inert.

Internal threats to the group's cohesion derive not just from historical accidents (the specific character of the component members) but from the limitations of the essential nature of the group-in-fusion. First, the group suffers from the fact that it is not an organism. United solely by the fact that each one freely chose to engage himself in the common praxis, making the achievement of the same goal his project, every member is aware that the engagement is not binding unless he reconfirms it. As he was free to join in the common endeavour, he is now free to withdraw. Second, without the urgency of the enemy's pressure, the group no longer has a common praxis. In a literal sense it has nothing to do. We know what happens. In order to protect itself against external threats which may come in the future, the group substitutes a new common praxis for the old one; it works on itself so as to ensure that it will remain a group, prepared to confront all dangers from without. In order to do so it must guard itself against dangers from within, not just against those few who might actually go over to the enemy but against everyone inasmuch as each member potentially has the free capacity to injure the group by withdrawing from it or even by simple passive non-engagement. Members of the group must deliberately protect themselves against their own freedom, must objectify the earlier spontaneous procedures. The instruments of this new fraternity are the pledge, the purge and terror. The members (orally, in writing, or by general understanding) pledge themselves not to leave the group and to abide by whatever agreements and regulations group action may impose. To mould free consent into a binding restriction, each third person invokes against himself and against all other Thirds a penalty (which may be a death sentence) to be imposed on himself or anyone else who may break the pledge. Now again it is the Third who mediates; the group itself functions as a Third. For self-protection the group proceeds to purge itself of the recalcitrant.

In the fused group (as opposed to the group-in-fusion at the moment of formation) seriality may be warded off for a while, but it is hard to see how it can be avoided completely for very long. Historically it has always returned; groups have always either disintegrated or degenerated into collectives or institutions. New pressures for group conformity may seem to many of its members to be more tyrannical than the seriality in the old collective. Persons who are impatient with restrictions or who want to improve the structures of the group by changing them are viewed with suspicion. All traitors are in the minority. A member of the minority is always a potential traitor.

For many readers the analysis of the rise and decline of the group-in-fusion is all too persuasive; they find *Critique of Dialectical Reason* even more pessimistic than *Being and Nothingness,* which at least left one with the feeling of an open future for those strong enough to face it. Two things are primarily responsible for the impression of the inevitable failure of all attempts at liberation. The first is Sartre's assumption that the group arises only in response to the threat of an external human enemy. Fear and hatred of others, however effective they may be in the initial mobilisation of revolutionary groups, are inadequate supports for the enduring community of free and re-sponsible persons that is Sartre's own goal. Second, at no point in the book does Sartre suggest any means by which a group based on trust and at peace might find the common praxis on which its existence depends.

If we look elsewhere in Sartre's work, we will not find explicit solutions to these problems. Yet it is evident that Sartre believed that a total transformation of human society is possible. Even in *Critique of Dialectical Reason* he makes it clear that he does not regard the conflict between groups as a permanent fact of our future history. Despite its dreary failures, Sartre claims that the pledged group is 'the beginning of humanity'. Insofar as we, its members, fashion our own conditions of living, we will be henceforth 'our own sons, our common creation'. He insists that the only acceptable basis for any acceptable ethics must have as its goal a We of humanity over-coming scarcity by developing the resources of the earth for the good of all humankind.[46] Although he never accepted any of the claims for a cosmic consciousness of a supra-individual transcen-dental self, Sartre did go so far, in a late interview, as to hold out the hope that we might rediscover the affective bond which led members of primitive clans to feel themselves to be linked by blood to a common ancestor. Our fraternity as members of the same species is an original fact of our existence; its affective realisation is necessary if we are to achieve universal liberation.[47]

Sartre's ultimate ideal for humanity is more radical than that of most Marxists. What he would have us all work to achieve would be a totally resocialised world with a minimum of established, centralised authority, a maximum of direct participation and responsibility for everyone. Even the family unit would be open to modification, for Sartre was as much concerned with the damage done by parents to their children as he was with our ill-being at the hands of educators and governments. It was his firm conviction that the removal of repressive conventional taboos would dissolve the fears that presently cause us to close in from one another. People would no longer have reason to keep secrets from others. A kind of transparency would diminish the opaqueness of the walls of our private worlds.[48] The gap between the emotional effusion of such utterances and the sombre analysis of the difficulties of sustaining a common praxis in the fused group is astounding. Yet while Sartre cannot be said to have filled it in, I do not think that we need to judge it unbridgeable— even within the framework of his own philosophical position. Two possibilities derived from Sartre seem to me essential and promising for communal efforts at liberation and social change.

The first is the necessity of combining the two positive dimensions of the personal look and extending them to the social sphere: the look as an exchange and looking-together-at-the-world. This seems to me to be essentially what Sartre has in mind when he says that political social planning must be accompanied by a developed affectivity.

A second idea from Sartre states, again in the form of an ideal, the requisites for a continually self-transcending society which would avoid the lapse into seriality and reification that historically have marked the death of the fused group and made of it a fraternity of terror, turned against its own members. In an essay, 'Materialism and Revolution', Sartre laid down a four-point credo for the New Revolutionary, whose aim would be the liberation of humanity in a classless society.[49] The following assumptions would be taken as true: (1) that people create their social structures, that no given pattern for humanity has been sanctioned by nature or by God or by universal reason; (2) that therefore any specific social organisation is subject to question and may legitimately be replaced by another; (3) that societies institute and conserve those values which tend to safeguard and preserve a particular social order; (4) that therefore a revolutionary movement may be inspired and guided by new values that will emerge clearly only in the course of the movement's own development.

Sartre did not, either in this article or later, spell out the steps whereby a society as a whole might pursue this ideal without the need for revolutionary action initiated by a minority. In fact, *Critique of Dialectical Reason* implies that an external threat is necessary to provoke any communal action and that groups historically have never allowed for their own transcendence. Yet I think the possibilities are there in what Sartre has written.

The difficulties in human relations and their possible resolutions show parallel structures at all levels; a resolution at a more simple level must precede a successful outcome at a higher one. Or perhaps it would be better to say that because of the parallelism we find a circle. A society not afraid to envision transcending itself must be made up of persons who are free and without fear, but individuals cannot live freely, creatively and safely except in a free and open society.

The parallels to which I refer are not the result of Sartre's having deliberately imposed any symmetrical pattern but derive naturally from his view of consciousness as a free process of relating itself to things in the world, making itself *be* in the world. We can see this continuity and development especially clearly with respect to Sartre's famous declaration that every human being wants to be God.[50] What Sartre meant by this was that we are overcome with anguish at not being able simply to be something once and for all, with the guarantee that this something is what objectively we ought to be and that it is meaningful in the universal scheme of things. We long to have the absoluteness of an instinct-guided animal or a genetically programmed plant or of a thing fashioned for a given purpose. But we would like to have and to be all this without ceasing to be a spontaneous, self-determining consciousness. We wish to be both cause and caused, to be the Self-Cause which the Scholastics called God. Although this self-contradictory goal cannot be achieved, we may pretend to ourselves that it can, and we may live as if we had attained it; that is, without ceasing to take personal credit for our accomplishments, we may (in bad faith, of course) assume that our values are externally supported, the meaning and purpose of our lives self-evident, our natures intrinsically correct. Thus to be true to ourselves would be automatically to fit into a prescribed pattern; and so far as the loss of free spontaneity is concerned, it does not greatly matter whether the model has been borrowed intact from others or has resulted from vows to oneself made in response to what once seemed right.

On the level of intimate personal relations, the comparable impossible ideal, portrayed at least as early as Plato's *Symposium*, is that the two should become one, or more exactly, that I should some-how become other while remaining wholly myself. The illusion that absolute oneness in otherness is both attainable and a self-sufficient answer to all of life's problems has wreaked havoc among countless Madame Bovarys of both sexes. Just as the first recognition of 'being in love' implied a promise to oneself, so lovers try to hedge their freedom with mutual vows. Each one swears to remain the same in relation to the other, a promise of fidelity which tacitly in-cludes a commitment not to change at all. The totally tyrannical relation, of course, is that in which one of the pair sets the parameters within which both will live. But fear of any possibilities which might modify the quality of the union may become a mutual self-imprison-ment.

As individuals cherish the futile desire to be God and lovers long vainly to become one, so the group suffers from its inability to become an organism. Once again it is our very freedom that threatens to undermine the hard-won unity. The pledge, freely given but intended to be irrevocable, is the bulwark against the group's future disintegration.

At all three levels we find an attempt to materialise a commitment as a means to ensure it. The individual makes firm resolves which he may record in a diary or proclaim in the presence of others; he does whatever he can to transform his emotional impulse into a permanent state, a resolution into a necessity. A marriage contract binds the couple. A sworn oath and constitution cement the bonds of the fused group. All of these are a consequence of the moment of reflection, efforts to fix and make permanent the results of pre-reflective choice or immediate emotion or spontaneous action in response to the threat or possibilities of a given situation.

Sartre would relate our defensive clinging to shame and fear of others to the negative moment of freedom. Any free action which brings something new into existence inevitably destroys something of what was there already. Selection is inseparable from exclusion, construction requires destruction. Sartre claims that historically human groups have tried to separate the positive from the negative with a resultant Manicheism that permeates our conventional morality and social structures. All that is good is identified with being and with conduct that will conserve present laws and customs. The rest is non-being and evil; it is relegated to criminals, subhumans and outcasts.[51] Individuals similarly label as good or safe whatever can be absorbed in their ego, without causing it to be no longer the same;

anything else is dangerous and wrong. Lovers try to convert and to reduce their own and each other's otherness into oneness. We are afraid to allow sameness and otherness to coexist. In principle we value growth but only in a given direction, not as a transcendence of present values.

As for a way out of these dilemmas with seemingly no exit, I believe that Sartre's credo for the New Revolutionary is appropriate for self-growth as it is for relations with other individuals and within groups. The goal is always to keep open the possibility for future self-transcendence while committing oneself concretely to the realisation of present fulfilment. The individual will question whether present values are sustained at too high a price or might be preserved in recognising 'the more inclusive claim'.[52] The loving couple will seek means whereby growing together does not restrict the stature of either one to its present height. Groups will learn that the only common praxis which will endure must be one shared with other groups and must eventually rule out the exclusion of any. Even Sartre's metaphor of the look continues to be relevant. I must look at, must examine and understand the ego my consciousness has built before I can alter it. But I must look outside at the world in order to do so. Similarly, if I want to enter into a lasting agreement with others, I must exchange with them the look of understanding before we can act effectively together to change the world, to get rid of tyranny.

It is evident that Sartre believes that the full utilisation of human freedom could result in a radical transformation of individual life and a total resocialisation. His vision of a We of humanity constructing a society of free individuals living with no need for secrecy does not propose the equivalent of the anthill. Sartre would be the first to argue that in our discovery of fraternity, our sameness as members of one species must not cancel out our individual and group otherness. We are brothers, he said, but not like peas in a can.[53] Sartre claims that conflict and not *Mitsein* is the origin of human relations.[54] Original sin is the existence of the Other.[55] But love and community are possible as a human triumph over the starting conditions.

## SUMMARY

Paradoxically, one could truthfully say both that ethical concern was the impetus for Sartre's entire philosophical enterprise and that he was uninterested, to the point of almost ignoring it, in the evolution of formal arguments which constitutes the history of ethics in western philosophy. One of the rare instances when he raises the question of the nature of ethics directly is an entry from *The War Diaries* which indicates clearly what for him ethics is and is not.

> [An ethics] is a system of ends; so to what end must human reality act? The only reply: to its own end. No other end can be proposed to it. Let us first observe that an end can be posited only by a being that is its own possibilities; that, in other words, pro-jects itself toward these possibilities in the future. . . . But in addition, human reality is limited everywhere by itself and whatever aim it sets itself, that aim is always itself. . . . Human reality exists for the purpose of itself—and it's that *self*, with its specific type of existence (as that which awaits it in the future to be realised by its freedom), which is *value*. There exists no value other than human reality for human reality.[56]

Sartre not only rejected all theological or cosmic support for ethics. He disavowed the existence of any biological norm which might represent what human nature is or should be. He was not concerned to search for a universal principle or principles on which to erect or by which to measure deontological claims. He was not in the slightest degree interested in the logical analysis of ethical propositions for truth value. He held that values are invented, not discovered, authored by individuals, not by the species. In his view the first and most important creative act for any person is in fact the formation of a value system by which one is willing to live and judge oneself.[57] If this statement, like the passage quoted, seems a curious admixture of relativity and normative prescription, that is because for Sartre the essential question is: What kind of life is appropriate for a being which is radically free and therefore responsible for what it makes of self and of the world? Sartre's phenomenological description of consciousness-in-the-world—that is, his ontology and his psychology—is as inextricably bound up with problems of ethics as Plato's view of the good, whether for the soul or for society, was the logical result of his idealist ontology and epistemology. Sartre's analysis of consciousness is designed to demonstrate that the individual *is* a responsible freedom. His literary works and political writing examine the kinds of responses which seek to evade, or which are consistent with, recognising this freedom and this responsibility in oneself and in others.

Such terms as authenticity and inauthenticity, good faith and bad faith, the injunction to respect the subjectivity of both the Other and myself in all human interaction may at first suggest the familiar harmonics of traditional morality. But Sartre's intention was to undermine, not to sustain the conventions of 'the serious world'. It is no accident that his view of the individual's relation with self and others had considerable influence on humanistic psychotherapy. His philosophical aim, like the therapeutic goal, is not to reveal unalterable structures but to throw light on self-imposed limiting patterns of thought and to release a creative consciousness. Sartre's insistence on what has been called a 'dreadful freedom'[58] is *per se* neither optimistic not pessimistic. To say that the future is open is not to view it as utopian nor as dystopian but simply to declare that it need not be like the past.

# Notes

1. Simone de Beauvoir, *The Prime of Life*, trans. Peter Green (New York: Lancer Books, 1962) p. 318. The chief sources for Sartre's biography, in addition to *The Words*, which is his own account of his childhood, and the four volumes of Simone de Beauvoir's autobiography, are: (1) a film scenario, *Sartre by Himself*, a film directed by Alexandre Astruc and Michel Contat, trans. Richard Seaver (New York: Urizen Books, 1978); (2) Beauvoir's narrative of the last decade of Sartre's life and her recorded conversations with him in 1974, *Adieux: A Farewell to Sartre*, trans. Patrick O'Brian (New York: Pantheon, 1984). For bibliographies for Sartre, cf. Michel Contat and Michel Rybalka, *The Writings of Jean-Paul Sartre*, trans. Richard C. McCleary (Evanston: Northwestern University Press, 1974), and François H. Lapointe, with the collaboration of Claire Lapointe, *Jean-Paul Sartre and His Critics: An International Bibliography: 1938–1980* (Bowling Green: Philosophy Documentation Center, 1981).
2. Ibid., p. 474.
3. Jean-Paul Sartre, *The War Diaries of Jean-Paul Sartre: November 1939/March 1940*, trans. Quintin Hoare (New York: Pantheon, 1984) pp. 222–29.
4. Beauvoir, *The Prime of Life*, p. 516.
5. Ibid., p. 13.
6. The text of *Bariona* is included in *The Writings of Jean-Paul Sartre*, by Contat and Rybalka, vol. 2.
7. Sartre, 'The Republic of Silence', trans. Ramon Guthrie, in *The Republic of Silence*, compiled and edited by A. J. Liebling (New York: Harcourt Brace, 1947) pp. 498–500.
8. Francis Jeanson reports on this speech in *Sartre par lui-même* (Paris: Editions du Seuil, 1957) pp. 158 ff.
9. Only one of these was completed. Ph. Gavi, J.-P. Sartre, P. Victor, *On a raison de se révolter* (Paris: Gallimard, 1974). The other was to have been *Pouvoir et liberté* by Sartre and Victor (who later wrote under the name of Benny Lévy).
10. For the most part Anglo-American philosophers in turn ignored Sartre (at least until very recently). An early two-part article by A. J. Ayer, based on what must have been a hasty reading of *Being and Nothingness*, was so filled with errors as to be embarrassing. 'Novelist Philosophers V', *Horizon* (July 1945) pp. 12–26 and (August 1945) pp. 101–10. On the other hand, R. M. Hare devoted serious discussion to Sartre's popular lecture, *Existentialism*, though I think he is mistaken in calling Sartre an absolutist in ethics; *Freedom and Reason* (Oxford University Press, 1963) pp. 38 and 48. Thomas Nagel has made the problem of meaning in an absurd universe a major concern although he is more interested in Camus' attempt at a solution than in Sartre's. 'The Absurd', *The Journal of Philosophy* (21 October 1971) pp. 716–27. Although Sartre was not notably influenced by American pragmatists, there are many interesting

near parallels between his position and theirs. Sartre's view of consciousness and of truth as something which becomes are reminiscent of William James. Sartre's emphasis on the role of philosophy in social action recalls John Dewey.

11. As a student Sartre also studied the work of two contemporary philosophers, Léon Brunschvicg and Alain (Emile Auguste Chartier) and was especially impressed by the latter. Steven Light claims that it was the Japanese philosopher Shūzō Kuki who first introduced Sartre to phenomenology in the 1920s rather than Raymond Aron in 1932 as Beauvoir has reported. *Shūzō Kuki and Jean-Paul Sartre: Influence and Counter-influence in the Early History of Existential Phenomenology* (Carbondale: Southern Illinois University Press, 1987).

12. Walter Kaufmann has discussed the influence of Nietzsche on Sartre's play *The Flies. Tragedy and Philosophy* (Garden City, New York: Doubleday, 1968) pp. 258–63.

13. Cf., Joseph P. Fell, *Heidegger and Sartre: An Essay on Being and Place* (New York: Columbia University Press, 1979).

14. Martin Heidegger, 'Letter on Humanism', trans. Edgar Lohner, *Philosophy in the Twentieth Century*, edited by William Barrett and Henry D. Aiken (New York: Random House, 1962) p. 293.

15. Sartre, *The Transcendence of the Ego*, trans. Forrest Williams and Robert Kirkpatrick (New York: Farrar, Straus and Giroux, 1957). Husserl, while rejecting the notion that the empirical personal ego was part of each one's basic consciousness, nevertheless retained the notion of a transcendental ego presiding over and ordering experience. Sartre denied the existence of any transcendental ego. He argued that the ego is structured *by* a consciousness that unifies experience; it is the product of consciousness, not part of its structure.

16. Contat and Rybalka, *The Writings of Jean-Paul Sartre*, p. 6.

17. The attitude of Sartre (and of two existential psychiatrists) towards Freud is the subject of a book by Gerald N. Izenberg, *The Existentialist Critique of Freud: The Crisis of Autonomy* (Princeton, N.J.: Princeton University Press, 1976).

18. Sartre, *Critique of Dialectical Reason*, trans. Alan Sheridan-Smith (New Jersey: Atlantic Highlands, 1976) and *Search for a Method*, trans. Hazel E. Barnes (New York: Alfred A. Knopf, 1963).

19. Sartre, *Cahiers pour une morale* (Paris: Gallimard, 1983).

20. For a fuller discussion of Sartre's attitude towards writing an ethics, see Hazel E. Barnes, *An Existentialist Ethics* (University of Chicago Press, 1978), preface and ch. 2. Recent work has been done on unpublished manuscripts in which Sartre attempted to work out an ethics consistent with Marxism. Particularly interesting are two things: his use of 'the integral human'—that is, full realisation of positive possibilities for everyone, as a social goal; and a distinction between pure or ideal norms, which keep open the possibility of integral humanity, and the repetitive norms of 'alienated morality'. Cf. Robert V. Stone and Elizabeth A. Bowman, 'Dialectical Ethics: A First Look at Sartre's Unpublished Lecture Notes', *Social Text Theory/Culture/Ideology* (Winter–Spring 1986) pp. 195–215.

21. Sartre criticises several of the traditional arguments for the existence of God in *The Flies*, albeit in the guise of opinions expressed by fictional characters. Cf. Hazel E. Barnes, *The Literature of Possibility: Humanistic Existentialism* (Lincoln: University of Nebraska Press, 1959) pp. 85–95.

22. Sartre, *Existentialism*, trans. Bernard Frechtman (New York: Philosophical Library, 1947) pp. 48–9.

23. Cf., Régis Jolivet, *Sartre: The Theology of the Absurd* (New York: Newman Press, 1967) and Thomas M. King, *Sartre and the Sacred* (Chicago: University of Chicago Press, 1974).

24. Giving a new interpretation to the phenomenologists' claim that all consciousness is consciousness *of* something, Sartre went on to define being-for-itself as a lack.

25. Sartre, *Being and Nothingness*, trans. Hazel E. Barnes (New York: Washington Square Press, 1972) pp. 101–2.

26. Misunderstanding of this point has resulted in discussions of whether or not the waiter is a legitimate example of bad faith. For example, cf. D. Z. Phillips, 'Bad Faith and Sartre's Waiter', *Philosophy* (January 1981) pp. 23–31, and Richard Zucker, 'Sartre's Waiter', *Kinesis* (Spring 1983) pp. 47–54.

27. Sartre, *Being and Nothingness*, p. 107.

28. The question of whether good faith in Sartrean terms in possible has been the subject of a large number of articles. See under entries 'Authenticity' and 'Bad faith' in Lapointe, *Jean-Paul Sartre and His Critics*, pp. 453–54.

29. Sartre, *Existentialism*, p. 19.

30. Sartre, *Being and Nothingness*, p. 523.

31. Sartre, *Saint Genet, Actor and Martyr*, trans. Bernard Frechtman (New York: New American Library, 1971).

32. Sartre, 'Itinerary of a Thought', *New Left Review* (November-December 1969) p. 45.

33. Critics have disagreed on the question of the unity of Sartre's thought. Mary Warnock finds a sharp cleavage, even an inconsistency, in moving from *Being and Nothingness* to *Critique of Dialectical Reason*. *The Philosophy of Sartre* (London: Hutchinson University Library, 1965). James F. Sheridan, more correctly in my opinion, argues for a natural transition and unity between the two. *Sartre: The Radical Conversion* (Athens: Ohio University Press, 1969). Perhaps the best analysis of Sartre's social theory is the book by Thomas R. Flynn, *Sartre and Marxist Existentialism* (Chicago, University of Chicago Press, 1984).

34. Sartre, *Critique of Dialectical Reason*, p. 124. I have slightly modified Sheridan-Smith's translation in passages quoted from this book.

35. Ibid., p. 34. The human organism is able to interact with the material environment only in so far as it 'makes itself matter'. In need of the inorganic (air, water, food), the human individual takes on an inorganic dimension; in turn the organism imposes on the environment a structure which reflects the organic (Sartre, *Critique of Dialectical Reason*, pp. 21–2). A man makes himself an instrument in order to render external objects instrumental to his needs.

36. Ibid., pp. 178–80.

37. Ibid., pp. 183–84.

38. Ibid., pp. 161–2.
39. Sartre distinguishes between consciousness and the ego. For him, the ego is the opaque product of a translucent, spontaneous consciousness that has organised its experiences into a unified collection of habitual responses and personalised traits. (Sartre would include in it both the 'me' and the 'I'.) The originating consciousness remains, as it were, apart, a controlling principle which may hide behind the structure of the ego but is never identical with it.
40. I suspect that the most frequent occasion for a consciousness confrontation with its fundamental project is the moment when we feel that we grasp the possibility of a thing to be done, a work to be created, and simultaneously recognise that something in us will impede its realisation. Persons who try to break through the limitations of the fundamental project are rare. Sartre was one of them, as attested by his well-known attempt to 'think against himself'.
41. Sartre, by way of illustration, shows how we move from one to the other when we first recognise that an immediate impulse of sexual desire or tenderness is an expression of the emotional state of love. To realise that I love (or hate) someone is to affirm that there is a feeling that remains fixed in me even when I am unaware of it, to expect that it will reappear and show itself as having already been there. It is to make a pledge to myself, to declare that something which I feel is the expression of a permanent state of my being. Cf. *The Transcendence of the Ego*, pp. 61–8.
42. I have discussed this idea in *An Existentialist Ethics*. In a conversation with Simone de Beauvoir in June 1984 she told me that in her opinion this was indeed a correct interpretation of Sartre's position.
43. This is the underlying assumption of *Critique of Dialectical Reason*. Arguments as to whether scarcity is the result of natural limitations or of psychological attitudes are likely to be non-productive inasmuch as we never deal with the physical world except in light of human projects. Obviously the space on earth and the quantity of its natural resources are limited, but just as evidently it is we ourselves who determine what needs have priority as we decide also what use to make of the land, development of alternative forms of energy and so forth. It is this second aspect which allowed Sartre to hope that scarcity will not dominate human history in the future as it has done in the past.
44. Sartre, *Critique of Dialectical Reason*, pp. 256 ff.
45. The study of the formation of the group-in-fusion, its problems and its ultimate disintegration or reification is the subject of most of the second half of *Critique of Dialectical Reason*. Alan Sheridan-Smith translates *groupe-en-fusion* as 'fused group', which is misleading. Strictly speaking, *groupe-en-fusion* refers to the group in process of its formation as it acts non-reflectively. The fused group emerges afterwards as its members reflect on their achieved unity and try to ensure its continued existence. Sartre usually refers to the latter as *le groupe assermenté*, the pledged group—which must be the form quickly assumed if the group is to continue to exist.
46. Sartre, *Critique of Dialectical Reason*, p. 249. Cf. *Being and Nothingness*, p. 550.

47. Sartre, 'Today's Hope: Conversations with Sartre', interviews with Benny Lévy, trans. Lillian Hernandez, George Waterson and Claire Hubert, *Telos* (Summer 1980) pp. 155–81.
48. Sartre, 'Self-Portrait at Seventy', *Life/Situations: Written and Spoken*, trans. Paul Auster and Lydia Davis (New York: Pantheon, 1977) pp. 11–13.
49. Sartre, 'Materialism and Revolution', *Literary and Philosophical Essays* (New York: Criterion Books, 1955) pp. 219–20.
50. Sartre, *Being and Nothingness*, p. 784. Value for Sartre is the synthesis of desire and its fulfillment, a goal towards which we are always reaching but which cannot be attained. The highest value, that which is fundamental to and expressed by every other value, is the synthesis being-in-itself-for-itself—or God. In my opinion Sartre vacillates between the belief that human reality *is* this impossible desire, that we *must* pursue this never-to-be-achieved being, and the view that it is possible to renounce the search. Perhaps the solution may be to say that insofar as this value is inextricable from our making ourselves be, it is indeed inevitable but that bad faith enters in only insofar as one feels that the ideal is achievable or has already been achieved. In other words, one may acknowledge that human reality is a pursuit of being and that the pursuit itself is the creative activity of freedom. The problem is central to Thomas C. Anderson's study of Sartre's ethics, *The Foundation and Structure of Sartrean Ethics* (Lawrence: The Regents Press of Kansas, 1979).
51. This is a principal thesis in Sartre's *Saint Genet, Actor and Martyr*. In this context Sartre shows that he has been influenced by Mircea Eliade.
52. The term is borrowed, of course, from William James, who argues that the problem of ethics is the just and wise balancing of existing claims, psychological and material.
53. Sartre, *Critique of Dialectical Reason*, p. 437.
54. Sartre, *Being and Nothingness*, p. 555.
55. Ibid., p. 531.
56. Sartre, *The War Diaries*, pp. 107–8.
57. Sartre, *Baudelaire*, trans. Martin Turnell (New York: New Directions, 1950) p. 44.
58. This term was first used by Marjorie Grene in the title for her book, *Dreadful Freedom: A Critique of Existentialism* (Chicago: University of Chicago Press, 1948).

# Bibliography

1. Anderson, Thomas C., *The Foundation and Structure of Sartrean Ethics* (Lawrence: The Regents Press of Kansas, 1979).
2. Barnes, Hazel E., *An Existentialist Ethics* (University of Chicago Press, 1978).
3. Beauvoir, Simone de, *La Cérémonie des adieux suivi de Entretiens avec Jean-Paul Sartre*: Août–Septembre 1974 (Paris: Gallimard, 1981). In English, *Adieux. A Farewell to Sartre*, trans. Patrick O'Brian (New York: Pantheon, 1984).
4. Contat, Michel and Michel Rybalka, *Les Ecrits de Sartre. Chronologie. Bibliographie commentée* (Paris: Gallimard, 1970). In English, *The Writings of Jean-Paul Sartre: A Bibliographical Life*, 2 vols. trans. Richard McCleary (Evanston: Northwestern University Press, 1974).
5. Fell, Joseph F., *Heidegger and Sartre: An Essay on Being and Place* (New York: Columbia University Press, 1979).
6. Flynn, Thomas R., *Sartre and Marxist Existentialism* (University of Chicago Press, 1984).
7. Greene, Norman N., *Jean-Paul Sartre: The Existentialist Ethic* (Ann Arbor: University of Michigan Press, 1960).
8. Jeanson, Francis, *Le Problème moral et la pensée de Sartre* (Paris: Editions du Seuil, 1965). In English, *Sartre and the Problem of morality*, trans. Robert J. Stone (Bloomington: Indiana University Press, 1980).
9. Lapointe, François H., with the collaboration of Claire Lapointe, *Jean Paul Sartre and His Critics: An International Bibliography: 1938–1980* (Bowling Green, Ohio: Philosophy Documentation Center, 1981).
10. Sartre, Jean-Paul, *Cahiers pour une morale* (Paris: Gallimard, 1983).
11. ——, *Les Carnets de la drôle de guerre. Novembre 1939–Mars 1940* (Paris: Gallimard, 1983). In English, *The War Diaries of Jean-Paul Sartre: November 1939/March 1940*, trans. Quintin Hoare (New York: Pantheon, 1984).
12. ——, *Critique de la raison dialectique* (précédé de *Question de méthode*), vol. 1, *Théories des ensembles pratiques* (Paris: Gallimard, 1960). In English, *Search for a Method*, trans. Hazel E. Barnes (New York: Alfred A. Knopf, 1963). *Critique of Dialectical Reason*, vol. 1, *Theory of Practical Ensembles*, trans. Alan Sheridan-Smith; Jonathan Ree (ed.) (Atlantic Highlands, N.J.: Humanities Press, 1976).
13. ——, *L'Etre et le néant* (Paris: Gallimard, 1943). In English, *Being and Nothingness*, trans. Hazel E. Barnes (New York: Washington Square Press, 1972).
14. ——, *L'Existentialisme est un humanisme* (Paris: Nagel, 1946). In English, *Existentialism*, trans. Bernard Frechtman (New York: Philosophical Library, 1947).
15. ——, *L'Idiot de la famille* (Paris: Gallimard, vols. 1 and 2, 1971; vol. 3, 1972). In English only part of vol. 1 has been published: *The Family Idiot*, trans. Carol Cosman (University of Chicago Press, 1981).
16. ——, 'Matérialisme et révolution', *Les Temps modernes* (June–July 1946).

In English, 'Materialism and Revolution', *Literary and Philosophical Essays*, trans. Annette Michelson (New York: Criterion Books, 1955).

17. ——, *Saint Genet comédien et martyr* (Paris: Gallimard, 1952). In English, *Saint Genet, Actor and Martyr*, trans. Bernard Frechtman (New York: Braziller, 1963).

18. ——, *Sartre: Un Film*, réalisé par Alexandre Astruc et Michel Contat avec la participation de Simone de Beauvoir, Jacques-Laurent Bost, André Gorz, Jean Pouillon. Texte intégral (Paris: Gallimard, 1977). In English, *Sartre by Himself*, trans. Richard Seaver (New York: Urizen Books, 1978).

19. ——, 'Self-Portrait at Seventy', *Life/Situations: Written and Spoken*, trans. Paul Auster and Lydia Davis (New York: Pantheon, 1977).

20. ——, 'Today's Hope: Conversations with Sartre', interviews with Benny Lévy, trans. Lillian Hernandaz, George Waterson and Claire Hubert, *Telos* (Summer 1980) pp. 155–81. These were originally published in French, the month before Sartre's death, in three parts, in *Le Nouvel Observateur* (March 1980).

21. ——, *La Transcendence de l'ego*, Introduction, notes and appendices by Sylvia Le Bon (Paris: Vrin, 1965). In English, *The Transcendence of the Ego: An Existentialist Theory of Consciousness*, trans. Forrest Williams and Robert Kirkpatrick (New York: Farrar, Straus and Giroux, 1957).

22. Stone, Robert V. and Elizabeth A. Bowman, 'Dialectical Ethics: A First Look at Sartre's Unpublished Lecture Notes', *Social Text: Theory/Culture/Ideology* (Winter-Spring 1968) pp. 195–215.

# 12

# Moore to Stevenson
## *Stephen Darwall*

### THE ANALYTIC TURN

No philosopher had greater impact on Anglo-American moral philosophy in the first half of the 20th century than G. E. Moore. Almost singlehandedly Moore changed even the dominant conception of the subject. What began the century as a synthetic and systematic discipline became, under his influence, a profoundly analytical one.

British moral philosophy of the late 19th century was dominated by two opposing traditions—the hedonistic utilitarianism of John Stuart Mill and Henry Sidgwick and the idealistic ethics of T. H. Green and F. H. Bradley, among others.[1] There were substantial differences between these groups, but they shared a broadly systematic conception of philosophic method.

Sidgwick's *Methods of Ethics*, for example, judiciously weighed the competing systematic strengths of the three main approaches in ethics as he saw them—egoism, utilitarianism, and intuitionism; and ultimately defended utilitarianism on the grounds that it both unifies defensible moral common sense and has its own deep philosophical appeal.[2] Moreover, both Sidgwick and Mill thought that ethics cannot fruitfully be pursued in isolation from other subjects. An acceptable moral philosophy, they thought, must fit with defensible views in political philosophy and economics to form a coherent system of ideas; and both writers actively investigated these connections.

For the idealists ethics was even more clearly a synthetic discipline. Reality itself, they believed, consists only of what can coherently be related in thought and experience. So ethical value and duty must also be related to mind, in this case to the willing self, and placed within a coherent metaphysical system. Ethics was part, therefore, of a whole systematic philosophy.

It was against this background that Moore's *Principia Ethica* appeared like a bolt in 1903. The book's first words, a simple commonplace from Bishop Butler which Moore placed facing the title page, were the most simple and direct challenge to idealism imaginable. The idealists had held that a thing's nature is determined by its relations to everything else. But Moore's motto was: 'Everything is what it is and not another thing'. These few words, though not Moore's own, reveal much of the style, method and even substance of *Principia*.

Moore's own first sentence was a more general challenge to the philosophical methods then current. 'It appears to me', he wrote, 'that in Ethics, as in all other philosophical studies, the difficulties and disagreements, of which its history is full, are mainly due to a very simple cause: namely to the attempt to answer questions, without first discovering precisely *what* question it is which you desire to answer.'[3] Ethics must begin with *analysis* before it can hope to be synthetic. Its first task is to identify and analyze the fundamental questions the discipline seeks to answer before trying to answer them.

It is difficult to overestimate the effect of this 'analytic turn'. Moore's methods took a while to catch on, but when they did they absolutely revolutionised the subject and made analytic ethics the dominant approach in Anglo-American moral philosophy through mid-century.

I shall discuss only three figures of this period in any detail. It is essential, of course, to begin with Moore. In addition to him I have chosen to focus on the two others who seem to have had the greatest lasting influence—W. D. Ross and Charles Stevenson.[4]

Ross was much influenced by Moore in general method, but ended up defending a radically different normative view. Where Moore was a consequentialist, holding that an act's being right or wrong depends only on the goodness of its consequences, Ross was a deontologist; he believed that many factors other than consequences are relevant to what a person should do.

The debate between consequentialists and deontologists has been a longstanding one in moral philosophy, but its terms have shifted in different periods. What was particularly interesting about the exchange between Ross and Moore was its location in a philosophical framework determined largely by Moore's *Principia*.

Stevenson was also much influenced by Moore. Indeed it could be argued that Stevenson's main project simply would not have been possible before *Principia*. Stevenson's interest in moral philosophy was not really in normative or substantive ethical theory at all. He was not concerned to advance any substantive views about what is good or right. What interested him was the question Moore had carefully distinguished and declared more fundamental than any substantive ethical question: How are the fundamental concepts of ethics themselves to be understood?

Stevenson shared Moore's belief that fundamental ethical terms cannot be analyzed in any way that makes ethical propositions identical to those of natural or social science, theology or metaphysics. The claim that something is good is different from the assertion that it is desired, pleasurable, loved by God or fully real. But where Moore had explained this by claiming, somewhat mysteriously, that goodness is a simple, unanalyzable, but 'nonnatural' property, Stevenson, as an empiricist, could not agree. He could see no grounds for supposing that there *are* any real properties distinct from those that can be studied by the natural and social sciences. His project, consequently, was to show how ethical terms and concepts can be irreducible, as Moore had thought, without being committed to Moore's metaphysics. And his solution was an elaborate and subtle theory of the emotive meaning of ethical language. Ethical terms are used not to ascribe any real property to things but to express the speaker's attitude and to influence the attitudes of others.

## G. E. MOORE AND ANALYTIC CONSEQUENTIALISM

What is initially most striking about Moore's approach to ethics, and what most impressed his contemporaries, were three things: first, his conception of the discipline as attempting to answer certain fundamental *questions*; second, his commitment to clarity in formulating these questions; and, third, his conviction that before either of these first two tasks could be pursued fundamental terms must be defined. Philosophers before Moore had taken an analytic approach to some extent or other, but none so resolutely, with such impressive results, and with so much influence as Moore. After Moore the analysis of fundamental ethical concepts came to be seen as a distinct area within moral philosophy, called metaethics, and for much of this century it was the dominant area.

What led Moore to approach ethics in this analytical and clarificatory way? Indeed, what led Moore to think of ethics as primarily concerned with answering certain *questions*? For that, after all, was his point of departure. We know Moore's explicit philosophical motives for analyzing ethical questions and concepts. He cites two main ones: only after analysis can it be clearly understood what ethical convictions are about or how to evaluate their truth and grounds.

But this simply raises a further historical question. What led Moore to appreciate these philosophical motives? Why was this approach salient for him in a way that it had not been for earlier writers? What was it about the concrete intellectual climate in which Moore philosophised that led him to the analytic method?

Surely part of the answer must be Moore's sense of the state of moral philosophy as he found it. As we shall see, he thought that both idealists and hedonistic utilitarians were seriously confused about fundamentals. Before headway could be made clarity had to be reached on the questions they were attempting to answer. But how was Moore in a position to render this diagnosis?

A very important part of Moore's intellectual development as an undergraduate at Cambridge resulted from his participation in a secret society known as the Apostles, a small, exclusive group of undergraduates who met regularly for lively and intense discussion of philosophical and social issues.[5] Some of England's most impressive minds of the late 19th and early 20th century belonged. Moore was introduced into the group by Bertrand Russell, and later men of such stature as J. M. Keynes, G. H. Hardy and Ludwig Wittgenstein were to join. It was within this group that Moore first really began to philosophise.

He was later to write:

I do not think that the world or the sciences would ever have suggested to me any philosophical problems. What has suggested philosophical problems to me is things which other philosophers have said . . .[6]

It is not unlikely that philosophical discussion within the Apostles and with Russell, gave Moore his initial stimulus to philosophy. Moreover, the Apostles' meetings regularly concerned the discussion of a specific *question*. For example, when Moore was inducted on 7 February 1894, the evening's question was: 'What ought Cambridge to give?' (What is the purpose of a Cambridge education?) Ordinarily, someone would present a paper taking a stand on the question, and then discussion would ensue, followed by a vote. Moore's first paper to the group, 'What end?', concerned what is good in itself.

We might well imagine, then, that Moore's propensity for concentrating on basic questions of ethics resulted to some extent from his participation in the Apostles.

But what about Moore's extraordinary commitment to clarification and analysis? Moore wrote in his autobiography that what interested him about what other philosophers had to say was:

> first, the problem of trying to get really clear as to what on earth a given philosopher *meant* by something which he said.[7]

This desire for clarity seems to be something Moore genuinely brought with him to the Apostles, and it was no small part of the initial charm and appeal he had for them, as he was to have later for so many other British intellectuals, especially the Bloomsbury group before World War I. He seems to have possessed from youth an ingenuous intellectual honesty and passion that would rest with nothing that was at all unclear. But it was apparently the meetings of the Apostles that provided Moore with the initial impetus for the project that would bear its first fruit in *Principia*: clarifying the fundamental questions of ethics.

Moore held that ethics attempts to answer two distinct questions: first, 'what kinds of things ought to exist for their own sakes?' (or, as he also put it, what is 'good in itself or has intrinsic value?'), and, second, 'What kinds of actions ought we to perform?' (*PE*, viii). Of these two, Moore believed the former to be more fundamental. Indeed, in *Principia* he held that the latter question, concerning right and wrong, really asks no more than which acts will actually bring about the most intrinsic value. Later he was to give up this 'analytical consequentialism', and maintain that while 'right' does not *mean* productive of the best consequences, nonetheless it *is* always right to do whatever will promote the most intrinsic value.[8] Moore never wavered from the position that the most important substantive question of ethics is: What is good in itself? What has intrinsic value?

Still, he thought, there is a question that is even more fundamental for ethics than this substantive one. And that concerns the nature of intrinsic goodness itself. Before we can assess attempted answers to the question of what is good, or even know what could count as evidence for and against them, we must first know what the question itself is *about*. So Moore argued that the issue of 'how "good" is to be defined, is the most fundamental question in all Ethics' (*PE*, 5).

Now it is important to appreciate that what Moore meant by 'definition' was a matter not of lexicography, but of elucidating the nature of *the property* to which 'good' refers. Moore thought it self-evident that when we wonder whether something is good we are wondering whether it has a specific property. And so the most fundamental question concerns the nature of that property: what is intrinsic value?

Moore's first answer, in *Principia*, may seem unlikely to provide much help in moral philosophy; for his thesis was that 'good' refers to a property that is simple and unanalyzable, one that can be given no contentful description at all. The property of goodness cannot be further analyzed. Nonetheless, Moore thought his discovery very powerful. Admittedly, it could not lead directly to knowledge of what is good, but it could demonstrate various proposed paths to that knowledge to be blind alleys.

The field of ethics was littered, Moore held, with attempts to argue for some substantive theory of good or other on the grounds that goodness simply *is* whatever property the theory identified as characteristic of what is good. So hedonists, Moore charged, had tended to argue that pleasure is the only intrinsic good on the grounds that 'good' simply means pleasurable, that being pleasurable is simply what it *is* to be good. But 'good' means no such thing. Indeed, Moore said, there is *nothing* contentful that it means. 'Whenever [a person] thinks of "intrinsic value" or "intrinsic worth," or says that a thing "ought to exist." he has before his mind the unique object—the unique property of things—which I mean by "good." ' (*PE*, 17.) That property is not identical with any of the properties with which philosophers have sought to identify it—not with being desired, nor being desired when fully informed, nor being desired by God, nor tending to promote survival, nor anything else. 'Everything is what it is and not another thing.'

Ethics, as a discipline, is concerned with 'the *only* simple object of thought which is peculiar to' it—the idea of intrinsic value (*PE*, 5). And since intrinsic goodness is irreducible, it follows that ethics is irreducible to any other subject—not to any of the sciences, nor to metaphysics, nor to theology.

Moore thought it followed from the unanalyzability of the concept of goodness that no evidence or reasons can be given for any proposition of intrinsic value at all. Strictly speaking, a proposition of, say, psychology can provide no evidence whatsoever for any proposition about what is intrinsically good. As a foundationalist, Moore thought that a proposition can only be evident in one of two ways: either it must be self-evident, or it must be deducible from some other self-evident proposition. If a property is complex and can be analyzed into simple parts, then its existence follows from the existence of the simples that form the complex. Moore gives the idea of a horse as an example: 'hoofed quadruped of the genus Equus'. From the propositions that x is a quadruped, x is hoofed, and so on, we can deduce that x is a horse. But since goodness is a simple property, there are no such propositions from which it can be deduced. A proposition about the good can be known, consequently, only if it is self-evident.[9]

But why was Moore so confident that goodness is not identical with any of the properties with which other philosophers had sought to identify it? Of course, everything is what it is and not another thing. But why such confidence that being good and, for instance being the object of informed desire are two things rather than one?

Given Moore's methodological emphasis on questions, it is perhaps fitting that his most powerful argument is known as the 'open question argument'. No definition can settle a question of ethics since 'whatever definition be offered, it may be always asked, with significance, of the complex so defined, whether it is itself good' (*PE*, 15). So, suppose someone suggests that goodness is identical to the property of being the object of informed desire. That this proposed identification cannot be correct, Moore argued, follows from the fact that the question, Is what we desire when informed good?, does not lack significance, though it would have to if 'good' and 'what we desire when informed' meant the same thing. Consider: since the word 'bachelor' means never married male adult, there is no significant question, Are never married male adults bachelors? But this is not the case with 'good'. It follows, Moore thought, that the fundamental concept of ethics, goodness, is indefinable.[10]

Moore dubbed the misidentification of goodness with any other property or set of properties the 'naturalistic fallacy'. But this term is misleading for two reasons. It is not really a fallacy, since strictly speaking it involves no mistaken inference, but rather a confusion of two distinct properties with each other.[11] Nor is what Moore meant to refer to essentially concerned with what is natural as opposed, say, to what is supernatural. Metaphysical idealists no less than naturalistically inclined hedonistic utilitarians had, he thought, made the same fundamental mistake of thinking that their respective ethical positions could be based on definitions. The naturalistic fallacy, he wrote, 'is to be met with in almost every book on Ethics' (*PE*, 14). So Moore writes of the idealists:

> The fact that the metaphysical writers who, like Green, attempt to *base* Ethics on Volition, do not even attempt this independent investigation [of whether something is good independent of its being the object of transcendental will], shews that they start from the false assumption that goodness is *identical* with being willed, and hence that their ethical reasonings have no value whatsoever. (*PE*, xxi)

The initial thrust of Moore's investigation into 'the most fundamental question in all Ethics' was, therefore, critical. With a single insight he thought himself in a position to discredit every attempt to provide some basis for a substantive ethical view. The worth of analytic ethics was thereby apparent. Failure to be analytical, to distinguish carefully between questions and assertions of different sorts, led to the naturalistic fallacy.[12]

This insistence on distinguishing, as logically independent, questions about ethical notions from substantive ethical questions, and on concentrating on the former as fundamental, set the pattern for analytic ethics in the 20th century.[13] But why did *Principia* have this influence? After all, Moore was not the first philosopher to attend to the meaning of ethical terms, nor to claim a fundamental ethical concept irreducible, nor even to identify the mistake he called the naturalistic fallacy. Actually, Sidgwick had already done both in *The Methods of Ethics*.[14]

One explanation of the analytic influence of *Principia* must surely be that Moore brought analysis onto centre stage and that he was able to persuade many of his readers that failure to be sufficiently analytical had brought both of the major moral philosophical traditions of his time, metaphysical idealism and naturalistic ethics, to ruin. Moore's analysis could not show that the substantive ethical views propounded by these traditions were false, but he was remarkably successful at persuading his readers that their proponents' arguments had no tendency to show them true and that moral philosophers must be analytical before they could hope to discover substantial ethical truth.

A second explanation is that *Principia* was only a part of a more general attack that Moore waged against idealism. In the same year

that *Principia* appeared, 1903, Moore published 'The Refutation of
Idealism'. There he accused idealist metaphysics and epistemology
of substantially the same fundamental confusion as the naturalistic
fallacy: 'the contradiction involved in both distinguishing and identifying the *object* and the *act* of Thought, "truth" itself and its supposed *criterion*'.[15] In epistemology and metaphysics, as in ethics, the
idealists failed fully to appreciate Butler's dictum. The act of thought
is one thing, its object is another.

Because idealism treated ethics as part of a coherent metaphysical
system, it could only be refuted convincingly in explicitly metaphysical terms. By engaging the idealists in these terms Moore,
together with Russell, helped to usher in a new period of metaphysical realism in England at the turn of the century.

To this point we have considered Moore's critical and methodological views. But what of his own positive views about the
nature of intrinsic value, about what has intrinsical value, and about
right conduct? These have been less influential, but they are very
interesting and important in their own right.

Some of Moore's most difficult and penetrating thought concerned
intrinsic value.[16] We already know that he believed the notion of
intrinsic value to be simple and unanalyzable and that he thought it
the fundamental idea of ethics. We know, moreover, that he held
intrinsic value not to be a 'natural' property, but, as he said, a non-
natural' quality. But what did he *mean* by these latter claims?

Part of what Moore meant was simply that intrinsic value was not
part of 'the subject-matter of the natural sciences and . . . psychology'
(*PE*, 40). But this cannot have been the whole of his idea. If it were,
goodness might be a supernatural property like 'commanded by
God' and be non-natural in his sense. But the very same thing that
led Moore to reject any identification of goodness with a natural
property led him also to reject any identification with such a supernatural property. To grasp his idea we must look deeper.

In particular, we must view *Principia* in the light of his later essay,
'The Conception of Intrinsic Value', and of his even later remarks on
the relation between these two works.[17] Moore was to write in 1942
that in calling goodness a non-natural property in 1903 he had been
attempting to say the very same thing that he came to express in
1922 by the mysterious, but ultimately telling, statement that while
intrinsic goodness is not an intrinsic property of anything, it is nonetheless a property that depends entirely on the intrinsic properties
of that to which it applies. Whether something is intrinsically good

depends solely on its intrinsic nature, otherwise the sort of good-ness, it has, if any, is not *intrinsic* goodness. Nonetheless, Moore thought that intrinsic goodness itself, though a property, was not among a thing's intrinsic properties. And it was to these latter properties that Moore had meant to refer as natural properties. If we are to credit Moore's later remarks, we apparently must conclude that in calling goodness a non-natural property, he meant to say that goodness is not part of the intrinsic nature of what is intrinsically good, though it is dependent on nothing other than that thing's intrinsic nature.

Now this is a deeply suggestive, but also a deeply puzzling view. The idea that intrinsic goodness depends solely on the intrinsic nature of what has it, does seem to suggest that intrinsic goodness cannot be an intrinsic property in the same sense. When pressed on the question of what makes a property an intrinsic property of some-thing, Moore responded that intrinsic properties 'seem to *describe* the intrinsic nature of what possesses them in a sense in which predicates of value never do'.[18]

Once we understand what intrinsic value is it is but a short step to Moore's famous 'isolation test' for determining what has it: 'it is necessary to consider what things are such that, if they existed *by themselves*, in absolute isolation, we should yet judge their existence to be good' (*PE*, 187). Isolating a thing in thought is necessary to assess whether it has value simply by virtue of what it intrinsically is.

Moore's own views about what actually has intrinsic value had decidedly less impact on academic moral philosophy in the first half of the 20th century than it did on the young British intellectuals who came to comprise the Bloomsbury Group—Virginia and Leonard Woolf, Clive Bell and J. M. Keynes, among others. When Keynes wrote that his reading of *Principia* 'was exciting, exhilarating, the beginning of a renaissance, the opening of a new heaven on a new earth', it was to Moore's chapter on 'The Ideal' that he referred.[19] But if this chapter had less of an impact on academic philosophers, that was because, ironically, *Principia* itself had shifted their focus almost entirely to what they called metaethics—the systematic study of fundamental ethical concepts.

One thing that did make an impact, however, was Moore's claim that many intrinsically valuable wholes have a value that cannot be analyzed into parts in such a way that the value of the whole is equal to the sum of the values of its parts. The Principle of Organic Unities, as it came to be known, played a very interesting role in Moore's overall position. If there was a significant residue of idealistic philosophy in Moore's ethics it was this. While Moore was staunchly analytic in philosophical method, and in insisting on the separation between substantive and metaethics, his substantive ethical views were themselves synthetic.

There are many valuable whole states of affairs, Moore believed, whose value is organic. In fact, the mistaken assumption that the intrinsic value of wholes can be analyzed into the values of their parts had, he thought, misled earlier thinkers, including Sidgwick, into fallaciously espousing hedonism; from the possibly true belief that every valuable state of affairs essentially involves pleasurable feeling, they concluded invalidly that a part of that whole, pleasurable feeling, is the only thing that is intrinsically valuable. When it is not simply based on the naturalistic fallacy, hedonism tends to be based on ignoring the principle of organic unities, or so Moore thought.

Moore's own view was that 'by far the most valuable things, which we know or can imagine, are certain states of consciousness, which may be roughly described as the pleasures of human intercourse and the enjoyment of beautiful objects' (*PE*, 188). In each case, what is valuable is an organic whole. For example, aesthetic enjoyment of genuine beauty is much more valuable, he thought, than the pleasure considered independently of whether its object really is beautiful.

'The pleasures of human intercourse and the enjoyment of beautiful objects.' These are things that have a value, simple in themselves, depending just on their nature and nothing else in the world. It was talk like this that was what inspired Bloomsbury.[20] Keynes was later to write that part of its appeal for him in his youth was its unworldly, timeless, almost religious quality. What made life worth living were certain contemplative states of consciousness in which time stood still and the world was transcended, except, of course, for its beauty and friendship.

Moreover, Moore argued that these truths about intrinsic value are:

> the ultimate and fundamental truth of Moral Philosophy. That it is only for the sake of these things—in order that as much of them as possible may at some time exist—that any one can be justified in performing any public or private duty (*PE*, 189)

This is heady stuff. It is hard to imagine a thought more likely to have seemed liberating to intellectually and aesthetically minded British upper class youth anxious to throw off the yoke of Victorian morality.

Consequentialism, the doctrine that what a person should do depends entirely on the consequences of alternative actions, or on the consequences of social acceptance of a rule or convention governing action, has generally been advanced as a reforming, if not radical, position. But there is an important difference between Moore's 'ideal utilitarianism' and the utilitarianism of the reforming 19th-century British moral and political philosophers such as Bentham, Mill and Sidgwick.

The primary thrust of the latter writers was political, social and economic. They were passionately concerned about such issues as freedom of speech and thought, universal education and the political and social position of women. And they used their utilitarianism as a basis to advance a liberal political programme. Moore's consequentialism lacked this political orientation, and his ideal did not inspire followers to social and political efforts. Granted, if personal affection and aesthetic enjoyment are intrinsically good, then the more the better. But it is quite unclear what political agenda would lead to that. It is more likely that, like the young intellectuals of Bloomsbury, adherents of this ideal will repair to their drawing rooms or other appropriate quarters.

The irony is that Moore's own views about public and private duty were pretty conventional and conservative. That he thought the objectively right act in any circumstance always to be the one that actually produces the greatest good, including his favoured intrinsic values, is true enough. But he also thought that we are almost never in a position to know what the long run consequences of any particular act will be. 'The individual', he concluded, 'can therefore be confidently recommended *always* to conform to rules which are both generally useful and generally practised' (*PE*, 164). This part of Moore's view, Keynes writes, he and his contemporaries simply ignored.[21]

Part of Moore's attraction for Bloomsbury and the Apostles was, of course, personal. His ingenuousness, intellectual passion and honesty were like a magnet to Keynes and his friends before the Great War. But as the war years came, worldly questions of war and peace, and whether to fight if called, could no longer be avoided. Bloomsbury and the Apostles were absorbed with them while Moore himself waffled until, without much passion, he took a moderate position with which he was more or less comfortable: he was opposed to the war, but he was not a pacifist and would fight if called up.

During this period, as his ideas seemed less compelling and relevant to Bloomsbury, so also was Moore growing out of touch with them personally. Moore married in 1916 (at the age of 43) and began a family. The special relationship with Bloomsbury was dead, an era ended.

Moore's impact on academic moral philosophy, however, was still in an early stage. Two strands of that influence are particularly notable. The deontological intuitionists, including W. D. Ross and H. A. Prichard, agreed with Moore that fundamental moral concepts are irreducible. And like Moore, they held that propositions involving such concepts can be known only if self-evident, and that there are indeed self-evident ethical propositions. They rejected, however, Moore's thesis that intrinsic goodness is the single fundamental concept of ethics, and they rejected the consequentialism it entailed. Propositions about moral duty are equally irreducible, and, they believed, some are equally self-evident.

The other strand, non-cognitivism of the sort typified by Stevenson, also agreed with Moore about the irreducibility of ethical concepts, and with his view that, were there any truths about ethics to be known, they would have to concern a sort of metaphysical property not subject to empirical investigation and cognisable only through direct intuition. But because they believed no such property or cognitive faculty to exist, and that the peculiar features of ethical concepts to which Moore had pointed are better explained by other facts concerning their actual *use*, the non-cognitivists held that there are no ethical facts to be known.

## ROSS AND DEONTOLOGICAL INTUITIONISM

Moore had written in *Principia* that while intrinsic goodness is an irreducible property of states of affairs, rightness and wrongness are not irreducible properties of conduct. An act's being the right thing to do in a particular circumstance *just is* its producing intrinsically better consequences than anything else that could be done.

This is a view that assaulted the common sense of Moore's day. If Moore was correct, any act deplored by common sense, any lie, betrayal, or broken promise, would be right so long as its consequences were better on balance. As we have seen, Moore himself was not inclined to draw very radical practical conclusions from his consequentialist views. His practical advice was, at least often, to cleave to conventional morality, despite its decidedly non-consequentialist prohibitions. Still, according to his *theory* the common sense view that certain things are wrong to do even if they would have better consequences, is not only false, but fundamentally confused, even unintelligible. If 'right' means productive of the best consequences, then it is *self-contradictory* to assert that it is sometimes wrong to do what would have the best consequences.

Common sense morality had its defender in W. D. Ross. In 1930 Ross published *The Right and the Good* in which he sharply attacked Moore's analytic consequentialism. Ross recalled Moore's own argument against any definition of 'good'. Moore had pointed out, Ross wrote, that if 'good' simply *meant* pleasant, for example, 'it would not be intelligible that the proposition "the good is just the pleasant" should have been maintained on the one hand, and denied on the other, with so much fervour; for we do not fight for or against analytic propositions; we take them for granted'.[22] Definitions lack the normative force of genuine ethical propositions.

But if this is so, Ross argued, and if *right* is also a genuine ethical notion, '[m]ust not the same claim be made about the statement "being right means being an act productive of the greatest good producible in the circumstances"?' (*RG*, 8); that is, if that definitional statement is true, then 'it is *right* to do what will produce the greatest good' cannot express a substantive ethical proposition. So Ross concluded that being right or wrong must be a property of acts that is distinct from the property of having or not having the best consequences. By using Moore's own analytic method he was able to argue against Moore that rightness, like goodness, is irreducible. To think otherwise, Ross might have said, is to commit a 'consequentialist fallacy'.

For the Moore of *Principia*, however, no ethical property existed that cannot be analyzed into the intrinsic goodness of states of affairs, if we include the performance of acts within the latter. And so, he might have replied to this argument that there is indeed no substantive ethical proposition that we ought to do what will have the best consequences; that *is* a mere tautology.

But this was not a position with which Moore could rest comfortably, and, as Ross noted, he retracted it in his *Ethics* in 1912. In the later book he agreed that it is not a 'mere tautology to say that it is always our duty to do what will have the best possible consequences'.[23] Still, even if it is granted that being right is not the *same thing* as producing the best consequences, it may still be true that what *makes* an act the right thing to do is always, and only, that it will produce the best consequences. And this *is* a view that Moore definitely wanted to maintain and Ross to deny. In Ross's view, Moore had put forward as appealing a consequentialist theory of moral duty as could be formulated. He called it 'the culmination of all the attempts to base rightness on productivity of some result' (*RG* 16). Nonetheless, Ross argued, deep problems beset any theory of that sort.

One problem, as Ross saw it, is that:

> the theory of Professor Moore seems to simplify unduly our relations to our fellows. It says, in effect, that the only morally significant relation in which my neighbours stand to me is that of being possible beneficiaries by my action. They do stand in this relation to me, and this relation is morally significant. But they may also stand to me in the relation of promisee to promiser, of creditor to debtor, of wife to husband, of child to parent, of friend to friend, of fellow countryman to fellow countryman, and the like. (*RG*, 19)

Common sense morality, of early 20th-century middle class Britain at any rate, was at least partly deontological. As against consequentialism, it held that what a person ought to do depends on factors other than the good results his acts might bring about. In particular, it held that a person has different obligations to others in virtue of the different relations in which he/she stands to them. So, for example, a parent might have a special obligation to educate her child as opposed to someone else's.

In defending common sense deontology against a revisionist and, as he saw it, overly simple consequentialism, Ross was entering into a debate that had been central in British moral philosophy since the 18th century. This time, however, the terms of the debate between deontology and consequentialism were set by Moore's *Principia*. While Moore had argued that common sense morality often deserved respect, it was only on the grounds of our ignorance about the potential consequences of our acts. Ross thought, however, that common sense morality could be defended directly, that personal and private duties do not depend on their furthering any ideal state, whether Moore's favoured ideal or anyone else's.

It is important to be careful here, though. Since Moore's ideal includes personal affection and friendship, it is not entirely correct to say that on his view a person's relation to others makes no difference to how he should act towards them. If one is in a position to confer a benefit on only one of A and B, it would not be morally irrelevant on Moore's view that A was a friend and B was not. Benefiting A would have an intrinsically valuable consequence that benefiting B would probably not—the advancing of a friendship.

Similarly, a consequentialist such as Moore *could* in principle hold that promise-keeping, truth-telling, in short, that keeping each of the traditional duties of common sense morality, has intrinsic value. Of course, most consequentialists would not say this. They would hold that these acts can be recommended only on the basis of their consequences, not including the act itself. Nonetheless, this is a possible position for a consequentialist to take. And a consequentialist certainly need not hold that the only morally significant relation in which others stand to the moral agent is that 'of being potential beneficiaries'. Only a 'nonideal' utilitarian must believe that.

Nonetheless, there is a deeper sort of criticism that Ross wanted to make of sophisticated consequentialisms such as Moore's. The problem with these views is that they do not bring in relationship-to-the-agent in the fundamental way that it seems to be morally relevant. What matters morally, Ross held, is not simply whether one's acts will promote intrinsically valuable states, even if these are thought to include the fulfillment of traditional duties. It also matters whether one's acts will keep the promises that *one* has made, keep faith with the friends who depend on *one*, and so on.

Moorean consequentialism is an example of what C. D. Broad called 'neutralism' in ethics, and what more recent writers have called, perhaps more descriptively, *agent-neutralism*.[24] Consequentialisms of either the utilitarian or more sophisticated Moorean variety are agent-neutral in the sense that they hold that any fact regarding *the agent* as such is fundamentally irrelevant to whether his/her acts are right or wrong. Considerations about the agent's position are, of course, relevant to determining what he/she is in a position to do, but they are not relevant to determining what states of affairs he/she should bring about were he/she in a position to do so.

An example may be helpful. Jones has made a promise to Smith to meet him at the station. Even if we suppose keeping a promise to have value in itself, that meeting Smith at the station would keep *his* promise is simply irrelevant to which act of Jones's would produce the most value. Of course, keeping his promise will usually be the only thing that Jones can do to bring about a promise-keeping. But it might not be. It is theoretically possible that Jones be faced with a choice between keeping his promise to Smith or breaking it but thereby bringing about a similarly valuable promise-keeping by someone else. According to an agent-neutral consequentialism, that the first act would be a keeping, and the second a breaking, of *his* promise is not morally relevant to what Jones should do.

Ross put his thesis that different relations the agent stands in to others have direct moral relevance to what he should do by saying that 'each of these relations is the foundation of a *prima facie* duty, which is more or less incumbent on me according to the circumstances of the case' (*RG*, 19).[25] If A is my child and B is not, then I have a *prima facie* duty to provide for A's well-being that I do not have to provide for B's (though I have some *prima facie* duty to promote any person's well-being). And the *prima facie* duty of parents with respect to their children is not a duty to promote the intrinsic value of parents providing for children. That would give me as much reason to promote another parent's provision for her children as I have to promote my providing for mine. It is a *prima facie* duty to provide for *my* child. ' "Right" ', Ross wrote, 'does not stand for a form of value at all' (*RG*, 122).

Ross's general picture was roughly this. Consider a specific act X, in certain circumstances, of which we want to know, is there a moral duty to do it? Or would doing it be wrong? Or neither? Various features of X will be relevant to answering these questions. Some features will be such that were they the only feature of X, there would be a duty to do it. Here Ross said that there exists a *prima facie* duty to perform acts with that feature. Other features are such that were they the only feature of X, it would be wrong to do X. In such a case, Ross said that there is a *prima facie* duty not to perform acts with such a feature. Whether X is right or wrong on balance depends on the relative stringency of the various right-making and wrong-making features of it. In his terms, it depends on the relative 'incumbency' of the various *prima facie* duties to perform and not to perform the act.

To illustrate: suppose Jones promises Smith to do X. This feature of X, that it would keep his promise to Smith, is morally relevant to whether Jones should do X, since were it the only feature of X, then X would be something he ought morally to do. Jones has a *prima facie* duty, consequently, to do X. There may, however, be other characteristics of X that are also morally relevant. Perhaps if Jones does X then he will be unable to aid some people who are in need. Or perhaps, he will have to lie. Of each of these further features it is true that were it the only feature of X then it would be wrong for Jones to do X. So each would, if it existed, create a *prima facie* duty for Jones not to do X. Whether X is the right thing for Jones to do in a given circumstance, all things considered, depends on the relative weight of the morally relevant features of X. It depends on the relative incumbency of the *prima facie* duties that exist for Jones to do and not to do X.

According to Moorean consequentialism everyone has *prima facie* duties to promote *the same* states of affairs, those that have intrinsic value, and to prevent the same states of affairs, those that have intrinsic disvalue. As against this, Ross argued that the agent's *own* promises, incurred obligations of gratitude and compensation, loyalties, and so on, directly create *prima facie* obligations *for him/her* that they simply do not create for others.

As we have noted, Ross's view was closer to the moral common sense of his day, indeed of ours, than was Moore's. And, Ross argued, that is positive evidence for it. In describing what he called 'the time-honoured method of ethics' he wrote:

my starting point [is] the existence of what is commonly called the moral consciousness; and by this I mean the existence of a large body of beliefs and convictions to the effect that there are certain kinds of acts that ought to be done.[26]

The job of the substantive ethical theorist is

to compare [convictions] with each other, and to study them in themselves, with a view to seeing which best survive such examination, and which must be rejected either because in themselves they are ill-grounded, or because they contradict other convictions that are better grounded; and to clear up, so far as we can, ambiguities that lurk in them.[27]

There is, then, a body of data to which ethical theory is responsible in roughly the same way that scientific theory is responsible to observations:

the moral convictions of thoughtful and well-educated people are the data of ethics just as sense-perceptions are the data of a natural science. (*RG*, 41)

The most coherent systematisation of common sense morality, Ross argued, is not a consequentialist theory, but a deontological theory that posits a plurality of *prima facie* duties that include: (1) duties of fidelity to promise and contract; (2) duties of reparation; (3) duties of gratitude; (4) duties of justice; (5) duties of beneficence; (6) duties of self-improvement; and (7) duties of non-maleficence. Moreover, while rough generalisations can be made about the relative incumbency of *prima facie* duties, for example, that it is more incumbent not to harm than to benefit, there are no hard and fast rules. So while we can know what our *prima facie* duties are in a particular instance, we generally cannot know with certainty which is most incumbent, what would be right on balance. Nor can ethics provide any certain standards here; that is beyond its competence. Ross was in the position, then, of defending common sense morality against Moore's consequentialism on the grounds that Moore's theory oversimplified the complexity that reflection on common moral convictions reveals.

Now any theory such as Ross's that accepts a *plurality* of fundamental right- and wrong-making characteristics, a *list* of *prima facie* duties, without any further explanation of that list, risks the charge of being unmotivated and unsystematic. Ross could say he had the support of common moral conviction for his list, but it could still be complained that his theory gave no deeper *explanation* of the list, of why there is, for example, a *prima facie* duty to provide for one's children. It only asserted these duties. Consequentialists, on the other hand, had always been able to argue that they at least had an explanation of why we should follow common sense morality when we should, that the conventions often have good consequences.

Ross was able to reply to these objections, however, that consequentialists such as Moore were in a poor position to make them. For they were pluralists about intrinsic goodness. Moore denied, after all, that there is any deeper unifying explanation of why what has intrinsic value has it, or why one thing is more intrinsically valuable than another.

Of course, monistic consequentialists, such as the hedonistic utilitarians, could claim to give a single explanation of what has intrinsic value and, consequently, of what acts are right. Whatever has intrinsic value involves pleasure, and whatever conduct is right, is so in virtue of maximising total net pleasure. The problem with these views, from the point of view of both Moore and Ross, however, was that they were simply implausible. Moore's passion for analysis led him to reject any identification of intrinsic value with, for example, pleasure, or any simple theory of the good such as hedonism. And Ross turned this same method to his own purposes, to argue, first, that rightness is irreducible to expedience, and second, that any simple theory of the right, such as consequentialism, must also be rejected. When we analyze the moral consciousness of common sense we see that our complex relations to others, and our individual histories inform what we should do in a way that an agent-neutral consequentialism cannot capture. In effect, Ross was able to turn Moore's own methods against him and in the defence of common sense morality.

## STEVENSON AND NON-COGNITIVISM

Although Moore and Ross disagreed radically about many things, there were also important points of agreement between them. Both were moral realists. Both thought that the fundamental terms of ethics refer to real properties of things and that ethical propositions are made true or false by virtue of whether a given act or state of affairs actually has the relevant property.

Moreover, both Ross and Moore believed that fundamental ethical propositions, could be known directly through what they called intuition. Both were foundationalists in moral epistemology; they believed that ethical convictions are justified if and only if they are self-evident or deducible from others that are. Ross likened ethical insight to the sort of insight a mathematician might have into the truth of mathematical axioms. He was careful to insist, however, that only propositions about *prima facie* duty can be evident in this way, and not propositions about what it is right to do, all things considered.

Intuitionism in moral epistemology and an associated non-naturalistic moral realism are only likely to appear plausible options in moral philosophy so long as two conditions hold. First, the surrounding philosophical environment must be more or less hospitable to metaphysics: to the belief that there are real properties and states of affairs that are distinct from the properties and states we can experience and the natural sciences can study. Second, there must be some hope of eventual agreement in ethical intuition and insight, at least among those who are likely to be credited with it. If ethical disagreements are sufficiently deep and unresolvable and if neither one side nor the other can make a creditable claim to better insight, then it will begin to be doubted that there is an objective truth to be seen.

Both conditions increasingly failed to hold in the first half of the 20th century. Partly, in fact, because of the initial analytic impetus of Moore and Russell, Anglo-American philosophy became more naturalist and empiricist. The required metaphysical underpinnings of both consequentialist and deontological intuitionism, consequently, seemed less plausible. But equally important was the increasing erosion of ethical consensus. Even as Ross defended it, common sense morality was undergoing profound changes.[28] The carnage of World War I, 'the seminal catastrophe of this century', as George Kennan has called it, had already shaken confidence in earlier values of patriotism and courage. And consensus about sexual *mores*, the rights of property, and social responsibility was also declining.

In such a cultural and philosophical climate, Moore's basic analytic programme seemed to lead not to intuitionism, but somewhere else entirely. And so in the 1930s a growing number of philosophers on both sides of the Atlantic came to believe that Moore's argument that ethical terms and sentences do not express properties or propositions that can be known empirically showed not that they point to some non-empirically knowable ethical order, but that, strictly speaking, they refer to nothing at all.[29] According to these 'non-cognitivists', ethics does not consist of a body of propositions about some objective moral order that are true or false as they correspond to that order or not. Ethics, rather, is an ongoing human activity of moral debate, praise, and blame that is complete within itself and not responsible to objective ethical facts. There are no ethical facts, they thought.

The most systematic and subtle of the non-cognitivists was Charles Stevenson, an American who, significantly enough, was first attracted to philosophy by Moore and Wittgenstein when he was studying English Literature at Cambridge in the early 1930s. In his landmark paper, 'The Emotive Meaning of Ethical Terms', published in 1937, and later in his systematic book, *Ethics and Language*, Stevenson argued that what makes the meaning of ethical terms irreducible, as he believed Moore had shown, is that they have an 'emotive meaning' that non-ethical terms do not.[30] Ethical terms are used both to express and to incite emotion. They 'are instruments', he wrote, 'used in the complicated interplay and readjustment of human interests' (*FV*, 17). So claims using ethical terms do not express propositions that are literally true or false. That is not what ethical language is for. It is used not to say something about the world, but to express an attitude towards it, and to encourage others to do the same.

With this rough characterisation of Stevenson's view we can already appreciate how it was a natural extension of Moore's analytic programme in the more general philosophical climate then current. First, recall what Moore said when he attempted to clarify what he had meant in saying that while intrinsic goodness is a property, it is not an intrinsic property. He said that intrinsic properties 'seem to *describe* the intrinsic nature of what possesses them in a sense in which predicates of value never do'.[31] Part of what was distinctive about ethical terms for Moore, then, was that they do not describe things in the ordinary way. To say of aesthetic enjoyment that it is intrinsically good is not further to describe what it is.

To accept Moore's view of the property of intrinsic value one had to be willing to believe that reality contains properties that are neither part of anything's (describable) nature nor capable of any sort of empirical confirmation. In the prevailing empiricist framework, which Stevenson very much accepted, this was impossible, however. So it was but a short step to the position that what is characteristic about ethical terms is that they are not used to refer to any aspect of reality at all.

Second, as an intuitionist Moore held that fundamental propositions of ethics do not admit of proof. This need not be problematic, he wrote in *Principia*, so long as there can be *agreement* on ethical matters. The mere fact that proof is lacking 'does not usually give us the least uneasiness. . . . [N]obody can prove that this is a chair beside me; yet I do not suppose any one is much dissatisfied for that reason.' We should, however, 'be uneasy, if some one, whom we do not think to be mad, disagrees with us' (*PE*, 75). What we seek in ethics is *agreement*, rather than proof. That is the goal that drives moral thought and debate. From this it was a short step for Stevenson to conclude that ethics just is the complex human activity of seeking such agreement, only he thought the sort of agreement desired was an agreement in attitude.

Moore had begun *Principia* with the charge that philosophical dispute in ethics was largely due 'to the attempt to answer questions, without first discovering precisely *what* question it is which you desire to answer' (*PE*, vii). Stevenson could not have agreed more.

His influential first paper begins by repeating the Moorean injunction that to answer ethical questions it is necessary, first, 'to examine the questions themselves'.

But there was an important twist to Stevenson's approach. Moore had assumed that what we mean by ethical questions and terms will be transparent to us if only we will reflect carefully.[32] Stevenson, however, was not willing to assume of *any* term of ordinary discourse that it has a clear meaning that is simply open to view. And given the rich and changing history governing the use of ethical terms, it seemed especially likely that whatever ethical questions we originally formulate with them will 'embody hypostatization, anthropomorphism, vagueness, and all the other ills to which our ordinary discourse is subject' (*FV*, 10–11). Clarification, then, must be partly a *creative* enterprise. To the extent that our original questions are subject to vagueness, ambiguity, or based on metaphysical confusion, 'we must *substitute* for it a question that is free from ambiguity and confusion' (*FV*, 10).

In particular, Stevenson was concerned not to be misled by the surface grammar of terms like 'good' and 'right' to suppose, as Moore had, that they refer to genuine properties of things. Perhaps most people *do* use ethical terms thinking, like Moore, that they are referring to metaphysically real properties. They take their terms to refer to an objective moral order. That people believe their terms to have this reference does not, however, secure it for them. And Stevenson thought on empiricist epistemological grounds that such an order simply does not exist. So if we are to give ethical questions a clear meaning we had better be able to do it without any such metaphysical assumption.

But how are we to decide when a question, however clear, is an adequate *substitution* for the ethical question with which we were initially concerned? To this Stevenson answered that an adequate substitution must be 'relevant' to its original meaning in the sense that 'those who have understood the definition [are] able to say all that they then want to say by using the term in the defined way' (*FV*, 11).

If it was Moore's influence that led Stevenson to seek clarification in ethics, it was surely the influence of Wittgenstein, as well as of the American pragmatist tradition, that led him to seek in a definition's usefulness a criterion of its adequacy.[33] During the time Stevenson was at Cambridge and attending his courses and discussion seminars, Wittgenstein was urging philosophers to beware of 'the fascination which forms of expression exert upon us' and look to their actual *use*:

'The use of the word *in practice* is its meaning'.[34] So it was to the human activities and practices within which ethical language is actually used that Stevenson looked to clarify its meaning.

He argued that any adequate, or 'relevant', clarification of ethical terms must meet three requirements. First, it must show how it is possible for people 'sensibly to *disagree* about whether something is "good"' (*FV*, 13). That ethical language is used to express agreement and disagreement of *some* sort is a datum which any adequate definition must explain. Moore, in fact, had argued that the Achilles heel of earlier empiricist subjectivist accounts of 'good', for example, that it means 'what the speaker desires', was that if they are correct disagreement over whether something is good is impossible. When two different people A and B utter, respectively, 'X is good' and 'X is not good', they would not be asserting conflicting propositions since one would be saying, according to the definition, 'I(A) desire X' and the other 'I(B) do not desire X'. As an empiricist, the challenge for Stevenson was to find some other empiricist account of ethical terms that explained how they can be used to express genuine agreement and disagreement.

Stevenson also accepted Moore's arguments that ethics is irreducible to natural or social science and that ethical terms are indefinable in naturalistic terms. So he held as a second requirement of 'relevance' that according to the proposed substitution 'the "goodness" of anything must not be verifiable solely by use of the scientific method' (*FV*, 13). Stevenson wanted to find an account of ethics that, like Moore's, avoided the naturalistic fallacy and could explain the phenomenon of ethical disagreement, but that, unlike Moore's, was consistent with an empiricist epistemology.

He found the crucial element of his account in a feature of ethical concepts that both Ross and Moore had largely ignored, what he called their 'magnetism'. The third requirement of an adequate account of 'good', he held, is that it entail that 'a person who recognizes X to be "good" must ipso facto acquire a stronger tendency to act in its favor than he otherwise would have had' (*FV*, 13). Ethical assertions have a distinctive *force* to them; if we sincerely and fully accept them we characteristically find ourselves moved.

Indeed, Stevenson argued, it is precisely this connection to motivation and feeling, 'the emotive meaning of ethical terms', that explains what Moore had discovered but could explain only with metaphysical and epistemological mystery: the irreducibility of ethical concepts to natural concepts. It is the emotive meaning of ethical language that explains why, given any description of something we can always significantly ask: But is it good? There is no need to think that goodness is a special kind of non-natural property. Moore's idea of a 'nonnatural quality', Stevenson wrote, 'must be taken as an invisible shadow cast by confusion and emotive meaning'.[35]

Put roughly, Stevenson proposed to substitute the following definition for 'x is good': 'I(we) like x. Do so as well'.[36] This met the three conditions. It showed how genuine ethical agreement and disagreement is possible as agreement or disagreement in expressed attitude. Second, it showed how the meaning of ethical terms was irreducible to the descriptive vocabulary of the sciences. And third, it explained the 'magnetism' of ethics—the connection of ethical judgement to feeling and motivation.

Stevenson held that ethical judgements could not be, strictly speaking, either true or false, but he did not think that reasons cannot be given for ethical opinions, nor that ethical disagreements are not subject to rational resolution, at least in a sense. Not every ethical disagreement rests on an ultimate or unresolvable disagreement in attitude. They may result from disagreements in belief. Two people may disagree violently about the morality of capital punishment because they disagree about its deterrent power or some other matter of fact. Stevenson was able to argue, consequently, that ethical debate can be rationally conducted through the presentation of reasons for ethical assertions. But by a *reason* he simply meant any consideration that when presented in discussion had an influence on an attitude.

There are, however, many different ways of influencing people in debate, many ways, even, of influencing them through the presentation of facts. The emotivist position invites the objection that it cannot distinguish between valid and invalid ways of influencing people, between rational and non-rational persuasion. After all, according to emotivism there is no truth in ethics, nor any evidence, in the sense of something which renders an ethical doctrine more probably true. 'Evidence' is whatever influences.

Stevenson's response was that the emotivist can indeed distinguish between valid and invalid ways of influencing people in the only way such a distinction makes sense. For the issue of which ways of influencing are appropriate and which are inappropriate is at bottom, he thought, an ethical question. In making that distinction in one way or another, a person takes an ethical stand and expresses an attitude. And being an emotivist does not preclude taking substantive ethical stands.

Another objection Stevenson faced was that we seem to use ethical concepts not simply when we are expressing our views or trying to influence others, but when, thinking to ourselves, we try to decide what to believe on some ethical matter. The emotivist theory seems tailor-made to explain the *interpersonal*, social use of ethical language; it is not, however, at all obvious how it can explain its *intrapersonal*, private use.

Stevenson's response to this challenge was ingenious. Ethical deliberation and soliloquising generally occurs, he argued, when our attitudes conflict in a way we want to resolve. Conflict of attitude within the self is a 'disquieting, half-paralyzing state of mind' and so we address ourselves in ethical vocabulary, now on one side of the issue, now on the other, in hope of resolving our conflict and getting on. In a brilliant passage he compellingly describes a vivid example:

> The use of self-persuasion is evidenced by the way in which certain people project their deliberations into some pretended social setting. They fancy themselves arguing with some superior or old friend, or revered teacher, and in the course of this mental dramatization find themselves apt in epigram, and masters of declamatory prose, until their opponent ends with an enthusiastic endorsement of their now decisive resolution. (*EL*, 149)

Stevenson notes that such soliloquies are rarely intended as a rehearsal for an actual exchange that will convince someone else:

> Rather, they make their opponent a fictitious character in a play, who lends them mainly the dignity of his name; and the epigrams and declamations which so effectively sway him are in fact serviceable in swaying themselves, with all the vigor of improvised narrative. (*EL*, 149)

Ethical deliberation, which has all the appearances of disinterested inquiry into ethical truth, is, he argued, but an internalised version of the mutual influence of social ethical debate, now on behalf of this attitude, now on behalf of that.

This gives some idea of the subtlety of Stevenson's thought. He was concerned to give an account of ethics that would do justice to Moore's insights about the irreducibility of ethical language, but also one that would firmly place ethics *within* the world and show its connections to actual human practice. The importance of this latter concern for Stevenson was shown by the passage he quoted from John Dewey at the beginning of *Ethics and Language*:

> a moral theory based upon realities of human nature . . . would put an end to the impossible attempt to live in two unrelated worlds [the ethical and the natural] . . . It would . . . link ethics with the study of history, sociology, law, and economics. (*EL*, vii)

Stevenson shared these two concerns with a generation of philosophers who were both foundationalist empiricists in epistemology and inheritors of Moore's analytic method in ethics and of his belief that ethical terms are irreducible. Non-cognitivisms of several varieties flourished from the 1930s through mid-century and beyond. It is still a viable doctrine today, though not nearly so widely accepted as a generation ago.[37]

Several things combined in the 20 year period beginning roughly in the early 1950s that tended both to undermine the relative dominance of non-cognitivist metaethics and to shift the focus of moral philosophy from analytical metaethics back to substantive ethical theory.

To begin with, the widespread assumption after Moore that moral philosophy should be primarily, if not exclusively, metaethical required one to believe that a fairly sharp line exists between analysis of moral concepts and substantive moral claims. But it became less clear that any such line could be drawn. In 1951 W. V. O. Quine argued in a landmark paper that there is no principled distinction between analytic and synthetic propositions.[38] The very distinction on which analytical metaethics had staked its integrity was imperilled.

Second, advances in the philosophy of science undermined the foundationalist assumptions of both empiricist and non-empiricist analytic ethics. Science no longer seemed to rest on a foundation of self-evident experience that was simply given. The very observations to which scientists appeal to confirm theory depend on theoretical assumptions. Justification in science, the empiricist paradigm of empirical knowledge, seemed no longer to be foundational but coherentist, a matter of fitting theories together with observations that themselves depend on theory.

If, however, epistemological justification is simply a matter of coherence, then it apparently was no longer a valid objection to the possibility of ethical knowledge that an 'ought' cannot be deduced from an 'is', that ethical propositions are not reducible to propositions that can be empirically verified. As in science, ethical beliefs might be justified if they can be fit together into a unified theory.

This thought led in two directions. First, it appeared to undermine a crucial source of support for non-cognitivism in ethics. Perhaps knowledge was no less possible in ethics than in science. And it led to the notion that moral philosophers can and should concern themselves with substantive ethical questions and develop substantive ethical theories, coherent systems of ethical thought. Roughly 30 years after Stevenson's first essay appeared the dominance of non-cognitivism was ended. And roughly 70 years after Moore introduced the analytic method into ethics, the singleminded pursuit of analytical metaethics was finished.

It was always somewhat ironic that *Principia* gave rise to a period in which systematic, substantive ethical theory was in eclipse. Moore pursued analysis, after all, only as a preliminary to ethical theory; but it was the earlier analytic chapters, and not the later substantive ones, that most influenced those who came just after him. As a later generation returns to substantive ethical theory, it will be to the neglected chapters that they will increasingly turn. Truncated by an earlier generation, *Principia* has proven a vital organic whole.[39]

# Notes

1. The major texts of these writers were, respectively, J. S. Mill, *Utilitarianism* (1861); Henry Sidgwick, *The Methods of Ethics* (1874); F. H. Bradley, *Ethical Studies* (1876); and T. H. Green, *Prolegomena to Ethics* (1883). Two other important figures of the period who do not fit neatly into either category are James Martineau, *Types of Ethical Theory* (1885), and Herbert Spencer, *The Data of Ethics* (1879) and *The Principles of Ethics* (1892–93).

   For an invaluable discussion of this period see J. B. Schneewind, *Sidgwick's Ethics and Victorian Moral Philosophy* (Oxford: Clarendon Press, 1977).
2. Intuitionism is the view that there is a plurality of self-evident ultimate ethical principles.
3. *Principia Ethica* (Cambridge University Press, 1966) p. vii. Further references to this work will be placed parenthetically in the text and abbreviated (*PE*).
4. Another important figure of the period was H. A. Prichard, an intuitionist and an Oxford colleague of Ross's. Prichard's work was perhaps more penetrating and more influential at the time than Ross's. As a matter of fact, Ross acknowledged that 'the main lines' of his view derived from Prichard's article, 'Does Moral Philosophy Rest on a Mistake?' in *Mind* 21 (1912). But his work was also somewhat idiosyncratic and unsystematic. Ross's *The Right and the Good* stands as a more enduring representative of Oxford intuitionism.

   John Dewey, who was also an important figure during this period, is treated in a separate chapter of the present volume.
5. Moore's relationships with the Apostles and later with Bloomsbury is discussed in Paul Levy, *Moore: G. E. Moore and the Cambridge Apostles* (New York: Holt, Rinehart, and Winston, 1979). I rely on this book for many of the historical details that follow. An illuminating picture of the relation of Moore's ethics to his personal life, and in particular to his dealings with the Apostles and Bloomsbury, is presented by Tom Regan in *Bloomsbury's Prophet: G. E. Moore and the Development of His Moral Philosophy* (Philadelphia: Temple University Press, 1987). This appeared too late, however, for me to take account of it in the text.
6. 'An Autobiography', *The Philosophy of G. E. Moore*, ed. P. Schilpp (La Salle, Ill.: Open Court, 1942) p. 14.
7. Ibid.
8. *Ethics* (New York: Oxford University Press, 1966) p. 89.
9. Moore's discussion recalls the view Plato has Socrates propose in *Theaetetus* 202d. This is by no means the only Platonic aspect of Moore's views, the most prominent being the idea that ethics is fundamentally concerned with the metaphysical property of goodness.
10. The formulation of the open question argument given in the text is the one most familiar in the philosophical tradition following Moore although it differs in details from the version Moore gave in *Principia*.

11. On this point see W. Frankena, 'The Naturalistic Fallacy', in *Mind* 48 (1939), pp. 464–77.
12. Significantly, Russell reports Moore's first contribution to an Apostles' discussion as a passionate defence of 'the enthusiasm for scepticism'. By this Moore meant not a scepticism that was final and incapable of relief, but a methodological scepticism, much like Descartes in the *Meditations*, necessary to pave the way for solid knowledge. (Quoted in Levy, *Moore*, p. 126.)
13. As late as 1970 a moral philosopher could expect to raise no eyebrows by writing:

> This book is not about what people ought to do. It is about what they are doing when they *talk* about what they ought to do. Moral philosophy, as I understand it, must not be confused with moralizing. A moralist . . . engages in reflection, argument, or discussion about what is morally right or wrong, good or evil . . . [A] moral philosopher . . . thinks and speaks about the ways in which moral terms, like 'right' and 'good' are used by moralists when they are delivering their moral judgments.

This statement from W. D. Hudson, *Modern Moral Philosophy* (Garden City, New York: Doubleday, 1970) p. 1, goes well beyond Moore in its focus on the use of ethical terms rather than on the ideas to which we use ethical terms to refer, and in its insistence that moral philosophy include no 'moralising'. Moore, after all, was concerned to begin with metaethical questions in order then to be able to address substantive ethical issues. Nonetheless, such a statement would surely have been impossible before *Principia*.
14. And the claims were well known to 18th-century British moral philosophers, many of whom were anxious to argue that ethical terms do not simply refer to the property of being willed or proscribed by God, or, as Hobbes believed, by the Sovereign. An excellent discussion can be found in Arthur N. Prior, 'The Naturalistic Fallacy: The History of Its Refutation', in *Logic and the Basis of Ethics* (Oxford University Press, 1968) pp. 95–107.
15. This passage is actually from *Principia*, p. xx, but it well expresses a central thesis of 'The Refutation of Idealism' (originally published in *Mind*).
16. See especially 'The Conception of Intrinsic Value', in *Philosophical Studies* (New York: Humanities Press, 1951) pp. 253–75. 'The Refutation of Idealism' is also included in this collection.
17. In Paul Schilpp (ed.), *The Philosophy of G. E. Moore*, p. 581.
18. 'The Conception of Intrinsic Value', in *Philosophical Studies* (New York: Harcourt, Brace & Co., 1922) p. 274.
19. 'My Early Beliefs', in *The Collected Writings of John Maynard Keynes*, v. x (Cambridge: Macmillan, St. Martin's Press, 1972) p. 435.
20. Interestingly enough, another philosopher who had a somewhat similar influence on the same generation of English writers and intellectuals was Friedrich Nietzsche. It is hard to imagine a thinker who differs

more from Moore in style. On Nietzsche's influence see Patrick Bridg-water, 'English Writers and Nietzsche', in Malcolm Pasley (ed.), *Nietzsche: Imagery and Thought* (Berkeley: University of California Press, 1978) pp. 221–58.

21. Keynes wrote: '[W]hat we got from Moore was by no means entirely what he offered us. He had one foot on the threshold of the new heaven, but the other foot in Sidgwick and the Benthamite calculus and the general rules of correct behavior. There was one chapter in the *Principia* of which we took not the slightest notice. We accepted Moore's religion, so to speak, and discarded his morals'. (*My Early Beliefs*, p. 435)

A careful reading of Moore's chapter on ethical conduct, however, reveals more leeway for the unconventional than might initially appear. Moore is careful to confine his recommendation of conventionality to rules that are both generally practised *and* generally useful. He mentions 'most of the rules comprehended under the name of Chastity' (*PE*, 158) as being only questionably useful. Moreover, he makes it clear that it is insufficient that a rule *would* be generally useful if practised, if it is not. And he says that when rules meeting the two conditions fail to apply, an individual should give preference to goods about which he presently cares most (on the grounds that he is likelier to realise them, and that the individual's own appreciation adds value (*PE*, 166–67).

22. *The Right and the Good* (Oxford University Press, 1930) p. 8. Further references will be placed parenthetically in the text and abbreviated (*RG*).

23. See note 8.

24. C. D. Broad, 'Certain Features of Moore's Ethical Doctrines, in P. Schilpp, *The Philosophy of G. E. Moore*, pp. 43–57. For recent discussions see Thomas Nagel, *The View From Nowhere* (New York: Oxford University Press, 1986) chapter IX; Samuel Scheffler, *The Rejection of Consequentialism* (Oxford University Press, 1982) *passim*; and Derek Parfit, *Reasons and Persons* (Oxford University Press, 1984) pp. 53–5, 95–114.

25. By a *prima facie* duty Ross meant something that would be a moral duty, all things considered, if no other morally relevant considerations applied.

26. *Foundations of Ethics* (Oxford: Clarendon Press, 1939) p. 1. The influence of Aristotle, of whose work Ross was a careful scholar, is clear here. Indeed, Ross refers to Aristotle as having given this method its best formulation. The debate between Ross and Moore echoes in some aspects that between Aristotle and Plato. The other main historical influence on Ross was Kant. Significantly, Ross published books on both Aristotle and Kant.

27. Ibid.

28. It is significant that even Ross's view might be described as 'situational' since he held there to be no certain general rules for determining which morally relevant considerations, which *prima facie* duties, are weightier in any given circumstance.

29. This group included A. E. Duncan-Jones, A. J. Ayer, Rudolph Carnap, and the linguists C. K. Ogden and I. A. Richards.

30. 'The Emotive Theory of Ethical Terms', originally published in *Mind*, was reprinted in a collection of Stevenson's essays, *Facts and Values*

(New Haven: Yale University Press, 1963). Further references to this volume will be placed parenthetically in the text and abbreviated (*FV*, ) *Ethics and Language* (New Haven: Yale University Press, 1944).

31. See note 18.

32. 'Whoever will attentively consider with himself what is actually before his mind when he asks the question "Is pleasure (or whatever it may be) after all good?" can easily satisfy himself that he is not merely wondering whether pleasure is pleasant' (*PE*, 16).

33. Wittgenstein would probably have had little sympathy with the project of reforming or regimenting ordinary usage. His idea was that one should focus on the actual use of language in context. Ordinary language is largely satisfactory as it stands.

34. *The Blue and Brown Books* (New York: Harper Torchbooks, 1965) p. 27. This volume consists of notes taken in Wittgenstein's courses at Cambridge in 1933–35. Stevenson received his B.A. in philosophy from Cambridge in 1933.

35. *Ethics and Language*, p. 109. Further references will be placed in text as follows: (*EL*, ).

36. This is what Stevenson called the 'first pattern of analysis'. Space does not permit discussion of his 'second pattern'.

37. The most subtle and influential current version is the prescriptivism of R. M. Hare, first presented in *Language and Morals* (Oxford: Clarendon Press, 1952), and further worked out in *Freedom and Reason* (Oxford University Press, 1963), and in *Moral Thinking* (Oxford University Press, 1981).

38. 'Two Dogmas of Empiricism', reprinted in *From a Logical Point of View* (New York: Harper Torchbooks, 1963).

39. I am indebted to William Frankena and Robert Cavalier for helpful comments and to W. D. Falk for years of illuminating discussion of Moore's views.

# Bibliography

1. Frankena, William, 'The Naturalistic Fallacy', *Mind* 48 (1939) pp. 464–77.
2. Hudson, W. D., *Modern Moral Philosophy* (Garden City, New York: Doubleday, 1970).
3. Levy, Paul, *Moore: G. E. Moore and the Cambridge Apostles* (New York: Holt, Rinehart, and Winston, 1979).
4. Moore, G. E., *Ethics* (New York: Oxford University Press, 1966).
5. ——, *Principia Ethica* (Cambridge University Press, 1966).
6. ——, 'The Conception of Intrinsic Value', in *Philosophical Studies* (New York: The Humanities Press, 1951).
7. Prichard, H. A., *Moral Obligation* (Oxford University Press, 1949).
8. Regan, Tom, *Bloomsbury's Prophet: G. E. Moore and the Development of His Moral Philosophy* (Philadelphia: Temple University Press, 1987).
9. Ross, W. D., *The Right and the Good* (Oxford University Press, 1930).
10. ——, *The Foundations of Ethics* (Oxford University Press, 1939).
11. Schilpp, Paul (ed.), *The Philosophy of G. E. Moore* (La Salle, Ill.: Open Court, 1942).
12. Stevenson, Charles, *Ethics and Language* (New Haven: Yale University Press, 1944).
13. ——, *Facts and Values* (New Haven: Yale University Press, 1963).
14. Urmson, J. O., *The Emotive Theory of Ethics* (London: Hutchinson University Library, 1968).
15. Warnock, Mary, *Ethics Since 1900* (London: Oxford University Press, 1963).

# 13

# Toulmin to Rawls
## *James P. Sterba*

There are several threads that make up the fabric of contemporary ethical theory from the 1950s to the present. One of these is the good reasons approach to ethics pioneered by Stephen Toulmin and developed by Kurt Baier.[1] Another is the revival of social contract theory begun by John Rawls and extended to a wide range of practical problems by David Richards, Charles Beitz, Norman Daniels, myself and others.[2] Recently, Stephen Darwall has argued that these two threads can be joined into one: that the good reasons approach can provide a rational foundation for a Rawlsian social contract theory.[3] But while establishing this linkage would clearly be an interesting result, it was never one of the stated goals of the major proponents of these views, and it is in terms of the stated goals of their major proponents that it seems best to begin to try to understand and to evaluate these views.

### THE GOOD REASONS APPROACH TO ETHICS

When Stephen Toulmin published *An Examination of the Place of Reason in Ethics* in 1950 his stated goal was to provide an alternative to what were then the three dominant approaches to ethics.[4] He labelled them the objective approach, the subjective approach and the imperative approach.

As one would expect, Toulmin saw the objective approach as epitomised in the work of G. E. Moore, who argued that goodness was a directly perceived, simple, non-natural property. According to Toulmin Moore was misled into thinking that goodness was an objective property because he believed that when two people disagree in their ethical judgements one must think that something has a certain objective property which the other thinks it lacks. This is a mistake, Toulmin argues, because disagreement in ethical judgements is perfectly explicable solely in terms of the opposing reasons which support those judgements. For example, if Mary says that X is good while John says that X is bad, there is no need to claim that Mary perceives a simple non-natural objective property that John fails to perceive. It suffices to claim that Mary knows of some good reasons for doing X of which John is ignorant. Furthermore, Toulmin argues that the degree of ethical disagreement that exists would hardly be possible if goodness were a directly perceived objective property like yellow. For if goodness were such a property, we could expect the kind of agreement we experience with respect to people's colour judgements.

Proponents of the subjective approach are seen by Toulmin to be making a mistake similar to proponents of the objective approach because they too assume that ethical judgements must refer to some property. In this case, it is a subjective property—the psychological state of the speaker—to which ethical judgements are said to refer. Yet, as Toulmin points out, if ethical judgements simply refer to the psychological state of the speaker, there is no possibility of ethical disagreement. For example, if Mary says that X is good (which means that she likes X) and John says X is bad (which means that he does not like X) then Mary and John do not really disagree—they just have different likes and dislikes. Thus the advantage of viewing moral judgements as supported by good reasons, Toulmin argues, is that such an approach provides for the possibility of ethical disagreement without assuming that ethical judgements refer to either a subjective or an objective property.

Now, according to Toulmin, proponents of the imperative approach recognise the errors of both the objective and the subjective approaches because they do not regard ethical judgements as referring to any property. Nevertheless, the mistake of proponents of this approach is that they regard ethical judgements as pseudo-statements analogous to commands. For example, according to this approach, when Mary says that X is good it means 'Do X', and when John says that X is bad it means 'Do not do X'. As a result, Toulmin claims, this approach cannot explain how ethical judgements can be true or false—a deficiency that Toulmin claims does not characterise his own good reasons approach to ethics.

In Toulmin's approach, good reasons are determined ultimately by reference to the very function of ethics.[5] That function, Toulmin claims, is 'to correlate our feelings and behavior in such a way as to make the fulfillment of everyone's aims and desires as far as possible compatible'. Frequently, however, there is no need to appeal directly to the function of ethics. For example, where there is no conflict of duties it suffices to appeal to the applicable conventional rules, such as the rules of the road, to determine what are the relevant good reasons. Thus facts which constitute good reasons in Toulmin's view do not do so in virtue of anything to which they refer but rather in virtue of the use to which they are put in supporting judgements which ultimately serve the very function of ethics.

But could not the function of ethics be different than it is? Toulmin does not think that this is possible without ethics ceasing to be ethics just as the function of science could not be other than 'to alter expectations' without science ceasing to be science.[6]

But surely we could ask, assuming that the function of ethics is fixed in this way, why should we engage in ethics? Yet, according to Toulmin, the only answer that we can give to this question is that we *are engaged* in ethics; it is not possible to give any further justification. This is because to ask for a further justification for ethics could not be a request for a moral reason to be moral because that would be circular. And if it is a request for a non-moral reason to be moral, what sort of justification could be given? As Toulmin points out, we could not give a self-interested justification for ethics.

Following the publication of his book, Toulmin's characterisation of the function of ethics was criticised first by R. M. Hare and then by others.[7] Hare asks why someone could not think that human development requires a conflict rather than a harmony of interests and then interpret the function of ethics to be the promotion of such conflict? Would such a person no longer be endorsing ethics or would he/she simply be endorsing a different kind of ethics? Hare thinks that the latter is the case, and it is not clear how Toulmin could respond to this criticism given that he rules out the possibility of providing any kind of overall justification for ethics. All he could say is that such a person would not be endorsing ethics as we normally understand it.

It is just at this point that Kurt Baier, who wrote his dissertation under Toulmin at Oxford, disagrees with Toulmin concerning the development of a good reasons approach to ethics. For Baier contends that it is possible to provide a justification for ethics that is compelling to all reasonable agents.

In *The Moral Point of View*, published in 1958, and in a series of articles continuing to the present, Baier has been attempting to construct such a justification for ethics by showing that moral reasons are superior to self-interested reasons.[8]

In *The Moral Point of View*, Baier begins by assuming that the very purpose of following reason is 'to maximize satisfaction and minimize frustration'. He then argues that the recognition of moral reasons as superior by everyone would produce greater satisfaction and lesser frustration than the recognition of self-interested reasons as superior by everyone. From this he concludes that moral reasons should be recognised as superior to self-interested reasons by everyone.

However, Baier's initial assumption concerning the purpose of following reason is ambiguous between a utilitarian and an egoistic interpretation. Under the utilitarian interpretation,

> reason requires the maximisation of satisfaction and the minimisation of frustration for everyone taken collectively.

Under the egoistic interpretation,

> reason requires the maximisation of satisfaction and the minimisation of frustration for everyone taken individually.

Yet only when the assumption is given the utilitarian interpretation does the conclusion follow. Unfortunately, this interpretation clearly begs the question against the egoist.

More recently, Baier has reformulated his justification for ethics in terms of a number of requirements of practical reason, the most important of which are the following:

**(1) Universality**

Since a fact F is a reason for someone to do A in virtue of his/her satisfying certain conditions D, F must be a reason to do A for anyone who satisfies D.

**(2) Empirical Substantiation**

The soundness of the belief that C is the criterion that is to determine whether or not F is a reason of a certain strength for X to do A is to be determined by the way acceptance of this criterion affects the satisfactoriness of the relevant lives.

**(3) Universalisability**

If F is a reason to do A for anyone who satisfies D, then F must also be capable of being a reason to do A for everyone who satisfies D.

Baier contends that only when moral reasons are taken to be supreme can these three requirements of practical reason be met, since only then would each person have the best reason grounded in the satisfactoriness of the person's own life that every person (not any person) can possibly have.[9]

To evaluate Baier's argument, let us consider whether the egoist can accept or reject all three of Baier's requirements without acting contrary to reason. For a fully adequate defence of morality in terms of practical reason must show that the egoist acts contrary to reason. Accordingly, for Baier's argument to go through, it must be the case that the egoist cannot accept or reject Baier's requirements without acting contrary to reason.

Now, at first glance, it would seem that the egoist would have no difficulty accepting at least the first two of Baier's three requirements. Certainly, the egoist could accept Baier's Universality criterion. The egoist could grant, for example, that if the fact that it would make them very rich (fact F) is a reason for them to steal given that conditions are such that he/she could easily get away with the theft (condition D), then F must be a reason to steal for anyone who satisfies D. Baier's Empirical Substantiation criterion also seems equally acceptable. How could the egoist deny that the soundness of egoism depends on the effect of taking egoistic reasons to be overriding in the lives of egoists? Hence, at least initially, only acceptance of Universalisability would seem to present a problem for the egoist.

Part of the problem is that Baier gives different interpretations to this proposed requirement. Sometimes he interprets the requirement to imply (1) that it must be possible for everyone always to be perfectly rational.[10] At other times, he interprets the requirement to imply, or at least suggest, the stronger claim (2) that it must be a good thing for everyone always to be perfectly rational.[11]

Now the egoist would have little difficulty accepting Universalisability under interpretation (1). The egoist would simply argue that once the directives of egoism are plausibly interpreted,[12] it is surely possible for everyone always to be perfectly rational by following the directives of egoism.

Yet accepting Universalisability under interpretation (1) does raise a problem for the egoist's initial acceptance of Empirical Substantiation. For the negative effects of the satisfactoriness of the egoist's life arising from everyone following the directives of egoism appear to violate it. However, there are at least two reasons for thinking that the egoist can meet this requirement while accepting Universalisability under interpretation (1).

First of all, the effects on the satisfactoriness of the egoist's life from everyone following the directives of egoism may not be as disastrous as they are sometimes made out to be. For under ideal institutional arrangements, a world where everyone pursues long-term self-interest may not be such a bad world to live in, although it would be different, of course, from a world where everyone always acted from or according to duty. Thus, Hobbes's war of all against all may be a poor model for a state of affairs where rational egoism reigns.

Secondly, the impact on the satisfactoriness of the egoist's life when everyone follows egoism must be evaluated together with the effects on the satisfactoriness of the egoist's life when almost everyone, save the egoist, follows morality. Obviously, for good self-interested reasons the egoist opposes the taking of self-interested reasons to be supreme by others. The egoist admits that such behaviour is fully rational but opposes it nonetheless. The egoist does not want others reaping the benefits of following self-interested reasons at his or her expense, and publicly endorses the following of moral reasons as strongly as anyone. The egoist observes that most people take a similar stand, and recognises that many with the 'proper upbringing' in fact come to care strongly for others and, as a result, follow moral reasons almost instinctively. Taking all this into account, the egoist is justified in concluding that it is improbable that circumstances will arise in which everyone followed the directives of egoism. Since the egoist can be assured that others will continue to follow the directives of morality even if the egoist follows those of self-interest, the egoist can reasonably expect that the overall effect on the satisfactoriness of his or her life from taking self-interested reasons to be supreme would be positive, and considerably better than the overall effect from taking moral reasons to be supreme.

Of course, someone might object to the introduction of probability assessments of other people's behaviour into the calculation of the overall satisfactoriness of the egoist's life.[13] But what is the ground for this objection? The egoist grants that it is possible for everyone to follow egoism. The egoist simply judges that this is unlikely, and that accordingly the expected overall effect on the egoist's life from following egoism would be quite positive, and considerably better than the expected overall effect from following the directives of morality. Unlike the prisoner in the well-known Prisoner's Dilemma, the egoist justifiably believes that others are more likely to do the mutually beneficial action (not confessing in the Prisoner's Dilemma). Hence, the egoist has good reason to think that the overall satisfactoriness of his or her life would be furthered by taking self-interested reasons to be supreme (confessing in the Prisoner's Dilemma).[14]

Give then that the egoist can accept Baier's Universality, Empirical Substantiation, and Universalisability under interpretation (1), Baier's defence of morality must ultimately rest on the claim that it is contrary to reason for the egoist to reject Universalisability under interpretation (2). That the egoist has to reject Universalisability under this interpretation seems correct. The egoist has to deny that it is a good thing for everyone to be perfectly rational and take the directives of egoism to be supreme. But why is that rejection contrary to reason? Why is it contrary to reason to recognise that people ought to do what is in their best interest and yet not to think it is a good thing for them all to do what they ought?

Here the 'oughts' found in most ordinary competitive games provide a useful analogy. For instance, tennis players can judge that their opponents ought to put maximum spin on their serves without being committed to thinking that it is a good thing for them if their opponents serve in this way and they counter with their best returns. For, if that occurred, it might be likely that they would lose the game. After all, not infrequently one side is victorious in a game only because the other side failed to execute its best moves.[15]

Of course, there is an important dissimilarity between these two types of 'oughts'. Since competitive games are governed by moral constraints when everyone does exactly what he or she ought to do, there is an accepted moral limit to what a person can lose. By contrast, when everyone takes self-interested reasons to be supreme, the only limit to what a person can lose is the point beyond which others would not benefit.

But, this dissimilarity does not destroy the analogy. For it is still the case that when judged from the individual player's or the egoist's point of view, it need not be a good thing for everyone to be perfectly rational. It follows, therefore, that the egoist cannot be convicted of acting contrary to reason for rejecting Baier's Universalisability criterion under interpretation (2). Thus, unable to show that the egoist acts contrary to reason, Baier's defence of morality fails to secure its obective.

Does this mean that all such attempts to rationally ground morality are doomed to failure? Many philosophers seem to think so. But accepting this conclusion also has its costs because it entails that morality and egoism are equally rational points of view, and this seems to deprive of us of adequate grounds for blaming and punishing people who consistently follow their self-interest at the expense of the requirements of morality. No wonder then that at least some philosophers continue to search for a justification for morality that can show that the egoist acts contrary to reason.

## THE REVIVAL OF SOCIAL CONTRACT THEORY

Except for the recent work of Stephen Darwall which attempts to show that a good reasons approach to ethics can provide a rational foundation for a Rawlsian social contract theory, there is little theoretical or historical connection between the good reasons approach to ethics and the contemporary revival of social contract theory. Indeed, in 1957 when John Rawls first employed a version of social contract theory in 'Justice as Fairness' to defend a conception of justice that was at odds with utilitarianism, he showed no interest whatsoever in providing an overall justification for ethics.[16] Rather he was concerned with a debate within moral theory between utilitarians and non-utilitarians. To this debate, Rawls sought to contribute a systematic account of a non-utilitarian conception of justice.

Now the basic idea of Rawls's social contract theory, as expressed in 'Justice as Fairness', is that

> A practice is just if it is in accordance with the principles all who participate in it might reasonably be expected to propose or to acknowledge before one another when they are similarly circumstanced and required to make a firm commitment in advance.[17]

For Rawls a social contract is a hypothetical not an historical contract. Thus Rawls does not claim that people actually agree to a particular set of morally defensible principles of justice. Rather Rawls claims that people *would agree* to such principles under certain specific conditions.

Later in 'Distributive Justice' and subsequently in *A Theory of Justice*, Rawls makes it explicit that the most relevant condition required for this hypothetical contract is a veil of ignorance which deprives people of the knowledge of the most particular facts about themselves and their society.[18] According to Rawls, morally adequate principles of justice are those principles people would agree to in an original position which is essentially characterised by this veil of ignorance.

Rawls's purpose in introducing this veil of ignorance is to remove from consideration certain particular facts the knowledge of which might lead people in the original position to favour principles which are not just. For this reason people in the original position do not know their place in society, their natural or acquired traits or abilities, what conceptions of the good they have, nor what their particular goals are. In addition, they do not know the particular political, economic or cultural characteristics of their own society nor do they know to which generation they belong. However, they do know that they are contemporaries, that they are in the circumstances of justice so that human cooperation is both possible and desirable and that they are each capable of a sense of justice. Moreover, there is no limit to their knowledge of general information such as is contained in political, social, economic and psychological theories. According to Rawls, the veil of ignorance has the effect of depriving persons in the original position of the knowledge they would need to advance their own special interests.

While the veil of ignorance does significantly restrict the knowledge of persons in the original position, Rawls believes that it still provides them with enough information to agree on just principles for regulating all subsequent criticism and reform of the basic structure of a society. This follows from the fact that when considering the basic structure of a society what is at issue are only primary social goods, that is, goods which are generally necessary for achieving whatever goals one happens to have. Thus persons behind the veil of ignorance would still recognise the importance of acquiring goods of this sort because they are the type of goods one would want regardless of whatever else one wants. Moreover, Rawls assumes that persons in the original position would ordinarily want more primary social goods rather than fewer. Allowing for an acceptable minimum, persons so situated would strive to maximise their index of primary social goods regardless of how others fared. This means that persons in the original position would not be influenced by affection, envy or rancour. For example, they would not choose to lower their expectations merely to avoid raising the expectations of someone else. Rather each would seek to maximise his own expectations even when this required that others have even greater expectations.

Rawls maintains that people in the original position would choose the following special conception of justice:

(1)  Each person is to have an equal right to the most extensive

total system of equal basic liberties compatible with a similar system of liberty for all.

(2a) Social and economic inequalities are to be arranged so that they are to the greatest benefit of the least advantaged and (2b) are attached to offices and positions open to all under conditions of fair equality of opportunity.

Rawls claims that the first principle would be taken to have priority over the second whenever the liberties guaranteed by the first principle can be effectively exercised by persons in all social positions. This means that when this condition is satisfied, liberties are not to be sacrificed for the sake of obtaining increased shares of other social goods. For example, it would not be considered just for a society to give up freedom of the press in order to achieve greater economic benefits. But when the liberties guaranteed by the first principle cannot be effectively exercised by persons in all social positions, Rawls argues that people in the original position would favour the following general conception of justice:

All social values—liberty and opportunity, income and wealth and the bases of self-respect—are to be distributed equally unless an unequal distribution of any, or all, of these values is to the advantage of the least favored.

Rawls also holds that a priority would be assigned between the two parts of the second principle, that 2b would be given priority over 2a, whenever the opportunities guaranteed by 2b can be effectively exercised by persons in all social positions. Thus, when this condition is satisfied, it would similarly be considered unjust to sacrifice basic opportunities to attain larger shares of economic goods. Similarly, Rawls allows that when this condition is not satisfied, people in the original position would be willing to dispense with this priority in favour of the more general conception of justice. According to Rawls, for societies that can satisfy the conditions for effective exercise of basic liberties and opportunities, it is these two principles, with their priority rules, that would be chosen by people in the original position.

Rawls believes these two principles would be chosen because the original position is a situation in which the maximin rule for choice under uncertainty applies. Since the maximin rule assumes that the best one can do is maximise the payoff to the least advantaged position, the principles that would be chosen by people in the original position are considered to be the same as those rational individuals would choose for the design of a society in which their enemy would assign them their position, which, of course, would be the least advantaged position. This is not to say that people in the original position believe that their place in society is so determined because then their reasoning would be based on false premises, and Rawls finds that unacceptable. Still the principles that people would select in both situations would be the same, according to Rawls, because both situations are such that the maximin rule for choice under uncertainty applies.

Rawls argues that the original position possesses, to a striking degree, the three features that make a choice situation appropriate for applying the maximin strategy. Those features are:

(1) There is some reason to discount the probabilities that are arrived at in the choice situation.
(2) The person choosing has a conception of the good such that he/she cares very little, if anything, for what he/she might gain above the minimin he/she can in fact be sure of gaining by following the maximin strategy.
(3) Alternative strategies have outcomes that the person choosing can hardly accept.

According to Rawls, the first feature is characteristic of the original position because people in the original position would not have any objective grounds for assigning probabilities to their turning up in different positions in society, and it would not be reasonable for people so situated to rely on any probability assignments in the absence of such grounds. In addition, Rawls argues that since people in the original position would want their choice of principles (and strategies) to seem reasonable to others, particularly their descendants, they would have still another reason for not relying on probability assignment that would be made in the absence of objective grounds.

In discussing the second feature, Rawls begins by arguing that his two principles of justice would guarantee a satisfactory minimum. He then goes on to claim that if the priority of liberty (and presumably the priority of opportunity) could be established in the original position, people so situated would have no desire to try for greater gains at the expense of equal liberties (or opportunities) and that, consequently, they would be content with the minimum provided by the maximin strategy.

To show that the original position possesses the third feature that characterises situations where the maximin strategy is said to apply, Rawls merely notes that, without priority rules, the principles of total and average utility, under certain conditions, might lead to serious infractions of liberty and that, consequently, the strategies which would lead to these principles would be unacceptable.

When asked to speculate concerning what might have influenced the development of his theory of justice, Rawls responded as follows:

> . . . I have, of course, as I suppose anyone does, reflected about what might have influenced me one way or the other. But so far I have never gotten very far on this, partly because it involves re-constructing one's intellectual bent and climate of ideas with which one was surrounded and that is hard to do accurately and without self-serving distortion (much of the latter unnoticed, if not represented). I recall that the idea of the original position goes back to the very 1950's since I have (or did have, should they have gotten lost) notes on that idea written up while I was at Oxford 1952–3. It was then a much more complicated situation than it latter become in *TJ*, believe it or not. In *TJ* what is found is the result of various attempts to simplify it. I suppose the first version of the idea was the result of combining ideas from game theory (very general intuitive ones) with some ideas from economics, plus an idea of Frank Knight's that one needs a constitution for political discussion, not to mention other things that might have been involved. I don't offer this as any help at all. It has never seemed to me worth it to try to answer the question; and in any case I don't think I know the answer, at any rate, not now.[19]

But while the particular source of the key ideas of Rawls's social contract theory may be difficult to uncover, nevertheless, the task of that theory was to explicate and to justify, if possible, a conception of justice that was, in fact, embedded in the political ideals of liberal democratic societies. So at least in this respect, Rawls's theory was closely attuned to contemporary culture.

In addition, events in society at large did influence the reception of Rawls's book in 1971. The Civil Rights Movement, the Black Liberation Movement and the Anti-Vietnam War Movement, which were flourishing at the time, all called for just the sort of examination and defence of the assumptions of a liberal democratic society that Rawls's theory provided. Moreover, among professional philosophers, there were many who had seen the need to address practical moral problems in their work and were looking for a theoretically satisfying way to do so without committing themselves to the prevailing utilitarian model theory—just the approach Rawls's theory recommended. All in all, Rawls's book could not have appeared at a more auspicious moment.

Needless to say, Rawls's theory has been challenged in various ways. Some critics like Ronald Dworkin, Robert Nozick and Michael Sandel have challenged the very idea of the original position. By contrast, other critics like Brian Barry, H. L. A. Hart and John Harsanyi have at least provisionally endorsed Rawls's contractual approach only to challenge Rawls's argument that his principles of justice would be derived therefrom.

In his early challenge to the very idea of the original position, Ronald Dworkin argues that hypothetical agreements do not (unlike actual agreements) provide independent arguments for the fairness of those agreements.[20] For example, suppose because I did not know the value of a painting I owned, if you had offered me $100 for it yesterday, I would have accepted your offer. Such hypothetical acceptance, Dworkin argues, in no way shows that it would be fair to force me to sell the painting to you today for $100 now that I have discovered it to be more valuable. Accordingly, Dworkin holds that the fact that a person would agree to do something in the original position does not provide an independent argument for his/her abiding by that agreement in everyday life.

But while it seems correct to argue that hypothetical agreement in the painting case does not support a demand that I presently sell you the painting for $100, it is not clear how this undermines the moral relevance of the hypothetical agreement that emerges from the original position. For surely Rawls is not committed to the view that all hypothetical agreements are morally binding. Nor could Dworkin reasonably argue that his example supports the conclusion that no hypothetical agreements are morally binding. For by parity of reasoning from the fact that some actual agreements are not binding (for example, an agreement to commit murder) it would follow that *no* actual agreements are morally binding, which is absurd. Consequently, to show that the specific agreement that would result from the original position is not morally binding, further argument is required.

Another challenge to the very idea of the original position developed by Robert Nozick and Michael Sandel is that it requires us to view persons stripped of their rightful natural and social assets.[21] Rawls, of course, explicitly designed the original position to reflect the judgement that 'no one deserves his place in the distribution of natural endowments or his initial starting place in society'. However, this judgement, when correctly interpreted, does not imply that a person's natural assets or initial social assets are undeserved, but only that the notion of desert does not apply to such assets. Nor does the judgement presuppose that the grounds of desert must themselves be deserved. Yet, according to Rawls, the judgement does imply that natural assets and initial social assets should be regarded, in effect, as common assets. For this reason, Nozick and Sandel, echoing Rawls's own complaint against utilitarianism, have claimed that Rawls's theory does not take seriously the distinction between persons.

Nevertheless, it is possible to interpret Rawls here as simply addressing a question every moral philosopher must address, namely: What constraints, if any, should apply to people's use of their natural and social assets in the pursuit of their own welfare? For example, should people be able to use such assets in pursuit of their own welfare, irrespective of the consequences on others. Egoists, of course, would say that they should, but most moral philosophers would disagree. Even libertarians, like Nozick, would object to such unconstrained use of people's natural and social assets. For Nozick, people's use of their natural and social assets is constrained by the moral requirement that they not interfere with or harm other people or at least that they do not do so without paying compensation. For others, particularly liberals, like John Rawls, the use of people's natural and social assets should be constrained not only when it interferes with or harms other people but also when such use fails to benefit others in fundamental ways, for example, by not providing them with an adequate social minimum.

So the charge that Rawls's view does not take seriously the distinction between persons ultimately comes down to the claim that although some constraints are morally justified, Rawls's view puts too many constraints on the use of a person's natural and social assets. But to make this charge stick, critics of Rawls's view need to provide an argument that only certain constraints on the use of natural and social assets are morally justified, and this is what Rawls's critics have yet to do.

Most critics of Rawls's theory, it turns out, have not challenged the conditions he imposes on the original position but rather have focused their attention on Rawls's argument that a particular conception of justice would be chosen by people in the original position. In challenging this argument Brian Barry and H. L. A. Hart both focus on Rawls's attempt to derive the 'priority of liberty' from the original position.[22] Barry and Hart question Rawls's grounds for claiming that beyond a certain point any additional increment of wealth is not worth the sacrifice of the smallest amount of liberty. Hart also questions how this priority is to work out in practice in the absence of any criteria of application.

Now much of Rawls's recent work responds to just these challenges.[23] What Rawls has done, in effect, is explicitly to introduce into the premises of his argument an ideal of a person which was at best only implicit in his earlier work. This ideal conceives of people in the original position as having two powers—the capacity for a sense of justice and the capacity for a conception of the good. The capacity for a sense of justice is the capacity to understand, to apply and to normally be moved by an effective desire to act from (and not merely in accordance with) the principles of justice as the fair terms of social cooperation. The capacity for a conception of the good is the capacity to form, to revise and rationally to pursue such a conception, that is, a conception of what we regard as a worthwhile human life. People in the original position are also said to have a highest-order interest in promoting the full exercise of these two powers.

Given the explicit introduction of this ideal of a person into Rawls's argument for the priority of liberty, together with his elaboration of that ideal, it does appear that people in the original position would favour the priority of liberty. Of course, critics might now want to argue that this result is attained only by means of premises that are unacceptably strong. In any case, by introducing the notion of fundamental cases and a standard of significance for particular liberties, Rawls seems to have answered Hart's question concerning how the priority of liberty would apply in practice.

Another critic of Rawls's work who accepts the idea of the original position but then rejects the argument that Rawls's principles of justice would be chosen by people so situated is John Harsanyi.[24] Harsanyi claims that people in Rawls's original position would first assign an equal probability to their occupying each particular position in society and then select the alternative with the highest average expected utility. To determine utility assignments, people in the original position are said to compare what it would be like to have particular distributive shares in society while possessing the subjective tastes of people who have those shares. Harsanyi further assumes that with the knowledge of the appropriate psychological laws and factual information, people in the original position would arrive at the same comparative utility judgements from which it would then be possible to determine which alternative maximises their average expected utility.

For example, consider a society with just the three members, X, Y and Z facing the following alternatives:

|   | Alternative A | Alternative C |
|---|---|---|
| X | 60 | 30 |
| Y | 10 | 20 |
| Z | <u>10</u> | <u>20</u> |
|   | 80 | 70 |

Given these alternatives, Harsanyi thinks that people in the original position would assume that it was equally probable that they would be either X, Y, or Z and, therefore, would select Alternative A as having the higher average expected utility. And if the utility values for two alternatives were the following:

|   | Alternative B | Alternative C |
|---|---|---|
| X | 50 | 30 |
| Y | 10 | 20 |
| Z | <u>10</u> | <u>20</u> |
|   | 70 | 70 |

Harsanyi thinks that people in the original position would be indifferent between the alternatives.

According to Harsanyi, any risk aversion that people in the original position might have in evaluating alternatives would be reflected in a declining marginal utility for money and other social goods. Thus, in our example, we could imagine that a yearly income of $100 000 may be required to provide a utility of 60 while only a yearly income of $5000 may be needed for a utility of 10. Similarly, a $40 000 yearly income may be required for a utility of 30 but only a $15 000 yearly income for a utility of 20.

But even if we assume that people in the original position were making judgements in terms of utilities and that declining marginal utility of social goods has been taken into account, people so situated would still have grounds for preferring Alternative C to both Alternatives A and B. This is because there are two factors that people would take into account in reaching decisions in the original position. One factor is the average utility payoff, and this factor would favour Alternative A. The other factor, however, is the distribution of utility payoffs, and this factor would clearly favour Alternative C. Moreover, given this set of alternatives, it is the second factor that would be decisive for people in the original position.

Of course, as Kenneth Arrow has pointed out, it is still possible to view the preferences of people in the original position as maximising average expected utility, provided that the distribution factor is allowed to enter into the calculation of utilities.[25] Thus, for example, the distribution factor (DF) might be incorporated into the calculation of utilities in the previous examples as follows:

|    | Alternative A | Alternative B | Alternative C |
|----|---------------|---------------|---------------|
| X  | 60            | 50            | 30            |
| Y  | 10            | 10            | 20            |
| Z  | 10            | 10            | 20            |
| DF | −10           | −10           | +5            |
|    | 70            | 60            | 75            |

Since the standard Von Neumann-Morgenstern procedure for assigning utilities in situations of uncertainty can incorporate such a distribution factor into the calculation of utilities, the preferences of people in the original position for Alternative C over Alternatives A and B can be viewed as maximising average expected utility.

However, interpreting the preferences of people in the original position in this way does nothing to establish the moral adequacy of utilitarianism as traditionally conceived. For introducing a distribution factor into the calculation of utilities over and above the individual utility payoffs only transforms utilitarianism as traditionally conceived into a form of ideal utilitarianism. In this particular form of ideal utilitarianism, the standard conflict between justice as a distribution factor and utility as the average individual utility payoff is transformed into a conflict between two types of utility. Yet the moral adequacy of utilitarianism as traditionally conceived is not established by the possibility of such a transformation because virtually any moral conflict can be represented as a conflict of utilities. Rather the adequacy of utilitarianism as traditionally conceived depends on showing that when utilities that are represented in forms of ideal utilitarianism conflict, the utility of the individual payoffs (either the sum or average utility of these payoffs) always has priority over other types of utility, in this case, the utility of the distribution factor. Since, as we have seen, people in the original position would reject such a priority by preferring Alternative C to Alternatives A and B, this clearly raises a serious challenge to the adequacy of utilitarianism as traditionally conceived.

Consequently, although it is possible to disagree with Rawls concerning exactly what non-utilitarian principles of justice would be chosen in the original position,[26] it does seem that he has been successful in achieving his basic goal of providing a systematic alternative to utilitarianism. In addition, other philosophers have extended Rawls's social contract theory so as to derive principles of punishment, welfare rights for distant peoples and future generations, a right to medical care, and even a solution to the abortion question.[27]

Obviously, this successful revival of social contract theory contrasts sharply with the apparent failure of the good reasons approach to justify ethics adequately. Hence, the importance of Stephen Darwall's recent attempt to employ the good reasons approach to ground a Rawlsian social contract theory.

Darwall begins with a general theory of practical reason in which reasons for action are characterised as having both motivational and normative dimensions.[28] As to their motivational dimension, reasons for action are described as:

(1) Facts the rational consideration of which would motivate an agent to act, other things being equal.

In contrast, as for their normative dimension, reasons for action are described as:

(2) Facts whose related norms it would be rational for anyone to impersonally prefer that all agents act on.

Darwall argues that facts must meet both dimensions before they constitute full-fledged reasons for acting.

For example, suppose that robbing People's National Bank would best serve my interest; and suppose that when I dispassionately reflect on the matter, I am motivated to rob the Bank, other things being equal. Thus (1) would presumably be satisfied. Yet surely I could not impersonally prefer that all agents act on the norm: Do whatever would best serve your own self-interest; I could not encourage general observance of this norm because such unconstrained pursuit of self-interest would be mutually frustrating, especially in Prisoner Dilemma situations. Consequently, the fact that robbing the Bank would best serve my own self-interest would not satisfy (2) and, hence, would not be a full-fledged reason for action on Darwall's account. By contrast, the fact that a particular welfare programme would provide an adequate social minimum to the truly needy would presumably satisfy both (1) and (2) and thus provide a full-fledged reason for action according to Darwall.

It is important to notice that in virtue of (1) Darwall's account is an internalist account of reasons for action. Such accounts regard motivation as internal to or constitutive of reasons for action; opposing externalist accounts regard motivation as external to or non-constitutive of reasons for action. Nevertheless, Darwall postulates such a weak connection between reasons for action and motivation (that is, reasons for action are said to presuppose only the capacity to motivate) that his internalist account would only be opposed to the most extreme externalist accounts. Consequently, opposition to Darwall's account is more likely to focus on (2).

As one would expect, moral philosophers have sought to incorporate a normative dimension into their accounts of reasons for action. But (2) represents a particularly ambitious attempt because Darwall sets out to characterise this dimension of reasons for action so that it will correspond with Rawls's original position.

His argument for incorporating Rawls's original position into his account of reasons for action begins with the seemingly uncontroversial principle that a rational agent ought to act as there is, all things considered, reason for him/her to act. Darwall then infers that since this principle applies to all rational agents, it must be impersonally based, and hence, symmetrically action-guiding for all rational agents. But if such a principle is impersonally based, argues Darwall, then, it must be preferred from the impartial standpoint of an arbitrary agent. In sum, if this seemingly uncontroversial principle which grounds our preferences is to be rational, then, it must be impersonally based, and if it is impersonally based, then, it must be impartial. Here is the heart of Darwall's defence of morality in terms of the requirements of practical reason.[29]

A basic difficulty with Darwall's defence concerns his claim that the principle that a rational agent ought to act as there is, all things considered, reason for him/her to act must be impersonally based. For why could not our commitment to this principle be personally based, assuming we were to understand the principle to be asymmetrically action-guiding so that the principle would not entail that other rational agents ought not to interfere with an agent's acting as there is reason for him/her to act, all things considered? (Consider again the analogy of the 'oughts' of competitive games.) If such a commitment to the principle is possible, practical reason would not have been shown to be, at its base, impartial. But is this not just what the defender of rational egoism claims is the case?

Darwall points out that if a rational agent's commitment to the principle that he/she ought to act as there is, all things considered, reason for him/her to act is impersonally based then his/her preference that he/she act on such a principle would be inseparable from a preference that others act on the same principle, that is, a rational agent would endorse this principle from an impersonal standpoint only if it were interpreted to be symmetrically action-guiding. But this does not show that if a rational agent's commitment to the principle were personally based, and, as a result, the principle were interpreted to be asymmetrically action-guiding, then, an agent's preference that he/she ought to act on such a principle would not be clearly separable from a preference that others act on such a principle.

Now other contemporary philosophers have also attempted to develop a good reasons approach to ethics.[30] Most recently, David Gauthier has attempted to combine a good reasons approach to ethics with his own version of social contract theory.[31] And while Gauthier's version of social contract theory owes more to Hobbes than it does to Rawls, it would be interesting if these two threads of contemporary ethics could somehow be joined, as Darwall envisioned, such that one provides the foundation for the other.

# Notes

1. Stephen Toulmin, *An Examination of the Place of Reason in Ethics* (Cambridge, 1950), Kurt Baier, *The Moral Point of View: A Rational Basis for Ethics* (Ithaca, 1958).
2. John Rawls, *A Theory of Justice* (Cambridge, 1971), David Richards, *The Moral Criticism of Law* (Encino, 1977), Charles Beitz, *Political Theory and International Relations* (Princeton, 1979), Norman Daniels, 'Health-Care Needs and Distributive Justice', *Philosophy and Public Affairs* (1981); James P. Sterba, *The Demands of Justice* (Notre Dame, 1980).
3. Stephen Darwall, *Impartial Reason* (Ithaca, 1982).
4. Toulmin, Part I.
5. Toulmin, Part III.
6. Toulmin, pp. 160–63, 98–101.
7. R. M. Hare, 'Review of An Examination of the Place of Reason in Ethics', *Philosophical Quarterly* (1951) pp. 372–75; George C. Kerner, *The Revolution in Ethical Theory* (Oxford, 1966).
8. Baier, pp. vi–vii.
9. Kurt Baier, 'The Social Source of Reason' in *Proceedings and Addresses of the American Philosophical Association* (1978); 'Moral Reasons and Reasons to be Moral', in *Values and Moral* edited by A. I. Goldman and J. Kim (Dordrecht, 1978); 'Moral Reason' in *Midwest Studies in Philosophy* III edited by Peter French and others (Morris, 1978); 'The Conceptual Link Between Morality and Rationality', *Nous* (1982).
10. See, for example, 'Moral Reasons and Reasons to be Moral', p. 240.
11. See 'Moral Reasons', p. 69.
12. See my *Demands of Justice*, chapter 1.
13. Baier, 'Moral Reasons and Reasons to be Moral', pp. 249–50. R. M. Hare makes an analogous claim in *Freedom and Reason* (Oxford, 1963) p. 93. John Rawls also wants to impose a similar restriction on choice in his 'original position'. But Rawls realises that he is importing a moral constraint. See *A Theory of Justice*, pp. 11–22.
14. The egoist's response to the occurrence of genuine Prisoner's Dilemmas would be to transform them, if possible, into choice situations favouring the practice of egoism.
15. When players fail to execute their best moves it may simply be due to their own lack of skill or ability, or they may have been simply tricked into not executing their best moves.
16. John Rawls, 'Justice as Fairness', *The Journal of Philosophy* (1957). This article appeared in an expanded version with the same title in *Philosophical Review* (1958).
17. Rawls, 'Justice as Fairness', pp. 659–60.
18. John Rawls, 'Distributive Justice', in *Philosophy, Politics and Society*, Third Series edited by Peter Laslett and W. G. Runciman (Oxford, 1969) p. 60; *A Theory of Justice*, pp. 136–50.
19. Personal correspondence.

20. Ronald Dworkin, 'The Original Position', *The University of Chicago Law Review* (1973).
21. Robert Nozick, *State Anarchy and Utopia* (New York, 1974); Michael Sandel, *Liberalism and the Limits of Justice* (Cambridge, 1982).
22. Brian Barry, *The Liberal Theory of Justice* (Oxford, 1973); H. L. A. Hart, 'Rawls on Liberty and its Priority', *The University of Chicago Law Review* (1973).
23. John Rawls, 'Kantian Constructionism in Moral Theory', *The Journal of Philosophy* (1980); 'The Basic Liberties and Their Priority', in Sterling McMurrin (ed.) *The Tanner Lectures on Human Values*, vol. III (Salt Lake City, 1982).
24. John Harsanyi, 'Can the Maximin Principle Serve as a Basis for Morality?' *American Political Science Review* (1975). Actually, Harsanyi himself helped revive social contract theory. See his 'Cardinal Utility in Welfare Economics and in the Theory of Risk-Taking', *Journal of Political Economy* (1953) and 'Cardinal Welfare, Individualistic Ethics and Interpersonal Comparisons of Utilities', *Journal of Political Economy* (1955).
25. Kenneth Arrow, 'Some Ordinalist-Utilitarian Notes on Rawls' Theory of Justice', *The Journal of Philosophy* (1973).
26. See, for example, my *Demands of Justice*, chapter 2.
27. See note 2.
28. Darwall, pp. 130, 225–26.
29. Darwall, pp. 208, 210–12, 225–26.
30. Alan Gewirth in *Reason and Morality* (Chicago, 1978) and my article 'Justifying Morality: The Right and the Wrong Ways', (Festschrift for Kurt Baier) *Syntheses* (1987).
31. David Gauthier, *Morals by Agreement* (Oxford, 1986).

# Bibliography

1. Baier, Kurt, *The Moral Point of View* (Ithaca: Cornell University Press, 1958).
2. Barry, Brian, *The Liberal Theory of Justice* (Oxford: Clarendon, 1973).
3. Bond, E. J., *Reason and Value* (Cambridge University Press, 1983).
4. Brandt, Richard, *A Theory of the Good and the Right* (Oxford: Clarendon, 1979).
5. Buchanan, James and Tullock, Gordon, *The Calculus of Consent* (Ann Arbor: University of Michigan Press, 1962).
6. Buchanan, James, *The Limits of Liberty* (University of Chicago Press, 1975).
7. Daniels, Norman, *Reading Rawls* (New York: Basic Books, 1975).
8. Darwall, Stephen, *Impartial Reason* (Ithaca: Cornell University Press, 1982).
9. Gauthier, David, *Morality and Rational Self-Interest* (Englewood Cliffs: Prentice-Hall, 1970).
10. Gauthier, David, *Morals by Agreement* (Oxford University Press, 1986).
11. Gert, Bernard, *The Moral Rules* (New York: Harper & Row, 1966).
12. Gewirth, Alan, *Reason and Morality* (Chicago University Press, 1978).
13. Grice, Geoffrey R., *The Grounds of Moral Judgment* (Cambridge University Press, 1967).
14. Kerner, Georg C., *The Revolution in Ethical Theory* (Oxford University Press, 1966).
15. Martin, Rex, *Rawls and Rights* (Lawrence: University of Kansas Press, 1985).
16. Monro, D. M., *Empiricism and Ethics* (Cambridge University Press, 1967).
17. Nagel, Thomas, *The Possibility of Altruism* (Oxford: Clarendon, 1970).
18. Norman, Richard, *Reasons for Action* (Oxford: Basil Blackwell, 1971).
19. Olson, Robert G., *The Morality of Self-Interest* (New York: Harcourt, Brace & World, 1965).
20. Rawls, John, *A Theory of Justice* (Cambridge, Mass.: Harvard University Press, 1971).
21. Raz, Joseph, *Practical Reasoning* (Oxford University Press, 1978).
22. Richards, David, *A Theory of Reasons for Action* (Oxford: Clarendon, 1971).
23. Schick, Frederic, *Having Reasons* (Princeton University Press, 1984).
24. Singer, Marcus, *Generalization in Ethics* (New York: Atheneum, 1961).
25. Sterba, James P., *The Demands of Justice* (Notre Dame: University of Notre Dame Press, 1980).
26. Toulmin, Stephen, *An Examination of the Place of Reason in Ethics* (Cambridge University Press, 1950).
27. Von Wright, Georg Henrik, *Norm and Action* (London: Routledge & Kegan Paul, 1963).
28. Von Wright, Georg Henrik, *The Varieties of Goodness* (London: Routledge & Kegan Paul, 1963).
29. Wolff, Robert Paul, *Understanding Rawls* (Princeton University Press, 1977).

# Index